PURSUING JUSTICE

An Introduction to Justice Studies

edited by

MARGOT A. HURLBERT

Fernwood Publishing
Halifax and Winnipeg

Editing: Jessica Antony and Brenda Conroy
Cover design: John van der Woude
Printed and bound in Canada by Hignell Book Printing

Published in Canada by Fernwood Publishing
32 Oceanvista Lane
Black Point, Nova Scotia, B0J 1B0
and 748 Broadway Avenue, Winnipeg, Manitoba, R3G 0X3
www.fernwoodpublishing.ca

Fernwood Publishing Company Limited gratefully acknowledges the financial support of the Government of Canada through the Canada Book Fund, the Canada Council for the Arts, the Nova Scotia Department of Tourism and Culture, the Manitoba Department of Culture, Heritage and Tourism under the Manitoba Publishers Marketing Assistance Program and the Province of Manitoba, through the Book Publishing Tax Credit, for our publishing program.

Library and Archives Canada Cataloguing in Publication

Hurlbert, Margot Ann, 1964-
Pursuing justice: an introduction to justice studies / Margot Hurlbert.

Includes bibliographical references
ISBN 978-1-55266-442-1 (pbk.).--ISBN 978-1-55266-457-5 (bound)

1. Justice. 2. Social justice--Canada.
3. Restorative justice--Canada. I. Title.

KE444.H87 2011 349.71 C2011-903223-6
KF385.H87 2011

Contents

Contributors ... vi
Acknowledgements ... viii
Introduction *Margot A. Hurlbert* ... 1
Formal Justice, Substantive Justice and Ethical Practice ... 2

Part I Framing Justice ... 7

1 Defining Justice ... 9
Margot A. Hurlbert and James P. Mulvale
Studying Justice ... 10
Searching for a Definition of Justice ... 13
Types of Justice Studies ... 18
Philosophers Theorizing Social Justice ... 20
Justice: Multiple and Changing Definitions ... 27
How Does the Law Fit into the Study of Justice? ... 28
Defining Justice ... 29
Glossary ... 30

2 Theorizing Justice ... 32
Margot A. Hurlbert
Social Problems ... 34
Theoretical Perspectives in Analyzing Social Problems ... 39
Neo-Liberalism and Justice ... 55
Glossary ... 56

Part II Social Justice ... 59

3 Social Justice, Stratification and Oppression ... 62
Loretta Gerlach and Margot A. Hurlbert
Formal and Distributive Justice ... 64
Social Justice and History ... 65
Analyzing Social Justice ... 66
Social Stratification and Status ... 68
Oppression ... 70
Occupational Stratification ... 71
It's Power Not Value: A Conflict Perspective on Stratification ... 73
Examples of Social Justice Issues ... 79
Framing Stratification and Social Justice ... 81
Glossary ... 82

4 Poverty, Economic Security and Justice 84
James P. Mulvale
What's Justice Got to Do with Economics? 84
How Should We Define "Poverty"? 85
The Dimensions of Poverty in Canada 87
Poverty and the Work Ethic 89
The Components of Economic Security 91
Eliminating Poverty and Economic Security 96
Glossary 98

5 Social Exclusion, Social Justice and Racism 100
Lisa Comeau
Diversity and Racism in Canada's History 101
Social Exclusion and Racist Ideology 105
White Privilege 109
Democratic Racism and Multiculturalism in Canada 114
Race, Racism and Social Justice 118
Glossary 119

6 Women and Injustice 121
Gillian Balfour
Who Are Criminalized and Imprisoned Women? 122
Retributive Justice and the Woman of Legal Discourse 129
Looking Forward: Restorative Justice 135
Getting Gender into Justice 139
Glossary 139

7 Environmental Justice 142
Margot A. Hurlbert
Thinking about the Environment 143
Changing Worldview of the Environment 144
The State of the Canadian Environment 149
What is Environmental Justice? 151
Social Environmental Justice 160
Glossary 161

Part III Legal Justice 163

8 Human Rights 166
Margot A. Hurlbert
Rights in Historical Context 167
A Brief Overview of the United Nations 169
Treaties and International Customary Law 173
Social Movements 180
Human Rights Law 181
International Indigenous Rights 185
Human Rights and Social Justice 186
Glossary 186

9 Equality Rights and Justice 188
Marilou McPhedran
What Is Equality? 189
Made in Canada Equality Rights 195
Canadian Constitutional Trialogue on Equality 199
Lived Equality 207
Equality Rights and Justice 211
Glossary 213
Acknowledgements 214

10 Law and Justice 215
Margot A. Hurlbert
The Law as a Social System 217
Structure of the Court System 219
Criminal Law and Civil Law 222
Crime and Intent 227
The Sources of Law 227
Perspectives on Law and Society 233
Neo-Liberalism and New Perspectives on Legal Justice 239
Glossary 241

11 The Criminal Justice System 244
Nicholas A. Jones and Allan L. Patenaude
Defining Crime 245
Measuring Crime 246
Reacting to Crime 248
Two Models: Crime Control, Due Process or Both? 249
Policing: The Law Enforcement Component 252
Criminal Courts: The Judicial Component 255
Corrections: The Punishment/Rehabilitation Component 261
The Criminal Justice System and Justice 264
Glossary 266

Part IV Pursuing Justice 269

12 Restorative Justice 272
Margot A. Hurlbert and Hirsch Greenberg
What Is Restorative Justice? 273
Restorative Justice Applications 282
Does Restorative Justice Work? 295
Restorative Justice and Social Justice 297
Glossary 298

References 301
Statutes 327
Cases 327

Contributors

Gillian Balfour is Associate Professor in the Department of Sociology at Trent University. Her research interests are the criminalization and punishment of Aboriginal women and neo-liberal responses to sexual violence. She has published "Re-Imagining a Feminist Criminology" in the *Canadian Journal of Criminology and Criminal Justice* (2006); co-edited (with Elizabeth Comack) *Criminalizing Women: Gender and (In)Justice in Neo-liberal Times* (2006); and co-authored (with Elizabeth Comack) *The Power to Criminalize: Violence, Inequality and the Law* (2004) and "Falling Between the Cracks of Restorative and Retributive Justice: The Victimization and Punishment of Aboriginal Women" in *Feminist Criminology* (2008).

Lisa Comeau completed her doctorate in the Faculty of Education, University of Regina, where she taught courses in anti-racism education and women's studies. She currently works on immigration issues for the federal government in Ottawa. She has published "Towards White, Anti-Racist Mothering Practices: Confronting Essentialist Discourses of Race and Culture," in the *Journal of the Association for Research on Mothering* (2007); "Contemporary Productions of Colonial Identities Through Liberal Discourses of Educational Reform," in the *Journal of the Canadian Association for Curriculum Studies* (2005); and the chapter "Re-inscribing Whiteness Through Progressive Constructions of 'the Problem' in Anti-Racist Education," in *The Great White North? Exploring Whiteness, Privilege and Identity in Education in Canada* (2007).

Loretta Gerlach has undergraduate degrees in psychology and human justice from the University of Regina. She has a master of arts, also from the University of Regina, in Canadian Plains Studies, and her thesis focused on community policing strategies as they pertain to Aboriginal communities. She is employed full time in the field of human resources and currently is working on a second master's degree in human resources management with a focus on labour relations and human rights issues. She has also been a sessional instructor at the University of Regina and Luther College since 2003.

Hirsch Greenberg has a master of social work from the University of Regina (1992) and is an Instructor/Practicum Coordinator with the Department of Justice Studies at the University fo Regina. Born in Montreal, he has spent the last forty-eight years in Saskatchewan working for community based organizations in Regina as a front line staff, senior administrator, and as a volunteer. He is actively doing research on housing and homelessness in Regina; works with a team of professors teaching inter-professional practice; is a member of the Regina Alternative Measurers Program; has been recognized by the local YMCA and Correctional Service of Canada for his work in restorative justice practice; facilitates workshops on trauma and recovery for victim service coordinators; and is the first chairperson of the newly constituted Saskatchewan Justice Institute at the University of Regina.

Margot A. Hurlbert is Associate Professor jointly appointed to the Department of Justice Studies and the Department of Sociology and Social Studies at the University of Regina. Margot became a full time faculty member of the university after practising law for eighteen years. Her research interests are justice for marginalized people, climate change and environmental justice.

Nicholas A. Jones is Assistant Professor in the Department of Justice Studies at the University of Regina. He completed his doctoral work at the University of Calgary in 2006. He published his dissertation, *The Courts of Genocide: Politics and the Rule of Law in Rwanda and Arusha*, in 2009. He is also working on a variety of research projects with various policing agencies in Saskatchewan. These projects are focused on Aboriginal issues in policing. His research interests include genocide, international law, restorative justice, transitional justice and policing.

Marilou McPhedran is a human rights lawyer now serving as the principal of the University of Winnipeg Global College. She founded the International Women's Rights Project (University of Victoria Centre for Global Studies) before being named to the 2007 Ariel Sallows Chair in Human Rights at the University of Saskatchewan College of Law. She was then appointed, in 2007, as Chief Commissioner of the Saskatchewan Human Rights Commission. A Member of the Order of Canada since 1985 in recognition of her contributions to strengthening equality rights in the Canadian Constitution, Marilou is a founding mother of LEAF — the Women's Legal Education and Action Fund — and provides strategic counsel on evidence-based advocacy and lived rights locally and internationally.

Allan L. Patenaude is Associate Professor and Head of the Department of Justice Studies at the University of Regina. A graduate of the School of Criminology at Simon Fraser University, Dr. Patenaude previously taught at the University of Arkansas at Little Rock and Westminster College in Salt Lake

City, Utah. Dr. Patenaude's publications have included articles and reviews in several scholarly journals and several chapters in scholarly texts concerned with corrections, Native North Americans and the administration of criminal justice and juvenile justice, including (co–authored with Darrel S. Wood and Curt T. Griffiths) "Indigenous Peoples in the Canadian Correctional System: Critical Issues and the Prospects of "Localized" Corrections" in the *Journal of Contemporary Criminal Justice* (1992) and "No Promises, But I'm Willing to Listen and Tell What I Hear: Conducting Qualitative Research Among Prison Inmates and Staff" in *Prison Journal* (2004).

Acknowledgements

I would like to thank our publisher, Wayne Antony, without whose guidance, reviews and comments this book would have never have come together. I would also like to thank the contributors for their patience and commitment to this project. Their hard work, insight, and contributions speak for themselves.

Many thanks to the two anonymous reviewers who provided detailed commentary and helpful suggestions. In addition, thank you to the students, Shayna Fisher and Yordanos Tesfamariam, who assisted in this project as well as the Fernwood folks who produced the final product: Beverley Rach and Debbie Mathers for production and layout; John van der Woude for cover design; and Jessica Antony and Brenda Conroy for copy editing.

Thanks as well to my family: to my husband for his steadfast encouragement and support, without which I am certain I would still be practising law; to my children for their understanding and support; and to my mother for teaching me I could do whatever I set my mind to. For my ability to write, and my ability to write a book, I owe my father a debt of gratitude.

Introduction

Margot A. Hurlbert

This book is about justice: its definition, its boundaries, its contradictions, its nuances. It is also about pursuing justice and the mechanisms and practices that may achieve justice. Justice is a tricky topic; just defining it is daunting. There are, for example, diverse and competing philosophies about what justice is, as well as several theoretical approaches to the study of justice. Adding to these complications, there are several social contexts within which justice is played out in our society: the Canadian justice system; the environment (including climate change); the perspective of women (including their contact with the criminal justice system); the law pertaining to equality, paid labour, poverty, the marginalization and colonization of Aboriginal people; and the oppression of racial minorities and the racial profiling practices conducted by the police. Furthermore, many academic disciplines make important contributions to the conceptualization of justice, including philosophy, law and sociology.

Every day, people make decisions which reflect their own individualized practice of justice. These individual decisions include whether to pollute by driving cars, shop at local farmers' markets or global food chains, purchase luxury goods contributing to our materialistic lifestyle (which someday will end up in our community landfill) or provide assistance to the poor. Decisions are also made in respect of social relations, occupations or volunteering activities. A career in helping people or a career in business might be chosen. Donations to charity, desistance from racial prejudice, jokes and practices or social activism through participating in local community non-profit organizations are all activities people choose which contribute to the practice of community justice. The summation of these individualized decisions and practices represent the justice practices of our community.

The primary objective of this book is to assist your thinking about what justice is and what it could be. By exploring justice in many different social contexts and topic areas, we can critically reflect upon our own individual practices that impact justice in our community. New ways of thinking about justice can affect a person's perspective, opinions and relationships. Another important objective of this book is to enhance critical thinking — not just the ability to criticize and argue, but to conceptualize, apply, analyze, synthesize and evaluate information. Most importantly, the aim of this book is to help you undertake these activities while recognizing your own preconceived opinions and biases and seeking to understand those of others.

Formal Justice, Substantive Justice and Ethical Practice

The book begins with an exploration of the definition of justice and some of the major philosophical approaches to defining justice. This sets the foundation and the framework of justice that informs the remainder of the book. This foundational conceptual framework of justice consists of three interconnecting themes: formal justice, substantive justice and ethical practice. This foundation rests on the thoughts of Aristotle.

Aristotle wrote about two types of justice: "rectificatory" justice and "distributive" justice (Aristotle 1985). Rectificatory justice in part lays the foundation for the first theme of justice — formal justice. Rectificatory justice was also referred to as "corrective justice" and focused on trying to restore to equality an unjust situation between people. For instance, restoring a victim of theft to the position they had been in prior to the act of theft by returning their money for such things as undelivered goods. Formal justice seeks to treat similarly-situated people similarly. For instance, all people, no matter who they are, who pay money for goods which a store or vendor fails to deliver, have their money returned. In this way formal justice embodies laws and rules of procedure or court processes aimed at achieving a fair trial (sometimes termed "procedural justice"). Within the corrective justice theme is the element of "just deserts." Does the victim of harm such as theft, or the perpetrator of that theft, deserve the outcome of correcting the situation? In an employment situation, does an employee receive a fair salary? Corrective justice seeks to redress these individualized inequalities.

An important distinction must be pointed out within the first theme of formal, or corrective, justice. This is the distinction between utilitarian and retributive corrective justice. Utilitarian corrective justice seeks the correction of injustices based on the goal of punishing people for misdeeds in a manner to achieve future social benefits such that the greatest consequences are achieved for the greatest number of people. By contrast, retributive corrective justice strives for reciprocity of action. An injustice should be responded to with a morally correct and fully deserved punishment equal in consequence to the injustice or crime to which it is responding.

In addition to writing that justice is treating equals equally, Aristotle argued that justice is treating "unequals" unequally, in proportion to their inequality (Aristotle 1985). This exercise of determining what is "unequal" and deserving different treatment is the genesis for another conception of justice — "substantive" justice, also known as distributive justice. Within the substantive justice theme, the two elements of fairness and equality are closely aligned. Substantive justice explores how rewards, goods and respect are distributed in society and whether this distribution is performed in a fair and equal manner.

Substantive justice is different than formal justice, or treating equals equally, in that it recognizes that individuals may need to be treated differently in order to achieve justice. For example, in terms of human rights (the topic of Chapter Eight), this may mean recognizing the inherent value of each individual human being as well as ensuring recognition and respect of their human dignity. In essence the theoretical application of "formal" equality is rejected in certain situations as sometimes special considerations must be taken into account for groups who have historically been disadvantaged and marginalized. These special considerations may result in special treatment in order that equality can be achieved in the future. Examples of special treatment to alleviate historical inequality are affirmative action in hiring decisions and special sentencing considerations (covered in Chapter Eleven).

In addition to the two themes discussed — formal justice and substantive justice — is the theme of ethical practice. Ethical practice includes moral righteousness, individual virtue and altruistic conduct. This theme explores our own individualized decisions and practices. Ethical practice includes matters of procedure, that is, allowing the input of all people in decision-making, granting all people respect and recognition, and finally making decisions which protect the least powerful, marginalized and most vulnerable in our community. This is the mechanism by which to achieve substantive justice; it is the act of recognizing, valuing and facilitating diversity. It is through the theme of ethical practice that social change is envisioned and oppressed minorities can be freed from exploitation by the most powerful in society, or the tyranny of the majority.

A philosophical foundation for ethical practice can be found in John Rawls' (1971) principle of maximin. In order to ensure that a person's social position did not determine their position on an issue of justice, Rawls sought to ensure objectivity through the performance of a mental exercise. This exercise consisted of a person suspending knowledge of their own individual characteristics, talents and social position and approaching issues in a manner to maximize fairness and welfare for all. We can modify Rawls' thinking here to propose that ethical justice practice requires one to consider and take into account the needs of the most vulnerable.

Many other methods can be employed for achieving ethical practice, not all of which were discussed by Rawls. While this particular ethical practice based on Rawls' thinking is quite individualized, it must be pointed out that institutions also have an ethical makeup and an ethical practice. One such institution is the Constitution of Canada, which supports values of liberal justice and equality for all and informs the ethical practice of many other Canadian institutions including courts of law, governments and public officials in Canada. Elaborating on all of these methods is not within the scope of this introductory text. However, it should be noted that ethical practice is about upholding values deemed important to a group or person, and consistent action that upholds these values creates morality. This book seeks to explore the dimensions of this individual and institutional morality.

A necessary precondition to ethical practice (discussed in Chapter One) is setting aside ethnocentrism (the inherent belief that one's own culture and ethnicity is superior to that of others). This is supplemented by viewing issues of justice not as debates between two opposite opinions, but as problematics to be explored and examined. Most importantly, in a problematic the positions of other people who have differing opinions are explored. Understanding the various theoretical perspectives to the study of justice (covered in Chapter Two) assists in developing the skills to understand differing opinions.

These three themes — formal justice, substantive justice and ethical practice — are not independent, unrelated or mutually exclusive. Often they interconnect and overlap and can be envisioned as three interconnected circles.

Consider the case of theft. Let us say that two people have been caught and convicted of stealing a significant amount of money: theft over $5000. The two people are both men, one of whom is a labourer with a relatively spotty record of employment, but working steadily over many years with bouts of unemployment; the other is a well-paid executive in a medium-sized Canadian corporation. Both men are in fact guilty of this misbehaviour and they both must pay a fine of $2000. By the standards and ideology of formal justice, justice is achieved because they are treated equally. Yet, this equal treatment obviously does not take into account the social circumstances of the two men, nor the consequences of the equal treatment. The manual labourer stole the money to pay his mortgage and buy food. Furthermore, the fine will ruin the labourer (as the CCPA has recently pointed out in its report on inequality in Canada, "The Growing Gap," most working class people are one paycheque away from bankruptcy). Most likely, if unable to pay the fine, the labourer will end up serving time in jail. This harms his current and future prospects for obtaining employment. For the corporate executive, while a $2000 fine is not insignificant, it will not bankrupt him, nor did he need that small amount of money to feed himself and his family. By the standards of substantive justice, justice is not achieved by equal treatment. Ethical practice might suggest that the equivalent fine for the corporate executive should be several times that amount paid by the labourer.

Summary Points

The three themes of justice are:

Formal justice, in which similar situations, cases and people are treated similarly;

Substantive justice, in which different people are treated differently in order to achieve justice; and

Ethical practice, which ensures that marginalized people are recognized, valued and have their needs taken into account in actions and decisions.

Part I

Framing Justice

Margot A. Hurlbert

Part I of *Pursuing Justice* defines terms, introduces ideas and establishes some frameworks for pursuing the study of justice. Many of these ideas and frameworks will be picked up on and developed further in subsequent chapters when particular areas of justice studies are explored, such as environmental justice, criminal justice and legal justice. These concepts are important in developing a base from which justice issues can be problematized later in the book. Chapter One, "Defining Justice," lays the foundation for the study of justice.

Although the study of justice is multidisciplinary, the thinking of historical and modern day philosophers about what justice is constitutes the majority of Chapter One. The chapter commences with some general thoughts about what justice is and how the study of justice should be approached. Philosophers have studied justice for many centuries, and their conceptions of justice have included such elements as "desert," "fairness," "equality" and "moral righteousness." In addition to the ancient Greek philosophers discussed in the introduction to this book and again in Chapter One, modern day philosophers have continued to define justice through rational critical thinking. Chapter One explores various approaches to social justice (having a just society), including religious perspectives, Aboriginal knowledge, social contract theory, utilitarianism or consequentialism, libertarian or free-market theories and some of the twentieth-century debates regarding social justice.

A multiplicity of social institutions and relations impact justice — or just relations between people—and, as such, a multi-disciplinary approach to studying justice is needed. No one discipline has a monopoly on the study of justice. Chapter One reviews several disciplines that inform and contribute to both the study of justice and to many of the subsequent chapters of the book.

Finally, Chapter One challenges the idea that law is the same as justice. The law is but one social institution that mediates relations between people and has influence on the actions and choices of people. Whether the outcomes of these choices and actions are "just" is a matter of one's norms, values and perceptions. Social institutions such as courts, governments (the state) or police forces also impact the justice equation when making determinations that affect the lives of individual people. The study of justice entails a study of all these institutions and how they impact social relations. The end of Chapter One explores the relationship of law to the study of justice and concludes by exposing the myth that law and justice are the same.

While Chapter One attempts to define justice by exploring the perspectives of philosophers, Chapter Two, "Theorizing Justice," expands thinking about justice by exploring techniques to broaden the analysis and understand the problematic of a justice issue. First, the method of investigating social problems that are the broader representation of a personal problem is introduced; this recognizes the intersection of individual problems in larger social contexts. For instance, the individual problems of hunger or job loss can be seen in the context of the social problems of poverty and unemployment. Understanding social problems allows us to understand different social contexts, places and groups and is foundational to pursuing substantive justice, the second theme of this book. Understanding social problems is necessary in identifying groups of people and individuals who are "unequals" and therefore should be treated "unequally."

After identifying broader social problems, these problems can then be explored by theorizing their causes. Several theoretical perspectives for analyzing social problems are reviewed in Chapter Two, including structural functionalism, conflict theory, symbolic interactionism, post-structuralism and feminism.

One of the preconditions to studying justice requires recognizing and respecting other peoples' perspectives; this can also be enhanced by exploring a diversity of theoretical perspectives. Understanding a variety of perspectives assists us in seeing a diverse, in-depth set of justice issues. Redressing injustice requires that consideration be given to all peoples' perspectives with special consideration to the less powerful in society (in accordance with the third theme of this book: ethical practice); comprehensive strategies to achieve justice also require that all theoretical perspectives be considered.

Chapter Two both commences and ends with a consideration of the ideology and the political strategy which perhaps inhibit one's ability to view individual problems within the context of social problems. Neo-liberalism is a set of ideas or a belief system that one's life chances in our society are determined by one's decisions. People who endorse this view tend to believe that the state has very little role to play in social relations and individuals should be given as much freedom as possible (including free and unregulated market places in which to trade). This discussion centres around whether the beliefs of neo-liberalism constitute part of our own individual ethnocentrism and, in accordance with one of the preconditions of studying justice, need to be set aside in order to fully embrace the problematics of justice issues.

1

Defining Justice

Margot A. Hurlbert and James P. Mulvale

At the end of this chapter, you will be able to:

- Define and discuss justice
- Understand some of the major philosophical approaches to justice
- List the different disciplines that comprise the study of justice, and describe how each discipline contributes to the multidisciplinary study of justice
- Discuss how law fits into the study of justice

Justice is a term often used in everyday speech, but what is "justice"? How is it defined and described? In this chapter, justice will be defined by considering what it is and the various approaches to studying it. The discussion will be expanded by reviewing certain aspects of justice including "desert," "fairness," "equality" and "moral righteousness." Philosophical theorizing about justice will be introduced and major philosophical approaches to defining justice will be reviewed. Law is often thought of as the ultimate expression of justice in society. But, justice is truly more than just the law.

Before pursuing a definition of justice, the rules of justice studies will be reviewed. These rules should not be forgotten when reading this book. These rules are meant to challenge thinking and, also, by opening and broadening perspective, prepare one for learning. Thinking of these rules when confronted with challenging and perhaps uncomfortable material within this book may prove helpful.

Main Points

As you read, highlight the answers to these questions:

Is it possible to agree on one definition of justice for all people, places and situations? For all time?

What do the various academic disciplines have to offer to the study of justice?

How are the various types of justice (for example criminal justice or restorative justice) informed by philosophical definitions of justice?

Studying Justice

Often when people think of the study of justice they think immediately of crime, perhaps a particular crime, the arrest of a person by the police, the courts and the eventual incarceration of an offender in jail and their possible rehabilitation. Another common theme is to describe justice in terms of the laws and rules of society. Crime and laws are part of the study of justice, but only part. Studying how these processes work together is the study of the criminal justice system. However, the study of justice entails more than just the operation of our criminal justice system and how to respond to a particular action by passing a law to make that activity a crime.

The study of justice is also concerned with how a person came to be in trouble with the law in the first place. Factors contributing to behaviour in contravention to society's laws from both an individual perspective and also on a broader societal level allow a much richer justice analysis. Studying this behaviour in relation to social factors such as poverty, racism and education can significantly inform our understanding of preventing crime and government law-making. Trying to understand why poor and marginalized people in our society fill our jails and our hospitals and have higher suicide rates than the rest of the population is also part of the study of justice.

A related pursuit is to study what is or is not labelled as crime in our society. Historically, being drunk or using recreational drugs was not a crime. In some countries prostitution is a legal activity. In many countries, and even in Canada, many workplace deaths and injuries completely preventable with proper safety equipment are labelled "accidents," not "crimes" (Rajan 2001: 385). Further, industrial discharges which have polluted drinking water and resulted in deaths and illnesses are not considered crimes (Nikiforuk 2008: 83). What is or is not a crime and who is and is not prosecuted for crime in our society are parts of the study of justice.

Studying justice is also concerned with many other aspects of our society. In fact, the study of justice by such people as Plato and Aristotle pre-existed modern notions of law and crime. How people are rewarded for their efforts in working, farming, creating and inventing and who profits from these activities such as corporations, retail stores and governments are also a concern of justice. Is the distribution of rewards fair? Are developing countries in other parts of the world paid a just price for their goods and services, or are their people employed in sweat shops, working long hours for very little compensation? How the environment of some of these developing countries supplying oil, rubber and other natural resources is affected and the impacts of climate change on these countries and their people in exchange for the exploitation of their resources are questions for justice studies. How this distribution is influenced by international human rights is also a paramount concern of justice studies.

In respect of the entire multitude of issues and topics pursued in justice studies, a few common rules exist, regardless of the topic. The first rule is that our own ethnocentrism (or preferences for practices and values reflective of our own culture) must be recognized. The potential of justice studies can only be achieved if we are able to break from our particular cultural background to take into account broader considerations that can affect the outcomes that we want to change. Recognition that we are ethnocentric and we think normatively (within the confines of our own values, norms, experiences and perspectives) is a first step in pursuing the study of justice, rather than just the study of law. If we are considering the destruction of the environment in a developing country supplying North America with oil and gas, it is necessary to consider the perspective of people living in that developing country. Similarly, if considering the appropriateness of a woman to wear a head scarf while playing soccer we would have to approach the issue from the woman's perspective. To disregard her perspective and consider only the thoughts, feelings and views of people where head scarves are not common, is not pursuing the study of justice. We must disengage from our personal emotion and recognize that we are products of our own cultural, religious and class background and, like most people, have a tendency to regard our own norms, values and standpoint as superior to all others.

The second rule in justice studies is recognizing that often the dominant viewpoint or the views of the majority are not the same as "justice." The idea of justice can't be captured by any single morality or standpoint but only emerges from the interaction among contending perspectives. Regard must be given to the perspectives of the marginalized, the poor and other minorities. Justice requires recognition that sometimes minorities and the oppressed must receive what may be regarded as "special status" and privileges to prevent what otherwise would be tyranny of the majority or tyranny of the most powerful groups or people in society. To only think from the perspective of one viewpoint and morality, especially when that perspective is the dominant standpoint or the majority of the population, limits meaningful contribution to broader issues of justice (Crank 2003: 2).

To fully understand the issues identified above, each of us must set aside our normative thinking. We have to be able to recognize when we are thinking normatively and understand that other viewpoints exist. Pursuing a full understanding of these viewpoints, even if they are held by a minority or only a few people, helps us to expand our understanding of a justice issue and approach it from more angles. In the example of the crime of drug possession, we can expand our understanding of the issues if we consider that in some countries the use of recreational drugs is not illegal. This exercise expands our consideration of this topic outside of the norms, values and culture that have determined that the use of and, therefore, possession of recreational drugs is illegal. We are able to recognize our own thought patterns, biases and perhaps prejudices. When we expand our thinking and begin to consider thoughtfully and respectfully the position, viewpoints, thoughts and opinions of the "other," we approach the study of justice not as a debate between two viewpoints, but as a problematic. This approach challenges our traditional thinking and makes us embrace a plurality of positions.

The study of justice is also multidisciplinary as it combines several usually separate branches of learning or fields of expertise. In this way, no one profession, be it law, philosophy, history or sociology, has an exclusive claim to the study of justice. Each of these disciplines, and several more, play an important role in the study of justice. Knowing about the contributions of each discipline to the study of justice provides an important base to understanding justice.

Philosophers, including Plato and Aristotle, have wrestled with defining justice for centuries, dating as far back as 600 BCE. The study of philosophy is the study of general and fundamental problems concerning matters of existence, including truth, beauty, law, validity and justice. It is an approach to these matters that is critical, generally systematic (or all-encompassing and not individualized) and reliant on reasoned argument. It does not rely on empirical or statistical methods or evidence but it is rather the pursuit of wisdom through rational and logical argument. Philosophy offers a meaningful starting point for defining justice as it has a long history in struggling with the concept of justice.

More recently, the philosophers' abstract speculation has been complemented by empirical ways of knowing manifested in social studies (such as psychology or sociology). Social scientists developed many disciplines in their efforts to understand human behaviour. Each discipline contributes to the field in its own way. History contributes by providing information on the past record of human social development with useful insights into patterns, regularities and irregularities. For instance, the historical treatment of people of Japanese ancestry during World War II, or the historical treatment of people from Africa enslaved several centuries ago, have important implications for understanding human behaviour and our own and others' conceptions of justice or fairness. Not only does this history still impact our society today, but it also illustrates how society's conception of justice has changed over time.

Similarly, political science and the study of the organization, structure, operation and administration of government is crucial for understanding the justice system, the role of courts, corrections and the development of laws. Often the media will portray a particular court decision as "outrageous" and blame either the judge or perhaps the lawyer. However, upon a closer analysis, students realize the government was responsible for writing and passing the law, which the court and the judge simply applied. Ultimately, the people elected the government.

Lastly, sociology, the systematic study of social structure, is crucial when studying justice or fairness within society. Law and the justice system of a society constitute a social structure that is influenced by other social structures in society. As an example, the laws surrounding marriage and divorce are influenced, at least in part, by the structure of the family. Changing norms and patterns of the family, or the definition of what a family is, have had symbiotic affects on the laws surrounding the family. The heterosexual nuclear family was historically the only recognized family unit with the status to receive the benefits accruing to a family unit such as insurance payments and matrimonial support. This nuclear family consisted of a father, mother and children. Now, however, benefits may accrue to same-sex couples, effectively giving a same-sex couple the status of a "family." Sociology focuses study on social structures and how human beings produce, reproduce and change social structures such as families and laws (Knuttila 2002: 21). The application of the principles of sociology to the study of law and the justice system improves and informs our understanding of justice.

Criminology makes an important contribution to the study of justice. Criminology is concerned with the study of the etiology or cause of crime. It looks at the role of the social setting and the interactions of various social groups in the cause of crime, as well as the biosocial and psychological causes of crime that tend to focus on the individual and their free will.

Searching for a Definition of Justice

One of the first written definitions of justice is that of the philosopher Aristotle, who lived approximately 2300 years ago (384–322 BCE). Aristotle stated that justice consists of righteousness, or complete virtue in relation to one's neighbour. He also espoused the idea of justice as a state of character, a cultivated set of dispositions, attitudes and good habits. Aristotle expands on justice by stating it consists of treating equals equally and unequals unequally, in proportion to their inequality. This is also known as distributive justice (Aristotle 1985). Although this first appears simple, its application becomes somewhat problematic. Are women and men different, therefore, unequal and to be treated unequally? Are people of different skin colour different, unequal or equal? Although most people today would say, "Of course these people are all equal. These are categories of difference that we should not take into account to exclude from privileges in society like voting, or riding at the front of the bus." This, however, was not always the case. In the first part of the twentieth century, women could not vote in the United States and Black people could not ride at the front of the bus.

Normative thinking, beliefs and value judgments form the basis for the determination of our categories of "equal" and "unequal." When we answer questions about equality, we answer them based on beliefs and biases that we learned from parents, teachers, peers and other subtle influences like media, television and the books we read. It is these influences that form internalized beliefs and values and a person's conception of "justice" and beliefs of what is fair and equal. As little as fifty years ago, many people did not think of themselves as racist, although they supported the laws of racial segregation (denying Black people the right to have full privileges of club membership, ride at the front of the bus or swim in a swimming pool); today we would consider these people and the laws segregating people on the basis of race as racist. Today, racist practices still occur. In Saskatoon, Saskatchewan, until very recently, police officers would take Aboriginal people out of the city and leave them in -40° weather without proper clothing instead of processing the necessary paperwork to charge them with a minor criminal offence. Several died (Wright 2004). Although this practice is clearly racist, many would not consider the Saskatoon police officers as racist. The challenge for justice studies today is to ascertain what practices in today's society are unequal and unfair but are regarded as normal.

The second type of justice that Aristotle contrasted with distributive justice was what he termed "rectificatory" justice or corrective justice, dealing specifically with the justice of transactions, whether they are voluntary (like buying, selling or lending) or involuntary (such as a victim of theft or violence). In this type of justice a judge tries to restore an unjust situation between parties to equality (Aristotle 1985). This theme receives most attention in the chapter on restorative justice.

The definition of justice is a moving target; conceptualizing justice is an ever-changing, subjective process of assessing the fairness of relations between individuals and groups of people. The following are four main popular or everyday meanings and understandings of justice.

Desert

This is the idea of "getting what one deserves." On the positive side, we may bestow an award or social recognition on someone for a good deed or unselfish behaviour (for example, a medal for bravery for risking one's life to save a drowning person or designation as "volunteer of the year" for providing valuable help without pay in a community service organization). Awards and honours may also be a way to recognize extraordinary talent (Album of the Year at the Junos or a gold medal at the Olympics) or great effort (designation as "the most improved student" or award for "the biggest loser" in a weight loss contest).

There is also a negative side to desert — punishment or bad consequences for harmful or immoral actions, laziness or incompetence. Sentencing in the courts through the use of fines, imprisonment and community service orders certainly fits this category — although there are numerous ongoing debates about the balance that should be struck in criminal sentencing with regard to retribution, restoration and rehabilitation (more on this question later). Other examples of getting what one deserves through negative consequences include children losing privileges for misbehaving, lazy students getting poor or failing grades and employees without the necessary skills for a job being demoted or dismissed.

Sometimes consequences are perceived to be genuinely deserved — for example, a repeat offender drunk driver who has his driver's licence taken away, or the athlete who avoids performance-enhancing drugs and still wins the gold medal. However sometimes credit or blame is ascribed in ways that are not deserved or fair. For instance, in regard to the distribution of wealth in society, sometimes people who are rich due to inherited wealth are highly regarded, and people who are poor due to circumstances beyond their control are seen as "lazy" or "stupid." In the latter regard, it is a common trend to distinguish between the "deserving" and "undeserving" poor in ways that reinforce invalid and negative stereotypes and that prevent us from adopting good policies and programs to combat poverty.

Fairness

This is the idea of treating equals equally. For example, two people doing the same job competently with the same amount of experience and training should get the same pay. There should not be distinctions in rates of pay based on gender, age, racial or ethnic background or any other factor not related to performance on the job. "Fairness," however, also means, in certain circumstances, treating people unequally in order to recognize and correct past injustices. For instance, if women or members of racial minorities have been historically excluded from certain (relatively well-paid and desirable) occupations, there may be a justifiable case for employment equity measures — giving suitable candidates from the disadvantaged group preference in hiring. Hence, there can sometimes be a distinction (and perhaps tension) between what is considered fair at the individual and collective levels.

This concept of justice also denotes "procedural fairness" — ensuring that everyone receives a fair hearing and due process in courts (for example, their case follows all the requirements of knowing the case against them, they have enough time to prepare and they have an impartial judge), tribunals, appeal boards and other formal decision-making bodies. For example, people with a low income should not be denied competent representation in court by a lawyer if they are charged with a serious criminal offence, even though they cannot afford legal fees. Legal aid schemes, in principle, are supposed to ensure such legal representation for all. Procedural fairness also demands a transparent process for decision-making that can be clearly understood by all, ready access to practical help to make one's case and the right to appeal a decision to a higher body in one feels that one has been unjustly treated.

Equality

This common understanding of justice is embodied in equal citizenship rights for all persons (for example, the right of all to vote in elections and run for political office and equal entitlement to universal public programs such as health insurance and education). Equality also demands that there be an equitable sharing of civic burdens, such as paying taxes (although "progressive" taxation schemes may require the wealthy to pay proportionately more, they are about fairness) or performing compulsory military service for a set period of time (in countries where this is required).

Equality also has economic and social dimensions. Does everyone enjoy adequate economic security through some combination of labour market earnings and income security programs provided through government? Do all people in society have ready access to adequate and affordable housing, sufficient, safe and nutritious food and other public goods such as transportation and green space?

These aspects of economic and social rights do not necessarily demand treating everyone exactly the same, or giving people equivalent shares of a social good. It can be acceptable to have differences in income levels, house prices and the consumption of goods and services. Such differences may in fact provide incentives that benefit individuals and society. For example, physicians tend to be well-paid in order to encourage people to complete long years of medical training and to provide this valuable service that benefits others. Economic and social differences also allow for individual preferences. For example, a person may decide to live in low-cost housing in order to save money for extensive travel. However, justice demands equality of access for everyone to adequate income, decent and affordable housing, food security and the other necessities of a modest but dignified life. A disabled person may require more resources than an able-bodied person for such things as transportation, communication or housing.

The social aspect of justice brings up questions of distributive justice — how resources (for example, money, natural talents, health care or political power) and opportunities (for example, places in the best educational institutions or access to the best jobs and the most lucrative business opportunities) are divided up among everyone in society. Unjust distributions may require corrective measures, in other words, "redistributive justice." For example, wealthy people may be required to pay more taxes than those with modest or low incomes, so that government can fund a reasonable level of public services for all. Educational institutions may have to take steps to recruit students and faculty members from groups that they have historically excluded, such as women, racial minorities and people with disabilities, so that these minority groups have access to the same educational opportunities as the majority. Once again, treating every individual exactly the same may not be possible or even desirable if we are to realize a collectively just distribution of money, social recognition and political power. Such a redistribution of economic resources, positive social status and the representation in decision-making bodies may serve the collective good of society by creating a fairer, more inclusive and more harmonious social order, even if some privileged individuals end up with less than they started with.

The process of redistribution, or, more specifically, arriving at a fair redistribution, involves participation. Participation in this context requires a societal decision mechanism or process that allows the meaningful participation of all people in society with recognition, mutual respect and an ethic of making decisions by taking into account the position of the least favoured or neediest in society. This idea introduces and bridges to the next conception of justice.

Moral Righteousness

This final aspect of justice encompasses the ideal of individual virtue and ethical conduct. Individuals are thought to be "just" when they engage in altruistic behaviour to help others or make society a better place and set an example of altruistic conduct in both their personal responsibilities (as a spouse, parent or friend) as well as civic and public roles (as an employee, elected politician or club president).

The four aspects of justice as described above are not mutually exclusive categories and often piggy-back onto one another. For example, a morally righteous person may work hard to achieve equality and fairness in broader society. We might think of famous people who fit this description, such as Nelson Mandela, in his public activities, who led the anti-apartheid movement in South Africa, or Nellie McClung who struggled for women's rights in Canada.

It is also true that these four distinct conceptions of justice may sometimes compete or run contradictory to one another. For example, advocates of social justice as equality often call for broad and generous social programs and are willing to accept relatively high taxes so that we can afford such programs. On the other hand, those who advocate for "justice as desert" in the marketplace tend to favour low taxes and highly differentiated rates of pay in order to provide financial incentives for the talented and hard working and to punish those who are seen as lacking in skills or effort. These two different camps will likely disagree on many aspects of how to distribute resources justly and on what a "just society" should look like.

Similarly, people in the "justice as desert" frame of mind often believe that criminals deserve retribution and harsh treatment. On the other hand, people who equate justice with equality or fairness may see the roots of criminal behaviour in social and economic marginalization and the lack of rehabilitative services for individuals in trouble with the law. So these two sides call for very different kinds of policies and programs in the criminal justice field.

Self Test

Are arguments founded on moral righteousness and desert always compatible? How do the rules of justice studies inform this answer?

What are the differences between the four meanings or understandings of justice?

Types of Justice Studies

Often we categorize the application of justice in a particular field as a special type of justice. For example, in respect to the environment, the area of environmental justice has developed. This area seeks to understand how the environment impacts our justice system and what aspects of the environment should be included in or protected by our justice system. Should sentient beings (entities with the ability to feel) have rights? Do horses or burrowing owls have rights? If we do grant them rights, are they the same as or different from the rights of humans? If their rights are different, how are they weighted against each other? Do we need to protect burrowing owls (an endangered species) from being trampled by horses? How do activities of development such as oil drilling, mining or manufacturing affect the environment and the people in the environment? Do these affected people determine what development is allowed to occur? How does the contribution of carbon emissions to climate change impact global distributive justice? These are all questions of environmental justice.

When people commit crimes, or offend the norms and morals of our society to the extent that the offence has been labelled as a "criminal" act, we state that they and their victims deserve criminal justice. In justice studies we examine the demarcation in society between acts that are deemed "criminal" and those that are not and how this changes over time. Up until 1969 the *Criminal Code* stated that it was an offence to engage in homosexual activity. Now, human rights statutes attempt to protect homosexuals from discrimination. Similarly, crimes in relation to occupational workplace safety (or running a business or place of employment in such a manner that it is dangerous and causes injury to employees) have just appeared in the *Criminal Code* in s. 217.1, illustrating the ways in which acts considered criminal change and evolve over time. The study of criminal justice explores how the criminal justice system operates and achieves the parallel of corrective justice and the goals of offender rehabilitation and retribution.

When we examine the restoration of a victim after a crime or injustice has been committed against them, we are speaking of the principle of restorative justice. Restorative justice also applies to more than just the victim — it also applies to the offender and the community. It can include reconciling harm done to a victim; restoring the relationship between the offender and victim after a criminal act; restoring the offender, victim and entire community after a criminal act; and also the restoration of two disputing parties (committing a wrong or several wrongs against each other, which are not necessarily criminal). Defining restorative justice is a difficult task. Narrow definitions focus on crime and resolving crime, while broader definitions focus on restoring community relationships (Marshall 1999; Zehr 2004; Braithwaite 2002). The final chapter of this book will pursue this task.

Social justice (very similar to distributive justice) is the broadest form of justice and relates to whether people have access to the things they need to live a secure and dignified life. Social justice refers to the conception of justice applied to our entire society; the idea of a "just" society is one in which individuals and groups receive fair treatment and a fair share of the benefits of society. Fair treatment often is termed "procedural justice" or the experience of fair processes in resolving disputes or processing an accused through the criminal justice system. Social justice works toward the realization of a world where all members of a society, regardless of background, have basic human rights and equal access to their community's wealth and resources.

An ideal definition of "social justice" might be:

> A set of ideas, values and social practices to ensure that all persons and groups enjoy economic security, can participate effectively in democratic decision-making, exercise mutual respect and caring for one another and live their lives in ways that protect and sustain the natural environment for future generations.

In Western democracies and in specific and concrete terms, social justice is implemented in part through democratically enacted law, effective public policy and programs delivered by governments and international organizations at all levels and, in part, through groups, organizations and social movements at the local, regional, national and international levels. This constellation of public institutions and activist groups strives to:

- overcome social exclusion or oppression of individuals and groups, including that which is based on gender, social class, racial-ethnic identity, cultural practices, religious belief, sexual orientation or disability;
- provide sufficient material resources to ensure an adequate standard of living for all, through some combination of decent, well-paying jobs in the labour market; readily accessible and non-stigmatized income security programs that recognize the socially valuable and unpaid work in the family and community; and high quality public services (including

health care, education and social services) available to all regardless of ability to pay;

- enable and support personal relationships of care, trust and nurturance based on an equitable distribution of care burdens between men and women;
- strike an effective balance between the full protection and realization of human rights (including civil, political, social, economic, cultural and environmental rights) and the fulfillment of social and civic responsibilities by individuals and groups;
- ensure that social diversity is respected and that tolerance is promoted throughout society;
- eliminate the unnecessary consumption of natural resources; radically minimize the harmful effects of human activity on the air, water, soil, climate, other species and natural habitats; and bring the scientific manipulation of life forms and genetic codes under democratic control through the application of the precautionary principle and the interests of the public good over profit and ownership rights;
- promote peace, respect and non-violence in communities and within and between nations.

Summary Points

The study of justice is the study of issues of fairness, equality, desert and moral righteousness in society as "problematics" not as debates between countervailing positions.

Recognizing our own ethnocentrism and seeking to understand other perspectives enriches our study of justice.

No discipline has a monopoly on the study of justice; the study of justice is informed by the social sciences and humanities, including philosophy, sociology, history and psychology.

Different types of justice studies have emerged in different fields, such as criminal justice, environmental justice and gender justice.

Philosophers Theorizing Social Justice

Main Points

As you read, highlight the answers to these questions:

Do the philosophers discussed employ all four understandings of justice or predominantly one over another?

Does the definition of social justice encapsulate all of the following ideas of the philosophers?

Earlier in this chapter, the definitions of justice put forth by Aristotle and Plato were discussed. Because many philosophers' work focused on defining justice and answering the question "what is justice?" directly, a good starting point in the search for a definition of justice is a review of a portion of this work. As this book pursues justice in the broadest sense — not limiting the inquiry to a particular subject, issue or set of relationships between people — philosophies pursuing social justice will be reviewed.

Centuries ago in the Western world, philosophers who were the predecessors of Plato and Aristotle struggled with defining justice. Many conceptions of justice were considered, explored and elaborated by these and other philosophers. Today, the discipline of philosophy outlines what justice is according to the perspectives of the ancient Greek philosophers, religious teachings, Aboriginal knowledge, social contract theory, utilitarian theory, libertarian theory and twentieth-century debates.

The Ancient Greek Philosophers

In Western intellectual history, the concept of justice is addressed in the writings of the philosophers Plato (427–347 BCE) and Aristotle (364–322 BCE) from ancient Greece. Plato's formulation states that justice applies to both the individual and society and incorporates, but also goes beyond, the law. While the concept of justice is applicable to all of society, it is also relevant to more specific settings such as the family, informal groups of friends or people working together in a place of employment.

Plato (1982) also conceived of justice as a virtue along the lines of moral righteousness. He had an expansive definition, seeing it as not simply paying debts we owe or carrying out prescribed rituals such as religious duties, but as acting with a moral spirit. He saw justice as a *comprehensive* virtue that bound together more specialized virtues such as courage, wisdom and self-control. He also saw justice as consistent with a sense of duty and doing as you are expected.

Aristotle saw justice as complex and explored many aspects of it. He divides justice into two categories: what he called "general justice," in which "all virtue is summed up," and "particular or special justice," which encompasses "the fair and equal" in social relations (Aristotle 1985: 1099a11, 1131a11–12). Particular justice includes distributive justice — people should get what they deserve in proportion to their "merit" or "worth." If we only have a limited number of flutes to go around, they should go to those who are accomplished musicians, not to those without musical ability or training. Distributive justice seeks an *intermediate* proportion between the two extremes. Neither sameness (where everyone gets exactly equal shares) nor preferential treatment for those in privileged positions (regardless an individual's merit and training) is just, according to Aristotle. We should strive to achieve maximum human flourishing based on distributing resources in proportion to the recipient's ability to use them well.

Religious Perspectives

The moral prescriptions of "justice" are key elements in major world religions. This is certainly the case in the Judeao-Christian tradition (the teachings that comprise the Jewish and Christian religious faiths). In the Old Testament of the Bible there are two different words in Hebrew that refer to justice. "*Mishpat*" refers to the correct decision or ruling that a wise judge would make. "*Tzedak*" refers to both righteousness, or being morally upright, and charity (Raphael 2001: 11). There is an evolution of conceptions of justice in the Bible. Early pronouncements emphasized the justice of retaliating in equal measure against someone who had harmed you (the "eye for eye" principle, as found in Chapter 21 of the Book of Exodus). Later on, in the New Testament, Jesus emphasizes the importance of love, forgiveness and "turning the other cheek." There is the parable, for instance, of the prodigal son who wastes his inheritance on wild living and then returns to his father poor and broken. Rather than being stern and retributive, the father thinks it is right and just to welcome his long lost son home with a sumptuous banquet and great celebration. The parable of Jesus's "miracle" of using a few loaves and fish to feed a vast multitude can be seen as a lesson about distributive justice — if we are willing to share with one another and trust in God, there will be enough of the necessities of life to satisfy everybody. In the Beatitudes, Jesus makes specific pronouncements about justice:

> Blessed are they that hunger and thirst after justice: for they shall have their fill. (Verse 6)
> Blessed are they that suffer persecution for justice' sake, for theirs is the kingdom of heaven. (Matthew, Chap. 5, Verse 10)

Other major world religions also emphasize the importance of sharing our wealth and helping others as a requirement of religious belief and as a foundation of a just and virtuous society. For instance, in Islam, one of the pillars of belief is "*zakat*," the giving of alms to the needy. This practice is, for Muslims, a faith-based form which can bee seen as distributive justice.

Aboriginal Knowledge

Aboriginal cultures each have a rich exploration of justice. Many Aboriginal cultures use a combination of stories and elder teachings. One perspective is represented by a circle of Aboriginal elders that were brought together by the Department of Justice Studies, at the University of Regina and the Department of Indigenous Studies of First Nations University in order to discuss and reflect upon their understandings of justice. Their discussion was captured in audio-visual format and highlighted aspects of justice from an Indigenous perspective such as the following:

- the importance of balance and harmony in oneself and in the community;
- recognition that group survival depends on such harmony in the community, and that individuals' unique and diverse talents and contribution all should be recognized by the group;
- respect for other people and for Mother Earth (including the plants and animals on which we depend for our survival);
- the community as a whole has an important role to play in resolving conflict and restoring harmony when harm has been done by one community member to another;
- we must impart our wisdom and insights to the next generation, especially through engaging children and young people in oral discussion and respect for cultural standards and spiritual beliefs;
- Aboriginal cultures must seek to combine respect for traditional teachings with adapting to the ways of the contemporary world; and
- justice must be understood holistically in a way that includes the above elements. (Handel, Asikinack and Mulvale 2002)

Another formulation of justice from an Aboriginal perspective is offered on the website of the Federation of Saskatchewan Indian Nations (2009):

> **Vision**
> The Justice Secretariat envisions healthy, safe, self-determined First Nations who have the capacity to govern themselves according to their ancestral laws, spiritual beliefs, values, customs and traditions in accordance with their inherent and Treaty rights.
>
> **Mission Statement**
> Strengthening First Nation communities by creating peaceful and harmonious relationships through the restoration of our traditional justice and governance processes, peacekeeping services and community based strategies that provide healing and community safety.

These are but two examples of worldviews of Aboriginal justice and should not be mistaken for being representative of all Aboriginal worldviews. Aboriginal worldviews respecting justice are inherently complex and multifaceted.

Social Contract Theory

Social contract theory is the view that morality and the political system are (or should be) founded solely on uniform social agreements that serve the best interests of those who make the agreements. Three well-known early proponents of this approach were Thomas Hobbes (1588–1679), John Locke (1632–1704) and Jean-Jacques Rousseau (1712–1778). Their respective conceptions of the foundation and workings of the social contract, though, were quite different.

Hobbes viewed human nature as being selfish and competitive, with all of us inclined to engage in "a war of all against all" to secure our own livelihood and maximize our own advantages (Hobbes 2000). Therefore, Hobbes argued that we need to cede control to a virtuous and wise ruler (called the "Leviathan") who can maintain social order and keep our nasty impulses in check. For Hobbes, a dictator (albeit a "benevolent" one) reflected a form of government for a just society.

Locke was less pessimistic about human nature and argued that we are capable of cooperation and that as individuals we possess natural rights — including, particularly, the right to private property. Locke emphasized that political authority is based on the consent of those who are governed. If a ruler or government becomes unjust or tyrannical, then the people have the right to act collectively to overthrow those holding political power (Locke 2000). Finally, Rousseau understood the social "compact" as a process whereby "*Each of us places his person and all his power in common under the supreme direction of the general will; and as one we receive each member as an indivisible part of the whole*" (Gagnebin and Raymond 1959: 361, emphasis in original).

In such a collectivist arrangement, Rousseau predicted that "the general will can direct the forces of the state" for "the common good" (Locke 2000: 94). This state would be governed democratically by all citizens (but just men, not women, according to Rousseau). In this way, we would be able to replace our current competitive and corrupt society with one that would be just and moral. Although Rousseau's vision of a society governed by such a social contract proved to be too idealistic and optimistic, aspects of this thought were very influential on later theorists of social justice.

Utilitarianism

Utilitarianism is a philosophical approach that argues that what is desirable for society is that which provides the greatest good to the greatest number of people. Behaviour and social arrangements are just and desirable to the extent that they enhance pleasure and reduce pain for individuals and society as a whole. The focus of what provides such pleasure and pain may be physical and sensory (for example, food when we are hungry and warmth when we are cold), emotional rewards or happiness (for example, love, a sense of pride in one's accomplishments or a sense of fulfillment in life) or more ideal conceptions of what is "good" or desirable (for example, freedom, beauty and inner or spiritual peace). Famous utilitarian thinkers who presented differing depictions of desirable consequences that should be maximized have included Jeremy Bentham in the 1700s (who emphasized sensory pleasure),

John Stuart Mill in the 1800s (who stressed social goods such as freedom and justice) and G.E. Moore in the 1900s (who emphasized "happiness" as found in aspects of life such as friendship and beauty).

Libertarian Theories

The libertarian conception of justice sees human fulfillment as, essentially, the ability to make free choices as an individual. This may be in the personal realm: who will I pick for a friend or a spouse? Where should I live? Who will I vote for in an election? What, if any, religion do I believe in? Liberty and freedom are also seen as essential in the economic realm, where buyers seek to buy at the lowest possible price, sellers seek to sell at the highest possible price, and the market for goods, services and labour are shaped by the forces of supply and demand. Human inclinations towards self-interest, competition and entrepreneurship are seen as natural and beneficial. In both the personal and economic realm, libertarians look upon attempts by government and other large social institutions to shape behaviour, regulate economic transactions or redistribute wealth with great suspicion. A "laissez faire" ("let it be") approach is seen as desirable in order to maximize human freedom and economic efficiency. Well-known theorists in the libertarian or free-market camp include Adam Smith (1976) from the late eighteenth century, and Friedrich von Hayak (1976) and Robert Nozick (1974) in the twentieth century. This perspective is foundational to the philosophy and political strategy of neo-liberalism, covered in Chapter Two. Neo-liberalism is a modern day resurgence of libertarian and free-market theories.

Twentieth-Century Debates about Redistributive and Social Justice

Twentieth-century theories and debates about social and redistributive justice were wide-ranging and complex. But, to a large extent, they revolved around the publication in 1971 of a famous book, *A Theory of Justice*, by the American philosopher John Rawls. Rawls (1971) proposed a new version of social contract theory, arguing that we have to rethink what a just society is from the ground up, putting aside our individual interests. He felt that it is possible to commit to equality and freedom, while at the same time recognizing that there are unavoidable differences in individuals' talents, resources and preferences. Working with both the "equality" and "difference" principles, Rawls argued that it is possible to design social arrangements and institutions in a way that will maximize fairness and welfare for all. We should start with no presuppositions about how society should be structured or how it should operate, but should understand that as human beings we are rational creatures and can act in cooperative ways to serve our own individual interests. This is what Rawls called the "original position." He also argued that in designing a just society, we should put ourselves behind the "veil of ignorance" — we should suspend knowledge of our own individual characteristics and talents (our gender, age and level of intelligence) and design social arrangements that benefit all (including the worst off) as much as possible. This is called the "maximin" principle.

Rawls' argument, to a large degree, set the terms of intellectual debate about justice for many years. He had "friendly" critics such as Ronald Dworkin (1973), who believed that the social contract was a hypothetical device that had to be constructed upon the more fundamental right of all persons to equal respect, and Susan Moller Okin (1989), who emphasized the need to make the discerning of justice truly gender-blind and founded on the equality of women and men. Rawls also had critics (such as libertarians, discussed above, and communitarians, discussed below) who fundamentally disagreed with his argument.

The communitarian school of thought on social justice proposed that "the standards of justice must be found in forms of life and traditions of particular societies and hence can vary from context to context" (Communitarianism 2009). What is just, fair or moral is determined collectively within our local neighbourhood, faith community, social class or ethno-cultural group. Communitarians tend to be skeptical about grand, universal theories of justice that involve state intervention in our everyday lives. They also emphasize moral responsibility and the importance of imparting our values and ethical standards to everyone in society and to the next generation. Well-known communitarian theorists include Alasdair MacIntyre (1981), Michael Walzer (1983) and Amatai Etzioni (1995).

Other social justice thinkers in the twentieth century emphasized freedom and equality for women and pointed out the misogynist assumptions and sexist pronouncements of White male theorists. Leading feminist theorists included Annette Baier (1986), who emphasizes the importance of trust, nurturance and vulnerability in human affairs; Martha Nussbaum (1999), who stresses human freedom, equality between women and men and a just international distribution that addresses the situation of poor women in poor countries; and Carole Pateman (1998), who focuses on how rights are constructed in such a way that privileges men and marginalizes women.

Other theorists, such as G.A. Cohen (1988), used Marxist theoretical assumptions to critique inequality and injustice as a function of the economic domination of the capitalist class (who own and control wealth) over those who work for them and produce goods and services. It can be noted that the original thinking of Karl Marx and his collaborator Friedrich Engels did not put much stake in the notion of justice, but instead emphasized that a revolution in the mode of production and distribution must take place, a revolution that will put an end to all class distinctions. Exploited workers would succeed if they understood the material necessity of this revolution, and "the conceptions of justice and injustice held by any armchair philosopher" were distractions at best (Engels 2000: 175). This quote reflects a narrow definition of justice, as something pursued by philosophers out of touch with real people and real issues. However, in this book, justice is defined much more broadly and their work is a central piece in this pursuit. The quote is an understatement of the contribution of Marx and Engels to the pursuit of justice. Their work will be discussed in more detail in later chapters.

Still, other theorists argued that traditional theories of social justice failed to adequately take account of the necessity of confronting racism (see Sharene Razack 1998) and building tolerant, multicultural societies (see Will Kymlicka 1995 and Charles Taylor 1994). Finally, towards the end of the twentieth century and into the twenty-first century, there has been a growing recognition that we must address the question of social justice and the distribution of wealth on a global basis. The work of Thomas Pogge (2008) is notable in this regard.

Summary Points

A discussion of justice is informed by the concepts of desert, fairness, equality and moral righteousness, which are not mutually exclusive and often contradictory.

Philosophers have struggled with defining justice for centuries. Major perspectives include ancient Greek philosophers, religious teachings, Aboriginal knowledge, social contract theory, utilitarian theory, libertarian theory and twentieth century debates.

Justice: Multiple and Changing Definitions

Just as society changes over time and place, so too does the definition of justice. Defining justice is an ever-changing, subjective process of determining whether the relations between individuals are fair, righteous and equitable. As illustrated in the last two sections of this chapter, philosophies and perspectives of justice are different for different people and different times. Justice has been of concern to society since its beginning. As stated by Bronowski (1973: 41):

> Justice is a universal of all cultures. It is a tightrope that man *(sic)* walks between his desire to fulfil his wishes, and his acknowledgement of social responsibility. No animal is faced with this dilemma: an animal is either social or solitary. Man alone aspires to be both, a social solitary.

Justice is constructed individually as well as in groups and societies as a whole; different individuals may completely disagree about whether a certain result is "just" or not. These individuals may use the same arguments based on desert, fairness, equality and moral righteousness to argue very different perspectives.

Two examples will be discussed here: divorce and law enforcement.

One's views on divorce affect one's views on the justice surrounding divorce laws. People perceive divorce laws in an individual manner based on their own views and life experiences. Those with a good relationship with both of their parents might view the law granting each parent joint custody and fifty percent access to children as just. Those with a poor relationship with one parent might perceive this same law as unjust.

Another example is one's relationship with law enforcement, or the legitimacy of the role of police officers in advancing justice. Those with a family member in law enforcement or a history of only good interactions with police may view the role of police officers as important and facilitative of justice. However, those who have had a poor experience with the police may perceive the role of police officers in the justice system somewhat differently or negatively. Educating yourself by reading about and exploring others' perceptions can change your own perceptions. Certain practices of police result in the over-policing of minority groups and are very unjust. If you are not a member of a minority group, this knowledge and view is gained from exploring others' perceptions, reading and researching.

How Does the Law Fit into the Study of Justice?

Often, people studying justice expect the content to include a large amount of study and learning about the law. It does not. The law is a skeleton or framework for justice. It sets out certain attributes of the justice system but it is only one social institution in the study of justice. Other institutions with significant influence over the law and important in our assessment of justice include the government, the economy, the education system, the family, marriage and religion, to name a few.

The law is often not the same thing as justice. Often, when "law" and "justice" are in the same sentence it is by way of contrast. A law may be unjust, immoral or not inclusive of all moral concerns. The legal response of Syncrude, a crude oil production company, to its killing of thousands of birds in its tar sands tailing ponds was that it "had a permit" (Henton 2010). These same tailing ponds have poisoned many people (Nikiforuk 2008). At the time of writing the legal case associated with the death of the birds has not yet finished so the legitimacy of this legal argument has not yet been determined. This illustrates the next problem in conceiving the institution of law as the same as or synonymous with justice.

In court, there is always a winner and a loser and often even the winner does not feel that justice has been achieved after thousands of dollars in legal bills and years of waiting for a court determination. There is a perpetual tension in each particular legal case between long-term stability, certainty and predictability on the one hand and equity, fairness and justice in the individual case. Many people believe Canadian society should reinstate the death penalty for murder. This, they believe, would discourage would-be murderers from committing the crime, as they would realize that they would lose their life if they were convicted of murder. Enforcing the death penalty for murder would be done consistently and therefore contribute to the stability, certainty and predictably of the law and criminal justice system. However, what of the fairness for a women who is battered, abused and confined to her home and eventually gains the courage to use her spouse's gun in the middle of the night to murder him in order to free herself from her confinement? Is this a case where the certainty of the death penalty would be exacted, or should the criminal justice system recognize her dire circumstance? Thus, this illustrates the tension between the certainty of applying legal "rules" and imparting justice. Lastly, law as an institution or social structure in society often represents the interests of the powerful, dominant interests and groups in society. This theme will be explored in many subsequent chapters.

Self Test

Is the law the same thing as justice?

What is a criticism of the manner in which philosophers pursue defining justice?

What have social studies added to the philosophers' pursuit of a definition of justice?

What philosophers incorporate aspects of the distribution of income or reward into their theories?

What is the weakness of this chapter's representation of Aboriginal views on justice?

Defining Justice

This chapter has opened a discussion about the definition of justice. The notion that the law is justice has been challenged. The law is but one social institution that mediates relations between people and has influence on the actions and choices of people. Whether the outcomes of these choices and actions are just is a matter of one's norms, values and perceptions. Social institutions such as courts, governments or police forces also impact the justice equation when making determinations that affect the lives of individual people. Whether one is arrested for an offence and convicted of that offence or whether there is a criminal law making something an offence are all determined by these institutions. Governments are also institutions affecting how much minimum wage earners make, whether unions are allowed to form and how much corporations are taxed (money that may contribute to social welfare programs). The study of justice entails a study of all these institutions and how they impact social relations.

The multiplicity of social institutions and relations impacting justice, or even relations between people, necessitates a multidisciplinary approach to studying justice. No one discipline has an advantage. Many approaches and perspectives must be pursued in studying justice and no simple, solitary definition of justice exists.

Philosophers have studied justice for many centuries. Conceptions of justice have included such principles as desert, fairness, equality and moral righteousness. Modern day philosophers have continued to explore the determination of justice through rational critical thinking, and this chapter has explored various approaches, including religious perspectives, Aboriginal knowledge, social contract theory, utilitarian theories, libertarian theories as well as some twentieth century distributive or re-distributive debates regarding social justice.

The study of justice must be pursued with two rules in mind. First, the recognition of one's own norms and prejudices must be made. Any justice issues should be analyzed with an acknowledgement of our own ethnocentrism. Second, it must be recognized that the perspective of marginalized people must be seriously considered, explored and given a voice if unjust social arrangements are to be uncovered and challenged.

Glossary

Charter – the short name for the *Canadian Charter of Rights and Freedoms*, which is a bill of rights entrenched in the Constitution of Canada. It is the first part of the *Constitution Act, 1982* and it guarantees the political and civil rights of people in Canada by enshrining them in the Constitution, where, if infringed upon or denied, people have the power to appeal to the courts.

common law – the body of law reflected in judicial decisions. The totality of these decisions is described as the common law.

Criminal Code – a statute passed by the federal government which contains a codification of criminal offences in Canada.

desert – the idea that a person should be rewarded or punished based on the desirability (or undesirability) of their behaviour.

distributive justice – the division of resources and opportunities fairly within society.

equality – treating people the same. For example, all people receive equal rights of citizenship such as the right to vote and be free from unreasonable search and seizure.

ethnocentrism – the tendency to view one's own ethnic group or culture as superior to other ethnic groups or cultures

fairness – treating equals equally, and unequals unequally; fairness achieves the correct balance in this formula.

multidisciplinary – composed of or combining severally usually separate disciplines at once.

normative – conforming to a standard of perceived correctness by adhering to rules of behaviour.

statute – an Act passed by the provincial legislature or the federal parliament. Usually dealing with one subject matter, for example, the *Environmental Protection Act* or the *Divorce Act*.

statutory law – law that is contained in a statute passed by either the provincial legislatures or the federal parliament in Canada.

2

Theorizing Justice

Margot A. Hurlbert

At the end of this chapter, you will be able to:

- Compare, contrast and link social and personal problems and view them in the context of neo-liberalism
- Identify individual problems in the context of social problems and recognize social problems based on individual problems
- Discuss and evaluate several perspectives used in analyzing social problems
- Understand the method of discourse analysis

Justice studies is intriguing and challenging because it involves multiple social dimensions. Moreover, comprehending the social problems coincident with justice issues helps to develop a broad, nuanced and contextualized analysis. A criminal act, for example, may be viewed as an unfortunate decision of an individual, and often people wish to focus on that individual's decision and a sentence that will deter such decisions in the future. However, a broader understanding of justice is always necessary, including understanding how a person came before the justice system, why a particular act is a "crime" punishable by the state, what the interests of the victim might be and how might society prevent reoffending. These issues are broader than just considering crime as an individual's choice.

Main Points

As you read, highlight the answers to these questions:
What is the difference between a personal problem and a social problem?
What is neo-liberalism?
Why is it important to approach problems as social problems?

A further example of this broader approach to thinking about problems is exploring the social nature of illness. A person diagnosed with tuberculosis is often viewed as having bad luck or the misfortune of poor health. However, when reconsidered in light of statistics, our view may change. Aboriginal and Inuit people have a tuberculosis rate seven times the Canadian average due to their crowded living conditions (Health Canada 1999). Thus, what may have been seen as only a personal problem of illness becomes a social health and justice problem associated with poverty. In Canada can it be said that such a significantly higher rate of illness is fair or just?

Understanding this broader scope of justice wherein personal problems are linked to social problems is necessary for viewing issues as problematics. Exploring the social dimensions of issues and problems opens the door for an expanded analysis of causes and contributing factors to an issue. By expanding the consideration of an issue beyond the realm of an individual's poor decision a deeper analysis can occur. This exercise is required to achieve substantive justice. Substantive justice might require implementing measures and approaches contextualized for a particular person in a particular situation, which may not be the same for another person because of the social problems surrounding them and their actions. Justice studies link the social problem of poverty and inequality to both personal health issues and the issues of individuals and their involvement with the criminal justice system (CJS). Both health issues and committing crime tend to be thought of as dependent on an individual and their personal choices, not dependent on the fact that someone is poor. However, being poor significantly increases one's chances of being involved with the CJS or having an illness. These are but two examples of society's justice issues; many more exist such as homelessness, society's treatment of disabled people and minority groups, and barriers to immigrants and refugees in Canada. James Mulvale, in Chapter Four, "Poverty, Economic Security and Justice," provides further analysis of this, illustrating how poverty impacts a person's life chances including their health and education.

Recognition of the social problems contributing to an individual's problems allows for an understanding that all people are not similarly situated; the contextualization of a person's problems within social problems informs how people situated differently should be treated differently. In this way it is a necessary precondition to determine what is required to achieve the second theme of justice identified in this book, substantive justice. Recognizing social problems informs the application of Aristotelian justice and the identification of what is a dissimilar situation because of social context, or that "unequals" should be treated unequally. This recognition is foundational to achieving substantive justice, recognizing and respecting an individual's human dignity through understanding that an individual's problems are not created solely due to bad luck and poor personal decisions. Identifying social problems allows the unequal distribution of benefits in society to be addressed, thus assisting in the goal of achieving substantive or distributive justice.

In the last few decades there has developed a trend to view problems as individual and not social. This is due to the increasing pervasiveness of the political ideology of neo-liberalism, which emerged in the 1980s (Ross and

Trachte 1990). Neo-liberalism is both an ideology (or set of beliefs, attitudes or opinions) of how modern society should operate and the foundation of a political strategy and platform about how society should be structured, termed "neo-conservatism." Although there are many different shades of neo-liberalism around the world, generally, the neo-liberal ideology is one that focuses on the individual as a social actor. Neo-liberal ideas support the self-regulation of the market economy; minimal involvement of the state in social programs, expenditures and regulation; privatization of government-owned industry (currently public services like water, power or insurance); "free" global trade; predominance and protection of individual property rights; and replacing the concept and practices of "the public good" or "community" with that of individual responsibility (Steger and Roy 2010). This last element pressures individuals and poor people to find solutions for their lack of health care, education and security by blaming them and labelling them as "lazy" if they are unsuccessful (Martinez and Garcia 2007). This ideology is reflected in mainstream politics and the strategies of many powerful financial institutions like the World Bank and International Monetary Fund (IMF). Because of its predominance as both an ideology and a strategy of political parties for the last several decades, neo-liberalism may contribute to the difficulty we have in thinking of issues and problems in today's society as "social" problems and not just personal problems.

Social Problems

Cases going through the criminal justice system are (most) often seen as representing individuals with problems. This isn't inaccurate, as particular individuals (accused, victims and others) proceeding through the CJS do have an individualized problem (whether it is an assault, a theft or a murder). In an analytical sense, viewing this as a personal problem suggests that "crime" can be explained in terms of the qualities of the individual involved — the offender has poor anger control, has ego issues, has had a poor moral upbringing and the like. From that it is a small step to conclude that solutions to crime lie within the immediate environment of an individual.

In justice studies, not only is the individual case proceeding through the justice system studied, but also how the individual case represents a wider social issue. In this way, it is not just the individual circumstance that is studied, but also how it is connected to a social problem. In a domestic assault, for example, the individual case is about the particular couple who have engaged in physically violent behaviour. There are particular details about the abused, the abuser, the history of the relationship, the level of violence, the number of previous violent incidents and previous criminal charges for assault. This is the individual problem or criminal justice case. However, the individual case does not occur in a social vacuum; it is connected to the larger social problem of violence in our societies, gender inequality and stereotypes, female economic dependency, childcare obligations and inequalities, and a pattern of familial abuse. These factors represent the social structures which contribute to domestic violence on a global and individualized basis. A social problem is one in which the causes and solutions lie outside of the individual and that individual's immediate environment; it is one rooted in our society's social structures and institutions.

The same analysis can be made with respect to health and illness. The significant link of poor health to poverty is well documented (Mitura and Bollman 2003; Health Canada 1999). Every day, however, the mentally ill are most often conceptualized and treated as individuals with the misfortune to be "ill" and in need of a cure. Good health is no longer supported in significant policy or programs (of nutrition and exercise) because of both the reduction of government programs and spending over the last few decades and society's increased endorsement of the belief that an individual's life choices determine one's own health. These principles are consistent with the political ideology of neo-liberalism.

When studying individualized problems and analyzing them as social problems, the concept and method of the "sociological imagination" is being employed. This term was developed by the American sociologist, C. Wright Mills, in his book *The Sociological Imagination* (1959). For Mills, in order to understand ourselves, our behaviour and the behaviour of others around us, near and far, we need to have the intellectual capacity of the sociological imagination. The relationship between (social) history and (personal) biography needs to be grasped. We need to be able to see ourselves and others within the wider context of the social structures which have influenced us. This is a broader context than just thinking about parents and friends and their influence on people (although this is part of the exercise). In order to truly understand individual lives, the social and historical processes that have shaped, structured and moulded society need to be considered. In this way, the personal biography and the biographies of others that have been affected by these wider social and historical processes can be viewed and analyzed. Utilizing the sociological imagination is seeing the relationship between an individual's experiences and the larger society in which those experiences are contextualized, that is, relating private troubles of individual people to the public issues of a society in a particular time and place.

Issues in society often appear as personal not just to non-participants (bystanders or observers), but especially so to people experiencing problems. One reason is that people tend to take responsibility for their actions and what happens to them, instead of blaming other events, people or circumstances. This, however, is a somewhat misguided reaction, albeit not completely erroneous. The object of thinking in broader societal terms is not to create "excuses"

Unemployment in Canada

Consider how the personal problem of losing one's job relates to the social problem of unemployment in Canada.

In 2008, the unemployment rate was 6.1 percent, hovering close to the lowest recorded unemployment rate at that time, which was experienced in the mid-1970s at 6 percent (Statistics Canada 2009a). By July of 2009 unemployed jumped to just over 8.5 percent of Canadians, with thousands losing employment (Statistics Canada 2010; Statistics Canada 2009b: 2). The unemployment rate had reached its highest levels in 1983 (12.0%) and 1993 (11.4%), following two major recessions in Canada (Statistics Canada 2009a).

During difficult economic times or times of high unemployment, the chances of losing a job are greater, given that a higher percentage of the population is without work. Consider the most recent recession, the "sub-prime mortgage economic downturn." This economic downturn was caused by the collapse of financial markets when investors lost faith in the stability of assets (or property) securing mortgages.

The situation occurred because of a conflict of interest whereby banks holding mortgages (loans on houses owned and occupied by people) had resold the mortgages as security to another financial institution and also at the same time valued the mortgage in the financial markets. What seller of an item wouldn't also want to be setting its price in the market!

When this conflict of interest and fraudulent practice was exposed, financial markets corrected devalued mortgages, which resulted in devalued house prices. Many people in the United States ended up with a mortgage loan well in excess of the value of their house. Banks began to fail (Guard and Antony 2009), which led to a downturn in stock markets and economies around the world, including Canada's.

Many bankers lost their jobs and people lost their savings; because people couldn't get loans they stopped buying cars and houses, stopped making their mortgage payments, and many in the automobile industry and housing industry lost their jobs. Automotive workers in Ontario lost their jobs. This reverberated through other parts of the Canadian economy. Because these people didn't have jobs and stopped spending money in stores, many storekeepers lost their jobs as well.

As a result, unemployment around the world has skyrocketed. In the United States unemployment is 9.4 percent: in Spain, unemployment has reached 20 percent (Visual Economics 2010). When viewed in the context of the social problem created by the interests of powerful banks in making money, losing a job clearly becomes situated in the context of the social problem, not the result of individual shortcomings.

for things such as being let go or committing a criminal act. The object is to be able to assess how social structures contributed to a particular circumstance and how to change life chances or opportunities in the future. Perhaps it is the social structure which needs to be assessed not (just) the individual.

By defining unemployment as a social problem, the appropriate ways to cope with the problem are different. Consider the statistics above that illustrate the level of unemployment in Canada over time. The rate of unemployment varies depending on the state of the economy, global competition and many other factors. When considering these statistics, the individual loss of a job is clearly part of a much bigger social picture. In the individualized situation only the individual feels the consequences and is left to deal with the problem. However, if we view the issue as a social problem it is possible to identify different causes (other than personal shortcomings) and identify appropriate solutions (hence the genesis of unemployment insurance or family-friendly workplaces). In order to make effective change in our society in a pursuit of social justice, it is important to analyze social problems.

When a newspaper reports on an individual in a community committing a crime, many people immediately personalize the offender's problem. The person is thought of as having made a bad decision. They may even be thought of as a "criminal" or a bad person. They may carry this stigma for the rest of their life. But committing a criminal act, just like our example of being fired, may be reflective of social problems as well as personal problems. When we individualize crimes we focus on the people committing them as bad people. This allows us to feel good about declaring a "war on crime." War, when carried out against "bad" people, is legitimated in our eyes. This

Crime Rates in Canada

Consider how the personal problem of getting in trouble with the law relates to the perceived social problem of crime in Canada.

When cases of crime are reported in newspapers and in the media the public perception that crime is a social problem in our community is fueled. However, the statistics don't support the notion that the social problem of crime is worsening. In 2008 Statistics Canada reported Canada's national police reported crime rate reached its lowest point in thirty years in both volume and severity. Canadian police reported approximately 2.2 million *Criminal Code* incidents (excluding traffic incidents); one in five of these incidents were violent (Wallace 2009: 6).

Together, seven offences accounted for about eighty percent of the volume of all reported crime in Canada: theft under $5,000 (twenty-five percent); mischief (seventeen percent); break and enter (ten percent); common assault (eight percent); administration of justice offences (such as breaching curfew or not reporting to a probation officer) (eight percent); motor vehicle theft (six percent), and disturb the peace (5 percent) (ibid.: 6).

Media reporting of crime paints a far different picture. Crime is sensationalized and readers' attention is drawn to individual incidents several times in each daily edition of newspapers. This media context allows political parties to build platforms calling for tougher responses to crime. In 2008, the Prime Minister of Canada continued to campaign to get tougher on crime, calling for harsher sentencing (McCulloch 2008).

allows focus on ensuring retributive justice, which is a particularly individualized response to justice.

Thinking of crime as a social problem includes recognizing peoples' social roles, in the ways they may both contribute to the crime rate and help redress crime. Take, for example, the problem of neighbourhood kids spray-painting graffiti on a garage. If it is thought of as an individualized problem, the kids are seen as "bad" and in need of some significant consequences in order to have their behaviour brought into line in the future. Often, people want these kids to suffer a consequence perhaps out of revenge or to satisfy a sense of "justice." If instead the youth are regarded as part of the community with not enough to do, or with parents who are forced to work long hours at minimum wage jobs who aren't able to afford childcare, we start to think of how the community contributed to the problem of them painting graffiti on a garage. Why are minimum wages so low that people can't afford childcare? Why is childcare so expensive? Why are these children ignored in the community? Why are there not more volunteers at schools and community centres to help run after-school programs? Pursuing this line of thought and inquiry allows crime to be viewed as a social problem. In order to restore communities to a state of health and vibrancy, the actions and roles of individual actors or people (other than the youth painting graffiti) must be included in the analysis and discussion. Recognizing the place of people in the community in the justice equation after a "crime" like the appearance of graffiti on our garage, moves the analysis from individualized retributive justice to restoring, repairing and rebuilding communities.

When answers are provided to the various questions such as these, theory-building begins. When questions are asked about why kids engage in graffiti and why the low level of minimum wage and lack of affordability of childcare exists, conclusions are being made based on observations, readings and perhaps even research. In this way, working assumptions are being developed based on various forms of generalization from experience and knowledge that will be used to guide situations in the future. We begin to engage in theoretical thinking when undertaking these exercises (Sears 2005: 9). As with all learning, a certain amount is drawn from personal experience. However, using the theorizing of others can help to develop analytical capacity. Already developed theories help by, in large part, suggesting the kinds of questions that need to be asked in trying to understand individual behaviour resulting in problematic situations and identifying surrounding social issues. Understanding the social issues surrounding these problematic situations is a necessary component in pursuing the study of justice by utilizing a broad definition of justice which includes social justice. If problems are only seen as personal, then the most vulnerable groups of individuals in society who need assistance in order to achieve a just society can't be identified.

Summary Points

Problems have both personal and social aspects.

Understanding social problems is important in order to respond appropriately with policy. Treating problems only as individual problems often does not address their root causes.

Responding to social problems through policy also requires theoretical thinking or the development of working assumptions based on generalization.

Theoretical Perspectives in Analyzing Social Problems

Main Points

As you read, highlight the answers to these questions:

Why do social science theories have qualifications and conditions?

Which theory is more critical of society?

Is any one theory superior to the others?

Everyday decisions are made by people about the simplest things, like what to eat and what to wear, to more enduring issues such as what program of study to embark on or which career to pursue. These decisions are based on understandings and beliefs about the possible benefits and costs of these decisions and an additional amount of embedded theory that is possessed about consequences of these decisions. A decision about what clothing to purchase may be informed by one's theory of which clothing manufacturer pays a fair wage to its workers. Different theories offer different tools to explain social phenomena. Expanding our knowledge of different theories can expand our understanding of social problems and inform the third perspective of justice in this book, ethical practice. This is because understanding a range of theoretical perspectives is akin to understanding a diverse set of people's perspectives, for, ultimately, theoretical perspectives represent different social movements or thinking from different backgrounds and places in the world. This broadens the problematic of an issue and, by illustrating different potential causes of the issue and therefore different potential solutions, allows for a more informed decision or ethical practice of how to remedy social problems in the future.

Formal theories, developed through social movement activism or scholarly studies, tend to reflect a broader view than theories based on personal experience. These academic theories are developed through interchange over time and a more rigorous set of requirements for internal consistency and fit with the world. An example of a theory is Darwin's theory of evolution. Many people (including his grandfather) had the idea of evolution prior to Darwin. However, Darwin developed a theoretical account explaining how and why evolution occurred over time, referring to broader scientific frameworks used for understanding life forms (Sears 2005: 19). A theory provides not simply a description, but rather an explanation of a phenomenon using some sort of broader framework of understanding.

In the social sciences, social explanations or theories generally will not hold without qualification for all time, all conditions and all cases, for at least two reasons:

a) The probabilistic nature of social inquiry
When predicting a social phenomenon (someone's future occupation, health and educational outcomes) it is impossible to do so with complete certainty. We can assign probabilities based on social class, education of parents and other factors.

b) The inherent pluralism in social causation
One is unable to say that a child who suffers child abuse and is raised in a home of criminal gang members will become a criminal. This is partly due to the second reason that scientific method is difficult to apply in the social sciences: the inherent pluralism in social causation (as many factors contribute to social outcomes). The abused child of criminals will have many other influences in their life, which may be positive and prevent that child from growing up to live a life of crime. Perhaps the child will excel in school because of thoughtful, caring teachers or will benefit from a particularly close relationship with grandparents. (Grabb 2002: 46)

There are many theoretical perspectives for studying social problems. Five will be discussed here: structural functionalism, conflict theory, symbolic interactionism, feminism and post-structuralism. These perspectives are a representative sampling of possible approaches. Each represents a different lens or analytic framework for approaching a social problem and is based on different values and different assumptions about how society functions. No one perspective is necessarily superior to the others; no perspective is wrong. Much can be learned from all of the perspectives.

Structural Functionalism

Structural functionalism is described as a school of thought rather than as a particular theory. This makes it difficult to define and describe in a manner all of its proponents will accept (Grabb 2002: 95). Structural functionalism is characterized by a particular strategy of inquiry. This strategy investigates society as if it were a system of parts that were interconnected to form various structures, each of which perform various functions for the system (Durkheim 1893: 49). Often the analogy of an organism is used, where society is envisioned just as a living (human) organism, with particular parts to fulfill particular functions and maintain a state of balance and social equilibrium. Just as a human body has organs such as a heart or liver performing different functions, so too does society have parts or structures performing functions. For example, the family is a structure that reproduces society through performing the function of having children and socializing them; politics is a structure that governs members of society; education is a structure that transmits society's skills and knowledge (Parsons 1937).

In analyzing society, structural functionalists may study "norms" (shared expectations about behaviour), "roles" (behaviour associated with a particular position in the social structure), "institutions" (collective means of dealing with basic social functions such as government, the economy, the family and education) and "values" (things preferred because they are defined as having worth) (Parsons 1951: 327; Williams 1960). All of these parts of society interrelate and work, according to structural functionalists, to maintain society as a functioning system (Parsons 1951). There are two types of function: manifest functions are those that society intends and are often formally set out as institutional goals; latent functions differ as they are functions that are unintended and almost always informal (Merton 1968).

Functionalism maintains that the ideal condition of any system is balance and stability, just like any living organism. Social problems arise when social institutions do not fulfill their functions and dysfunction occurs. Dysfunctions are undesirable consequences of an activity or social process that inhibits a society's ability to adapt or adjust (Merton 1968). Social disorganization in the entire society is caused by dysfunctions in social institutions. Social problems result from rapid social change from things such as technological advancement, which causes stress on institutions.

Illness is seen from a functionalist perspective as a dysfunction or a threat to social institutions operating as they should. This is easily analogous to the organism metaphor as illness causes an imbalance and is counterproductive to a healthy thriving organism. People who are ill cannot fulfill their appropriate social roles: their responsibilities to family, employers and larger society. According to Talcott Parsons (1951), a founder of this perspective, illness is a form of deviance that must be controlled. Sick individuals are seen as not responsible for their incapacity, exempted from their usual role and task obligation, expected to "get well" and obligated to seek and comply with directions of a medical professional. In this way, physicians are agents of social control by certifying a person is physically or mentally ill and specifying how they are to behave and treatment they are to undergo.

Structural functionalism would view crime as a social problem resulting from rapid change in society which has weakened social solidarity and social institutions like the family so that insufficient order is maintained. Our correctional and penitentiary institutions have become breeding grounds for gang members starting with Hell's Angels to the more recent Native Syndicate members. This is a latent function (arguably a dysfunction) as it is unintended and not a formal function of these correctional and penitentiary institutions. The manifest function is to retrain and rehabilitate offenders.

Structural functionalists have two main theories of crime. The first is that deviance functions to maintain society (Erikson 1966). By "criminalizing" behaviour which is inconsistent with social norms, social norms of cohesion are endorsed and social solidarity is expressed when those who do not conform are stigmatized. This is a view that was expressed as early as 1927 when studying social problems of immigration (Thomas and Zraniedi 1927) and again the in the 1960s when relating crime to the disintegration of traditional institutional authorities like the church, family, legal system and community (Nisbet 1969). This is an approach to crime which is often seized by some political parties to form part of their "get tough on crime" campaign. However, the reality is that crime is often committed in moments of passion or desperation with very little thought as to criminal consequences. As such, having a law against a certain act does not provide an incentive to a person to hold off in performing the act in that particular moment of passion.

A second functionalist theory of crime focuses on norm violation as a disruption of natural order and equilibrium. This perspective sees this disruption as a natural occurrence and an indication of social change. Philip Hauser (1969) argued that observable social problems such as housing, pollution, crimes of violence, protest and war were all related to "social morphological revolutions" or the transition of the small, intimate community life of the past to the large, mass society of today. This change, he believed, was in part due to increased population, increased diversity of cultures in populations and increased urbanization (such that people live in close proximity to one another).

One of the founding structural functionalist scholars, Emile Durkheim (1858–1917) studied the solidarity of industrial society. Durkheim conceptualized the notion of society in a state of "anomie" — a condition where there was an absence of social regulation resulting in a state of normlessness. This he considered a pathological state indicating a breakdown in social order and solidarity. In a healthy society people know exactly what goals are appropriate for their particular social positions and precisely how they are supposed to realize those goals. A state of anomie is a state of confusion about the legitimacy of various social aspirations and the propriety of certain ways of pursuing those aspirations (Durkheim 1895). For example, studying hard and doing well in school to pursue one's choice of career makes a healthy contribution to society; however, a state of anomie is being a member of a gang and pursuing economic reward through selling harmful drugs to young people.

Durkheim distinguished physical needs from social needs. Physical needs are regulated by nature such as eating until one's hunger is satisfied; social needs are not so regulated. A person has an unlimited desire for wealth, power and prestige if they are not checked by external and social constraints. Unregulated, they escalate until they are unattainable. Unsatisfied social desires without social norms results in disappointment, unhappiness and frustration. This increases stress and an individual propensity to commit suicide. In times of rapid economic change such as an economic decline, recession or depression, the suicide rates escalate (Durkheim 1897). Although Drukheim studied suicide, Merton borrowed the concept of anomie to explain deviance in the United States (1938). Often, communities with high suicide rates also have very high crime rates. A recent newspaper article documents the high suicide rate of Nunavut, which also has high crime rates (Paperny and Minogue 2009; Statistics Canada 2008).

Durkheim's theories of anomie and suicide have been revised to a more general theory of social deviance and crime in more recent times (Yablonsky and Haskell 1988). In North American society youth are taught the value of being successful by making money and acquiring material wealth. The media assist with this materialism and the embracement of this lifestyle. However, the reality is that our society does not provide equal opportunities to all to attain this lifestyle. In fact, a differential opportunity exists depending on one's social status, ethnicity and background.

The overemphasis on ends (being wealthy) and lack of emphasis on means (ensuring equality of opportunity) produces an imperfect state of affairs or an anomie. With the overemphasis on the end goal of winning, the way people play the game or the means of achieving that goal is less important and people feel less bound to rules, laws and social norms. This mal-integration or anomie in turn produces strain which is most acutely felt by lower-status individuals. Society encourages these individuals to aspire highly but denies them equal access to legitimate avenues of opportunity to attain these goals through education and work. These individuals experience frustration, differential opportunity and strain, and this encourages deviance as a way of

Suicide in Northern Aboriginal Communities

The suicide rate among First Nations youths, 10 to 19 years, was 4.3 times greater than for other Canadians in 2000. There were 28.2 suicides per 100,000 First Nations people while the suicide rate for non-First Nations youth was 6.5 deaths per 100,000 (Health Canada 2005). Moreover, as a result of colonialism and residential school systems, Aboriginal peoples in Canada have lower socio-economic status than the rest of the population. As Durkheim's theory of anomie suggests, the rate of suicide among Aboriginal peoples is much greater than that of the rest of the Canadian population.

adapting to the gap separating social goals and the means of attaining them (Merton 1938). This theory of deviance is sometimes referred to as "strain theory." These late twentieth century versions of structural functionalism reflect the pervasive neo-liberalism discussed earlier in the chapter. Their focus has centred on the individual, with the individual as the source of all behaviour. The next theory shifts away from this neo-liberal focus.

Conflict Theory

Conflict theory evolved from the work of Karl Marx and focuses on issues of power, oppression and exclusion. Whereas structural functionalists view society as different parts working together, the conflict perspective views society as a struggle between different groups and interests competing for power and resources. Karl Marx viewed society as having progressed through a series of class/power struggles: the slave with the master; the serfs with the lords; and finally the worker with the owner of the factories (Marx and Engels 1848: 58, 92). At the time Karl Marx was writing, in the nineteenth century, industrialization was rapidly occurring and capitalism had emerged as a dominant economic form. Capitalism is an economic system characterized by private ownership of "property," by which Marx meant the "means of production," or the elements that contribute to production such as buildings, machines, labour or raw materials. From this private ownership, profits, which are actually created by the labour of workers, accrue disproportionately to capitalists, the owners of businesses (Marx and Engels 1848: 84).

Karl Marx saw society as divided, fundamentally but not completely, into two broad "classes": the workers (the "proletariat") and the business owners (the "bourgeoisie") (Marx and Engels 1848: 58). These were the two classes having the power struggle within the era of industrialization that Karl Marx was analyzing. This division benefited the business owners in two main ways. First, paying workers wages that were less than the value of the goods they produced, wealthy owners had access to many resources not available to workers. But, as well, their ownership and control of the means of production (the economy) gave business owners the means to control the other institutions of society (such as the state and the media) to their advantage (Marx and Engels 1846: 59). An example of this is the laws against vagrancy (loitering in public places) that penalize unemployed people as not contributing to the capitalist system of work and consumerism, while they were unemployed through no fault of their own (Chambliss 1994). For Marx, capitalism is fundamentally, at its very core, an unjust society.

Neo-Marxist conflict theorists today have further developed the ideas of class inequality inherent to capitalism and the rise to dominance of the ideology of neo-liberalism and the social problems linked to poverty; others focus on race/ethnicity or gender. An example would be a focus on corporate crime or wrongs committed in the pursuit of profits without regard to other considerations such as worker or consumer safety. In a neo-Marxist analysis, worker and product hazards are inherent in capitalism because the fundamental goal is profit-making.

The resolution of these issues is the creation of a classless society, changing work to make it safer and more fulfilling for everyone and applying stronger controls over corporations to ensure the economy serves society rather than social life existing to serve the economy. In relation to justice, the conflict approach would argue that powerful groups in society — particularly the economically powerful — have at their disposal the means to, if not define, then to disproportionately influence the kind of behaviour that is defined as criminal. Instrumental Marxists see capitalists as having direct access to those who run the state because of elite upper-class connections; structural Marxists see this influence as a result of the predominance of the economy (with the capitalists and the state actors all consistently pursuing the advancement of the economy and maximization of profits as goals). The result of these connections is that, most often, socially harmful behaviours that are key to profit-making (like unsafe, dangerous work) will not likely be criminalized. In an inequitable society, such as capitalism, they would argue, much crime results from the lack of opportunities for the poor and for racial or ethnic minorities. Again, a classless society would not define crime in a manner detrimental to those who are poor or not meeting the needs or interests of the powerful capitalist class in society.

In respect of health, the conflict perspective concludes that the medical complex of a societal health care system rooted in the capitalist economy creates social problems. Not only do the poor all over the world experience poor health because of their highly stress-filled lives (where the soup kitchen is a pay cheque away) but also their lack of access to resources for good health care such a medicine and doctors. In another example, pharmaceutical companies are known to put profits before health. Pharmaceutical companies have been exposed for activities that advance profit-making at the expense of the health of society in general. For instance:

a) In the non-Western world, some pharmaceutical companies investigate indigenous knowledge of traditional healing. Upon making a discovery, the pharmaceutical company will patent the discovery and prevent even the original indigenous people from practising their own form of healing. Then, the pharmaceutical company will sell their patented "discovery" for a profit not shared with the indigenous people (Shiva 1997).
b) Health professionals have documented that some pharmaceutical companies put profits first and have actively prevented the publication of research exposing harmful effects of their patented drugs (Lexchin 2002; Thompson, Baird and Downie 2001).

Other conflict theorists focus less on social classes and more on conflict arising from groups with opposing values and interests. Value conflicts occur between diverse categories of people including non-Whites and Whites, heterosexuals and homosexuals, environmentalists and industrialists, and young and old. These conflict theorists sometimes term their theory as "oppression theory." Oppression entails the domination of subordinate groups by more powerful groups and their exclusion from full participation in society. An example of this is the treatment of Aboriginal peoples in Canadian society after centuries of colonialism (Mullaly 2002: 17).

Conflict theory is, like structural functionalism, concerned with the social world at an aggregate, "big picture" or macro level. Broad aspects of society, such as institutions and large social groups are studied.

Symbolic Interactionism

Symbolic interactionism focuses on the individual in society or the micro level of society. It examines the individual and how the individual is shaped and influenced by the society they are living in. An individual's identity is shaped by symbolic interaction — that is, social behaviour based on the meanings that are created and attached to behaviour. In other words, actual behaviour is less important than the meaning attached to behaviour. Max Weber (1864–1920) asserted that to understand individual and group behaviour one needs to see the world from the eyes of that individual or group. When conducting social science research, scientists must try to understand others' views of reality and the subjective aspects of their experiences, including their symbols, values, attitudes and beliefs (Mead 1934). When trying to understand the individual being studied, the researcher is trying to understand that individual's "construction" of social life, or how that individual perceives the world and themselves. The influence of social structures on this perception or individual construction is the paramount object of study (Cooley 1902). Social problems are studied and analyzed from the aspect of how certain behaviours come to be defined as social problems and how individuals and groups come to engage in activities that a significant number of people, or a number of significant people, view as a major social concern (Becker 1963).

For symbolic interactionists, the way that people conceive of themselves, their society and specific situations, affects their behaviour. The labelling perspective is the classic symbolic interactionist perspective on deviance. From this point of view, a social group or behaviour is viewed as problematic if it is labelled as such. Symbolic interactionists would argue that mental illness is most importantly a label (a social construction) conferred on individuals who are "different" and who don't conform to particular definitions of appropriate behaviour. A growing number of behaviours and conditions are being labelled as medical problems, such as hyperactivity, attention deficit disorder and learning disabilities. Even some natural aspects of life, such as aging, menopause and birth, have been transformed socially into medical events.

In respect of crime, two questions are important. First, how do crime and deviance come to be defined as such (Becker 1963) or, more specifically, "labelled" as crime? Second, what are the effects of being labelled as criminal or deviant? With respect to the former, Becker explains that deviance can often be in the eye of the beholder because various groups have different conceptions of what is right and proper in certain situations. That is, deviance is discovered by a dominant group that does not share a belief in the appropriateness of another group's behaviour. For example, during the first half of the twentieth century, the Aboriginal tradition of potlatch was illegal. This was a traditional ceremony and practice of sharing one's worldly goods and wealth with others. In his classic statement, Becker (1963: 9) explains:

> Social groups create deviance by making the rules whose infraction constitutes deviance, and by applying those rules to particular people and labelling them as outsiders. From this point of view, deviance is not a quality of the act the person commits, but rather a consequence of the application by others of rules and sanctions to an "offender." The deviant is one to whom that label has successfully been applied; deviant behavior is behavior that people so label.

With respect to the impact of being "labelled" as criminal and the creation of further deviant behaviour, two paths were identified. First, the label catches the attention of the labelling audience, causing the audience to watch and continue to label the individual. Second, the label may be internalized by the individual, leading to an acceptance of a deviant self-concept (Wilkins 1965). After an individual commits a criminal act and is caught and convicted, that person is stigmatized as a criminal. This deviant label then dominates that person's social identity and is thus the primary basis on which the person is defined by others. Being labelled deviant then may deny that person opportunities for engaging in non-deviant behaviour and causes the person to develop a deviant self-concept and act accordingly (Wilkins 1965; Schwartz 1962).

The labelling perspective can be seen in youth involved in crime. Teenagers who commit acts of crime are often expelled from school or placed in custody. This causes them to be denied opportunities to participate in sports and activities that regular students are able to participate in and affects their self-image as being a "druggie" or "gang member." Resolving social problems sometimes involves changing the meanings and definitions attributed to people and situations (Goffman 1963).

All three perspectives covered have their strengths and weaknesses.

Table 1 Comparison of Theoretical Perspectives

	Structural Functionalism	**Conflict Theory**	**Symbolic Interactionism**
Representative Theorists	Emile Durkheim Robert Merton	Karl Marx C. Wright Mills	George H. Mead Erving Goffman
Society	Society is a set of interrelated parts; cultural consensus exists and leads to social order; natural state of society is balance and harmony.	Society is marked by power struggles over scarce resources; inequities result in conflict; social change is inevitable; the fundamental inequality of capitalist society results in a constant state of imbalance.	Society is a network of interlocking roles; social order is constructed through interaction as individuals, through shared meaning, make sense out of their social world.
Individuals	Society's institutions socialize individuals; socialization is the process by which social control is exerted; people need society and its institutions.	People are inherently good, but societies based on capitalism and patriarchy institutionalize and reward negative aspects of humans such as materialism and wealth accumulation.	Humans are interpretative and interactive; they are constantly changing as their "social beings" emerge and are moulded by changing circumstances.
Cause of Social Problems?	Rapid social change: social disorganization that disrupts the harmony and balance; inadequate socialization, weak institutions, or a combination of these.	Inequality: the dominance of groups of people over other groups of people; oppression and exploitation; competition between groups.	Different interpretations of roles: labelling of individuals, groups or behaviours as deviant; definition of an objective condition as a social problem.
Social Policy Solutions	Repair weak institutions; assure proper socialization; cultivate a strong collective sense of right and wrong.	Minimize competition; create an equitable system for the distribution of resources.	Reduce impact of labelling and associated stigmatization; alter definitions of what is defined as a social problem.

	Structural Functionalism	Conflict Theory	Symbolic Interactionism
Criticisms	Called "sunshine sociology"; supports the maintenance of the status quo; needs to ask "functional for whom?"; does not deal with issues of power and conflict; incorrectly assumes a consensus.	Utopian and simplistic model; Marxist states have failed; denies existence of cooperation and equitable exchange; can't explain cohesion and harmony.	Concentrates solely on micro issues; fails to link micro issues to macro level concerns; too psychological in its approach; assumes label amplifies problem.

Source: Adapted from Mooney, Knox and Schacht 2008:16.

Although scholars often are drawn to one particular theory and reject others, it should be noted that there are scholars who study and apply each of these theories. No one theory has been endorsed as the superior theory; it would be impossible for a consensus such as this to be achieved. All three, though, have come under heavy criticism in recent years. Feminists have shown that all three ignore a fundamental fact about all societies — their division into two genders and the almost universal inequality between the genders. Post-structuralism criticizes the structural functionalist and conflict theories for over-emphasizing society and social behaviour and, in the process, ignoring the individual variation in behaviour and attitudes within society; symbolic interactionism is criticized for being too focused on a psychological analysis at the individual level.

Summary Points

Structural functionalism is often illustrated using the example of an organism. It is a macro level theory.

The conflict perspective focuses on power differences and conflict in society.

Symbolic interactionism differs from structural functionalism as the focus is on the perspective of the individual and effects of social structures on this perspective.

Feminism

Main Points

As you read, highlight the answers to these questions:

How is feminism significantly different from the three previous theoretical perspectives discussed?

Which of the three theoretical perspectives is most similar to feminism?

What is discourse analysis?

Feminists aim to make what appears "natural" questionable. The dominant Western belief is that capitalism is the best economic institutional arrangement; the neo-Marxist conflict perspective seeks to denaturalize and question this. Feminism aims at "denaturalizing" beliefs, thought and behaviour patterns that are patriarchical — those that give males privileged access to society's resources and social attitudes and see males and masculinity as superior to females and femininity. A patriarchical belief would be akin to the belief, started in the nineteenth century Victorian upper class, that a woman's place was in a home, giving birth to and caring for children (supportable by the fact that women have children, not men). Feminists seek to denaturalize this belief and the current parallel beliefs in today's era, for example, the notion that certain occupations like engineering are better suited to men. The task of defining feminism is controversial and difficult because of its depth and breadth, but understanding its goals and methods is illuminating (Beasley 1999). At its most general, feminism can be understood as both a body of knowledge and a political movement aimed at understanding and alleviating the inequality of women (Comack 2006: 42). Put simply, feminists argue that male-dominated societies are fundamentally unjust.

European and male perspectives, such as conflict theory and symbolic interactionism, are valid, but only partially. Feminists were pioneers in exposing this. For example, the Marxist conflict perspective centres on the class struggle between workers and capitalists. This theorizing did not reflect the perspective of women in the work force and the economy, for example. Women's issues of maternity leave and gender equality in pay and promotion were all omitted. Theoretical frameworks of feminism were able to analyze these issues.

Another feature that feminist theorizing shares with the conflict perspectives is its insistence on analyzing power within relationships (both interpersonal relations and societal relations). The feminist focus is on gendered power and patriarchy. Patriarchy can be defined as the domination of women by men. This domination occurs in two key and inter-related ways. Men dominate through their privileged access to the public institutions of social power — men occupy the key positions in the economy and politics. Men also dominate in the attitudes that privilege masculinity — that is, the attributes of men (strength, aggression and so on) are seen to be superior to those of women (nurturance, cooperation and so on). The privileging of masculinity leads many of societies' institutions to reflect masculine attributes. Because there are many women, in many areas of the world, with many perspectives, there is no one feminist theoretical perspective. As well, there is no singular feminist issue per se. Feminists analyze all issues from a feminist, gendered power analysis. Sometimes this perspective is termed "reflexive." This means that the feminist perspective is constantly evolving through the process of reflection and a working and reworking of the different types of feminism in relation to the dominant social structure of patriarchy (a survey of which is beyond the scope of this chapter). Many other theoretical approaches today are also reflexive.

This constant reflection and reevaluation is a common feature with theoretical perspectives that reject the view that all knowledge rests on scientific method, which holds the key to truth about human behaviour. The disciplines of science (physical), medicine and psychology are some of the disciplines that rely heavily on these positivist assumptions (positivism is attributed to Auguste Comte and has come to be known today as the idea that society can be studied objectively and rationally and without values, beliefs, feelings and opinions). Feminism is a world view which challenges these all-knowing, objective claims to truth based on totalizing structures formulated on aggregated statistical data, for example, theories of total structures of capitalism or patriarchy. Structural functionalism and the neo-Marxist conflict theory often make such totalizing claims. Feminism instead tends to focus on the standpoint of the individual person or racial or ethnic minority and attempts to deconstruct totalizing claims, exposing their socially constructed and patriarchical claims of truth.

Within the health field, a paramount concern of feminists has been the relatively small numbers of and treatment of women within the medical profession. Until only very recently it had been very difficult for women to enroll in medical faculties to become doctors, and it is still somewhat difficult for women to attain the lucrative professional specialties of doctors. In addition, the majority of nurses are women fulfilling the care giving, less well-paid positions in the health care field. Many of the traditional functions of midwives in labour and delivery have been taken over by doctors, reducing their work load and paid compensation (Van Teijlingen et al. 2000). This was done, not because the practice of midwifery wasn't a safe medical practice, but because it didn't medicalize birth. These issues could be analyzed both from a feminist perspective and a conflict perspective. From a feminist perspective, the place of women within the field of health and practices of health care are marginalized; from a conflict perspective the medical profession now controls, directs and profits from what used to be a natural maternal process of giving birth.

Self Test

Why is recognizing social problems surrounding personal problems essential for achieving substantive justice and formulating policy? Give examples.

What are the differences between how structural functionalism, conflict theory and symbolic interactionism explain crime in society? Which perspective is most accurate and why?

Which theoretical perspective might best explain why young women join gangs? How could more than one perspective be used?

Post-Structuralism

Post-structural theorists reject the grandiose macro theories of structural functionalism, conflict and symbolic interactionism based on totalizing structures such as capitalism. Some refer to these theorists as "post-modern" as well; however, there is controversy on whether society has ever been "modern" and thus could ever be "post-" modern. For this reason, the term this book employs is "post-structural."

Privilege is embedded and replicated in practices of social structure and social interactions through the exercise of power, which is everywhere (Foucault 1979). Instead of focusing on power itself and who holds that power (as some neo-Marxist conflict theorists do), post-structuralists employ Michel Foucault's focus on the mechanisms of power (Comack 2006: 61). For example, regulatory environments exist outside the formal purview of the "state" or government, but nonetheless regulate and control individual behaviour. This occurs in all aspects of our lives, including poverty, unemployment and health.

According to Foucault, a new social mentality of regulation developed in the sixteenth century contrasting and eventually replacing regulation by absolute submission to a sovereign king or queen (Foucault 1978: 137). This new mentality exerted a much less visible, more internalized and less physically coercive influence and comprehensive regulation of behaviour without the sovereign state's mechanisms of control. This change in how society is ruled, from sovereign monarch to government, was characterized by the increase in the liberty of the individual. Foucault saw neo-liberalism as a mentality of rule, representing a method of rationalizing the exercise of government through techniques for leading and controlling individuals without being responsible for them (Foucault 1997: 74). By increasing individual liberties and freedoms and freeing individuals from subjugation by a monarch, societal norms and expectations of individual behaviour conforming to these norms increased. Many new mechanisms of control relied heavily on individual perception and ideas of reality.

New mechanisms of control emerged in neo-liberal ideology as well. Social risks such as illness, unemployment and poverty became viewed not as the responsibility of the state, but as something lying in the domain of the individual (Lemke 2001: 201). Long gone were the days of absolute monarchy and feudalism wherein everyone had a role (serf or lord). Individual freedom brought individual choice and individual responsibility. An individual is seen as having the responsibility to obtain an occupation for financial support to be free from poverty and unemployment; an individual is also seen as having the responsibility to eat healthy food and attend a gym to remain free from illness.

These theorists often employ deconstruction as a method to expose mechanisms of control. Modernist thinking relies on binary oppositions (for example, racism and non-racism, or Black and White). Deconstruction allows for the illumination of how a particular category such as Whiteness is socially constructed. This method explores the various privileges that are accorded to being White and how these privileges are embedded in everyday practices and interactions between people. Deconstruction also criticizes the forces of hierarchy that are present in such binary constructions or boundary formations implicit in social structures and language.

Discourse analysis is often utilized as a way to deconstruct. Discourses are forms of language use or ways of making sense of the world and its social practices (Phillips and Hardy 2002). Discourses are reflected in the language of people represented in all manner of forms, whether they be letters, newspaper articles, trial transcripts, laws, art or even music — what discourse analysts call social "texts." Discourse methodology assumes that meaning made by a speaker or writer is structured by language. This language is such that everyone has their own subjective experience of what the language means and consequently constructs texts differently, but within their own particular time, place and community. For example, most texts written prior to the 1970s used the term "he" to refer to an individual. All laws prior to this time were written using the term "he." Feminists then pointed out the gendered place of privilege this form of language attributed to the male, or the "he." The utilization of the word "he" subtly assumed that an individual was always a "he" and only in exception would be a "she." This language practice was one of the ways that male domination was perpetuated. Now, the practice has become to use "he or she" or "they" or omit the pronoun altogether. This language practice reflects equality.

Through a process of examining and analyzing the discourses found in various texts from a standpoint or place of the "other," the marginalized or the "de-centred," the structures of power and influence that are the centre of mainstream society can be revealed. Specific forms of discourses that claim to speak the truth and thus exercise power in a society are de-centred to reveal the fact they reflect the truth of the writer or speaker, but do not reflect the truth of all people. For example, many schools still teach that North America was "discovered" by various European explorers. Although this may reflect the fact that Europeans discovered a land across the ocean of which they were previously unaware, to say they discovered North America reflects a White Eurocentric belief very different from the reality of all of the Indigenous peoples living in North America at the time whose ancestors had known North America since time immemorial. Just as importantly, using the language of discovery is an exercise in oppression, if only in that this language continually supports the idea for White people that they have a right to the land their ancestors "discovered."

The deconstruction of discourses reveals the various "centrisms" that are

Discourse of Denial: Racial Profiling Exposed

Police generally deny any racism in their practices, procedures or work force. On October 19, 2002, Police Chief Julian Fantino was quoted in the *Toronto Star* as saying, "We do not do racial profiling... there's no racism" (in Henry and Tator 2006: 157). These sentiments were reiterated in the media by the President of the Ontario Association of Chiefs of Police, the Toronto Police Association, the Toronto Police Services Board and the Mayor of Toronto (Henry and Tator 2006: 157). However, the *Toronto Star* had studied data (based on arrests, tickets and detentions) which confirmed racial profiling was taking place. As well, the Ontario Human Right Commission conducted an inquiry in 2003, reporting on the costs and impacts of racial profiling, and two other reports also confirmed the practice of systemic racial profiling in the Toronto Police Department (Henry and Tator 2006: 158).

The statements of the Chief of Police and heads of significant crime control organizations represent the "discourse" or story and language told by powerful members of our society that racism is non existent. This is an example of the "discourse of denial." This is the story that Canadians like to hear and believe. However, the hard factual evidence represented by the research reports represents the reality of racism existing within police practices.

embedded and naturalized so as to not be questioned. These centrisms may be many and include ethnocentrism (the belief in the superiority of one's own culture and ethnicity), anthropocentrism (the belief in the superiority of humans) or theocentrism (the belief in the superiority of a particular religion). The deconstruction of discourse can also reveal various myths that mainstream society likes to believe, but which are inaccurate. These myths are also termed "discourses of denial."

As an example, churches and government operated residential schools in Canada for many years. It can only be assumed that a discourse of denial was in existence at the time that these schools were described and thought of as "educating" Aboriginal people. Now, decades later, the discourse of denial has been exposed as a "myth." A Truth and Reconciliation Commission is exposing the lived experience of oppression and horror that many of these students faced through acts of violence perpetuated against them within these schools (Sinclair 2010).

By critically engaging and deconstructing structures in society, post-structuralists expose mechanisms of power that oppress groups of people. Often these mechanisms are thought of as "natural" to many and not questioned. When this occurs the "discourse of denial" is at work making structures of oppression and domination appear quite natural. Without the exposure by post-structural academics, students and citizens, these totalizing structures of oppression would continue to oppress and marginalize. In order to assist the marginalized and least well-off in society and achieve social justice, discourses of denial have to be questioned and replaced with practices that can achieve justice.

Summary Points

Feminism seeks to uncover or decentre the embedded power relations of patriarchy in everyday social interaction.

There is no one feminist theoretical perspective.

Post-structuralists analyze mechanisms of control, regulation and power.

Discourse analysis deconstructs the meaning of language in texts to show that powerful groups can dominate covertly through perpetuating, reinforcing and saturating society with their "centrisms" or implicit beliefs. It also discloses myths privileged groups like to believe, which are inconsistent with the lived experience or reality of disadvantaged groups.

Neo-Liberalism and Justice

The pervasive ideology of neo-liberalism insists that people in our society view troubles of health, loss of employment and crime as problems of an individual. This ideology has many parallels to both the political strategy of political parties in the latter half of the twentieth century that are termed neo-conservatism and the focus on cutting state welfare programs and the reliance on individuals and free markets. Viewing matters as individual problems downplays their social dimensions and implications. Social dimensions are illustrated by the evidence that poor people predominantly have problems of health, crime and unemployment. Health, crime and unemployment are but three illustrations; many other social problems exist in respect of many other social structures. The inequity of these social structures casts into doubt the social justness of our society.

Understanding the inequity of social structures inherent in social problems is an important step in assessing the second theme of this book, substantive justice. Viewing problems as social allows for a richer policy response to assist people in alleviating problems and imagining new patterns of distributing societal assets such as education, health care and employment benefits. Shifting the analysis from individual problems to social problems focuses policy discussion to strengthening community or social cohesion and strategies to make our society more socially just.

Applying a theoretical perspective to a social problem allows a broader and deeper analysis of both its causes and the potential remedies; it expands the problematic of an issue. This chapter introduced five theoretical perspectives. It should be kept in mind that there are many theoretical perspectives applied by many people in many contexts, not just these five. No one theoretical perspective is the only correct theoretical perspective. Our knowledge of our society and of the people in it is expanded by understanding all theoretical perspectives. We will not have the diverse, multicultural, anti-racist and anti-sexist society we wish without first acknowledging the anti-racist and feminist theoretical perspectives. Acknowledging this is a first step in informing the third theme of justice in this book, our own ethical practice, and also in thinking about structural and institutional ethical practices that might end structural or systemic racism. This theme will be pursued further in Chapter Four.

Discourse analysis is one method employed to expose and de-centre the privilege embedded in the meaning of the language we use. This form of analysis illustrates that often privilege is subtle, hidden and not even fully understood (especially by those with privilege) until exposed through the standpoint of another perspective. Discourse analysis is a method that allows the many facets of power relations in society to be revealed and various "centrisms" uncovered.

Glossary

anomie – a state of normlessness.

class – refers to groups of people who live in similar economic circumstances. There is a disagreement about which economic circumstances are primary. Some define class as groups who have similar levels of material wealth and purchasing power, such as upper, middle and lower classes; while others see class as based on similar positions within the structure of production, such as capitalists, managers and workers.

conflict theory – a theory of society that views society as an aggregate, focusing on power dynamics between groups in society.

deconstruction – the exposure of centrism and embedded power structures through analysis.

discourse – forms of language which reflect ways of making sense of the world and social practices.

feminism – a doctrine that suggests that women are systematically disadvantaged in modern society and a social movement that advocates equal opportunities for men and women.

ideology – a set of beliefs, attitudes or opinions organized around certain values in respect of anything from religion, economics or scientific knowledge regardless of whether they are accurate or not.

labelling – the societal process of assigning a status to an individual such as the status of "criminal" or "troublemaker." Positive labels are also possible with similar effects as negative ones such as "best student" or "most likely to succeed."

modernity – the term commonly used to describe the time period ushered in by intellectual changes associated with the Enlightenment, rise of science, emergence and expansion of capitalism and expansion of western Europe. The central political and analytical assumption of modernity included the notion that knowledge is progressive, cumulative, holistic, universal and rational (Knutilla 2002: 18).

neo-conservatism – a political strategy founded on neo-liberalism.

neo-liberalism – the ideas and opinions often termed an "ideology" that focus on individuals as responsible for their social circumstances. Neo-liberal ideals are many and varied but tend to support the self-regulation of the market economy; minimal involvement of the state in social programs, expenditures and regulation; the privatization of government-owned industry (of currently public services like water, power and insurance); "free" global trade; the predominance and protection of individual property rights; and the replacement of the concept and practices of "the public good" or "community" with that of individual responsibility.

oppression – domination of subordinate groups by more powerful groups and their exclusion from full participation in society.

patriarchy – a social situation where men are dominant over women in status and power.

personal problem – a problem explained in terms of an individual's choices.

positivism – the idea that society can be studied objectively and rationally without values, beliefs, feelings and opinions.

post-structuralism – a perspective that rejects totalizing structural views of society (such as those encapsulated in theories of structural functionalism) and instead seeks to set aside or challenge predominant viewpoints and mechanisms of power in society.

social problem – a problem explained in terms of an individual's choices.

social structure – patterns of relationships or interaction among the various components of society that are relatively enduring.

structural functionalism – a theory of society wherein each aspect of society has a purpose and function contributing to the whole.

symbolic interactionism – a theory of society wherein an individual and their self-perception is shaped by social interaction with others.

Part II

Social Justice

Margot A. Hurlbert

Social justice is a set of ideas, values and social practices to ensure that all persons and groups enjoy economic security, can participate effectively in democratic decision-making, exercise mutual respect and caring for one another and live their lives in ways that protect and sustain the natural environment for future generations. Social justice is predominantly concerned with achieving the second pillar of justice: substantive or distributive justice. However, in nations like Canada, social justice is integrally intertwined with our democratic institutions that, in theory, enshrine the first theme of justice: formal, procedural justice.

Some advocates of social justice in Canada often fail to mention this important interconnection. This omission is in part due to the necessity of rejecting the theory of formal justice, or the practice of treating all people alike in all situations. In order to achieve substantive justice, however, different rules must apply to different people and different situations at certain times. For example, Canada's work force should fairly represent Canada's ethnic, cultural and gender diversity; to achieve this, a period of hiring preference for those groups historically discriminated against might be needed. This is termed "affirmative hiring" or "employment equity." The situations warranting different treatment, such as affirmative hiring practices, for people to achieve social justice, are built on a foundation of procedural justice, democratic institutions and human rights. Understanding when formal justice or procedural justice should apply and when substantive justice or the differential treatment of people should apply is the pursuit of justice; no one theme of justice, formal or substantive, is superior or can be practised to the exclusion of the other.

In order to achieve equality in Canada, more than formal justice is required. In 1985 Canada repatriated its Constitution and expanded it to include the *Charter of Rights and Freedoms*, whereby the right to equality became a "constitutional" right (something greater than a human right). The right to equality provides that no person can be discriminated against or treated differently. For example, this ensures "colour blind" practices: all people are treated equally regardless of the colour of their skin such that no one may be discriminated against or be the object of prejudice. This is a version of formal/procedural equality and justice. However, another constitutional right protects practices that are aimed at alleviating historical oppression or discrimination by requiring different practices for different people, such as affirmative hiring practices. These practices achieve substantive equality. That is, more is needed than these legal remedies; even if they are necessary, they are not sufficient to achieving social justice, and Part II of this book provides a foundation for understanding why. Achieving social justice also requires the ability to critically analyze society to generate solutions to current injustices. Setting aside preconceived biases and opinions is a requisite. Strategies to achieve social justice may be generated by approaching social problems with numerous analytic and theoretical perspectives. This book starts such a discussion. Part II addresses economic inequality through paid work, poverty, racism, social exclusion, the marginalization of women (particularly in the criminal justice system) and finally the environment.

Chapter Three, "Social Justice, Stratification and Oppression," by Loretta Gerlach, explores how people are ranked according to value (most often associated with their paid labour), resulting in social categorization by worth, or what is often termed "social stratification." How this process occurs in society is analyzed using theoretical perspectives introduced in Chapter Two. James Mulvale in Chapter Four, "Poverty, Economic Security and Justice," picks up on this analysis, illustrating how economic stratification impacts a person's life chances, including their health and education. With the goal of achieving substantive justice through economic redistribution, a specific strategy for combating poverty and achieving social justice—a basic income for all—is proposed. Implementing this strategy is an example of the ethical practice of taking into account the needs of the most vulnerable.

In Chapter Five, "Social Exclusion, Social Justice and Racism," Lisa Comeau explores social inequality in respect of race and ethnicity. In order to change the processes and structures of exclusion more is needed than eliminating prejudice or discrimination and practising inclusion. Focusing only on strategies of inclusion to achieve equality prevents true changes to the processes and structures of exclusion. In order to effect real change, an understanding and recognition of the privilege that exists in society for some groups of people that excludes and oppresses others is required. Lisa Comeau explores this privilege and its perpetuation through "democratic racism," a mechanism of discourse in society that masks racist practices.

Racist practices are most readily identified by marginalized and oppressed groups, whose knowledge is often crucial to exposing democratic racism. By listening to, seeing and understanding the perspectives and experiences of marginalized and oppressed peoples these practices can be indentified and exposed. Once exposed, there is at least the possibility democratic racism can be changed. Being oblivious to these perspectives prevents understanding and the possibility of acting in a manner that challenges democratic racism, which is a form of systemic discrimination. An obligation rests on those with privilege to act. In Chapter Six, "Women and Injustice," Gillian Balfour exposes practices of formal or procedural justice within the criminal justice system which oppress women. Of concern is the fact that, increasingly, women are being criminalized, punished and incarcerated. Gillian Balfour demonstrates that formal criminal justice and the rights-based adversarial court system, in its professed blindness to gender (and race and class) stereotypes, do not achieve substantive justice for women. That is, by not seeing the gendered nature of crime, the criminal justice system perpetuates gender oppression in society.

The last chapter in Part II, Chapter Seven, "Environmental Justice," surveys various definitions of environmental justice. Formal procedural environmental justice is illustrated through the legal system and substantive environmental (in)justice is illustrated through an analysis of how environmental resources and negative impacts of development such as pollution are unequally distributed in society. Achieving environmental justice requires both aspects of formal and substantive justice, as well as an ethical practice of taking into account the interests of the neediest. The interaction of all three themes of justice is demonstrated through the example of climate change. This chapter proposes a practice of environmental justice, based on a procedure of interconnection and real democratic participation, which attempts to combine all three elements of justice.

3

Social Justice, Stratification and Oppression

Loretta Gerlach and Margot A. Hurlbert

At the end of this chapter, you will be able to:

- Explore dimensions of social justice
- Illustrate labour market and social stratification
- Describe economic reward (labour or occupational stratification) and low income or poverty using the theoretical perspectives of structural functionalism, conflict, symbolic interactionism and feminism

Social justice, like justice itself, is one of those terms that we all use and probably claim that we'd know when we saw it, but it almost defies definition. It certainly is about how the many things that we value in life — money, prestige, schooling, good health and so on — are distributed among the people that make up a community, country, society and the world. It is also about how the things that we don't like — polluted water or hard or dirty work — are distributed amongst us. Social justice asks, in either case, if that distribution is fair. How do we determine what is "fair" and what is not? At the same time, social justice is also about what we think about how those things are distributed.

In very general terms, we could say that social justice is the perceived fairness of the division of rewards and burdens in society. It is less concerned with the codified forms of law than with the assessment of how a given society distributes its social and material goods (Pojman 2006). This distribution has been studied for hundreds of years. For example, Aristotle developed a concept of justice that explored proportionality — he viewed justice as whether people got what they deserved or had earned (Solomon and Murphy 2000). Beginning in the eighteenth century, Immanuel Kant and others proposed that, when looking at situations of distribution, people use a moral foundation to make decisions, and these philosophers felt that there may be some universality in how rational people apply these moral assessments and therefore what is right for one, should be right for all (Johnson 2008). This argument supports the political notion of rule by the majority. This book seeks to set aside the notion that majority rule imparts justice.

At the beginning of the twentieth century more philosophers began to explore the idea of "moral relativism," which countered the principle of universal morality (or majority rule) by stating that individual morals are products of their cultural, geographical and/or religious and other environments (Gowans 2008). This is akin to the idea of recognizing and respecting difference. As a result, while the material measure of the distribution of material goods among a society may be objective, the moral assessment of division is complex. This complexity is what pursuing social justice is about. The study of social justice refers to conceptualizing, analyzing and synthesizing how the good and bad things in our communities are distributed amongst us. This chapter will expand upon the definition of social justice offered in Chapter One.

Main Points

As you read, highlight the answers to these questions:
What is the definition of social justice?
How and why do social justice issues change over time?
Which of the three interlocking frames of justice is social justice most concerned with?

When we study social justice, we utilize a multidisciplinary approach that enables us to gain insight into the unique and complex challenges facing societies throughout the world. In a world increasingly characterized by conflict, on a global and a national level, as well as a growing gap between the rich and poor, there is a need to bring systematic analysis and a greater depth of understanding toward our most pressing social, economic and political problems. The study of social justice borrows from a number of disciplines, including sociology, philosophy, political science, cultural studies, psychology and history. For example, the philosophical roots of social justice were referenced earlier in this chapter. Philosophers continue to debate the question today as to whether there is an objective or universal test of social justice, or whether it is determined by power or the lack of it. History teaches us many lessons about social justice including the processes of colonization endured by Indigenous peoples the world over, international relationships between nations, and physical and political battles over access to wealth and power that have occurred throughout the ages. Sociology helps us understand how we are socialized by the influencing forces around us to form common views of right and wrong, good and bad, worthy and unworthy.

Social justice embraces a wide berth of topics which all relate to how the good and bad things in society are distributed. Just a few examples include:

- the unequal distribution of economic rewards including income and wealth;

- discrepancy in the availability of quality health care to people including pharmaceutical care, home care and emergency medical attention;
- the increased incidence of poverty among senior citizens or elderly people;
- the decreasing likelihood that our youth will obtain secure, well-paying careers or affordable housing, especially in relation to that of their parents;
- workplace wage gaps and the gendered division of paid work;
- barriers in employment faced by gays, lesbians or transgendered individuals; and
- the reduced participation in post-secondary education of people from lower-income families.

This chapter will focus on distribution, or what is often referred to as stratification, in relation to economic rewards: wealth, money and income. These elements of economic stratification are linked to broader social justice issues.

Formal and Distributive Justice

Procedural justice is a part of formal justice, the first overarching theme of justice in this book. Procedural justice is concerned with the fairness of processes (Heffernan and Kleinig 2000). It is useful to make a distinction between procedural justice and distributive or substantive justice. A procedural justice view will explore the processes by which decisions are made, through which rights and resources are allocated in a society. Those who promote procedural justice advocate that the same, fair procedure will always lead to just outcomes because everyone is treated the same and has the same opportunity to succeed. For example, let's say a big multinational department store is looking to hire people to work as department managers. A formal justice approach would say as long as the application forms used when people apply are the same, the criteria used to assess people's qualifications are the same and the interview questions asked of all the candidates for the job are the same, then everyone has a fair chance to get the job, and therefore any end decision is just. As stated in the introductory chapter, this is problematic because equal treatment does not always result in just outcomes. There is more on this in subsequent chapters.

Distributive or substantive justice views are concerned with what is "just" or "right" as it pertains to the allocation of goods (or utility) and benefits in a society (Drislane and Parkinson 2005). A distributive justice perspective measures the outcomes of a given situation and thus concentrates on whether or not results of what happens in a given society are just. Returning to the examples of hiring processes, for many years policing and firefighter organizations hired based on specific fitness criteria that involved high standards of strength and aerobic capacity. This resulted in an unintended outcome whereby significantly more men were successful in competitions than women, who generally have less upper body strength and aerobic capacity. Even though fitness testing was administered the same for everyone, it did not lead to a fair outcome because women were unable to succeed. After much review, policing and firefighter organizations have adapted these standards to ensure that candidates are physically fit enough to do the job, but the fitness standards are fair and reasonable to ensure that both men and women can succeed with proper fitness training. Distributive or substantive justice is associated with social justice more often than formal or procedural justice because both distributive justice and social justice are fundamentally concerned with the balance associated in the allocation of social rewards and burdens among people.

Determining whether outcomes are just, or whether the distribution of good and bad things in society is just, draws on ethical practice — the third pillar of justice — that is, taking into account the needs of the most vulnerable. This chapter will commence the discussion by critically examining how distribution occurs in society and defining and exploring oppression. Understanding oppression in society allows for the identification of the vulnerable and least favoured. Later chapters will draw attention to the least favoured in society: the poor (Chapter Four), those who are racially discriminated against (Chapter Five) and women in relation to the criminal justice system (Chapter Six).

Social Justice and History

Social justice issues are dynamic over time. Matters of grave importance a hundred years ago may or may not remain equally significant today. For example, one hundred years ago, the women's suffrage movement was concerned with women's right to vote, which is no longer an issue. At the same time, there are social justice issues that concern people today that people a century ago had never thought of. For example, a hundred years ago, Canadians would not have worried about ensuring equality in law for same-sex couples or about the health implications of continued asbestos exposure (Snider 2006: 187). As we evolve as a society, so do our values and our knowledge, and therefore our perspectives of social justice change over time. Some important social justice issues may still hold the same weight and merit but may in fact have changed in substance.

Let us consider our views on work and workplace issues. In the early years of the twentieth century, many Canadians were worried about various aspects of their working life, including access to jobs, good wages and benefits and safe working conditions (issues that Canadians still face). Through periods of industrialization and urbanization, workers in factories and in the trades wanted to ensure that they were being paid well enough, and many started to form unions and engaged in very difficult and dangerous struggles with owners of businesses and governments to gain rights such as the eight-hour work day and minimal health and safety protection. Canada's history is filled with struggles between working people and governments to ensure better working conditions for working people. For example, in May and June of 1919, more than 25,000 workers in Winnipeg walked off the job for six weeks in support of the principles of collective bargaining, better wages and the improvement of working conditions (Peirce and Bentham 2007). This resulted in the largest general strike in Canadian history. Unfortunately, the strike ended after very serious violence between police and strikers, and worker's rights were not advanced for several more years (ibid.). Today, Canadians are less active in and concerned with unions, and most are not terribly afraid for their safety at work (although many people are still killed on the job today and unfortunately many of them are under the age of twenty-five) (ibid.). Today many people are concerned about finding a full time job, with benefits and a good wage that will be flexible enough for them to balance their work and family lives (especially when you consider that most women now work outside the home). Specifically, we know that women and younger workers in Canada share more of these concerns since they are more likely to experience "precarious" employment — work that is part time, seasonal, piece work, home-based or contract (Beaujot 2004; Statistics Canada 2003).

Summary Points

Social justice is primarily concerned with substantive or distributive justice, but it is informed by ethical practice.

The study of social justice draws upon many academic disciplines.

Social justice issues are dynamic and change over time with social conditions.

Analyzing Social Justice

When studying social justice issues, we are compelled to look for the different elements of the problem. One is the so-called objective element, which refers to the quantifiable and observable aspects — both positive and negative — of a given social condition. Another is the subjective element, which refers to the perceptions of a social condition and its impacts and whether or not it should be considered a "problem." This relates to the moral nature of the problem — that is, in determining whether or not a particular social condition is harmful to society or to a segment of society and if the condition should and can be changed. For instance, we can objectively describe the growing gap between the rich and poor, and we could demonstrate objectively that the growing gap and increasing inequality has negative impacts on those who are becoming poorer and on society as social cohesion breaks down and poor health and crime increase. Yet, there are many, including some social theorists, who would argue that the growing gap is not unjust and is not a social problem. That is, they do not perceive it to be an issue that can and should be addressed or changed. So, the objective element is measuring the growing gap and its impacts, and the subjective element is determining whether or not this is a social problem that results in social harm and requires any change. Theoretical approaches to analyzing these elements of social issues and problems assist in discussing and recognizing subjective elements. Theorizing about labour stratification later in this chapter will illustrate this.

The third frame of justice, ethical practice, enters into social justice when exploring the subjective aspects of social issues and problems. In analyzing social problems, the interests of the least favoured or marginalized must be considered. The following example illustrates how the interests of the least favoured must be considered.

If an ethical practice is not part of the framing of justice, identifying and remedying social problems will be a contest or debate between different

The Growing Gap

The "growing gap" refers to the growing economic gap between the rich and the poor, which in recent years has reached unprecedented levels. This means that, both globally and nationally, the top income earners continue to earn increasingly more, while the lowest income earners are experiencing equally rapid decreases in their income (Mooney et al. 2008). According to the World Bank, the average income of the richest twenty countries was thirty-seven times that of the poorest twenty countries and this gap had doubled from 1960 to 2000 (ibid). Closer to home, the 2006 Canadian census indicates that this gap is also reflected among individual Canadian income earners (Beauchesne 2008). The top 20% of earners had a 6.2% increase in earnings since the 2000 Census, while the bottom 20% of earners experienced a 3.1% decrease over the last several years (ibid). This means that those who have the most money in Canada continue to gain more money and therefore improve their economic circumstances in life while those with the least amount of money continue to struggle.

The growing gap has occurred during the period of expanding globalization of economic systems across the world. Today the economic systems of countries around the world are more integrated than ever with the rise of trade treaties — organizations like the World Trade Organization (WTO) and the Asia-Pacific Economic Cooperation Forum (APEC) — and government cooperation such as that seen among the G20 and the G8. This is all part of the process of globalization, which is a social, economic, cultural and political process that makes it easier for people, goods, ideas and capital to travel around the world (Brym 2004). Supporters of globalization argue that this disparity is a natural result of market forces and an inability of the unsuccessful to properly adapt. However, critics of globalization claim that this capitalist free market model of globalization inherently creates a growing inequality. (Ghorayshi 2007: 217) groups having different moral views of social problems. This is an interesting dilemma for students of justice because, without an ethical practice, people disagree on what issues should or could be addressed and changed and even whether or not a condition is harmful. In fact, if people don't believe poverty is a social problem, then studies such as the growing gap would never be conducted. The problem outlined above is a social problem when approached from the ethical practice of considering the needs of the least well-off, the poor, who are growing poorer. When approached from the perspective of structural functionalists and neo-liberals, who believe in individualism, the growing gap is not a social problem but an illustration of poor people being treated justly for having made poor employment decisions (this will be explored in more detail below).

Often, varying perceptions are rooted in the fact that people differ in their values, beliefs and life experiences. Thus, what is seen as and publicly defined as a social justice issue will vary within a society, among societies and across historical periods.

Social Stratification and Status

Main Points:

As you read, highlight the answers to these questions:
What is social stratification?
What is status and how does this concept inform social stratification?
How does labour stratification interrelate with social stratification?

One of the central elements of the social structure of our society, as the growing gap so clearly illustrates, is inequality, or "social stratification," as sociologists often call it. Social stratification refers to the systematic process by which individuals, groups and places are categorized and ranked on a scale of social worth. This results in a hierarchy of individuals and groups and a resultant inequality of social relationships that determines who gets different rewards and burdens in society and why (Kerbo 2006).

Stratification is the division of society into layers based on social characteristics such as power or socio-economic status. Inequality and stratification are nothing new to society; they have been around for many centuries and are features of almost all societies (Porter 1970: 7). This inequality and stratification marks the relationships between the groups that make up the various elements of the social structure of our society: family (mothers, fathers, sisters, brothers); education (principals and university presidents, teachers and professors, students, support staff); government (prime minister and premier, cabinet ministers, bureaucrats, clerks, garbage collectors). All these groups relate to one another in many ways, but there are differences of power, authority and responsibility between them. Those differences of stratification express the distribution of rewards and burdens in society.

Social stratification is institutionalized (and backed by norms) and is based on statuses rather than personal attributes. Sociologists and anthropologists often refer to the positions people hold with a social group within the social structure as "status." Unfortunately, some people view specific racial populations to have more social worth than others. The same can be said of gender, as often men tend to be ranked as more valuable — evidenced by pay inequities in Canada. Professional athletes, rock stars and famous writers are often viewed as valued members of society. High school drop outs, criminals and the unemployed often are not. Finally, senior citizens seem to have less value and we provide less resources and attention to their needs and contributions than we do to other adults.

Some statuses are ascribed, that is, assigned on the basis of factors over which the individual has no control, and are often present from birth. Being born female and Aboriginal is an example of ascribed status. Achieved status, on the other hand, is assigned on the basis of some characteristic or behaviour over which the individual has some control. Most occupations, like doctor, daycare worker or welder, have an element of achieved status (Porter 1970: 7.).

"Master status" is the status that is the most significant in a person's social identity and the one which dominates all other statuses they may hold (ibid.). For example, a person might be a friend, a son, a father, an excellent basketball player and a physician. Due to the prestige associated with being a doctor in Canadian society, physician may be their master status. However, two doctors may not both regard their occupation as their master status; an Aboriginal doctor may regard "Aboriginal" as her master status.

Finally, the status value is the value that some characteristics impart to those who possess them, causing those individuals to be regarded and treated as more valuable or more worthy than persons who possess features from other categories. Thus, in our society, a physician has more status value than a maintenance worker. Status is important to social justice because it describes how we rank citizens relative to one another. The question for justice analysis is why some social positions have more status value than others and whether or not those status value differences are fair.

As should be obvious there is a subjective element in status value. Different statuses are afforded different value in the way they are regarded by others, which creates the perceived inequality between statuses. The status value afforded different statuses may not coincide with the actual value of the status to individuals and to society. That is, the ranking system in society — stratification — is as much about what statuses are perceived to be important as it is about their actual social value. To extend the example above, we certainly perceive professional athletes to have higher status value than maintenance workers, but, as garbage worker strikes demonstrate, our society can probably last longer without professional athletes than it can without maintenance workers.

Oppression

It is conceivable that all societies will have some kind of stratification system, one that distinguishes individuals based on their abilities and contribution to society. But, where stratification is systemic, long standing and cruel, it becomes oppression. This means that, when a conscious decision to use power and/or authority to ensure those who experience less social recognition are deliberately held back from the benefits in society in such a manner as to cause harm, pain and/or distress, it is unjust. Moreover, when stratification is structured in such a way that groups, not just individuals, benefit — where a dominant group exercises long standing and unjust power over a subordinate group — it is very likely oppression. Thus, for feminists, gender stratification is oppression and for Marxist conflict analysts, class stratification is oppression. Stratification based on race, disability or sexual orientation is oppression.

People can experience oppression at many different levels simultaneously. Aboriginal people experience oppression in Canada as evidenced by the processes of colonization and their contemporary inequalities of income and health. However, as we will see, there is evidence that women experience oppression as well. Thus, Aboriginal women may experience multiple oppressions compared to Aboriginal men or Caucasian women. People may experience oppression at many levels, and where these levels intersect the oppression can be particularly disempowering.

There is a correlation in North America, and most modern liberal capitalist societies, between socio-economic status, social stratification (Kerbo 2006) and oppression. The upper classes, as denoted by occupation, property ownership (wealth) and access to power and other resources, fare better in regards to society's distribution of rewards and benefits (ibid.). Those with lower socio-economic status — the working class, poor and homeless — have limited access to resources, little power and fare poorly in respect of society's distribution of rewards and benefits. This limits opportunities for these people as well as their children, effectively denying or excluding them from opportunities, such as good health.

Indicators of mortality and morbidity (that is, the incidence of ill health, including heart diseases, cancers and cardiovascular diseases) strongly relate to socio-economic status. The poorer one is, the poorer their health and the younger they die (Raphael 2010; Segall and Chappell 2000). Degenerative diseases are predominantly experienced by lower socio-economic groups. Thus, oppression is not just about lack of access to material wealth and income, it has intimate and life-threatening consequences for individuals. It also has negative societal consequences. Not solving poverty ultimately costs all Canadians health dollars. Canada spends 10.4 percent of its gross domestic product, or $142 billion, on health care (Veenstra 2009: 364), and most of these dollars are spent on reactive health costs responding to degenerative diseases. So health care funds are ultimately reactive in responding to poverty, not preventing poverty.

Summary Points

Social justice is the study of fairness in society. It is an area of study that considers how society divides rewards and burdens among its citizens and how it addresses any related inequalities.

Social justice is an inherently interdisciplinary study of justice borrowing from many social sciences.

Stratification or the division of society into layers based on social characteristics (such as power or socio-economic status) expresses the distribution of rewards and benefits in society.

Oppression occurs when a group of people in society are denied or excluded from opportunities.

Occupational Stratification

One of the key kinds of stratification in society is labour or occupational stratification. Put simply, our society is layered in terms of the kinds of work or occupations that exist. Different work is distinguished by the respect given to the work, the power and authority some occupations have over other occupations and the monetary rewards that accrue to various occupations. Note the wages in Table2 associated with various occupations.

Sociologists and others have debated the structure of occupational prestige and income for many years. Their debates illustrate very well the main lines of diverse views about the justice of labour stratification and social stratification in general.

Table 2 Occupational Remuneration in Canada

Occupation	Average Hourly Wage
Management occupations	$35.50
Social science, education, government, service and religious occupations	$29.97
Art, culture, recreation and sport occupations	$23.33
Trades, transport and equipment operators and related occupations	$22.84
Sales and service occupations	$15.53

Source: Statistics Canada 2011

They Get What They Deserve: Structural Functionalists on Occupational Stratification

One of the most notable structural functionalist approaches to occupational or labour market stratification was put forward by Kingsley Davis and Wilfred Moore in 1945. Davis and Moore postulated that some level of inequality was necessary in society (Davis and Moore 1945). They indicated that certain jobs in a given modern society are more important to the functioning of society than others and only a limited number of people can be trained, or have the talent, to do these jobs. Usually, those who succeed must sacrifice to do so (in terms of spending long years in educational pursuits) and, therefore, in order to induce the most talented members of society into those jobs, we must provide differential access to the rewards of society, which are already limited. Key jobs are those that are functionally important and take training or talent to achieve. Rewards for jobs are based on compensation in monetary terms, status (or ego) and humour or diversion (how fun a job is). Therefore, we have no choice but to live in a society that accepts some level of inequality.

Structural functionalists would favour the models of formal or procedural justice. They would relate to the idea that if everyone is given an equal opportunity (that is, the process is same for everyone) to compete for society's rewards, justice will prevail. An environment of equal opportunity would mean that those who succeed would do so on their own merit. Those who fail would do so due to their own defect. In this way, people receiving the key jobs in society would do so based on their own merit (talent and training).

As a result, you can see that some structural functionalists would say that some level of poverty, or low-paying jobs, in our society can be acceptable as it contributes to stability when people strive harder to avoid experiencing poverty and/or low-paying jobs themselves. Furthermore, functionalists are aware that there are limited resources in any given society to be allocated so they indicate that some competition for those resources is acceptable. As members of society compete for those scare resources (and in this example, good jobs) some will succeed and some will fail. However, if there is too much poverty and too many people are dissatisfied, eventually there may be a threat to the overall social stability. As structural functionalists are concerned with the overall equilibrium in a society, they will only consider matters social justice issues if there is a disruption to social stability. Thus, the growing gap is only a concern if it causes rioting or political instability. Once disruption occurs, functionalists will turn their attention to correcting the problem. Therefore, structural functionalists generally argue that modern, Western capitalist societies reflect an appropriate balance, and hence equilibrium, in the current level of poverty and equality of opportunity. Consider the fairness of labour stratification and the structural functionalist arguments in the following illustration of the "income parade."

It's Power Not Value: A Conflict Perspective on Stratification

Conflict theorists take issue with the arguments and conclusions of Davis and Moore, viewing labour market stratification quite differently. Conflict theorists view society as comprised of different groups and interests that compete for power and resources. Marx, for example, saw the division of the economy into an owning class and a working class as fundamentally unjust because the owning class controlled the economy and, thus, the distribution of economic rewards and burdens, which they did their best to ensure would benefit them over the other class(es) in society. He argued that because of their economic power, the owning class and the wealthy had the resources to more strongly influence state policy, the media, schooling and the other structures of what he called the "social superstructure."

Issue is taken with the idea that the rewards, including occupational income, flows from differences in functional importance (Tumin 1953). Is a garbage collector really less important than a sales manager and less important to society than a professional athlete? If garbage isn't cleared, negative health and environmental consequences result. If fewer goods are

The Income Parade: Emergence of a "Winner Takes All" Society

Not only does Canada have a growing gap between rich and poor people (defined as the top ten percent of Canadian earners and the bottom forty percent), it also has an increasing rise in the income of the very wealthy including chief executive officers running companies and hedge fund managers investing money in stock markets. This phenomenon has been described as representing a "winner takes all" mentality in which this pursuit of astronomical income is sought after and regarded as acceptable.

Yet, this state of income inequality is actually quite recent.

In the 1970s the average pay of a CEO compared to an average worker was a gap of about 30 to 1; by 2007 this gap had risen to 340 to 1. If just the top 100 highest paid CEOs are considered in relation to the average worker, in the 1970s the gap was 45 to 1; by 2006 that gap was 1,723 to 1. In respect of hedge fund managers, the top 25 hedge fund managers in 2009 made more than 24,000 times that of the average worker. (McQuaig and Brooks 2010: 7–8)

One way to visualize the distribution of income is as a national parade in which everyone in the country marches and the height of the marcher is determined by their income.

If the parade was to last a total of sixty minutes, in the late 1970s the first six minutes people would be less than a foot tall earning less than $7,000, including welfare recipients, part time workers and old age pensioners. Gradually, height would increase, so by about fifteen minutes they would be three feet tall, representing fast-food workers, retail clerks and parking lot attendants. After about forty minutes people standing at normal height reflecting average income levels would appear and only in the last ten minutes would really tall people appear such as doctors, lawyers, accountants and engineers standing seven or even eight feet in height. In the last six minutes the marchers would be fourteen feet tall. In the last minute the marchers would hit thirty feet and the last few seconds some real giants, including Edgar Bronfman, chairman of Seagram's with a take home pay of $397,582, standing 199 feet tall would appear.

In 2009 the parade would be very similar until the last few seconds. The faces of the CEOs and hedge fund managers would be so high up, we wouldn't be able to see them. For instance, Siegfried Wolf, CEO of Magna International with an income of $13 million, would stand 2,054 feet tall and the CEO of Research in Motion (the creator and distributor of Blackberry products) Michael Lazaridis, would stand 8,058 feet tall, more than a mile and a half high.

Most Canadians regard extreme inequality as a thing of the past when kings and nobles of pre-industrial times enjoyed a lavish and grand living compared to the poor of that day. However, relatively speaking, was that state of affairs so much more extreme than the inequality of today?

If the parade was to occur in 1688 there would first be some very tiny characters: vagrants, gypsies, rogues and vagabonds followed by paupers and cottagers. After about fifteen minutes household servants and common labourers would appear, measuring about two feet tall. Eventually, the middle class of blacksmiths, silversmiths, masons, tailors and cobblers would appear, standing normal height. Just slightly taller are prosperous shopkeepers and innkeepers, followed by naval officers at about ten feet tall. Only in the last few minutes are some giants, successful merchants and sea traders measuring about fifty feet. Then in the last seconds are heavily armoured knights standing 108 feet tall followed by archbishops and bishops standing 175 feet tall and finally a couple dozen magnificently attired dukes and earls standing 815 feet tall, a fraction of the height of today's mile-high giants. (McQuaig and Brooks 2010: 10–13)

sold, what harm would result? Given the propensity of sales people and marketers to prey on the insecurities of people and especially children, some would say that they are actually dysfunctional for society! In the case of professional and elite athletics, some would argue that the huge amount of resources that go into those kinds of sports are actually part of the growth of an overweight, inactive population of spectators; hardly functional for the health of the population.

Issue is also taken with the idea that education is freely available to all and not predominantly a privilege of the wealthy, given the costly nature of post-secondary education — costs that are borne increasingly by individuals and families. Further, people usually don't seek jobs with the most monetary reward, but with work that attracts them. People chose work as a "calling," not necessarily based on monetary reward (Tumin 1953). Studies of job satisfaction, for example, consistently show that it is dignity, freedom and input into the decisions about work that are utmost in people's minds, not just wages (Toynbee 2003; Hachett 1994). For example, arts and culture are extremely important to the quality of life in a society, and most artists, writers and musicians live on very meagre incomes.

Instead, an argument can be made that reward or compensation for a particular job reflects aspects of social and economic power, not social functionality. Those with power are able to run society in a manner reflective of their needs, wants and interests which leads to inequality (and conflict) among people. Consider the case study below and how the interests of the powerful are rewarded in higher pay. For example, conflict theorists would say government authorities and decision-makers (who have access to power and reflect the elite in society) let problems like poverty, systemic racism in employment, violence against women and other issues go deliberately unaddressed.

This inequality and its perceived and real unfairness often leads to physical, political, economic or social struggles that may result in a change of power. Less powerful groups may have access to some or all of the resources necessary to be able to enact change for their benefit and to reverse an injustice. Trade unions began forming in Canada shortly after Confederation and, especially from 1945 to the 1970s, were successful in increasing wages and improving work conditions for workers (Peirce and Bentham 2007). However, since the mid 1970s, corporations have moved operations to various low-wage, non-union countries (they have globalized) and to places with neo-liberal state policies that make it more difficult for unions to certify and with back-to-work and other laws that have curtailed strikes and reduced union power (ibid).

Poverty has also been an issue that has waxed and waned over the same time period. Since the mid 1970s, with the advent of rampant globalization and ascendant neo-liberalism, the ranks of the poor have swelled (as the above case study implies). The increasing inequality of incomes has led many poor people and their allies to speak about the effects of poverty on the lives of poor people and their children. As a result of this social conflict, awareness has increased about issues those in poverty face, including inadequate access to food and housing, even while poverty has not abated in Canada.

In sum, from a conflict perspective, the main levels and kinds of stratification in our liberal, capitalist society are unjust. The inequalities that make up our stratification system do not, as the functionalists claim, stem from processes that are good for society (that are "functional"), but rather from the use of their social, economic and political power by the already advantaged to maintain their privileges and life comfort.

Economic Power

In Canada, an "economic elite" exists. At the end of 2001 Canada's 100 wealthiest citizens were worth approximately $120 billion. At the other end of the spectrum, wealth equivalent to $120 billion would require the sum of the wealth of 504 million Canadian families (Canada only has approximately 33 million people) (Hurtig 2001: 271). This elite is increasingly a unified and class-conscious group. This is a result of the elite's solid organizational unity and coordinated lobbying efforts (Brownlee 2005: 8). Corporate power has taken hold of the state and public spheres, influencing decisions about who governs and how, the production process, the distribution of resources, the nature and generosity of social programs, the quality and quantity of jobs and the extent of environmental pollution (ibid.). Sources of organizational unification include policy organizations, advocacy think tanks and free-enterprise foundations. Mechanisms of unity of the elite include social class backgrounds, connections to major political parties and interlocking directorships of companies (Brownlee 2005; Carroll 2005).

Is it any wonder that in 2007 after two decades of overall economic expansion, the top 5 percent of earners saw average incomes leap from $133,000 to $178,000 while middle income earners saw average incomes frozen at $25,000 with family income nudging up from $42,000 to $43,000 (Beauchesne 2008)?

The public is not willing to have this continue in the future. In an Ipsos Global Public Affairs survey in 2009, 80 percent of Canada's citizens stated large companies have too much influence over government decisions (Barrera 2009).

It's All in How You Look at It: Symbolic Interaction on Stratification

From the perspective of symbolic interactionism, if members of a given society are not concerned with the problems associated with low-paying jobs and, perhaps specifically, the resulting child poverty, then child poverty would not really be a social justice issue. So, while the individual living in poverty may view child poverty as a problem, child poverty is only seen as a social justice issue if collectively citizens view it and label it as such. For interactionists, it's all in how a problem comes to be socially defined that is the real basis of what is or is not an issue of social justice. Looking at child poverty in another way, while there may be poor children in a society and their lives may be dangerous and uncomfortable, if citizens do not see this or the process that created this situation as unjust, they will not act in ways to undo it. It will, for all intents and purposes, not be a social justice issue.

Sometimes this process is called "social constructionism." This is the view that reality is socially constructed by individuals who interpret the social world around them, and, through this interpretation, issues come to have meaning. If people are unable to relate to, or are unaware of, issues in the social world around them, they are unlikely to view the problems as injustices. For example, if individuals do not realize that many children in

Canada don't have adequate resources to meet their basic needs of food, clothing and shelter, they will not be concerned about it, and thus it is not advanced as a social issue. If the public is not aware, they are unlikely to put more pressure on the media, governments or community-based organizations to raise awareness about the issue and encourage solutions. Or, if they are aware but they have not interpreted that information as a social problem, it may be that they construe it as a personal problem of the children living in poverty. For example, there is a widespread attitude that defines child poverty in Canada as less serious compared to the abject poverty of children in other parts of the world. There is also the perception that Canada has a very generous social safety net (though, in this regard, it is likely that not many people know that social assistance payments have increasingly fallen farther and farther below the poverty line over the past two to three decades) (National Council on Welfare 2008).

Symbolic interactionists are concerned with how definitions and meanings are created and maintained. Thus, they are interested in how information about a social issue is created and disseminated throughout society. In this regard, the media, interest groups and the state become key institutions of study. In the child poverty example, well-funded think tanks, such as the Fraser Institute, play an important role. Over the years the Fraser Institute has consistently claimed that Canada's poverty line is much too high, thereby creating a large group of poor people who are not actually poor (Sarlo 2008). Symbolic interactionism is more individualistic in that the individual's subjective viewpoint determines their perspective on the problem rather than the more ideological or philosophical view of problems evident in the previous theories. In general, then, for symbolic interactionists, the specific nature of the stratification system in a society is, in some senses, irrelevant, as whether or not it is just depends on whether or not each of us perceives it as just.

Social Justice Is Gendered: Feminism on Stratification

Feminism is another conflict perspective but feminists are concerned with the nature of women's global oppression and subordination to men, which is known as patriarchy. In other words, where Marxists are concerned with class inequality inherent to a capitalist system, feminists are concerned with gender inequality inherent to a patriarchal society. In terms of labour or occupational income inequality, feminists would point out that all the other perspectives have overlooked the fact that there are substantial gender issues of pay inequality within occupational groups, and that there are substantial gender imbalances in unpaid labour. While there have been some improvements to the inequalities that exist between men and women in Canada, there are still serious inequalities in existence today. Most Canadians would admit that men and women are not treated equally in the workplace, in politics, in the home or in other social spheres. Women continue to experience occupational segregation resulting in women working in occupations where other women are more likely to also hold jobs (Kerbo 2006; Wilson 2001: 225). Specifically, women are often over-represented in "pink collar" jobs, which are female-dominated jobs that have low pay, fewer benefits and little prestige (Tyler 2002: A18; Nelson 2006). At the same time, male-dominated positions requiring the same knowledge, skills, working conditions and responsibilities as female-dominated positions tend to be higher-paying (Nelson 2006: 229). As a result, there is a significant gender wage gap. Women who work full time earn just over 72.1 cents for each dollar earned by their male counterparts (ibid.). This inequality cannot be explained by the functional differences between occupations because it applies to the same occupations.

At the same time, women tend to do a disproportionate amount of unpaid labour (Marshall 2006; Nelson 2006). Whether they work full time in the labour force or not, Canadian women overall still maintain primary responsibility for childcare, housework, elder care, shopping and food preparation (ibid.). This is commonly known as the "double day" or "second shift" (ibid.). This is most pressing on women who have childcare and elder care responsibilities in addition to their responsibilities in the labour force. Women who are meeting the needs of children and elderly relatives are often referred to as "the sandwich generation," as they are sandwiched between caring for their children and caring for their elderly relatives. (Kendall et al. 2008).

Feminists question why the gender imbalances exist in the first place as well as why those who have power to address the problems (usually the government) have not, and what alternatives are available to enact social change. From this perspective, such inequalities, which permeate our stratification system, cannot be seen as just because they are based on an ascribed status — gender. For feminists, justice can only be achieved when the inequalities (not the differences) between women and men are eradicated.

Self Test

When would the way labour is stratified in society be viewed as a social problem to people employing the symbolic interactionist paradigm?

When would the way labour is stratified in society not be a problem to people employing the conflict perspective?

Summary Points

Occupational stratification informs and intersects with social stratification.

Oppression is the result of unjust social inequality which has created social problems.

Global social issues involve an analysis of the fairness of the distribution of good and bad things in the world community.

Examples of Social Justice Issues

Other examples where socio-economic status impacts social stratification can be seen in the interaction of people with the criminal justice system (CJS). Chapters Six, Eleven and Twelve will expand on poor and marginalized people's interaction with the CJS. Stratification results in social inequality and the reduction of the life chances of those people who occupy the lower echelons of stratification and are less valued. Stratification reflects the manner good things (like income, benefits, opportunities and life chances) and bad things (like systemic discrimination, lack of resources, reduced occupational opportunities and pollution) are distributed in society based on a person's status and social worth. To illustrate the broad gambit of social justice, consider the following examples.

Interestingly, many of the things that people consider benefits to our modern lives are also at the root of social injustices around the world. In expanding the definition of community beyond those people who come in contact with each other from day to day, to a global community where all people live in the same world, aspects of distributive justice, or the distribution of good and bad things throughout the world, broadens the analysis. The scope of social justice issues is large and diverse.

One example of this expanded analysis is that of globalized consumerism. Many of us wear clothing that was made in a factory outside of Canada, most likely in a developing nation like China, Burma, Bangladesh, El Salvador, the Philippines or Thailand. Clothing is made in countries that pay low wages and is transported across the globe and sold in places like United States and Canada in large retail stores. Sometimes, these clothes appear on the rack in the store at very low prices. This can be a real benefit for consumers, especially for people with low incomes, including, but not limited to, single mothers and seniors. Yet, what do we as consumers really know about the conditions in which our clothing and shoes were made? Do we know what wages were paid to the workers who made them for us? Do we know how many hours they worked in a day or how safe their workplace was? Sometimes, these clothes may have been made in so-called "sweatshops" and, in these cases, Canadians may be unaware. Sweatshops involve long hours, low wages and often treacherous working conditions such as being locked in the factory and unable to leave until the end of the shift (for a detailed discussion, see Sluiter 2009). Some people may be concerned about these working conditions and feel that people should not be subjected to such difficult circumstances. These people may be concerned that North Americans are taking advantage of low-priced products created by workers that labour under conditions more difficult than we experience in our own countries. However, others may feel that although these are conditions we would not tolerate in Canada, we need to consider the different environments in which these factories exist in developing countries. They might say that it is better to have some work under these conditions than no work at all, and, therefore, even though the conditions are not what we would expect in Canada, these overseas workers are still benefiting from having any kind of job. This conflict in views — whether workers should be subjected to conditions substandard to those in North America versus the benefit of creating jobs in developing countries that may not otherwise exist — can also be applied to many of the other goods we consume today, such as electronics, toys and household goods like sheets, towels and carpets.

Another example of a social justice issue is limited access to mental health care in Canada. Canadians enjoy a universal health care system that includes many aspects of health care, such as visits to the doctor and hospital and being publicly administered and provided for. However, there are still many aspects of health care that are not met by this universal system. Mental health counselling is among those unmet needs (Statistics Canada 2003b). Mental health counselling can be costly, and Canadians may have difficulty accessing counselling due to long wait lists and limited service provision (ibid.). In some rural and northern communities there may be no local mental health counselling available at all. As you can see, Canadians have chosen, through their political voices, to ensure that some medical services are provided for while others are not.

Of interest is the correlation between low socio-economic status and the prevalence of mental health problems (Dickinson 2002: 376). Depression and substance abuse rates are higher among those in the lower socio-economic classes (ibid.). One explanation for this is that that those from the lower classes experience greater stress due to economic pressures. Another explanation is that those from lower socio-economic backgrounds are more likely to have their (odd, sometimes disruptive) behaviours labelled and treated as mental illness (ibid.). In essence the trappings of being poor apparent in a person's clothes, geographical place and hygiene allow those in higher socio-economic classes to stereotype and label behaviours as mental illness. For example, finding a man drunk and asleep in his jaguar at the side of the road would be treated very differently from finding a man drunk and asleep underneath newspapers at the side of the road

The last example of an issue of social justice is that of systemic discrimination. There is much evidence that our society is stratified along racial lines. Aboriginal people in Canada have higher rates of unemployment, lower rates of educational attainment and less access to housing than other Canadians (Statistics Canada 2006). In the case of recent immigrants to Canada, as a group they have lower average earnings and higher rates of workplace discrimination and injury (Pierce and Bentham 2007). Like women, Aboriginal people, visible minorities and new Canadians are under-represented in positions of power and authority in Canada. They also have less of a voice among elected officials and law makers, corporate managers, education policy makers and media outlets. Because of this, these groups are oppressed or are treated unfairly in Canadian society. Identifying the causes of this oppression will be explored further in the next few chapters.

Framing Stratification and Social Justice

The study of social justice involves an examination of how society distributes rewards and burdens — that is, the way it is stratified. Understanding the values and judgments that underlie stratification, as well as how society stratifies itself, forms the foundation for determining whether or not something is socially just. The difference between formal (or procedural) and distributive (or substantive) justice allows us to understand that even when the rules are the same, the outcome may not be just. Distributive justice, or determining what situations are unequal or require unequal treatment, is expanded upon with an understanding of stratification and oppression in society.

Stratification means that we assign different values to different people based on their achieved and ascribed statuses. Based on those assigned values, we treat people accordingly. As a result, we have assigned high social values to certain occupations like physicians, rock stars and CEOs. As a society, we treat these people very well, providing them with many of society's rewards and resources. On the contrary, we assign relatively little social value to other occupations in society, such as teachers, garbage collectors and artists, as well as homeless people, drug users and disabled people.

As a society, we have not allocated many resources to particular groups of people and seemingly are more or less content to let them bear more of our social burdens. What results is a social spectrum of people; a person's place on that spectrum will determine how they will experience society's rewards and burdens. We can see that some individuals who belong to specific groups consistently bear more of society's burdens while others seem to consistently bear more rewards by virtue of the status we attribute to their role. For example, and as stated above, some groups in Canada, such as Aboriginal people, experience more burdens across social life, including in the realms of economic attainment, employment and education.

All in all, social justice issues are complex and often ambiguous. Social debates are often portrayed in the media, including the issues exemplified in this chapter. In the end, there is a social choice made: whether or not to offer a service, spend money on a social good, support a systemic change, invert the balance of power or purchase a certain item. This is why they are often considered moral problems, a debate between two opposite viewpoints or political interests. These are serious debates about the nature of the injustices involved. Given that our society is made up of a number of diverse and interrelated groups, there can often be powerful interests at work in any of these issues, including individuals and groups who do not see injustice in any of the above situations. Often these powerful interests benefit from not having social problems recognized and prefer to see them as political debates. These groups may work hard to maintain things as they are.

Many justice issues are systemic in nature or involve social, not just individual, problems. In order to be both recognized and addressed as justice issues, the social element inherent in the problems must be identified. Social justice issues often require long-term, deeply structural solutions. This is why treating social justice issues only as moral debates between two opposing viewpoints does not address underlying issues and achieve justice. However, when social justice issues are approached as a problematic, an issue to be understood with each perspective explored and given both a voice and recognition, they are more than just a "debate" of two viewpoints. As we saw in the discussion of social perspectives on stratification, there are differing emphases on formal and distributive justice. Conflict theorists, feminists and, to some extent, social constructionists emphasize the importance of distributive justice, arguing that the stratification system in our society is unjust and oppressive. Structural functionalists (and neo-liberals) claim that ours is a stratification system that is open and free so that it is formally just.

Oppression is the unjust exercise of power or authority by one group over another and the exclusion of this group from opportunities. Understanding stratification and oppression assists in the identification of the least powerful in society, ultimately informing the third justice theme, an ethical practice. When a social problem is analyzed as an issue of distributive justice and with an ethical practice of protecting the least powerful and vulnerable in society, distributive justice can be achieved.

Glossary

discrimination – different treatment of an individual on the basis of such characteristics as class, poverty, national or ethnic origin, colour, religion, age, sex, sexual orientation, marital status, family status or physical or mental disability.

occupational stratification – the division of jobs and occupations in society into layers based on status and the corresponding allocation of rewards in the form of monetary compensation, humour or diversion and respect.

objective element – refers to the quantifiable and observable element of a given social condition. For example, the objective element of occupational stratification is a statistical survey of incomes paid for different occupations.

oppression – the unjust or cruel exercise of authority or power by a majority group (or powerful group) over a minority group (or less powerful group) resulting in the less powerful group being denied opportunities in life.

procedural justice – concerned with fairness and consistency of procedure. This is a rule-based focus of justice based on the premise that if fair and consistent rules are followed, justice will emerge from decisions.

status – the position or level of social prestige a person holds within the social structure based on characteristics such as occupation, race, ethnicity, education, wealth and power.

status value – the worth, esteem and importance society attributes to a person based on characteristics such as employment, gender, race, ethnicity or education.

stratification – the systematic process by which individuals, groups and places are categorized and ranked on a scale of social worth.

subjective element – the subjective element refers to the perception(s) of a social condition and its impacts and whether or not it should be considered a "problem." This relates to the moral nature of the problem — that is, in determining whether or not a particular social condition is harmful to society or to a segment of society and if the condition should and can be changed.

substantive justice – a concentration on what is just or right with respect to the allocation of utility, resources or goods in a given society. It focuses on just outcomes. This is akin to distributive justice.

4

Poverty, Economic Security and Justice

James P. Mulvale

At the end of this chapter, you will be able to:

- Define poverty in several different ways
- Understand the dimensions and effects of poverty
- Describe strategies to redistribute income and achieve justice and economic security for all

What's Justice Got to Do with Economics?

If justice incorporates the concepts of fairness and equality, then we must also apply these concepts to the economic realm. Is "fairness" realized when some members of society are not able to meet their basic economic needs while others are very wealthy? Does "equality" demand some sharing of the collective economic resources of society, which will necessitate levelling huge discrepancies in income and wealth between the rich and the poor?

These economic dimensions of justice are described as "distributive justice" (the fairness of how income and wealth are distributed among everyone in society in the first place) and "redistributive justice" (what needs to be done in order to more equally share economic wealth and ensure that everyone has a decent material standard of living). In addition to examining how income and wealth are distributed among individuals, families and specific occupations in the labour market, justice demands that we ask *how the rules of economic distribution are set.* For instance, is the collective voice of average working people too weak to ensure adequate wages and work-related benefits? Do economic elites — particularly large corporations devoted to maximizing their own profits — have too much power in determining taxation systems (which can transfer wealth from the rich to the poor) and funding levels for universal public services (which can especially benefit lower income groups)?

In this chapter, we examine

- the unjust circumstances of those who are economically insecure — those who live in poverty;

- what economic security might look like in a society that does better than we do in redistributing wealth to ensure that all have a decent life; and
- the need to ensure economic redistribution in the context of environmental limits and lowering overall consumption of the resources of the planet.

How Should We Define "Poverty"?

Main Points

As you read, highlight the answers to these questions:
How many ways can poverty be defined?
What is the best measure of poverty and why?

The most obvious way to define "poverty" is in monetary terms. If one's access to money from all sources (paid employment or that of a family member, earnings through self-employment, income from social benefits, investment income and accumulated or inherited wealth) is not sufficient to cover the cost of the necessities of life at a level that ensures a minimally acceptable standard of dignity and choice, one can be said to be "poor." The necessities of life needing to be purchased include food, housing, clothing, utilities such as power and heat, household items, toiletries, transportation, education and medical needs. The scope of this list and the specific items which should or should not be included are sometimes contentious questions. Should "necessities" include the cost of an annual vacation? Or an internet hook-up? Or life insurance premiums? Most social justice advocates and people working in the social welfare field tend to argue for a relatively broad and inclusive list of items to include as necessary for a minimal but adequate standard of living.

There are also different approaches to determining the income level below which an individual or family is considered to be below the "poverty line" (Ross et al. 2000: 13–44; Statistics Canada 2008). Relative measures of poverty take into account differences in income across an entire population and set an income threshold below which people are classified as poor. The Statistics Canada Low Income Measure (LIM) operates in this manner (although StatsCan uses the term "low income" rather than "poverty" to describe what it is measuring). Absolute measures of poverty set a level of income that is supposed to meet the total cost of a predetermined list of necessary items for a minimally acceptable standard of living (for example, food, housing, utilities, transportation, personal and household items, etc.). Unlike relative measures of poverty, the absolute approach is not based on the overall income distribution (like those in the lowest 30 percent of earners) or on a predetermined cut-off point (like those earning less than $30,000) that determines who falls above or below the poverty line.

Both types of measurements of poverty typically take account of family size (a large family needs more money to live than a childless couple or a single person, although there also "economies of scale" in the some costs, such as groceries and housing); place of residence (large cities tend to be more expensive than smaller towns or rural areas); and income levels before and after income tax and receipt of government transfers (such as the GST/HST rebate or National Child Benefit). Some poverty measurements combine the two approaches. The Market Basket Measure (MBM) and Statistics Canada's Low Income Cut-Off (LICO) are two such broadly used methods. Although LICO is the most common measurement of poverty in Canada, unlike many other countries, we do not have an "official" method that is adopted by political leaders and widely accepted by public policy experts. To give an illustration of where the LICO poverty line falls, the (before-tax) LICO for a family of four living in Regina in 2007 was set at $34,671. The figure for cities under 30,000 population (for example, Yorkton) was $31,529 and for rural areas was $27,714.

Canadians often engage in heated debate about how and where to draw the poverty line, which in turn determines the actual number of people living in poverty. Right-wing think tanks such as the Fraser Institute (Sarlo 2008) set the line at a much lower level that the LICO and other measures. In so doing, lots of people are no longer classified as poor — although the daily hardships of their lives do not change at all!

In recent years, there has been growing interest in "deprivation indexes," which take account of multiple dimensions, in addition to income, of a person's life in defining and measuring economic marginalization. For instance, the Index of Multiple Deprivation (Department for Communities and Local Government 2007: 9), developed in the United Kingdom, is comprised of "seven domains which relate to income deprivation, employment deprivation, health deprivation and disability, education skills and training deprivation, barriers to housing and services, living environment deprivation, and crime." A similar approach has been employed in Ireland (see County Galway 2005). Deprivation indexes are useful for mapping where geographic regions, local municipalities or specific neighbourhoods fall along the continuum from most deprived to most affluent.

Broader Definitions of Poverty

While most efforts to define and measure poverty deal with cash income and the monetary cost of the material necessities of life, there are also calls for a deeper understanding of the social dimensions of involuntary poverty.[1] Poverty is certainly about the lack of access to the material necessities of life, but it also has negative emotional, psychological, behavioural and health-related consequences for individuals, families and communities. Poverty is usually accompanied by a lack of opportunities for positive social interactions and relationships, exclusion from participation in political decision-making and the disparagement of a person's culture and social identity. Reducing or eliminating poverty involves not just ensuring that people have an adequate income but that they are connected with supportive communities and benefit from inclusion in society as a whole.

One such broader definition of poverty (which has been especially influential in conceptualizing poverty in developing countries) is Amartya Sen's "capability approach" (UN OHCHR 2004: 6–8). It takes a multidimensional view of poverty that goes beyond lack of income and focuses on "the non-fulfillment of human rights." Sen is concerned with "how well a person can do or be the things she has reasons to value." For this to be achieved, "the goodness of social arrangements [must] be judged in terms of the flourishing of human freedoms" — which include being free of "hunger, disease and illiteracy." Poverty defined in this broader way goes beyond "low income [to include] the broader concept of inadequate command over economic resources," such as "publicly provided goods and services," "communally owned and managed resources" and "resources that are made available through formal and informal networks of mutual support." Poverty may result from "non-economic factors," such as discrimination against women, ethnic minorities or other groups. The capability approach to understanding poverty as the non-fulfillment of human rights also avoids the adoption of "a uniformly low level of command over economic resources" as its minimum criterion. It seeks to account for individual differences in needs (for example, for food or health care) and for cultural variation (for example, in the amount of clothing considered normal).

The Dimensions of Poverty in Canada

The overall poverty rate in Canada (based on after-tax LICO lines) has changed very little over the last quarter century (National Council of Welfare 2007a). The figure in 2004 (11.2 percent) was almost identical to the 1980 figure (11.6 percent). Rates rose to the 14 percent range during the recession of the early 1980s. In the 1990s an economic slowdown increased unemployment, which, combined with severe government cuts to social programs, drove the poverty rate into the 13–15 percent range. According to the Organisation for Economic Co-operation and Development (OECD), Canada's rates of poverty have been rising relative to other countries and is above the OECD average (Hay 2009: 4).

Contrary to popular perceptions, a large proportion of poor people are in the work force. In 2001, a careful statistical analysis found that 40 percent of low-income people were living in families classified as "working poor" (Fleury and Fortin 2006: 17). In terms of prevailing wage rates, Saunders (2005: iii) notes:

> Almost one-sixth of full-time workers in Canada earn very low wages — below $10 per hour in 2001 dollars. Most low-paid workers are part of households with more than one wage earner, and so manage to escape poverty. However, almost one-third of low-paid workers are poor, because wages below $10 per hour are insufficient to allow a single-earner living in a large urban centre to avoid poverty, even if he or she were working full-time throughout the year.

It is also important to measure the "depth" of poverty — how far poor individuals and families fall below the poverty line. Raphael (2007: 43–44) states that the poor on average fall about 30 percent below the poverty line, although single unattached adults tend to be in deeper poverty (falling approximately 40 percent below the threshold), while seniors tend to be less badly off (falling less than 20 percent below). Another factor is the "persistence" of poverty. A high proportion of people transition in and out of poverty over short periods of time, even though the overall rate of poverty across the population stays relatively stable. Single males, single females and lone-parent females tend to undergo longer term bouts of poverty (127).

Poverty is especially prevalent in certain segments of the population, including "women (particularly young mothers and unattached seniors), recent immigrants, people with disabilities, and Aboriginal people" (Hay 2009: 5). There is also evidence that income advantages and disadvantages are transmitted from one generation to the next and that good outcomes for children (such as normal physical and cognitive development, success in school and good mental health) are related to higher income levels of parents (Raphael 2007: 122).

The effects of poverty on the Aboriginal people of Canada — including First Nations, Métis and Inuit people — are particularly serious and appalling (Centre for Social Justice 2007–2010). Poverty among Aboriginal peoples is related to our history of colonialism and racist assumptions and practices (now often subtle and systemic, rather than blatant). This poverty has serious negative social outcomes for the first inhabitants of the land we share, such as poorer health status, lower educational attainment and grossly inadequate housing in many Aboriginal communities.

The Growing Gap

The old saying, "the rich get richer and the poor get poorer" appears to be exactly the case right now in Canada, according the Growing Gap project (Canada Centre for Policy Alternatives n.d.). The increasing difference between high-income and low-income earners is a consistent trend across the country. To take Saskatchewan as an example, Gingrich (2009: 41) reports:

Inequality of earnings increased among Saskatchewan families over the thirty years from 1976 to 2006. Over this period, the richest 10 per cent of Saskatchewan families took home the lion's share of the province's economic growth, increasing its share of earnings from twenty-three to twenty-eight per cent. The bottom half of Saskatchewan families found themselves shut out from economic gains and their share of earnings dropped from twenty-six to twenty-three per cent. There is a growing divide between the top half of Saskatchewan families and those in the bottom half: in the 2003–2006 period, the share of earnings going to the top half was four times greater than earnings going to the bottom half.

Health Status

Poverty quite literally makes us sick. Lightman et al. (2008: 2) point out:

> The poorest one-fifth of Canadians, when compared to the richest twenty percent, have:
>
> - more than double the rate of diabetes and heart disease;
> - a sixty percent greater rate of two or more chronic health conditions;
> - more than three times the rate of bronchitis;
> - nearly double the rate of arthritis or rheumatism.

The poorest fifth of our population face a staggering 358 percent higher rate of disability compared to the richest fifth. The poor experience major health inequality in many other areas, including 128 percent more mental and behavioural disorders; 95 percent more ulcers; 63 percent more chronic conditions; and 33 percent more circulatory conditions.

Summary Points

Poverty is especially prevalent amongst young mothers, unattached seniors, recent immigrants, people with disabilities and Aboriginal people.

Poverty impacts life chances including health and success in school.

Poverty and the Work Ethic

There is a widespread belief in Canadian society that everyone needs to "work for a living" — that it is morally objectionable for healthy adults to be furnished with the material necessities of life without expending efforts on their own behalf to provide for themselves and those who depend upon them, such as their children. This belief is related to what is called the "reciprocity" norm — if we receive benefits from others (be they family members, friends, groups to which we belong or our government), we should also contribute something in return. This is a belief that lines up with the Christian "golden rule" — do unto others as you would have them do unto you.

While we value work and reciprocity in contemporary Canadian society, we also consider it to be right and just to pay taxes to government so that it can provide services that we cannot reasonably be expected to provide for ourselves. Our tax money is invested in schools for our children, health care for when we are ill, roads and highways that take us where we want to go and public media (such as the Canadian Broadcasting Corporation (CBC)) that help us communicate with one another and define ourselves as Canadians.

Widely held beliefs in the work ethic and the reciprocity norm are sometimes expressed, unfortunately, in negative attitudes towards individuals and groups who receive specific types of income support from government. Thus, public opinion tends to draw lines between the "deserving" and "undeserving" poor. For instance, senior citizens are thought to deserve a public pension after a lifetime of work, and children with life-threatening illnesses are thought to deserve expensive medical treatment paid for with public funds. Other categories of people, however, such as single mothers on social assistance and seasonal workers in fishing or forestry, are often suspected of taking unfair advantage of benefit programs, of being "lazy" or of having made poor life choices.

Such moral judgments, based on negative stereotypes and untested, broad assumptions, are inaccurate and unfair. To be sure, all of us have moral obligations to contribute to our families, communities and places of employment and to act as citizens who have responsibilities as well as rights. However, the construction in the public's mind of broad categories of the "undeserving poor" completely submerges individual differences in circumstances and fails to take into account the complexities of people's lives. Is the woman with young children who applies for social assistance because she must leave an abusive husband not deserving of this support? On the other hand, do wealthy people who take advantage of tax write-offs and tax shelters (which are also "benefits" granted by the government) require such support?

Negative assumptions about who deserves social benefits are often aimed at groups of people who are already victims of inequality and marginalization (such as women, Aboriginal persons and people of non-European ancestry). Such popular calculations of who should be entitled to income support also tend to define "work" (as the criterion of who "deserves" benefits) in a narrow way — restricted only to paid work in the labour force. The unpaid work done (mostly by women) in the home – caring for children and elderly family members, cooking, housecleaning, laundry and so on – is not counted in determining entitlement to income support programs.

The Components of Economic Security

Main Points

As you read, highlight the answers to these questions:
What is economic security?
What specific changes could be made to eliminate poverty?
How does environmental sustainability relate to economic security?

Let's accept a broad definition of work that includes unpaid work in the home, volunteer work to make our communities better places to live and subsistence work to grow or gather our food in urban gardens or in rural and northern Canada. Starting with this more expansive understanding of work, we can also begin to think of economic security in broader terms. The question then becomes: how should people be justly compensated for socially necessary and useful work through a variety of mechanisms, including but not limited to the paid labour force? Several areas of public policy and types of social programs must be considered if we are to ensure social justice in the context of a broad understanding of work and economic well being.

A Just and Equitable Labour Market

Ensuring a sufficient quantity of "good jobs" in the paid labour market means the adoption of public policies and laws that create and sustain well-paying, secure employment with decent working conditions. To achieve this goal, governments must undertake or strengthen actions in the following areas:

- direct creation of jobs in the broad public sector (education, health care, social support, environmental protection, government services, etc.);
- indirect creation of jobs in the private sector through various mechanisms with corporations and small businesses (tax incentives, subsidies for job creation, conditions placed on new investment, adoption of economic development strategies, etc.);
- raising the minimum wage to meet or exceed the poverty line;
- setting and enforcing employment standards (hours of work before overtime rates are paid, avenues of complaint about unscrupulous employers, occupational health and safety rights and requirements for employers, etc.);
- employment and pay equity laws to ensure fair access and equal pay for groups who have historically been excluded from more desirable occupations (particularly women, persons with disabilities, racial minorities and Aboriginal people); and
- laws governing the formation and bargaining rights of labour unions, to ensure that workers can have an effective collective voice with their employers in regard to wages, benefits and conditions of work.

Farm Survival and Food Security

Economic survival of the family farm is another component of overall economic security. The National Farmers Union (NFU 2005: 3) points out that since the mid-1980s market-based farm income (before government farm subsidies are factored in) has been around zero, with this figure dipping below zero after 2000. Beyond the immediate difficulties facing Canadian farmers as reported in the media (such as the outbreak of "mad cow disease," the rise and fall of commodity prices, heavy government subsidies for farmers in the United States), the NFU (2005: 8) calls for a focus on the "real causes" for the lack of economic viability for family farms, especially "the rise of corporate power and consolidation." The "vertical integration" of food processing and distribution in transnational food companies and huge retail grocery chains means that these powerful players in the agribusiness sector can dictate commercial terms to farmers. These large corporations "snatch away profits that would otherwise end up on our family farms" (11). The NFU (2005: 12–25) also outlines a detailed plan "to quickly and affordably end the farm income crisis." The proposed remedies include the following:

- guaranteeing farmers their costs of production;
- careful management of land, production levels and marketing to ensure a rational economic system in food production and distribution that provides farmers with a decent living;
- controlling the power and profits of companies that sell fertilizers, chemicals, seeds and machinery to farmers;
- food labels that disclose "the farmers' share" of the price paid in the supermarket (for example, "each time [consumers] paid $1.40 for a loaf of bread, they [would be] reminded that the farmer got only 5¢ and the remaining $1.35 went to huge retail and processing corporations"). Such labels could also alert consumers to the presence of genetically modified ingredients in food products and the number of "food miles" that the product travelled from the point of production, which contributes to global warming through the production of greenhouse gases in the transportation sector;
- emphasizing production of organic and local food as an alternative to production for the global commodity market; and
- involving farmers in campaigns to "end hunger in Canada" and "deal with the growing epidemic of obesity, diabetes and other health problems created by our food system."

Ensuring the economic viability of the family farm is closely linked to the goal of food security, which is defined by the Food and Agriculture Organization of the United Nations as

> a condition in which all people, at all times, have physical and economic access to sufficient, safe and nutritious food to meet their dietary needs and food preferences for an active and healthy life. (Centre for Studies in Food Security n.d. and n.p.)

Part of the equation of food security is having cash in one's pocket to buy groceries, and in this sense food security is tied to the discussion on income security which follows. But taking food security seriously also demands a critical look at the availability of nutritious food in one's immediate locality, the affordability and quality of these local food supplies and public education on food storage and preparation and healthy eating choices. Food security leads to us to questions such as: why do school children have easier access to junk food than to fresh fruits and vegetables in the school cafeteria? Are there ways to distribute nutritious foods that bypass large corporations and follow a shorter and more direct route from the farm gate to the kitchen table? Do chemical additives and genetically modified ingredients in food products threaten our health? Why have we become so reliant on food banks, when they barely existed and were not considered necessary in Canada before 1980?

Income Security

One of the functions of the social safety net in Canada has been to provide an adequate cash income to people who, for various reasons, are temporarily or permanently unable to earn a gainful living in the labour market. Income support programs such as unemployment insurance, pensions for the elderly, child benefits, workers' compensation and social assistance grew in scope in the thirty-year period from the mid-1940s to the mid-1970s. However, over the last thirty-five years, cuts in and restructuring of the welfare state have left our social safety net tattered and full of holes. The one exception to this trend has been public pensions for the elderly, which have remained more or less intact and kept poverty rates among seniors relatively low.

There are several schemes on offer by defenders of the Canadian welfare state to reconstitute a viable income support system (for example, Scott n.d.; Freiler et al. 2004; Battle et al. 2006). Unfortunately, there appears to be little appetite at this point in time among Canadian political leaders from any party for substantial improvement in income support programs, let alone generous and comprehensive measures to tackle poverty and ensure economic security for all.

A Basic Income for All?

There has been international interest and debate over the last twenty years about the desirability and practicality of a "basic income" (Van Parijs 2004). Such a program would provide all members of a society with an unconditional income from the government that would be adequate to meet basic needs and ensure a modest but dignified standard of living. A basic or guaranteed income could in principle take the place of many existing income support programs, such as unemployment insurance, social assistance and public pensions for the elderly. As a universal program for which everyone qualifies, a basic or guaranteed income could eliminate the need for costly and bureaucratic administration and "policing" procedures in existing programs, which are supposed to ensure that eligibility criteria are met by recipients of benefits.

This debate about the desirability and feasibility of a basic or guaranteed income has been livening up in Canada in recent years (Mulvale 2008a). While a stand-alone, comprehensive guaranteed income (GI) program is not on the immediate political horizon, a case can be made for a gradual, step-by-step advance towards a GI "framework" as an innovation in Canadian social welfare that would promote social justice. Moving towards a GI framework would entail improvements in the rates and range of coverage of existing income support programs, as well as new programs to fill holes in the current system (Young and Mulvale 2009). Even if an unconditional, universal and adequate basic income program were in place, most people would still no doubt be engaged in the paid labour force. However, workers would have the option to cut down on their hours of work, take breaks from paid work for family or personal reasons, refuse or quit undesirable jobs and seek re-training or further education if they want to advance their careers.

Elements of an overall GI scheme are already in place for children and seniors in Canada. Money to finance a GI framework could come from a variety of sources, such as higher taxes on the wealthy (which would help us achieve redistributive justice) or by sending a portion of natural resource royalties that now go to provincial governments directly to individuals. A partial basic income is paid to everyone in the American state of Alaska using this approach. Research conducted in Saskatchewan (Mulvale 2008b) suggests that people involved in efforts to fight poverty are willing to entertain the idea of guaranteed income as a worthwhile and feasible public policy goal.

Adequate and Affordable Housing

An adequate and affordable place to live is an essential component of quality of life and security. The Wellesley Institute (n.d.). points out that "the lack of housing is directly linked to higher morbidity (illness) and higher mortality (death)" and that "homelessness and insecure housing are at record levels in Canada." This situation was brought about in no small way by the complete withdrawal of the federal government from funding social housing (provided by the public sector and a variety of community-based and non-profit organizations), as part of government cost-cutting in the mid-1990s. There has been *some* government re-investment in social housing in recent years, but it has not matched the level of the earlier cuts.

An adequate supply of publicly funded social housing can have both direct and indirect benefits. It can provide directly to lower income people more rental units that are decent places to live and with affordable rents. Indirectly, by increasing the supply of housing available, it can moderate the rapidly inflating cost of renting or buying accommodation in the private marketplace.

Accessible and Affordable Health Care

Our system of universal and readily accessible health care in Canada is a vital element of our economic security system. The costs of physician and hospital care is very high and can devastate the finances of those who experience the common circumstance of serious or prolonged ill health. Our "medicare" system was pioneered in Saskatchewan in the 1940s and 1950s and was established as a national program across Canada in the 1960s. It provides medical and hospital care at no direct cost to the person requiring care, through a "single payer," government-administered insurance plan that covers all Canadians and reimburses a wide range of direct care providers. Medicare is not a perfect system and faces challenges, such as the rising cost of serving an aging population, over-crowded emergency rooms and long wait lists for medical specialists and surgery. Nonetheless, medicare has been a remarkable success story (Campbell and Marchildon 2007) and is very strongly supported by Canadians. Our American neighbours often look to Canada as an example, as they struggle to reform their market-based and profit-oriented health care system, which is much more costly than ours and leaves millions of people with inadequate or no health care.

Self Test

What types of social programs currently exist to alleviate poverty?
Why are government policy measures such as a basic income not yet implemented?
What strategy could be used to eliminate poverty?

Economic Security and Environmental Sustainability

In Canada and on the global level we face immediate and grave problems posed by our abuse and destruction of the natural environment. These problems include global climate change, depletion of natural resources, loss of natural habitat, species extinction and threats to our health from pollution and environmental toxins. It is therefore essential to link any discussion of economic security to the question of environmental sustainability of the planet. Social justice and ecological justice are now inextricably linked, both in moral and material terms. Economic security will only be achievable if there is wide and deep economic redistribution that provides everyone with what they need and at the same time lowers overall consumption levels, resource extraction and environmental damage. Environmental sustainability and social equality can be mutually reinforcing goals, and both are essential in building a more just society.

Our traditional approach to extending prosperity in Canadian society has been to rely on economic growth to increase wealth, thereby enabling those with less to take a relatively bigger slice of the pie. But we have now reached critical environmental limits, and open-ended, indiscriminate economic growth is no longer viable. The rules of the economic game must change. We now need to regulate and reduce consumption through measures such as "green taxes" (on fossil fuels, for example) and the restriction of non-essential activities that leave a big environmental footprint (for example, recreational use of snowmobiles and ATVs). In particular, we must ensure that economic elites roll back their standard of living and accept lower profit margins — through such measures as large tax increases on the wealthy, limits on corporate profit-taking and calling a halt to economic investment or production that causes environmental destruction.

Our focus must shift from pursuing economic growth to acting as careful stewards of economic resources. We must find ways to provide people with the material necessities of life in the context of a "steady state" economy that maximizes emotional and social well being (Mulvale 2007). We now need to be much more strategic and in tune with the ecological imperatives of the Earth as we plan and carry out economic activities. All of us (including those on very low incomes and the working and middle classes) need to adjust our lifestyles and consumption patterns in order to minimize our environmental footprint. Of course the "well off" might have more to give up in this regard, as they tend to be the ones who own monster homes and summer cottages, travel to far off destinations for their vacations and generally live more extravagant lifestyles than those with more modest economic means.

Summary Points

Economic security has important implications for paid work, farm survival and environmental sustainability.

A basic guaranteed income could replace income support programs and fill gaps in government policies.

In addition to redistribution, economic security also requires a reduction in overall consumption to achieve environmental sustainability. Programs for income security can't be funded from economic growth.

Eliminating Poverty and Economic Security

The above ingredients in this recipe for universal economic security call for fundamental changes in Canadian society and on the broader international level. Many social movements (such as organized labour, feminists, environmental activists and anti-racism groups) and advocacy organizations (such as anti-poverty groups, faith-based social justice bodies, peace and international development groups, human rights watchdogs and fair trade advocates) continue to struggle for economic security for everyone, here in Canada and internationally. These movements and organizations must continue and increase their struggles, working in concert with one another whenever possible, and using new research data and innovative campaigning strategies as they become available.

Two specific examples of practical organizing to address poverty and extend economic security in Canada are worth examining. The first campaign is called Dignity for All: The Campaign for a Poverty-Free Canada, and it was launched at the Canadian Social Forum in Calgary in May 2009. This campaign brings together a variety of social justice groups under the leadership of Canada Without Poverty (a national organization directed by people who have personal experience with living in poverty) and Citizens for Public Justice (a faith-based advocacy organization). The vision of the Dignity for All initiative is "to make a poverty-free and more socially secure and cohesive Canada a reality by 2020." The campaign sets three goals:

1. a comprehensive, integrated federal plan for poverty elimination;
2. a federal act to eliminate poverty, promote social inclusion and strengthen social security; and
3. sufficient federal revenue to invest in social security.

The first goal (which calls for poverty *elimination*, not just reduction) identifies the following aspects that a federal plan must address, which are similar to some of the components discussed in this chapter:

- income security;
- food security;
- housing security;
- childcare and early childhood development;
- education and training;
- labour standards;
- job creation, including a green jobs strategy;
- unemployment insurance;
- health supports; and
- particular supports for vulnerable populations.

The second example of organizing on-the-ground efforts to tackle poverty from a social justice perspective is the work going on across Canada to formulate and actualize poverty reduction strategies. This approach involves developing and implementing a comprehensive and systematic plan to reduce poverty by a broad range of partners (including government, people living in poverty, organizations providing social service, health care and education, social justice advocates, labour unions, faith-based groups and the business sector). A poverty reduction plan must address income security, job training, affordable housing, food security and early childhood development and care. Poverty reduction strategies set highly specific goals with timelines over an extended period in order to lower overall poverty rates and to lessen the depth and breadth of poverty. Progress or problems in meeting these goals are reviewed regularly and reported on publicly in order to hold governments and other actors accountable.

The National Council of Welfare (2007b), which calls for the formulation of such a strategy at the national level, provides a clear blueprint of the essential ingredients of a poverty reduction strategy and how it should be carried out. The Canadian Council on Social Development has usefully catalogued recent efforts to reduce poverty in each province and territory across the country (Scott 2009). As of late 2009, actual poverty reduction strategies were in place in six provinces in the eastern part of the country (Newfoundland and Labrador, Nova Scotia, New Brunswick, Québec, Ontario and Manitoba). Groups were active in the four other provinces (Prince Edward Island, Saskatchewan, Alberta and British Colombia) and were working to convince their provincial governments and other key players to commit to poverty reduction strategies.

Ensuring universal economic security in the context of a green, sustainable society would, needless to say, be a fundamental transformation. Work to bring about such radical change must take place though small, pragmatic steps in the here and now. Such work must also be energized and guided by a bold vision of social justice and the sharing and redistribution of social and material resources, so that each and every one of us has access to what we need for a good life, in harmony with the Earth and one other.

Glossary

depth of poverty – the degree to which someone's income falls below the poverty line; the farther one falls below the poverty line, the "deeper" is the poverty that one experiences.

economic security – a condition in which individuals and families have access to appropriate forms of paid employment, government benefits, income derived from personal assets and access to land, raw material and other productive resources so that they have their basic material needs (for example, food, shelter and clothing) met at an adequate level and on an ongoing basis.

environmental sustainability – a set of conditions in which we can ensure the economic survival and social well being of all species (including human beings) at local, regional and global levels in ways that do not degrade the environment or exhaust natural resources and that can be maintained over the long run.

guaranteed income (GI) – a program or set of programs provided by the state that provides a minimum level of income to everyone on a continuing basis. Everyone would be entitled to GI irrespective of their personal circumstances or need and would be subject to no or very few conditions of eligibility. GI from the state would be typically combined with income from paid employment and access to public services to guarantee economic security for all.

Low Income Cut-Off (LICO) – defined by Statistics Canada as "income thresholds below which a family will likely devote a larger share of its income on the necessities of food, shelter and clothing than the average family. The approach is essentially to estimate an income threshold at which families are expected to spend 20 percentage points more than the average family on food, shelter and clothing."

Low Income Measure (LIM) – set by Statistics Canada at 50 percent of the median household income — "median" being the middle of the distribution from highest to lowest. Those whose income falls below the LIM are officially considered to be "low income."

poverty – in monetary terms, poverty is having insufficient income from all sources to cover the cost of the necessities of life and to ensure a minimally acceptable level of personal dignity and choice. It is usually accompanied by the lack of opportunities for positive social interactions and relationships with others, exclusion from participation in civic affairs and community life and low status in the eyes of others.

poverty line – a predetermined and specific level of income separating those above the line (the non-poor) from those below the line (people living in poverty). Poverty lines are typically adjusted to individual circumstances that affect the cost of living, such as family size and composition, and the average cost of housing and food in the local area. The LICO and the LIM are examples of poverty lines used in Canada.

Note

1. Excluded from this discussion are those who embrace *voluntary poverty* — those who for religious belief, political commitment or values based in social justice choose to live with a bare minimum of material resources. Voluntary poverty adherents often have communal living arrangements (for example, a convent or monastery, or a rural self-sustaining commune committed to radical ecological values).

5

Social Exclusion, Social Justice and Racism

Lisa Comeau

At the end of this chapter, you will be able to:

- Confront the ways you are personally affected by racism
- Identify and explore White privilege
- Understand the distinctions between individual and systemic racism, and how each manifests in contemporary Canada
- Confront democratic racism and grasp how it operates in Canada

It may seem like an obvious claim that racism is an example of injustice. However, the specific ways that racism manifests in individual, societal and structural domains and how it impacts formal and substantive justice and ethical practice are not as straightforward as they may at first appear. Whether racism even exists at all as a societal force in Canada is highly contested, and how racism ought to be defined and understood and where and how it manifests are also points of considerable debate. That this is the case may itself be testimony to the general acceptance in Canada of liberal principles that align justice with the equality of all people and the right of all people to be treated as equals. To claim that racism exists in a foundational way in Canada is to acknowledge that serious racial injustice persists in this nation in spite of our commitment to such liberal principles. Moreover, this claim raises questions about who and what practices might be implicated in such injustice. Exploring the often subtle ways that racism is maintained is a difficult but necessary first step to making changes in ourselves and our society that will help to effect greater equality and justice for all.

For this reason, this chapter not merely provides information *about* racism but requires you to begin to confront the ways in which you are personally affected by racism. The issue of social justice and racism is a deeply complex topic, which emerges out of Canada's history as a colony of the British Empire and ultimately as a White settler society. This history shapes not only who we are and how we think about ourselves as a nation and as citizens but also the social and power relations amongst groups within Canada. Understanding racism historically helps us identify and explain racism today. Identifying and confronting how the privilege of some racialized groups in society is connected to the social exclusion and oppression of other racialized groups is central to understanding racism in Canada.

Diversity and Racism in Canada's History

Main Points

As you read, highlight the answers to these questions:
Historically, how was racism inherent in Canada's immigration policy?
What evidence of racism exists in Canada today?
How has the *Indian Act* discriminated against Aboriginal people in Canada?

Through policies and legislation such as the *Indian Act* (1876) and explicitly race-based immigration laws that limited and even prohibited the entry of some groups, Canada was constructed as a nation of White European settlers and as a colony within the British Empire. In the early years after Confederation, huge waves of Europeans were recruited to settle and populate the young nation. Immigrants from non-European countries also attempted to come to Canada during this time, but many faced significant barriers due to the immigration policy of the time, and those who managed to immigrate faced racial hostility. During this era, non-British immigrants were considered a major "problem," and much effort was made in educating/assimilating diverse settlers from Scandinavia, Eastern Europe and Russia, and Southern Europe to the ideals of British character and ways of living. This included teaching the English language and Protestant values and ethics (Anderson 1918; Woodsworth 1909). The assimilation of non-European immigrants was considered a much greater problem because they were deemed to be racially inferior to White people (Anderson 1918; Woodsworth 1909). Hence, there was less certainty about the possibility of assimilation and a great concern that they would dilute British purity. Canadian Heritage (2004), the federal department responsible for multiculturalism and other cultural issues, claims that Canada has been diverse from its very beginning. In a literal sense, this is true. However, diversity (the wide variety of people and their cultural practices) has not by any means been embraced from the beginning.

In the aftermath of World War II, the world entered a period of major political and ideological change that led to the expulsion of colonial governments in some countries and to the development of widespread social and political movements, such as the civil rights movement in the United States. Canada also made significant changes during this time. Although Canada remains a settler society and the *Indian Act* continues to define the relationship between Aboriginal people and the Crown, the *Indian Act* has been amended in several important ways. Residential schools have been closed, Native women and their children can now retain their Indian status even though married to a non-status person, and many of those who historically lost Indian status have been able to regain it. Through continuing processes of both struggle and negotiation, a general movement towards Aboriginal self-government and self-determination is currently underway.

Canada's explicitly race-based immigration laws have also been changed. The 1962 *Immigration Act* shifted the focus from an admissions policy based on country of origin to a policy of entry for skilled immigrants and family reunion. In 1967, the "points system" was introduced, according to which admission is granted on the basis of an objective assessment of individual attributes and qualifications rather than on race or nationality. Prior to this change, Canada had a sad history of making entry for some immigrants incredibly difficult. For example, between 1923 and 1947, the *Chinese Immigration Act*, popularly referred to as the "Chinese Exclusion Act," banned Chinese immigration outright except for students, who had to return upon completion of their studies, merchants with money, Chinese children born in Canada and members of the Chinese government. As a consequence, fewer than fifty Chinese immigrated to Canada between those years (Boyko 1998: 54). In an example of Canadian anti-Semitism, which points to the significance of religion as an element of "race" (something that manifests currently in Islamophobia), Canada permitted the entry of only 5,000 Jewish refugees during World War II. By contrast, the United States accepted 200,000; Britain, 70,000; Argentina, 50,000; Brazil, 27,000, China 25,000; Bolivia, 14,000; and Chile 14,000 (121).

As a result of changes in policy and legislation, the Canadian population has become increasingly diverse in its ethno-racial make-up. The Canadian census reveals that in 2006, 19.8 percent of the Canadian population was foreign born — the highest this percentage has been in seventy-five years (CBC 2007). Moreover, the highest numbers of recent immigrants are now coming from countries in Asia, Africa and Central and South America rather than Europe. Demographic projections to 2031 by Statistics Canada (2010a) reveal that the Canadian population is moving from a European to an Asian foreign-born population, that there will be a rapid increase in the proportion of people belonging to so-called "visible minority" groups among the Canadian-born population, that visible minorities will constitute close to 90 percent of Canadian population growth and that visible minorities will comprise approximately 60 percent of the populations of Toronto and Vancouver (Statistics Canada 2010a). These changes also suggest that the very term "visible minority," arguably offensive because it contains an inherent reference both to skin colour and to a White majority, is also quickly becoming inaccurate.

In addition to opening its doors through changes in immigration law, Canada embraced multiculturalism as official policy in 1971 and enshrined this policy in law through the *Multiculturalism Act* in 1988. Multiculturalism is now a significant aspect of Canadian national identity, and Canada is heralded as a world leader for its commitments to multiculturalism. While multiculturalism may have many positive effects, it is also the object of important critiques, explored later in this chapter.

In spite of the increasing ethno-racial diversity of the Canadian population and although Canada's commitment to multiculturalism is often understood as both the evidence and the means of achieving "non-racism" in Canada, racism remains a major barrier to the equality of all Canadians. As one example, poverty in Canada is becoming increasingly racialized (Galabuzi 2006; Pruegger, Cook and Richter-Salomons 2009). Galabuzi (2006: 17), for example, shows that in 1995, 35.6 percent of members of racialized groups lived under the poverty line, twice as high as the 17.6 percent in the mainstream Canadian population. The situation worsens among racialized women, single-parents and specific ethno-racial groups. In its *2005 Report Card on Child Poverty*, Campaign 2000 indicates that, in 2001, the poverty rate among Aboriginal children was 40 percent; among visible minority children it was 33.6 percent; and among visible minority immigrant children arriving between 1996 and 2001 it was 49 percent. According to the Canadian Council of Provincial Child and Youth Advocates (2010: 4), 49 percent of off-reserve First Nations children under six years of age lived in low-income families compared to 18 percent of non-Aboriginal children, and 57 percent of off-reserve First Nations children in large cities also lived in low-income families. By correlation, Aboriginal children are also disproportionately involved in the youth criminal justice and child protection systems and face increased serious health problems including poor housing, food insecurity and poor water quality. Regarding immigrants, research (Picot, Hou and Coulombe 2007) indicates that in spite of the rising educational and skill levels of immigrants (many of whom, as we saw above, are visible minorities) in the late 1990s and early 2000s, the low-income rates of new immigrants rose to as high as 3.5 times that of the Canadian-born in 2002, falling slightly to 3.2 times as high in 2004. These rates were higher than at any time during the 1990s. Moreover, the probability of new immigrants entering poverty rose, and the probability of leaving poverty fell. In the context of the 2031 demographic projections referred to above, if these poverty gaps are not addressed as a priority and diminished as quickly as possible, they have the potential to cause tremendous problems both for people who will be excluded from the wealth of the country and for the country as a whole.

Before going any further, it is important to challenge the mistaken notion that the terms "racism," "prejudice" and "discrimination" are synonymous. While prejudice and discrimination may be expressions of racism, it is overly simplistic to reduce racism to either or both of these. As Wetherell and Potter

(1992) explain, accounts of prejudice are psychological accounts. What these authors refer to as the "prejudice problematic" (1992: 201) stresses the failings of individual characters and the irrationality of individual motives, which permits people who don't consider themselves prejudiced to adopt the "moral identity of tolerance" (211). Approaching racism as primarily a question of individual prejudices and discrimination encourages "failure to engage with social structural change" (210). By contrast, Wetherell and Potter define racism as "the symbolic and cultural expression of a society which is systematically organized around the oppression of one group and the dominance of another" (198).

The distinction between what can be understood as "individual racism," the prejudiced attitudes and discriminatory behaviours exhibited by some individuals, and "systemic racism" is important in the context of statistics about the racialization of poverty. Although "individual racism" persists in

The Indian Act

In 1876 the Canadian federal parliament passed the *Indian Act*. The language employed in the statute illustrates the time, place and status of Aboriginal people. First, the term "Indian," used in error by early European explorers who believed themselves to be in India, is completely a European construct. Illustrating the tenacity of discourse it remains in use today. The term also reflects the racist misperception that the people who first inhabited North America are/were a homogeneous, uniform people, essentially different from other groups of people. Another interesting term employed in the act is "band," again a foreign concept to Aboriginal people, who might have referred to themselves as a "people" or a "nation," often associated with a specific geographical location (see Poser n.d.).

The rules established in the Act were also foreign to Aboriginal people. In the same year the *Indian Act* was passed, treaties were being negotiated in western Canada on a nation-to-nation basis. This unilateral federal legislation set new and different rules, defining who would qualify as a real "Indian" within Aboriginal communities and how Aboriginal governments would operate. It established reserves controlled by federal agents. More importantly, it imposed severe restrictions on the activities of Aboriginal people, which included the following:

- Indians were prohibited from taking part in many traditional cultural practices;
- Indians couldn't own land; the federal government owned it in trust for them;
- Indians couldn't hire a lawyer;
- Indians couldn't vote; and
- Indians were prohibited from developing land, selling produce from land (crops) and leaving the reserve without a permit from a federal Indian agent.

Although the *Indian Act* has been amended, it still governs many aspects of the lives of people who fall within its ambit.

Canada (see for example the 35 percent increase in police-reported hate crimes (Statistics Canada 2010b) and the resurgence of the Ku Klux Klan in Saskatchewan (Regina *Leader-Post* 2007)), the prejudices and discriminatory behaviours of individuals cannot fully explain the social inequalities referred to above. Rather, statistics of poverty amongst Aboriginal and visible minority people provide evidence of "systemic racism," a form of racism which operates at a societal and structural level. Systemic racism manifests in inequalities between racialized groups of people as a result of the cumulative effect of a wide range of public policies, social practices and persistent racist ideologies. Systemic racism is a particular form of oppression that excludes some groups of people from opportunities in society on the basis of their "race" or ethnicity. The *Indian Act* and the early to mid twentieth-century race-based immigration policies are prototypical examples of public policies which constituted the racist foundation upon which the new country of Canada was built. Such policies, together with the socially accepted racist discourses of the time, produced systemic racism as a social and political reality which benefited White Canadian citizens while severely and blatantly oppressing Aboriginal peoples and non-White, non-European immigrants. Systemic racism, which continues to dispossess and disadvantage Aboriginal people, immigrants and Canadian-born people of colour in twenty-first-century Canada, is directly connected to this history.

Summary Points

Prior to World War II, laws discriminated against people of different ethnic backgrounds. The *Indian Act* and immigration laws are examples.
Systemic racism still exists in Canada today.

Social Exclusion and Racist Ideology

Main Points

As you read, highlight the answers to these questions:
How do various forms of oppression such as racism, sexism and poverty interact to produce social exclusion?
Do the concepts of "race" and "racial hierarchy" exist in a biological way?
What is White privilege?

Systemic racism is complex and often subtle. It can't be easily understood in and of itself because it is also deeply interconnected with other forms of systemic oppression, such as poverty and sexism. For instance, quite possibly a wealthy, male Aboriginal lawyer experiences some form of racism in spite of his position as a well-educated, professional man. However, it is almost certain that his experiences of racism are significantly different than those of an Aboriginal teenaged mother living in poverty. In both cases, racism is mediated by the person's sex and social class. It can be difficult to determine exactly whether an experience is due to racism, sexism, poverty or another systemic oppression such as heterosexism, ageism and so on.

Underscoring the complexity and interconnectedness of racism with other forms of systemic oppression, Galabuzi (2006: 173) uses the term "social exclusion" to refer to "the inability of certain groups or individuals to participate fully in Canadian life due to structural inequalities in access to social, economic, political, and cultural resources arising out of the often intersecting experiences of oppression relating to race, class, gender, disability, sexual orientation, and immigrant status." The term refers to "both the structures and the dynamic processes of inequality among groups in society that, over time, structure access to critical resources that determine the quality of membership in society and ultimately produce and reproduce a complex of unequal outcomes" (176). The multiple dimensions in which social exclusion manifests include, but are not limited to, education, health, employment, the economy, the media, civic and political participation and the criminal justice system.

The concepts of "social exclusion" and "social inclusion" originated in France in the early 1970s. Since then, several governments in Europe, and to a lesser extent in other jurisdictions including Canada, have used these concepts to expand their understanding of "social disadvantage" beyond the simple definition of lack of income. Through these efforts, a richer understanding has been emerging of the complex interconnections between multiple social and economic factors that result in poverty and other forms of social marginalization among specific social groups. These groups include Aboriginal people, recent immigrants, lone parents, unattached people between forty-five and sixty-four years old and people with disabilities.

Although social inclusion and social exclusion are often understood relative to one another, Galabuzi (2006: 175–76) emphasizes what he sees as important distinctions between them as frameworks for understanding and addressing social inequalities. "Social inclusion" is rooted in the liberal tradition that assumes the equality of all people. The objective of the social inclusion framework is to address the extreme manifestations of social inequalities that threaten social cohesion — to bring "the excluded into the tent" (175). However, he argues that efforts at social inclusion rarely attempt to change the processes and structures of exclusion; as long as these remain intact, social inclusion remains illusory. The reality is that Canadian society is not now, nor has it ever been, a colour-blind, gender-blind and classless society wherein all individuals operate on a level playing field. Social inclusion may allow some individuals from marginalized groups into the centre of society. As an example of formal justice, White women in Canada won the right to vote federally and in most provinces between the years 1916 and 1925.

However, women still don't make up 50 percent of elected representatives, they are still over-represented in part-time, contractual and poorly paid jobs, and they continue to earn approximately 70 cents for every dollar earned by men. Nevertheless, the situation is far worse for Aboriginal women, who didn't get the right to vote until 1960, at the same time Aboriginal men did, and for women of colour, who experience much higher rates of social exclusion of all sorts. Galabuzi claims that a social inclusion framework fails to address these complex intersections of oppression and the historical assertion of economic, political, social and cultural privilege which occurs at the expense of others.

By contrast, a social exclusion framework draws from those traditions that emphasize conflict in society, and it acknowledges the construction and operation of persistent social hierarchies of race, class, gender and so on. The social exclusion framework confronts the connections between the social exclusion of some groups of people and the dominance and privileges of other groups. Dominance requires subordination: if everyone were actually equal, nobody would enjoy the privileges of dominance.

It bears repeating that privilege doesn't accrue only to racial or cultural groups but also to gender groups, class groups and to any social group which claims to be, or is treated as if it is, superior to other groups. Individuals may be a member of several privileged groups at the same time. For example, White, male, upper- and middle-class men between the ages of twenty-five and sixty-five are privileged by virtue of race, sex, class and age. Consider how many Canadian politicians, past and present, at all levels of government, fall into these categories. Privileged groups create systems and structures that reflect the values, embody the characteristics and embrace the interests of the members of the privileged group. Social exclusion and privilege can be hard to identify because they are normalized through the operation of the dominant ideology in society.

Henry, Tator, Mattis and Rees (2000: 15) define ideology as "a set of beliefs, perceptions, assumptions and values that provide members of a group with an understanding and an explanation of their world." According to Fleras and Elliott (1992: 54), ideology also provides a framework for "organizing, maintaining and transforming relations of power and dominance in society." More specifically, *racist ideology* can be understood as central to how we view ourselves in the context of society and how our social institutions operate. According to Henry et al. (2000: 16),

> racist ideology… organizes, preserves, and perpetuates the power structures in a society. It creates and preserves a system of dominance based on race and is communicated and reproduced through… the mass media, schools and universities, religious doctrines, symbols and

images, art, music, and literature. It is reflected and regenerated in the very language we read, write, and speak.

The dominant ideology created by privileged groups is reflected in many institutional structures, and, ironically, racist ideology can manifest in ideas and practices considered democratic and even progressive. As an example, the front page of the Regina *Leader-Post* on February 5, 2003, featured a large picture of precisely this phenomenon. In it were several visibly White children, some with "war painted" faces, some with Halloween costume feather bonnets and plastic bows and arrows, and others sitting on colourful, woven South American rugs in front of large construction paper tipis. The caption below identified them as a grade four class "learning about Plains Cree culture." While the inclusion of First Nations culture in an elementary school curriculum is a mark of progress over its earlier absence, this picture of the dominant group "dressing up as" the subordinate group was reminiscent of the caricaturing of Black people through the popular blackface routines in American minstrel and vaudeville shows (Rogin 1996). It permits a repetition of stereotypes and a collapsing of the heterogeneity of Aboriginal peoples into a single, inaccurate entity. Turned into spectacle through its publication on the front page of the newspaper, this picture served as an invitation to all of Regina to participate in this consumption of "traditional" culture, and in so doing, perform themselves as tolerant, liberal and essentially "good" people and confirms the stereotype of who "real Indians" (St. Denis 2004) are or were.

Privileged and dominantly positioned people (including politicians) are not necessarily malicious individuals who intentionally and consciously subordinate others for their own gain. Rather, privilege and dominance operate in far more subtle ways. Individuals may be quite unaware of their privilege and of the ways of thinking and acting through which their own dominance is maintained. Hence becoming aware of systems of privilege and learning how privilege is constructed and maintained is a vital step in being able to challenge systemic oppressions. This is why Galabuzi maintains that a social exclusion framework, which can confront the idea that some groups benefit *at the expense of* other groups, is a crucial part of actually *restructuring* social structures that exclude and oppress people.

Self Test

Can a person be a member of only one social group?
If social exclusion exists, does social privilege exist as well?
Does systemic racism require the intentional act of racism?

White Privilege

For people who identify as White and therefore enjoy the benefits of White dominance and privilege, confronting White privilege for the first time can be an uncomfortable experience. They will often experience feelings of shame and guilt. It is also common for people to react with angry indignation, feeling that they've been unfairly accused of some wrongdoing. Other reactions include a denial of any unearned privilege or even an insistence that they are victims of "reverse racism" (Henry et al. 2000: 26–28). Regardless of whether a person is racialized as White or as "of colour," the recognition of systemic racial privilege has implications on both a personal and an institutional level. For White people, confronting White racial privilege means acknowledging that they reap the benefits of centuries of injustices perpetrated against Aboriginal peoples and other people of colour. For people of colour, the recognition of White racial privilege (which generally occurs very early in life) confirms that life is not yet fair for all people. Either way, this can be deeply disturbing. Yet recognizing that society is still structured along a racial axis allows for purposeful individual and institutional efforts to work towards greater social equality and justice.

The terms "Whiteness," "White privilege" and "White" are capitalized in order to refer to a specific socio-political location of dominance. When the term "white" is not capitalized, it is used as a descriptive reference to skin colour. Although so called white skin colour is one of the primary characteristics by which individuals identify with Whiteness and gain entitlement to White privilege, it bears emphasizing again that not *all* white-skinned people enjoy the privileges and dominance of Whiteness in the same way or to the same extent, just as not all people of colour experience racism in the same way. Gender, socio-economic class, sexual orientation, mental and physical dis/ability and age, among other factors, also play a role in privilege.

One of the most important elements of White privilege is that it is very often invisible to those who benefit from it (McIntosh 1988). However, people of colour are often quite well aware of how White privilege operates in White people's lives. In part, White privilege still has to do simply with having "white" skin, together with other White-identifying physical attributes such as the texture of hair, the colour of eyes and hair, and the shape of eyes, nose and lips. People who look White may be treated well simply *because* they look White, while people of colour may experience discriminatory treatment simply on the basis of not looking White. Many people of mixed racial ancestry attest that among siblings, those who pass for White are often treated better by society at large than those who are visibly not White. Kinewesquao (2009: 120) refers to the practice among many Métis families of trying to protect their children from racism by "passing" (for White) or "keeping one's head down" or living "under the radar." All of these terms refer to the active management of identity in order to be recognized as White rather than Aboriginal, in an attempt to avoid the racism so often experienced by visibly Aboriginal people.

However, Whiteness and White privilege are more complex than mere skin colour. It is now well understood that race is not a biologically essential category. That is, there is no single gene or set of genes responsible for the characteristics commonly understood as "race." Of course we all inherit physical characteristics from our ancestors — we have our mother's eyes or our father's nose, and our skin colour also reflects our ancestry. However, these things, in themselves, do not constitute race. Instead, race is the meaning that for centuries has been assigned to specific groupings of physical characteristics (California Newsreel 2003). Whiteness is a socially constructed location of dominance. Throughout several centuries of European imperialism and colonialism, White Europeans constructed themselves as racially superior to all other people (Feagin 2006: 11; Goldberg 1993), thus justifying the theft of lands and the enslavement, genocide and attempts at cultural genocide of colonized peoples (Feagin 2006: 14). In early colonial America, Europeans saw themselves as Christians and only later came to identify themselves as White, in opposition to Negro and Indian (15). This emerging distinction between people on the basis of skin colour also enabled the assignment of non-physical abilities, moral virtues and character traits. As Goldberg (1993) explains, this process was nothing less than the social construction of a racial hierarchy, sanctioned by emerging scientific disciplines such as anthropology and biology as well as the Judeo-Christian thought of the time.

According to this racial hierarchy, White people were constructed as the most fully human, intelligent, virtuous and capable of leadership and governance, while other groups were constructed as less than fully human and less capable of human rationality and self-government (Goldberg 1993) — and as inherently dangerous to the racial and moral purity of White people (Anderson 1918; Stoler 1995; Woodsworth 1909). These allegedly essential differences were attributed to the emerging category of "race." Goldberg explains that because the race concept is an essentially "empty" social construction, it has been flexible and adaptable to several scientific and political agendas — various and multiple "racisms" — that resulted in the exclusion of various non-racialized social groups, including women and poor people. For example, in Canada, the concept of race has been employed to distinguish between the deserving poor and undeserving paupers (Valverde 1991) and between respectability and degeneracy (Fellows and Razack 1998: 346). Throughout Canadian history, the term "race" has been applied to a range of differences beyond skin colour, including nationality, language and religion. In contemporary Canada, these differences are now framed in the language of culture. The fact that "race" doesn't really exist as a physical

Identifying White Privilege[3]

One of the earliest and clearest articulations of the concept of White privilege was written in 1988 by Peggy McIntosh. In this often re-published and widely taught text, McIntosh reflects on her perception that, as a White woman in her workplace, she has many conditions of advantage that her colleagues of colour can't count on. She describes her White privileges as "an invisible package of unearned assets that I can count on cashing in on each day, but about which I was meant to remain oblivious"(1988: para. 3). Her list of forty-six unearned advantages, her White privilege, is autobiographical. McIntosh makes clear that her list is specific to her time and place, and derived from observing the differences between her experiences and those of her colleagues of color in the same workplace. She does not speak for all White people everywhere relative to all people of colour. Included here are twenty-six examples drawn from her original list of forty-six:

1. I can if I wish arrange to be in the company of people of my race most of the time.
2. If I should need to move, I can be pretty sure of renting or purchasing housing in an area which I can afford and in which I would want to live.
3. I can be pretty sure that my neighbors in such a location will be neutral or pleasant to me.
4. I can go shopping alone most of the time, pretty well assured that I will not be followed or harassed.
5. I can turn on the television or open to the front page of the paper and see people of my race widely represented.
6. When I am told about our national heritage or about "civilization," I am shown that people of my color made it what it is.
7. I can be sure that my children will be given curricular materials that testify to the existence of their race.
8. If I want to, I can be pretty sure of finding a publisher for this piece on White privilege.
9. I can go into a music shop and count on finding the music of my race represented, into a supermarket and find the staple foods which fit with my cultural traditions, into a hairdresser's shop and find someone who can cut my hair.
10. Whether I use checks, credit cards, or cash, I can count on my skin color not to work against the appearance of financial reliability.
11. I can arrange to protect my children most of the time from people who might not like them.
12. I can swear, or dress in second hand clothes, or not answer letters, without having people attribute these choices to the bad morals, the poverty, or the illiteracy of my race.
13. I can speak in public to a powerful male group without putting my race on trial.
14. I can do well in a challenging situation without being called a credit to my race.
15. I am never asked to speak for all the people of my racial group.

16. I can remain oblivious of the language and customs of persons of color who constitute the world's majority without feeling in my culture any penalty for such oblivion.
17. I can criticize our government and talk about how much I fear its policies and behavior without being seen as a cultural outsider.
18. I can be pretty sure that if I ask to talk to "the person in charge," I will be facing a person of my race.
19. If a traffic cop pulls me over or if the IRS audits my tax return, I can be sure I haven't been singled out because of my race.
20. I can easily buy posters, postcards, picture books, greeting cards, dolls, toys, and children's magazines featuring people of my race.
21. I can go home from most meetings of organizations I belong to feeling somewhat tied in, rather than isolated, out-of-place, out-numbered, unheard, held at a distance, or feared.
22. I can take a job with an affirmative action employer without having co-workers on the job suspect that I got it because of my race.
23. I can choose public accommodation without fearing that people of my race cannot get in or will be mistreated in the places I have chosen.
24. I can be sure that if I need legal or medical help, my race will not work against me.
25. If my day, week, or year is going badly, I need not ask of each negative episode or situation whether it has racial overtones.
26. I can choose blemish cover or bandages in flesh color and have them more or less match my skin. (para. 9)

category, even though it carries a very important social meaning, means that there really isn't a racial hierarchy either. Unfortunately, many people still accept the notion of a cultural hierarchy (just as some even still accept the idea of a racial hierarchy), that is, that some cultures and cultural practices are better, more developed or more civilized than others. This idea underlies the moral justification of contemporary Western imperial practices, such as the imposition of Western-style democracy and capitalism on foreign nations (Bisharat 2003; Klein 2007). Similarly, under Canadian multiculturalism, typically accepted are only those benign cultural differences such as food, costume and dance that don't pose any threat to the normative Canadian way of life (Bannerji 2000; Henry et al. 2000: 30).

Because of the history of the concept of race and the emergence of a racial hierarchy in Canada's colonial beginnings, Whiteness became (and remains) the social location of cultural and institutional dominance, according to which White people continue to be constructed as "normal," are able to assume a sense of superiority and are granted privileges, which in a cyclical manner confirm their dominance. Whiteness, as a location of dominance, is something that European immigrant groups have been able to access throughout Canadian history. Recall from above that in the early years of the twentieth century, the assimilation of non-British Europeans to British ideals was considered a serious challenge (Anderson 1918; Woodsworth 1909). Although these immigrants had white skin, they were considered distinctly inferior to British settlers and colonizers. Many European immigrants attempted to integrate and to reap the promised rewards of life in Canada (at least for their children) — and some even Anglicized their names. In many instances, their children were fair-skinned, Canadian-born people with Anglicized names who spoke English with Canadian accents; this second generation had "become White." They had been assimilated into the norm and thus were granted access to the privileges available to members of the normative group — privileges from which many of their parents would have been excluded. However, because the race category was fluid enough to adapt to various political agendas, some immigrant groups, in spite of being European and white-skinned, were subjected to gross injustices on the basis of race, understood variously as nationality or religion, and so on. For example, during World War I, over 8,500 Ukranian immigrant men (and much smaller numbers of women and children) were imprisoned in internment camps because they weren't considered truly Canadian, but rather Ukranian, and as such, enemies in the war context (Boyko 1998).

Many Canadians are familiar with the "grand narrative of Canadian history" (Stanley 2002), that romanticized story of White European immigrants coming to Canada in search of a better life and, by the sweat of their brow, actually creating that better life for themselves. In the context of this story, many Canadians also accept the notion that Canada is a "meritocracy" — that is, that no matter who you are, if you have enough raw talent and you work hard enough, you will reap the rewards of your efforts. Accordingly, people often conclude that those who don't have many benefits simply haven't applied themselves very well. Meritocracy is exposed as a myth (McIntosh 1988) when we acknowledge that, historically, Aboriginal people and immigrants of colour were excluded from the possibility of *becoming White* — hence they were excluded from the social and economic benefits of being a White Canadian. This is not to suggest that Aboriginal people and immigrants of colour have ever wanted to reject their identities and heritages. Rather, it underlines the historical reality that by virtue of being constructed as racially inferior to White people, they were excluded (with few individual exceptions) from the possibility of attaining the social and economic benefits and privileges of being White. Because the accumulated wealth and social status of one generation have typically been the starting point for successive generations, the effects of the history of social hierarchies continue to be felt today (California Newsreel 2003b; Feagin 2006). This leaves contemporary White Canadians with a considerable responsibility: first to learn to see their White privilege and second to work to transform those social structures that continue to privilege White people at the expense of people of colour.

Democratic Racism and Multiculturalism in Canada

Main Points

As you read, highlight the answers to these questions:
What is the fundamental contradiction of democratic racism?
What are some important critiques of the discourse and practice of multiculturalism in Canada?

This chapter began with the acknowledgement that there is much disagreement and debate about *whether* racism exists at all as well as how it manifests in contemporary Canada. Yet this chapter provides several examples of the persistence of both "individual racism" and "systemic racism." The increasing and increasingly racialized gaps in poverty and income between White Canadians and both Aboriginal people and immigrants of colour is clear evidence that systemic racism is alive and well in Canada. In sum, racism is a social structure of power relations that advantages White people, emerges out of colonial history, is often unintentional and invisible to White people and is mediated by class, gender and other social characteristics.

Yet how is it possible that in a country such as Canada, committed to the liberal and democratic principles of justice and equality, there is so much evidence of widespread "injustice" and "inequality"? If the explicitly racist laws and practices from Canadian history have changed and if, as a nation, Canada is truly committed to multiculturalism and the valuing of diversity, then by what means are current forms of racism perpetuated? Henry et al. name this paradoxical situation "democratic racism," arguing that this is the most appropriate model for understanding how and why racism continues in Canada today. They define democratic racism as

> an ideology in which two conflicting sets of values are made congruent to each other. Commitments to democratic principles such as justice, equality, and fairness conflict but coexist with attitudes and behaviours that include negative feelings about minority groups, differential treatment, and discrimination against them. (2000: 23)

Utilizing a method of discourse analysis introduced in Chapter Two, Henry et al. (2000) present twelve discourses of democratic racism,[1] all of which have the effect of supporting this co-existence of fundamentally conflicting sets of values. They are ways of thinking and speaking about social problems, values and practices that are in common use. While they all refer in some way to the importance of equality among individuals, they also often result in a lack of support for policies and practices that might ameliorate the low status of people of colour. As Henry et al. suggest, such policies tend to require changes in the existing social, economic and political order, usually by state intervention. The intervention, however, is perceived to be in conflict with and a threat to liberal democracy. As an example, the discourse of political correctness is likely familiar to most Canadians, who are likely to have some understanding that political correctness refers to a limiting of how language is used, for instance, the avoidance of racist and sexist names, slurs and jokes in order not to offend people. Yet there is also a backlash against or resistance to political correctness, evident in questions about what certain groups want to be called now. Henry et al. (2000: 25–26) point out that what is at stake here is the power of naming. By deriding politically correct language, which aims at disrupting oppressive speech, this backlash works to maintain for privileged groups the power to name people and socio-political structures. As another example, employment equity, or affirmative action, is a highly contentious policy and practice that might actually lead to more equitable employment of people of colour. In Canada, under the *Employment Equity Act*, there are four designated "equity groups": women, people with disabilities, Aboriginal peoples and visible minorities. Employment equity goes beyond mere non-discrimination and requires that these specific groups be targeted for proactive treatment. Employment equity is a strong example of the practice of substantive justice because it recognizes that in order to achieve fairness for these four groups, which have long histories of unequal access to meaningful and well-paid employment, such proactive effort is required. Yet it is often denounced as "reverse racism" (Henry et al, 2000: 28) because it is claimed to be providing an unfair advantage to people of colour, thus disadvantaging White people and working contrary to the principles of a meritocratic society, according to which individuals succeed or fail on the basis of their own merit.

In this section, I focus on explaining how multiculturalism operates as a discourse of democratic racism. According to Henry et al. (2000: 29–30), "the concepts of tolerance, accommodation, sensitivity, harmony, and diversity lie at the core of multicultural ideology and are firmly embedded in multicultural policy and discourse." When Prime Minister Trudeau introduced multiculturalism policy to Parliament in 1971 he claimed that it would "break down discriminatory attitudes and cultural jealousies" and that such a "vigorous policy of multiculturalism… [could] form the base of a society which is based upon fair play for all" (Ungerleider 2009: 182). Multiculturalism is intended as a form of what Lentin (2009) calls state-sanctioned anti-racism. It may also be intended as formal justice in its attempt to treat every individual as equal in their diversity. The fact that people from around the world speaking many languages and professing many faiths manage to live in Canada in relative peace and harmony is quite an accomplishment.

At the same time, multiculturalism produces a range of conflicting effects. Henry et al. (2000: 30) argue that the terms "tolerance" and "sensitivity" imply that there is a dominant norm against which "difference" is measured and that there is a limit to how much difference, and what kinds of differences, will be tolerated. This issue was the explicit topic of exploration in Québec in 2007 as the Consultation Commission on Accommodation Practices Related to Cultural Differences (otherwise known as the Bouchard-Taylor Commission for its co-chairs Gérard Bouchard and Charles Taylor) worked through a province-wide public consultation process taking stock of accommodation practices. The same issue is discussed across the country, although not yet through such a formal process.

One serious critique of multiculturalism is that it de-historicizes and depoliticizes the social constructs of race and racial difference. Bannerji (2000) argues that the timing of the introduction of multiculturalism policy in 1971 was politically astute as it was announced in the context of two monumental political challenges by groups with long histories of claims and grievances against Canada as a British colony. Briefly, in 1969, Indian Affairs Minister Jean Chrétien released a white paper proposing the necessity for Aboriginal people to become fully participating and equal members of Canadian society. Aboriginal groups across the country were enraged at the lack of consultation in preparing what they saw as yet one more attempt by the federal government to assimilate them and refuse to honour treaty obligations. In 1972, the National Indian Brotherhood released *Indian Control of Indian Education* — the so-called "Red Paper"[2] — wherein they insisted on the protection and revitalization of Aboriginal cultures and languages. At approximately the same time, separatist sentiment was building in Québec, the Parti Québécois was formed, and the FLQ crisis occurred. In response Prime Minister Trudeau infamously implemented the *War Measures Act,* resulting in the arrest and detainment of thousands of separatist sympathizers. In 1971, the *Official Languages Act* was passed, making both English and French official national languages. By this time, immigration policy had been changed, and for the first time in its history, Canada was receiving large numbers of immigrants from so-called "non-traditional source countries" in Africa, Asia and Latin and South America. Bannerji (2000) argues that in this political context, the introduction of multiculturalism policy served to weaken the political claims of Québec separatists and Aboriginal people by reducing their cultural demands. Multiculturalism enabled a political discourse that relied on ideas of cultural differences rather than the historical and political constructions of differences along a racial hierarchy. Bannerji argues that multiculturalism sets Francophones, Aboriginal people and immigrants of colour apart from each other *and* apart from "mainstream" Canadian culture. In this way, multiculturalism "rests on posing 'Canadian culture' against 'multicultures,'" with Whiteness marking the difference between the core culture and the others (2000: 10). Consider that only the others have hyphenated identities

— French-Canadians, Aboriginal-Canadians, African-Canadians — while those in the centre remain "Canadians" (Mackey 1999: 3).

Another important way that multiculturalism enables democratic racism is that the emphasis on the distinction between Canadian culture and other cultures has the effect of essentializing and commodifying culture. The multicultural focus on cultural diversity and its encouragement of people to retain their "traditional" cultures essentializes those other cultures, usually in some primitive and romantic formulation (St. Denis 2004). In Said's (1978: 32) words, "this object [culture] is a 'fact' which, if it develops, changes, or otherwise transforms itself in the way that civilizations frequently do, nevertheless is fundamentally, even ontologically stable." Through this process, questions of *authenticity* have to do with *not* having been influenced by modern, Eurowestern culture. Maori scholar Linda Tuhiwai Smith (1999: 74) writes: "What counts as 'authentic,' is used by the West as one criteria to determine who really is Indigenous, who is worth saving, who is still innocent and free from Western contamination." By this logic, *traditional* cultures aren't recognized as having the inherent, organic ability for growth and change, while modern Western culture retains the capacity for progress in various arenas. Smith continues: "At the heart of such a view of authenticity is a belief that indigenous cultures cannot change, cannot recreate themselves and still claim to be indigenous. Nor can they be complicated, internally diverse or contradictory. Only the West has that privilege."

Under multiculturalism, "traditional" cultural practices tend to be commodified as the stuff of celebrations: food, clothes and dances. As Henry et al. assert (2000: 30), these are the differences that are "tolerable" to the dominant culture. The celebration of multicultural diversity usually involves the consumption of these commodified cultural differences at public festivals and school potlucks, where culturally "diverse" people wear their "traditional" dress, perform "traditional" dances and share "traditional" food. The consumption of these differences — the "eating of the other" as hooks (1992) says — has the simultaneous effect of confirming the tolerance of the consumer and the essential difference of the other. None of this demands any acknowledgement that these "traditional" ethnicities "are themselves the constructs of colonial — orientalist and racist — discourses" (Bannerji 2000: 9).

In the context of Canadian multiculturalism, culture ceases to be an organic process, a way of living that is dynamic and flexible and to which *all* people are subject. Because culture is regarded as the property of others, the discourse of multiculturalism also has the effect of leaving those who don't identify with any particular cultural heritage — primarily White, Eurowestern Canadians — feeling rootless, cultureless and even experiencing some "innocent yearning" for an experience of "authentic" culture that is characteristic of what Rosaldo (1989: 70) calls "imperialist nostalgia."

The discourse of multiculturalism is a site of struggle over the truth of Canadian history, identity and virtue. By subjugating Canada's racist histories and silencing the language of race, the discourse of multiculturalism masks the operation of power, hiding the threads of political continuity between the past and the present and collapsing race into ethnicity. Racism is thus reduced to an individual's intolerance of cultural diversity. In this way, multicultural discourse serves to protect privileged White people from having to confront their own complicity in systemic racism and poverty — and to maintain them in positions of dominance and normativity. Multiculturalism allows Canadians to detest racism – and the racists within their midst – without ever having to confront the normalized, systemic embeddedness of racism or the complicity of those Canadians who occupy positions of racial and cultural dominance in maintaining racism.

Self Test

Historically, how have White people been constructed in Canada?

What are the implications of the discourses of democratic racism for attempts to achieve racial justice?

In what ways do the practice of multiculturalism in Canada perpetuate rather than challenge racism?

Race, Racism and Social Justice

Many people understand racism as primarily an individual problem that is rooted in ignorance and stereotypes and that manifests through prejudice and discrimination against people of different racial and cultural groups. While this may be one form of racism, racism is, more importantly, a deeply complex form of systemic oppression that emerges out of Canada's history as a colony of the British Empire and through the construction of Canada as a nation of White European settlers. Canada was built on a foundation of racist legislation, including the *Indian Act* and race-based immigration policies. This history continues to shape who we are and how we think about ourselves as a nation and as citizens of that nation. This history also continues to mediate the social and power relations amongst various groups within the Canadian population, in spite of, and even through, official multiculturalism.

Racism has been presented as a social structure of power that is based on the socially constructed idea of race and that privileges White people as a group while disadvantaging people of colour as a group. Because racism has been deeply embedded in Canada's social structure for centuries, it is often normalized and rendered invisible — especially by those people who are the beneficiaries of systemic racism. Racism is reproduced through the discourses of democratic racism such as multiculturalism that fail to challenge the construction and operation of social hierarchies of race, class and gender, among other factors.

In this chapter, we have begun to confront the ways in which we are personally influenced by racism. Regardless of how we identify and are identified in racial terms, the recognition of systemic racial privilege can be deeply disturbing. By acknowledging that society is still structured along a racial axis and exploring the various ways in which systemic racism is maintained, we also encounter a moral imperative to work towards greater social equality and justice in our capacity as individuals, community members and citizens.

Glossary

Aboriginal – persons who have Indigenous ancestry, including First Nations, Inuit and Métis.

democratic racism – an ideology in which two conflicting sets of values are made congruent to each other. Commitments to democratic principles such as justice, equality and fairness conflict but coexist with attitudes and behaviours that include negative feelings about minority groups, differential treatment and discrimination against them (Henry, Tator, Mattis and Rees 2000: 23).

First Nations – persons designated as Indian and Inuit under the federal *Indian Act*.

individual racism – the prejudiced attitudes and discriminatory behaviours exhibited by individuals.

ideology – a set of beliefs, perceptions, assumptions and values that provide members of a group with an understanding and an explanation of their world.

multiculturalism – both the official policy and legislation in Canada that ensures the rights of individuals from diverse cultures to protect and maintain their culture; and more generally the cultural and ethnic diversity among the Canadian population.

racism – a structure of power relations that advantages White people as a group while marginalizing people of colour as a group. Racism is fluid, dynamic and context specific; therefore it is possible to identify various different manifestations of racism in different locations.

racist ideology – a set of beliefs, perceptions, assumptions and values that creates and preserves a system of dominance based on race.

social exclusion – a framework or way of thinking about social inequalities that refers to both the structures and the dynamic processes of inequality among groups in society that, over time, structure access to the processes of production, wealth creation and power, and ultimately produce and reproduce a complex of unequal outcomes. A social exclusion framework acknowledges the construction and operation of social hierarchies of race, class, gender and so on.

social inclusion – a framework or way of thinking about social inequalities that is rooted in the liberal tradition that assumes the equality of all people. The objective of the social inclusion framework is to address the extreme manifestations of social inequalities that threaten social cohesion. Efforts at social inclusion rarely attempt to change the processes and structures of exclusion.

systemic racism – a form of racism which operates at a societal and structural level. It excludes some groups of people from opportunities in society on the basis of their "race" or ethnicity, and manifests in inequalities between racialized groups of people as a result of the cumulative effect of a wide range of public policies, social practices and persistent racist ideologies.

Whiteness – the socially constructed location of cultural and institutional dominance according to which White people are "normal," are able to assume a sense of superiority and are granted privileges which, in turn, confirm their dominance.

White privilege – the various ways in which White people benefit from their location of cultural and institutional dominance. White privilege emerges out of colonial history and is normalized such that it is often invisible to those who benefit from it. White privilege is mediated by the effects of socio-economic class, gender and other social locations, such that not all White people enjoy White privilege to the same extent or in the same ways.

Notes

1. Discourse of political correctness; discourse of denial; discourse of colour blindness; discourse of equal opportunity; discourse of blaming the victim; discourse of White victimization; discourse of reverse racism; discourse of binary polarization; discourse of moral panic; discourse of multiculturalism: tolerance, accommodation, harmony and diversity; discourse of liberal values: individualism, truth, tradition, universalism and freedom of expression; discourse of national identity. A full discussion of all of these is beyond the scope of this introductory text.
2. The Assembly of First Nations released a revised version of this document entitled *First Nations Control of First Nations Education: It's Our Vision, It's Our Time* in July 2009.
3. Excerpted from Peggy McIntosh, 1988. "White Privilege and Male Privilege: A Personal Account of Coming To See Correspondences through Work in Women's Studies." Working Paper 189, Wellesley College Center for Research on Women, Wellesley MA. Copyright fees are donated to National SEED Project on Inclusive Curriculum (Seeking Educational Equity and Diversity).

6

Women and Injustice

Gillian Balfour

At the end of this chapter, you will be able to:

- Understand the key principles of feminist engagement with criminal justice
- Understand the limits of retributive justice for women
- Discuss the implications of restorative justice for victimized and criminalized women

A key strategy for achieving social change and substantive equality for oppressed peoples has been to turn to the law. The power of the law is its presumed objectivity and impartiality, where facts and evidence of harms, needs and rights are heard before a court of highly trained lawyers and judges. The idealized aim of formal justice is to treat everyone the same and to denounce discrimination. However, as is discussed in other chapters, the presumed procedural correctness of formal justice does not allow for substantive justice because of its very intention *to be blind to difference*. Social justice — the provision of resources and opportunities based on specific or different needs and experiences — can only be realized through a contextualized understanding of oppression. Feminist-inspired legal strategies have tried to address sexism in society (such as pay inequities for women workers or the invisibility of marital rape) through removing gender from the law. The aim of this "liberal feminist" tactic has been to make men and women equal before the law. "Radical feminists" countered that the "myth of liberation" (Firestone 1970) presupposed by liberal feminists would only buttress the patriarchal intention of the law: to protect the rights and power of men by erasing the unique societal, cultural and economic realities of women's lives: their vulnerability to sexual violence, motherhood and the public/private spheres of paid and unpaid work. As this chapter demonstrates, the liberal feminist tactic of using formal justice to protect the privacy rights of rape victims has been successfully challenged as being a threat to the Constitutional rights of men accused of rape. In this way the rights of men (who are almost always those accused of rape) are seen as more important than the rights of women (who are almost always the victims of rape). How then can feminists seize law to achieve substantive justice? Unfortunately, the recent history of feminist legal activism to address gendered violence and poverty has been to position women as victims in need of protection by the state. This has created institutions of surveillance and monitoring of women on social assistance and women who report domestic violence and has done little to achieve substantive equality of women: for example, though access to a living wage and affordable housing and childcare. Feminist-inspired legal strategies have also left behind and harmed racialized women, women living with mental illness, women addicted to drugs, women in prison and women who use violence. This group of the most marginalized women are at the centre of this chapter. The social exclusion of these women has been exacerbated by how feminists have engaged with law and how feminists have in some cases not engaged in the ethical practice of social inclusion of all women.

This book takes up the discussion of justice from a variety of standpoints to address a complex array of issues. This chapter, however, focuses on one site of the law: the criminalization and punishment of women. Racialized women constitute the fastest growing prisoner population in the world. Women are increasingly confined in immigration detention centres, psychiatric institutions, jails and penitentiaries (Sudbury 2005). In Canada, the rate of imprisoned Aboriginal women jumped 72.5 percent between 1996 and 2004 (Pollack 2009: 84). In the U.S., the country with the highest rate of imprisonment in the world, there has been a 2800 percent increase in the number of women in prison since 1970; in the U.K., women prisoner rates have increased 173 percent between 1992 and 2002 (Balfour 2006: 165). How do we make sense of this global trend towards greater punitive treatment of women? Have women become more dangerous? In what follows we explore women's social and criminal histories, theorize how criminal law has responded to women's lived experiences and consider the implications of restorative justice for criminalized and victimized women.

Who Are Criminalized and Imprisoned Women?

Main Points

As you read, highlight the answers to these questions:

How do statistics and the lived experience of imprisoned women relate to popular consumer culture and media reporting?

What is the prison industrial complex, and what is its impact on criminalized women?

What have been negative consequences of liberal feminist strategies?

Much of our common-sense understanding of the social world comes to be defined through the narratives and images in movies, books and news media. Very few of us have been inside a courtroom or a prison. Instead, much of our awareness of criminalized and imprisoned women comes from dominant discourses that privilege certain explanations and solutions of social problems. In this chapter we explore cultural stereotypes of criminalized women that are reproduced in the media and also consider how such images and narratives are echoed in the administration of criminal justice.

Much of what we read in newspapers and watch on movie screens depicts women and girls as butch-like lesbians or prostitutes, like Charlize Theron in the blockbuster movie *Monster*, or Ali Larter as a vindictive sexualized stalker in *Obsessed*. Bookstores feature displays of Stephanie Meyers' *Twilight* book series and popular teen fiction writer Sean Olin's *Killing Brittany*. In *Twilight*, Bella — a chaste young White woman — falls in love with a vampire and a werewolf. Both of these masculine characters pursue Bella, vying for her virginity. In *Killing Brittany*, a young woman kills her family and boyfriend amidst book cover images of blood-spattered lipstick kisses.

The lines between popular consumer culture and newspaper crime reporting blur in the journalistic accounts of criminalized young women. Media coverage of the trial and conviction of a fifteen-year-old "puppet master" who directed her boyfriend to stab his former girlfriend to death, abounded with claims of her sexual jealousy, body image problems and delayed toilet training. In one article, the accused is said to suffer from "borderline personality disorder and resemble Glenn Close's character in Fatal Attraction" (Hewitt 2009). Similarly, a twelve-year-old girl in Medicine Hat, Alberta, was convicted for convincing her twenty-four-year-old "boyfriend" to kill her family in exchange for sex. In a *Globe and Mail* article, Christie Blatchford (2009) pities the male killer in this case as a product of an alcoholic mother and a series of her abusive partners and possibly a sufferer of fetal alcohol syndrome. Blatchford riles against "the seemingly studious, obedient, intelligent girls of good background who moved boys about like chess pieces."

Are criminalized and imprisoned women who they seem to be in these images and narratives — White, middle class, hypersexualized and dangerously capable of wielding control over older men for sex? Orthodox or conservative criminological theories have long cast the "bad girl" as driven by her hormones, inherent immorality or ability to seduce men to do her bidding. Otto Pollock (1978), writing in the 1970s, authored the first sociological treatise on female delinquency, stating that women's ability to fake an organism is evidence of their criminal tendencies to deceive. Thus, women were likely to be as deviant as men, but their wrongdoing was underreported due to chivalry by police and judges. In the 1980s, Hagan (1987) and his colleagues wrote of delinquent girls as being inadequately supervised in families where mothers worked outside of the home, as they failed to instill appropriate norms and controls of domesticity. The reality is, however, that most women in trouble in Canada are young Aboriginal women living in poverty, many as single mothers, with little education and with histories of profound victimization, including childhood sexual abuse, rape and domestic violence (Balfour and Comack 2006; Comack 1996). The Canadian Human Rights Commission (2003) noted that 80 percent of all federally sentenced women report having been physically and/or sexually abused; this percentage rises to 90 percent for federally sentenced Aboriginal women. Federally incarcerated women (and men) tend to have lower educational attainment than the Canadian adult population as a whole. While more than 80 percent of women in Canada have progressed beyond grade nine, for women prisoners the figure is closer to 50 percent. The Canadian Association of Elizabeth Fry Societies — a feminist prisoner advocate network — reported that two-thirds of federally sentenced women are mothers, who are more likely than men to have primary childcare responsibilities; about 25,000 children have mothers who are in either federal prisons or provincial jails in Canada each year (CAEFS 2009). Many women in prison also struggle with the mental health effects of trauma, such as post-traumatic stress disorder, anxiety and depression (Laishes 2002). In short, the criminal histories of women in trouble are at odds with what we hear in the news and see in movie theatres.

In Canada, persons can be charged and prosecuted for summary or indictable offences; the former can result in a sentence of less than two years in a provincial jail, whereas the latter can result in a sentence of greater than two years to be served in a federal penitentiary. Once charges are laid against a person, the court can decide to confine the accused to pre-trial custody in a remand centre or to release her on bail or under an order to appear before the court at a later date. According to the principles of fundamental justice, the deprivation of liberty (imprisonment) is to be administered only in the direst circumstances (the accused is a flight risk or presents an imminent threat to themselves or others). However, in Canada, the greatest increase in prisoner populations has been at the pre-trial level, and disproportionately, women accused of non-violent crimes are held in remand centres. Between 2001 and 2007, the growth in the number of women admitted to remand has been greater than the overall growth in remand: the number of adult females held in remand centres rose by 36 percent between 2001/2002 and 2006/2007, while the total number of adults admitted to remand was up 14 percent (Bambooram 2008).

Between 2001 and 2006, the number of adults admitted to provincial and territorial sentenced custody decreased by 9 percent, but the number of females admitted increased by 11 percent; and the share of female offenders admitted to sentenced custody rose from 9 to 11 percent between 2001/2002 and 2006/2007 (Bambooram 2008). Statistics Canada reported that "the number of females admitted for robbery rose from 16 percent in 2001/2002 to 23 percent in 2006/2007" (Bambooram 2008). However, more than half of all charges for which federally sentenced women are convicted are non-violent, property and drug offences. Property offences account for 47 percent of all charges against women (CAEFS 2009). The recidivism rate for federally sentenced women is approximately 21 percent, as compared to 59 percent for men. Only 1–2 percent of federally sentenced women are returned to prison as the result of the commission of new crimes and less than 0.5 percent is for a violent offence (CAEFS 2009). Prisoner data also indicate that there has been a greater percentage of offenders convicted of non-violent property related offences — disproportionately women — sentenced to longer terms of imprisonment, thus confined to federal prisons; and between 2003/2004 and 2006/2007, 30 percent more women were admitted to provincial and territorial jails, most often for "other *Criminal Code*" offences: mischief, disturbing the peace, arson, prostitution and offensive weapons (Bambooram 2008)

Women are charged for drug-related offences at a rate higher than are men. For example, some women living in poverty with children to support agree to transport drugs across the border into the United States or Canada. Susan Boyd (2006: 138) reports that 14 percent of all drug charges involved women, yet 30 percent of women prisoners were serving federal sentences (greater than two years) for drug offences, compared to 18 percent of men. In 1996, a provincial commission established to examine systemic racism in the Ontario criminal justice system reported that between 1986 and 1993, the number of women admitted to provincial jails for drug-related offences increased by 667 percent for White women and 5200 percent for Black women (138). Correctional Services Canada data show a 20 percent increase in the number of federally sentenced women serving drug-related sentences since 1997 (139).

Thus, criminalized and imprisoned women are very different from those depicted in the narratives and images of popular culture and crime reporting. Rather than "girls gone wild," criminalized women are amongst the most marginalized, are generally convicted of non-violent crimes and are least likely to reoffend (Kong and AuCoin 2008).

Self Test

Which of the following claims are true with regards to women's criminal histories?

- Women are more likely to be held in pre-trial custody than men.
- Women are more likely than men to be imprisoned for drug-related offences.
- Women are increasingly imprisoned for "other *Criminal Code*" offences, such as mischief.
- Women are less likely to be repeat offenders than men.

- What has contributed to the significant increase in the number of women in prison in Canada over the last decade?

How can we begin to understand the paradox between the social histories of victimization, social exclusion and criminal histories of women in trouble, and the increasing rates of women's imprisonment? Shouldn't the courts take into consideration the unique circumstances of women in poverty and women who have been victims of sexual violence? Unfortunately, throughout most of Canada, liberal, conservative and social democratic provincial governments alike have worked to dismantle key public institutions created to address crime through reducing poverty, increasing education and providing preventative community mental health services. In addition, the capacity for oversight of police and prisons has been increased. Much of these significant changes have been strongly supported by White, middle-class voters who denounce rehabilitation of offenders, harm reduction approaches to drug addiction and welfare supports for the poor. The "prison industrial complex" is an economic opportunity for rural and Aboriginal communities as prisons become job creation opportunities. Yet these prisons are increasingly used to house persons who are homeless and/or unemployed or living with mental health problems. As outlined in the previous chapter, racialized women, immigrant women and single mothers comprise the largest proportion of the underclass in Canada. The Auditor General of Canada (2003) reported that 77 percent of Canadians accessing social service agencies, such as income assistance, public housing and daycare, are women. As neo-liberal reforms have restricted eligibility to welfare and increased levels of surveillance of those on assistance, women have been increasingly vulnerable to criminalization for welfare fraud (for example, failure to report additional income such as student loans or saving accounts). As well, zero tolerance mandatory charging practices in cases of domestic violence have resulted in dual charging of some women who call police to report being assaulted. A study conducted by Pollack, Green and Allspach (2005) of charging by police in Toronto found that two-thirds of their sample of women before the courts for domestic violence charges had been solely or dually charged by police responding to their calls to report assault. Together, neo-liberal economic policies and neo-conservative law-and-order reforms have adversely impacted women in poverty and living with violence. As imprisonment is a form of punishment to be proscribed by the criminal justice system as proportionate to the seriousness of the offence and the moral blameworthiness of the offender, we should be greatly concerned about the use of prisons because of failed social policies.

What is the connection between race, class, gender and the criminal justice system? Conditions of social inequality and social exclusion heighten the likelihood of police charges, criminalization and imprisonment. The principles of fundamental justice that underpin the "official version of law" (Naffine 1990) (discussed in Chapter Ten) are purported to ensure a rights-based adversarial system of justice to protect the accused's rights to security of the person and freedom from arbitrary detention by the state. Indeed, the image of the blindfolded maiden of justice suggests the sacred right to procedural fairness, thus protecting against the influence of racial, class and gendered stereotypes in the administration of justice. Regardless of the constraints of due process proscribed in law, such cultural stereotypes appear to enable or shape the administration of justice. Indeed, as is illustrated in the following case study of two women convicted of drug trafficking for couriering cocaine from Jamaica to Canada, attempts by the sentencing judge to contextualize the women's choices was overturned on appeal in order to uphold the retributive principles of deterrence and denunciation. This case reveals how women's lived experiences of structural inequality and racism are not recognized through the law's method of objectivity and impartiality.

In 2001, two women were arrested at Toronto's Pearson International Airport for trafficking and possession of cocaine. The provincial court judge in this case asserted that the women should not be sentenced to prison because gendered social conditions of poverty, single parenting, minimum wage employment and lack of family support led to their offence. The following is an excerpt from the judge's written decision:

> Cocaine courier importation cases are, almost invariably, not about greed in the sense of an offender reaping profits to maintain a lavish lifestyle or to acquire luxuries. These individuals, highly dispensable throwaways of elusive overseers, live in the despair of poverty — single mothers and subjects of systemic racism. The reward for the risk taken pays rent, feeds children, and supports a subsistence level existence… On… the cocaine importation offence… women constitute a third to one half of those charged. It is apparent that women, and especially African Canadian women, like the offenders here and so many others, are virtue tested by drug operation overseers deliberately preying on their social and economic disadvantage.
>
> Each of the offenders in this case has three young children. Each is a single mother with no financial assistance from their children's fathers. Each requires welfare to survive. In Canada, the feminization of poverty is an entrenched social phenomenon with a multiplicity of economic barriers faced by women. Courts have long recognized the economic disadvantage of the female partner in a domestic relationship. The impact of childcare on women's financial ability and independence is equally well known. Offenders like those before the court are subject to both the systemic economic inequality of women caring on their own for young children and the compounding disadvantage of systemic racism securing their poverty status. These individuals, almost inevitably

> without a prior criminal record, are in turn conscripted by the drug distribution hierarchy targeting their vulnerability. Poor, then exploited in their poverty, these women when captured and convicted have been subjected to severe sentences perpetuating their position of disadvantage. (*R.* v. *Hamilton and Mason* 2003))

The judge in this case decided upon a conditional sentence (a prison term to be served in the community) for the two women because of their remorse, the personal circumstances (poverty) that led to their crimes and the impact of imprisonment upon their children. In response to the judge's attempt to achieve substantive justice within the administration of formal justice, the province of Ontario appealed the sentence, seeking a term of imprisonment. The following is an excerpt from the appeal judge's written decision:

> Sentencing is not based on group characteristics, but on the facts relating to the specific offence and specific offender as revealed by the evidence adduced in the proceedings. A sentencing proceeding is also not the forum in which to right perceived societal wrongs, allocate responsibility for criminal conduct as between the offender and society, or "make up" for perceived social injustices by the imposition of sentences that do not reflect the seriousness of the crime... The trial judge stepped outside of the proper role of a judge on sentencing and ultimately imposed sentences that were inconsistent with the statutory principles of sentencing. He rested his conclusion that conditional sentences were appropriate primarily on his finding that the [women] because of their race, gender, and poverty, were particularly vulnerable targets to those who sought out individuals to act as cocaine couriers. Ms. Hamilton received a conditional sentence of twenty months on terms that provided for partial house arrest in the first year of the sentence and a curfew for the remainder of the sentence. Ms. Mason received a conditional sentence of two years less a day on terms that provided for partial house arrest in the first fifteen months of the sentence and a curfew for the rest of the sentence. The trial judge lost his appearance of impartiality. While no doubt well-intentioned, the trial judge effectively took on the combined role of advocate, witness, and judge, thereby losing the appearance of a neutral arbiter. The Crown submits that the women received conditional sentences because they were poor, black, and female, and that none of these factors diminish the seriousness of the offence or justify a conditional sentence. Counsel further argues that the imposition of conditional sentences based on the race and gender of the respondents will only reinforce the prevailing wisdom among drug overlords that young black women make ideal drug couriers, thereby

> perpetuating and exacerbating the vulnerability of the very group the trial judge sought to assist.
>
> The trial judge's role as the arbiter of the respective merits of competing positions developed and put before the trial judge by the parties best ensures judicial impartiality and the appearance of judicial impartiality. Human nature is such that it is always easier to objectively assess the merits of someone else's argument. The relatively passive role assigned to the trial judge also recognizes that judges, by virtue of their very neutrality, are not in a position to make informed decisions as to which issues should be raised. It is also important that the trial judge limit the scope of his or her intervention into the role traditionally left to counsel. The trial judge should frame any issue that he or she introduces as precisely as possible and relate it to the case before the court. This will avoid turning the sentencing hearing into a *de facto* commission of inquiry. (*R.* v. *Hamilton and Mason* 2004)

Self Test

In your view, what should the purpose of sentencing be in this case with regards to the two women charged?

Do you agree that judges should take social problems of systemic racism and feminization of poverty into consideration in the sentencing of criminalized persons, or focus solely on the moral blameworthiness of the offender and seriousness of the offence?

If only moral blameworthiness is focused on, how can social problems be addressed?

Retributive Justice and the Woman of Legal Discourse

Main Points

As you read, highlight the answers to these questions:

How can the over-representation of marginalized women in the criminal process be explained?

What strategies have feminists used for law reforms?

What have been the results of these strategies?

The cases above, of Marsha Hamilton and Donna Mason, reveal the limits of the law as a site of social justice and the hegemony of the official version of the law: the criminalization process is one which unfolds in a context of rationality and objectivity. In this view, the legal system is founded on a series of procedural requirements and technical exercises to protect the rights of the accused balanced off against the role of the state to denounce conduct that is not in the public interest. That is, according to the procedural requirements of the law, persons are criminalized and condemned solely on the basis of their behaviour and its harmfulness. In the view of the law, gender is not and should not be considered.

Yet, the over-representation of marginalized groups in the criminalization process reveals a paradox between the law and the administration of justice. The disconnection between "what the legal world would have us believe about itself" (Naffine 1990: 24) and the law in practice raises the possibility that the criminalization process is influenced by gendered, as well as racialized and class-based, presuppositions. Smart (1992) argues that much of early liberal feminism saw the "law as sexist," or discriminatory towards women, and sought to engage with the law through rights-based reforms to the black letter of the law to demand equality with men with regards to material resources and opportunities. Radical feminists rejected the equity argument and instead asserted a "law as male" paradigm, drawing on the re-victimizing experiences of raped and battered women by the police and before the courts. Feminist lawyers and anti-violence activists have tackled the law's sexist treatment of raped and battered women through appealing lower court rulings and filing Constitutional challenges of such decisions before the Supreme Court of Canada.

Feminist-Inspired Law Reforms

Feminists have long argued that the laws concerning rape have been framed by mythologies that normalize women as liars and sexual temptresses (Busby 1999; Smart, 1989). Drawn from wider patriarchal culture, these myths have played a significant role in Canadian jurisprudence. Rape myths that frame our everyday common sense include "a woman who dresses in sexy clothes is asking for it"; "rape is caused by men's natural impulses once a woman has turned him on"; "no means yes: when a woman flirts with a man, what does she expect?"; "if yes to one then yes to all"; "women cannot be trusted, they make false accusations and blackmail ex-boyfriends"; and "real rape is when you have physical injuries" (Comack 2000: 139–42). In the context of these myths, the law is male in that it protects men's sexual access to women and blames women for rape. Seen from another perspective, in cases of robbery it is never suggested that the robbery victim is to blame because he left his door unlocked. Numerous reforms have been made in Canadian criminal law as a result of feminist legal activism to combat the place of rape mythologies in the strategies of lawyers and decisions of judges. For example, in 1983 feminist lawyers challenged the sexism of rape laws and won changes to the legal category of rape: the offence was changed to sexual assault, husbands could be charged with sexually assaulting their wives, vaginal penetration was no longer required as corroborating evidence necessary for conviction, and lawyers' ability to ask questions about a woman's sexual history was restricted.

These reforms were designed to acknowledge rape as a violent crime, not a crime of passion, and to shield women from humiliating experiences before the courts. Other changes to the form of law achieved by feminist lawyers included changes to protect child victims of sexual assault and clarification of when consent to sex can be obtained (for example, a woman cannot consent to sex if she is intoxicated). Finally, the defence of "mistaken belief in consent" based on a woman's sexual history, lifestyle or dress was struck down as discriminatory against women, although provisions were implemented to allow judges to consider some evidence under certain conditions. One of the key Supreme Court decisions in sexual assault case law is *R.* v. *Seaboyer; R. v. Gayme* (1991), as it was the first Constitutional challenge of section 276, the rape shield provision. At issue was whether two men convicted of sexual assault should be allowed to cross-examine a victim as to her sexual history and to use a defence of mistaken belief in consent. The Supreme Court agreed with the accused men and ruled the rape shield provision unconstitutional, but upheld the convictions. The dissenting opinion of Justice Claire L'Heureux-Dube, who argued strongly against the ruling to strike down the rape shield provision, is presented here in part:

> Sexual assault is not like any other crime. It is for the most part unreported and the prosecution and conviction rates are among the lowest for all violent crimes. These statistics indicate that prejudicial beliefs may distort our perception of what actually happens. Rape myths still present formidable obstacles for complainants in their dealings with the very system charged with discovering the truth. From the making of the initial complaint down to the determination of the issue at trial, stereotype and mythology are at work, lowering the number of reported cases, influencing police decisions to pursue the case, thereby decreasing the rates of arrest, and finally distorting the issues at trial and, necessarily, the results.
>
> The concept of relevance has been imbued with stereotypical notions of female complainants and sexual assault. This is plain from the common law which held that evidence of "unchasteness" was relevant to both consent and credibility The irrelevance of most evidence of prior sexual history is clear once the mythical basis of relevancy determinations in this area of the law is revealed. Nevertheless, Parliament has provided broad avenues for its admissibility in setting out exceptions to the general rule in s. 276. Moreover, *all* evidence of the complainant's previous sexual history with the accused is prima facie admissible under those provisions. Evidence that is excluded by these provisions is simply irrelevant in a decision-making context free of myth and stereotype.
>
> The exclusion of "pattern" evidence and "habit" evidence is not unconstitutional; the mythical basis of these arguments denies their relevance. "Pattern of conduct evidence" usually occurs where the com-

> plainant has had consensual sexual relations in circumstances that look much like those supporting the assault allegation. Such evidence is almost invariably irrelevant. Arguments in its favour depend for their vitality on the notion that women consent to sex based upon such extraneous considerations as the location of the act, the race, age or profession of the alleged assaulter and/or considerations of the nature of the sexual act engaged in. Consent is to a person and not to a circumstance.
>
> Such arguments are implicitly based upon the notion that women will, in the right circumstances, consent to anyone and, more fundamentally, that "unchaste" women have a propensity to consent. Evidence characterized as habitual, as being more specific than character and as denoting one's regular response to a repeated situation, too, is inadmissible. Adopting such an argument here would lend support to the stereotypical proposition that "unchaste" women have a propensity to consent. No analogy can be drawn between this behaviour and volitional sexual conduct. The relevance of evidence of mistaken belief in consent in some cases does not conclusively demonstrate the infirmity of the provision. No relevant evidence regarding the defence of honest but mistaken belief in consent is excluded by the legislation under attack here. Evidence of prior acts of prostitution or allegations of prostitution are properly excluded by the provision. This evidence is never relevant and, moreover, is highly prejudicial. A prostitute is not generally more willing to consent to sexual intercourse and is no less credible as a witness because of that mode of life. There is no understandable reason for asking complainants in sexual assault cases if they are prostitutes.
>
> The evidence excluded by s. 276 is simply irrelevant because it is based upon discriminatory beliefs about women and sexual assault. The importance of Parliament's objectives in the reform of the law of sexual assault is amplified by the nature of the harm done and by the fact that its legislative effort gives voice to values that are paramount in a free and democratic society. (*R.* v. *Seaboyer; R.* v. *Gayme* 1991))

Following this decision, feminist lawyers proposed a revised rape shield provision to ensure the protection of the accused's rights to a fair trial and a woman's equality and privacy rights. However, despite feminist-inspired reforms to constrain the place of rape myths in sexual assault trials, rates of sexual violence have not declined, rates of successful prosecution have not increased, and rates of imprisonment for sexual assault remain the lowest of any violent crime. Furthermore, a series of formidable challenges by the defence bar against these reforms have resulted in a reassertion of the accused's right to make a full defence to the charge of rape over women's equality and privacy rights. For example, defence lawyers rely upon third party evidence aimed at discrediting the victim (personal diaries, therapeutic counselling records and school records). In 1999, such anti-feminist backlash reappeared with a vengeance in *R.* v. *Ewanchuk* (1999). A provincial court judge ruled that the perpetrator, accused of sexually assaulting a young woman he was interviewing for a job, was entitled to the defence of implied consent — although no such defence existed in law — because the victim did not actively resist the attack. The victim claimed that she was terrified of the perpetrator and said no repeatedly but did not physically resist. The Supreme Court overturned the lower court's acquittal of the accused and threw out the defence of implied consent and expressed in its decision a feminist analysis of "sexual violence as a matter of equality as it is an offence against human dignity and violation of human rights" (para. 7). Although the Court recognized the importance of protecting women's Constitutional rights, the lower court rulings in the Ewanchuk case reveal the contested terrain of rape law reform and how the form of law can reproduce rather than remedy gender inequality. Why is the form of law not more effective in its denunciation of rape and recognition of raped women's rights? Is it perhaps that law is sexist or male in its treatment of victimized women? If understood in this way, does law also engender criminalized women?

Self Test

These two examples of case law (*R.* v. *Seaboyer* and *R.* v. Ewanchuk) reveal the seemingly irreconcilable differences between an accused's right to a fair trial and a victim's equality and privacy rights. Should there be a hierarchy of rights imposed by the rule of law?

Why have goals of equality and objectivity not resulted in less sexism in the law's treatment of raped women?

The Practice of Law as a Gendering Process

Smart (1992) claims that feminist socio-legal theory needs to reconsider the law's treatment of women as a gendering process — a series of processes or strategies that weave together various cultural constructs of masculinity, femininity, dangerousness, blameworthiness and victimization. Smart goes on to explain that women do not enter the criminal justice system already gendered or sexed; rather, women's identities as rape victims or murderers are scripted according to dominant discourses of femininity. Daly (1994: 433) extends Smart's notion of the law as gendered to argue that the law is also "colour coded and class compounded." For example, prostitutes are rarely viewed by the courts as rape victims regardless of the brutality of the violence perpetrated against them. Razack's (2000) analysis of the rape and murder of a prostituted Aboriginal woman, Pamela George, in Regina Saskatchewan, helps us make sense of law as gendered and racialized. Razack claims that under law, Aboriginal peoples are culturalized; for example, addiction and violence are understood to be a normative part of Aboriginal relationships, culture and communities. Razack cites examples of lawyers' strategies at the trial of the two White, middle-class university students accused of killing George after she refused to get into the car with them. The site of the murder was described as "a romantic place where couples are often necking or petting in vehicles" (114) and George herself was referred to as the "hooker" or the "Indian" whereas the accused men were referred to as "boys who did pretty darn stupid things" (117). Razack argues that these strategies constitute the identities of the men and Pamela George as well as where the death occurred in such a way that "no one could really be held accountable for her death, at least not to the extent that there would have been accountability had she been [White]" (117).

Through the analysis of the practice of law, we are able to see how Aboriginal women are constituted as "drunken squaws," as such cultural presuppositions make up the ideological content of the law. According to Kline (1994: 458), these "squaw narratives" of Aboriginal women developed out of colonialism (*Indian Act*, reserve system, residential schools) and have become "abstracted and indeterminate in law." Through the law's appearance of neutrality, its power to naturalize and legitimize racist ideologies is obscured. Nahanee (1994) and Nightingale (1991) have shown how stereotypes of the "drunken Indian" have influenced how the courts minimize the culpability of Aboriginal men accused of sexual assault. Alcohol abuse is often raised as a mitigating factor when sentencing a man convicted of rape, "even as the root cause of violence against women" (Nahanee 1994: 198). Similarly, the law as a gendering and racializing strategy comes into view when examining how Aboriginal women's credibility is assessed according to the image of the "drunken Indian." Nightingale (1991) suggests that either an Aboriginal woman is not likely to be believed by the police or band leaders when she alleges to have been raped because she was intoxicated, or her claim of being passed out during the rape is over exaggerated to enable lawyers to argue that the rape was less traumatic. In more recent research on the law's treatment of violence against Aboriginal women in the context of sentencing circles, Cunliffe and Cameron (2007) point out how procedural requirements for evidence and victim impact statements take control of women's victimization by deciding what is credible testimony and the necessary punishment. In their study of sentencing circles in cases of domestic violence, women's victimization narratives are often omitted from sentencing decisions, at best interpreted by judges as to their meaning and significance. So, despite efforts to take gender into account in the sentencing process, the context of women's experiences and needs for safety are overshadowed by the form of the law.

Looking Forward: Restorative Justice

Is it possible to engage with law to resolve the problem of women's increasing rates of imprisonment and the persistence of violence against women? Compulsory criminalization of domestic violence has had the unintended consequence of locking up women who call police for help (Snider 1994). Similarly, rape law reforms to protect women's rights and to challenge rape myths in the form and practice of law appear to have done little to stem the rate of sexual violence against women and improve conviction rates. Moreover, given that the ethos of criminal justice is punishment not social justice and that its process is entrenched in a rights-based adversarial model, feminists have rightly reconsidered the law as an effective means of resistance to patriarchy and furthering social change. For some socio-legal scholars and anti-violence activists, restorative justice offers a new paradigm of justice. Over the past two decades, restorative justice policies and practices have been implemented in most industrialized countries and many developing nations. Broadly speaking, the restorative justice framework brings together people in a model of justice where crime is the action that harms specific people and relationships, which in turn creates needs and obligations. Crime is then handled within a framework where victims, offenders and communities work together to repair the harm (Cheon and Regehr 2006). Throughout the process of reparation, the offender must accept responsibility for her actions and make amends, whereas the community is expected to ensure the safety and support of the victim and offender (Braithwaite 2001). Morris (2002: 600) asserts that in some countries, such as New Zealand, restorative justice has come to emphasize a human-rights perspective that seeks to restore the victim's security, self-respect and dignity:

> Restorative processes and practices, therefore, should empower offenders and victims by giving them a sense of inclusion in and satisfaction with these processes and practices; they should enable victims to feel better as a result of participating in them; and they should hold offenders accountable in meaningful ways by encouraging them to make amends to their victims. If all these occur, we might expect the restorative justice processes to impact on reoffending and reintegration and to heal victim's hurt.

New Zealand has also begun to implement restorative justice in the context of serious crimes such as sexual assault and domestic violence. In Canada, the Aboriginal community of Hollow Water is responding to the high rate of intergenerational child sexual abuse with a holistic, community-centred strategy that addresses the trauma of abuse experienced by the victim and the victim's family, as well as the needs of the victimizer. The aim is to restore the capacity of the community to care for the needs of its members, not vengeance or retribution through the incarceration of the perpetrator. Proponents of restorative justice in the violence against women context point to how retributive justice (mandatory charging, vigorous prosecution and minimum sentencing) has not addressed low reporting and prosecution rates and the re-victimization of women under vigorous cross-examination. Successful convictions and punitive sentences are achieved only in cases where women are viewed by the courts to be chaste, respectable, sober and physically injured in her resistance against the attacker (Christie 1984; Hudson 2002). Women must adopt the identity of "victim" and relinquish their autonomy and self-determination (Lacey 1998). Moreover, the punitive sentencing of men may create conditions of endangerment for women as their abusers seek revenge upon women for calling the police or testifying in court (Snider 1998). Proponents further assert that the principles of restorative justice can address women's needs for safety and denunciation of the violence. "Restorative justice can empower a woman to define herself and the harm that has been done; she is at the centre of events, in control and telling her stories and in her own way" (Hulsman 1991, cited in Hudson 2002: 624).

In contrast, opponents of restorative justice for rape and domestic violence assert that such a criminal justice response is "cheap justice" (Coker 2006) that does not take seriously the impact and prevalence of gendered violence. Oftentimes, communities have a limited capacity or willingness to respond to the safety needs of women who have been victimized (Cameron 2006; Daly and Stubbs 2005; McGillvray and Comaskey 1999). Razack (1998) argues that sentencing circles do not take into account complex historical, economic and political contexts of gendered violence perpetrated against women, especially those who are Aboriginal. Such debates question the safety of women who may feel pressure from the community to support the offender and the risk of trivializing gendered violence and returning it to the domestic sphere as a relationship problem (Coker 2006). In Canada, the response of women's organizations to the implementation of restorative justice in response to gendered violence has been mixed. Cameron (2006) calls for a moratorium in cases of domestic and sexualized violence, especially within the Aboriginal community, as tradition is not always respectful of women's status in the community and in some instances can fail to protect women from their abusers. Overall, most feminist, Aboriginal and critical race scholars are uncertain as to the potential of restorative justice practices to address the root causes of gendered violence.

Conditional sentencing is one example of an alternative intended to lessen the rate of incarceration in Canada. This sentencing option was created by Parliament in 1996 as part of sweeping reforms to the *Criminal Code*.

Conditional sentencing has been recognized by some legal scholars as an attempt to move towards a restorative justice paradigm (Roberts and Roach

1996 Sentencing Options

Statutes of Canada 1995 Chapter 22
An Act to amend the Criminal Code (sentencing) and other Acts in consequence thereof

BILL C-41 Assented to 13th July, 1995
742.1 Where a person is convicted of an offence, except an offence that is punishable by a minimum term of imprisonment, and the court

(a) imposes a sentence of imprisonment of less than two years, and

(b) is satisfied that serving the sentence in the community would not endanger the safety of the community,

the court may, for the purpose of supervising the offender's behaviour in the community, order that the offender serve the sentence in the community, subject to the offender's complying with the conditions of a conditional sentence order made under section 742.3.

Firearm, etc., prohibitions
742.3 (1) The court shall prescribe, as conditions of a conditional sentence order, that the offender do all of the following:

(a) keep the peace and be of good behaviour;

(b) appear before the court when required to do so by the court;

(c) report to a supervisor

(i) within two working days, or such longer period as the court directs, after the making of the conditional sentence order, and

(ii) thereafter, when required by the supervisor and in the manner directed by the supervisor;

(d) remain within the jurisdiction of the court unless written permission to go outside that jurisdiction is obtained from the court or the supervisor; and

(e) notify the court or the supervisor in advance of any change of name or address, and promptly notify the court or the supervisor of any change of employment or occupation.

Optional conditions of conditional sentence order
(2) The court may prescribe, as additional conditions of a conditional sentence order, that the offender do one or more of the following:

(a) abstain from

(i) the consumption of alcohol or other intoxicating substances, or

(ii) the consumption of drugs except in accordance with a medical prescription;

(b) abstain from owning, possessing or carrying a weapon;

(c) provide for the support or care of dependants;

(d) perform up to 240 hours of community service over a period not exceeding eighteen months;

(e) attend a treatment program approved by the province; and

(f) comply with such other reasonable conditions as the court considers desirable, subject to any regulations made under subsection 738(2), for securing the good conduct of the offender and for preventing a repetition by the offender of the same offence or the commission of other offences.

2005), whereas others claim that such sentencing practices are designed to alleviate the cost of imprisonment for the state. Little empirical research has been conducted to examine the gendered impact of conditional sentencing upon criminalized or victimized women. Rather, impact studies conducted by the federal government's Centre for Justice Statistics indicate that courts tend to utilize conditional sentences for property related offences, although there is some evidence that it is being used in cases of sexual assault. Indeed the Supreme Court of Canada has ruled that a conditional sentence is not precluded by the seriousness of the offence; rather sentencing decisions should be based on the offender's needs for treatment and successful reintegration into the community (*R.* v. *Gladue* 1998).

The promise of conditional sentences to reduce the high rate of imprisonment has not been realized for criminalized women, whose incarceration rates continue to climb. Preliminary research indicates that conditional sentences are sought by defence counsel in cases of intimate partner sexual violence (Balfour and Du Mont 2011). In determining the implications of conditional sentencing to denounce sexual violence and protect women from harm, we need to consider lessons learned from earlier feminist-inspired legal reforms. In a study of sexual assault cases in Ontario between 1993 and 2001, Du Mont, Hyde and Badgley (2008) found that in two-thirds of the cases, despite vaginal and/or anal penetration, physical force or coercion, the median sentence was twenty-seven months. Sentence length increased significantly if the perpetrator was a stranger and a weapon was used or threatened. Such data tell us that despite hard won reforms, rape myths about who is a rape victim, who is a rapist and what is real rape remain embedded in the law. If rape myths continue to underpin the strategies of lawyers in rape cases, should we be content to think of sentencing reforms as capable of addressing the incarceration spiral of women in trouble? After all, many women in trouble are victimized, criminalized and have "fallen between the cracks of restorative and retributive justice" (Balfour 2008). In other words, law reforms to denounce violence against women and sentencing reforms to slow the rate of incarceration have not benefited the population of women most likely to be victims and prisoners. Feminist socio-legal theory and anti-violence activists need to consider in their work those women whose lives are lived at the crossroads of punishment and victimization.

Summary Points

Often feminist law reform measures are met with anti-feminist backlash so ultimately little progress is made.

Law is gendered, colour coded and class compounded.

Restorative justice has had mixed responses from scholars and commentators for meeting the needs of marginalized women: some assert its potential and benefits, others assert it as "cheap justice," while others say it trivializes gender violence.

Conditional sentences have not reduced the incarceration rates of criminalized women.

Getting Gender into Justice

Despite popular cultural narratives of "bad girls" that depict young women in trouble as violent and manipulative, criminalized women are amongst the most marginalized and vulnerable people in Canadian society. Their criminal histories reveal the impact of poverty, addiction, mental illness and single parenting. Most women prisoners are convicted of non-violent crimes, such as fraud, drug and prostitution related offences, and are more likely to be imprisoned in pre-trial custody and sentenced to prison for a first offence than are male offenders. Moreover, women offenders are a very low risk to commit another offence. A disproportionate number of federally sentenced women are Aboriginal or Black women convicted of serious crimes that resulted from impacts of social exclusion, sexual violence, addiction and mental illness. Despite these realities about women in trouble, we have witnessed a global lockdown of women. Feminist engagement with law has resulted in reforms to sexual assault laws, asserted the human rights of women prisoners and challenged the sexism inherent in welfare reforms. Yet, the form and practice of law has yet to create real systemic changes to the criminal justice response to women in trouble. In cases of restorative justice and sexual assault, victimized and criminalized women fall between the cracks. Although some feminists believe that while the law remains sexist or male, it is an important power resource to articulate and defend women's rights. However, it appears that law reforms are of little consequence or benefit to women and should not be the central strategy of feminist politics. It is important to broaden the site of struggle against gender oppression and to bring the law to bear upon political and economic practices of injustice. Violence against women has been a key site of feminist legal activism, yet prisons are filled with women who have been criminalized for fighting back or surviving on the streets because of poverty and mental illness. Perhaps it is time for feminists to consider and condemn economic oppression and political disenfranchisement as state violence against women.

Glossary

anti-feminist backlash – the response to feminist-inspired victories to denounce gendered violence, achieve pay equity and mount significant legal challenges against the state to protect the rights of women, by (mostly male) critics who see feminist politics and policies as a threat to family values, as underestimating violence against men and the seriousness of women's own violence, and undermining the rights of men before the law.

Canadian Association of Elizabeth Fry Societies – a network of feminist prisoner advocacy and prison abolition organizations which provides support to women and girls in conflict with the law, as well as challenging government policies with regards to the conditions of confinement in women's prisons.

conditional sentence – a sentencing option created by the federal government in 1996 to allow offenders receiving sentences of less than two years to serve their sentences in the community under strict conditions. The intent was to decrease the high rate of incarceration especially for non-violent offenders and to encourage judges to be creative and flexible in their sentencing practices.

Hollow Water – an Aboriginal community in Manitoba that has created a holistic community-based healing process that seeks to address the intergenerational impact of sexual abuse through the combined power of community and law. An abuser may plead guilty and be sentenced to probation requiring full cooperation with the healing process, or be abandoned to the courts, with jail as the probable outcome.

law as sexist – a viewpoint of liberal feminists that law perpetuates discrimination against women by allowing for differential treatment on the basis of sex. Instead, liberal feminists believe women and men should be seen as individuals.

law as male – a perspective of radical feminists that law perpetuates patriarchal oppression by protecting men's entitlement to women's bodies by failing to criminalize men who sexually exploit women through prostitution, pornography and sexual violence.

liberal feminism – a feminist perspective that formal equality can be achieved through law and policy reforms that are gender neutral and create individual opportunities.

official version of the law – how the law sees itself: rational, objective and impartial and unaffected by stereotypes or biases. The official version of law is best portrayed by the image of the blind-folded maiden of justice holding the scales of justice weighing the factual evidence put before her.

orthodox/conservative criminological theories – explanations of the causes of crime that focus on individual pathology or immorality. Such theories presuppose that social problems are caused by individuals. Solutions to crime are rehabilitation and punishment, not social transformation.

prison industrial complex – a phrase coined by Angela Davis (1997) to describe the rapid expansion of the U.S inmate populations and the political influence of private prison companies and businesses that supply goods and services to government prison agencies. It is seem as equalling the military industrial complex, which emerged out of the World War

II. Activists describe the prison industrial complex as perpetuating a belief that imprisonment is a quick fix to underlying social problems such as homelessness, unemployment, drug addiction, mental illness and illiteracy.

radical feminism – a perspective that claims that women are oppressed under patriarchy (male centred political and cultural system) through sexual violence and reproduction.

rape shield – a legal provision in the *Criminal Code* that protects women from having to testify about their sexual history. This provision has been challenged by defence lawyers who claim a woman's sexual history can lead the man to believe she consented to sex, thus violating a man's right a fair trial.

recidivism – the recriminalization and/or re-imprisonment of people who have been previously in trouble with the law. Recidivism rates refer to people convicted of new crimes as well those who have broken the conditions of their probation or parole.

sentencing circles – a restorative justice sentencing practice that takes place in the community where the crime happened and involves the victim and the victimizer. The community decides the nature of the sentence to be handed down. Circles are typically practised in small rural Aboriginal communities.

victim impact statement – a legal provision created in 1987 to allow victims of crimes to formally document the impact of their victimization. However, impact statements are rarely taken into account in sentencing hearings, as judges are more likely to sentence according to principles of general deterrence and denunciation.

7

Environmental Justice

Margot A. Hurlbert

At the end of this chapter, you will be able to:

- Describe different cognized environments and world views respecting the environment
- Outline current environmental challenges
- Understand different approaches to environmental justice locally and globally and arrive at a definition of environmental justice

Environmental justice, or what some prefer to call ecological justice, expands our consideration of justice beyond the realm of inter-human relationships. Traditionally, analyses of justice issues predominantly focused on relationships between individuals or groups of people. Environmental justice, on the other hand, turns our focus towards aspects of both the physical environment in which we live — particularly how we, as humans, interact and relate to that environment, how this impacts relations between humans and how these relations are, in part, justice issues.

The analysis that follows will show that, in studying environmental justice, the task is more difficult than simply adding environment into the justice mix and stirring. Consider the following illustration of environmental justice when we utilize our current conception of human rights and add in the idea of the Earth having rights, or plant and animal rights.

This chapter explores environmental justice outlining various possible definitions of environmental justice (legal, procedural and participatory) and ultimately arguing for a broad approach to environmental justice combining these definitions. This broad definition, which combines various dimensions of environmental justice, arrives at a place of social environmental justice, which is both a formula to analyze environmental issues in assessing "justice" or "injustice" and a mechanism to apply to environmental issues to achieve societal justice. This definition contains aspects of formal justice, substantive justice and ethical practice, the three themes of justice envisioned in this book.

> **Ecological Justice: The Rights of Plants and Animals**
>
> Can environmental justice be approached by simply adding the Earth, plants and animals into our current considerations of justice (Wenz 1988)? Do animals (both sentient and non-sentient organisms) have rights and are they part of our justice equation? In other words should dogs, cats, horses and cows have rights? Should all animals have rights, or only the ones humans rely on? If they should, must we become vegetarians? Must carnivorous animals, such as wolves become vegetarians? If not, rabbits will never have meaningful rights unless domesticated, but would they then be happy? What about the rights of the wolves to make an honest living (meal)?
>
> Is the concern to protect future human generations who rely on these entities or to protect those entities because of their own right to existence?
>
> Some prefer the term "ecological" justice when expanding the gambit of justice beyond human relationships to recognize this broader focus.
>
> The addition of the environment in our consideration of justice is more complex than expanding our notion of whom and what should be included in our structures of legal justice. It often challenges our preconceived beliefs about justice and people's relationship to the environment, all of which requires a reconsideration of the relationship between people in a global context. This is particularly evident when the specific environmental justice issue of climate change is considered.

Thinking about the Environment

Main Points

As you read, highlight the answers to these questions:
What is a cognized environment?
What is a worldview? How have worldviews changed over time?
Does the new ecological paradigm represent our current worldview?

What do we mean by "the environment"? We could start with our immediate environment at work or at home using characteristics of both our physical surroundings and our social and emotional surroundings. For instance, some workplaces are described as "toxic environments" to work in (this may mean that the people at the workplace are having interpersonal relationship issues or it may mean that there are toxic chemicals present). A common starting point is to think of the environment as the "natural" world. Perhaps this is even reduced to the notion of pristine wilderness and rainforests. Here the term environment is being used in the broad sense which includes the environment within which we are living and working as well as the environment beyond our doorstep, our community and even our country. It includes the wide open spaces of the country, the vanishing wilderness and rainforests, the Arctic and the oceans and seas. In this sense, environment means the biophysical environment or that which is contained in the biosphere, or the part of the Earth and its atmosphere in which living organisms exist and that is capable of supporting life. The biophysical environment contains all variables that comprise it, including the physical environment (such as oceans, deserts, land and cities) and biological life forms (such as plants, animals and people).

The particular focus in environmental justice is on the relationship between people and the natural environment (found in our balcony, backyard and park as well as in various rural and urban landscapes). Significant focus is also on the environment itself and how the characteristics of the environment create a unique relationship with people. For instance, Canada's environment has always been very rich in natural resources such as oil, gas, uranium and forests. These natural resources, their existence, their exploitation and their sale, have had significant impacts on Canadian society. This reciprocal relationship is important as people both affect the environment by their actions and are affected by the environment in many aspects of their lives from how they make their livelihood to the state of their health.

Often when discussing the relationship between people and their environment, the notion of "cognized" environment is used. This refers to the ways humans define and interpret the biophysical environment and is distinguishable from the "real environment," or the external biophysical environment independent of how people think about it. The cognized environment recognizes that people may live in natural environments but they live and act in worlds mediated and constructed by cultural symbols (Harper 2004: 38). Societal attitudes to genetically modified crops are illustrative. In some cultures these crops are acceptable and have been incorporated into societal food systems as a mainstay. Genetically modified corn can be found in hundreds of processed foods in North America. In other societies, such as certain countries in Europe, genetically modified crops are seen as hazardous, risky and unacceptable and the farmers refuse to grow them and the people refuse to eat them. For the people who embrace genetically modified crops, their cognized environment embraces human ingenuity; for the people who do not embrace genetically modified crops, their cognized environment embraces what is "natural." Because a cognized environment is cultural, in a broad sense, it is helpful to understand that it is a possible component of a larger societal ideology or world view.

Changing Worldview of the Environment

A world view is a view shared by people. It is the totality of a group of people's cultural beliefs and belief systems about the world and reality (Harper 2004: 39). The concept of world view usually requires a great degree of generalization so is somewhat obscure as there is always a certain amount of diversity of opinion. However, in recognizing this, a discussion of how world views have changed historically allows for both an example and an analysis of current world views.

When humans existed in small bands of hunter gatherers, travelling as nomads hunting small game and fishing, tracking migration and eating roots and berries, their world view was thought to be one of a state of being "embedded in nature" (Harper 2004: 40). Their cognized environment was that of a living natural world of things being governed by spiritual forces or a natural living wilderness. When people discovered how to cultivate crops and domesticate and breed animals they transitioned to settled agricultural communities and eventually took up intensive agriculture, growing crops year after year in the same place. A more complex set of social relationships and a world view of people controlling (or opposed to) nature emerged (Harper 2004: 44). The cognized environment was more that of a garden with people depending upon, but dominating for human purposes, the natural system. Finally, when industrialization began and humans were able to use machines to increase productive processes, the relationships between humans to produce goods, distribute wealth and use natural resources changed significantly. The world view of humans dominating nature for their purposes has been amplified to the point that instead of just tending the garden, humans are remaking it (Harper 2004: 48). The creation of human-made materials such as plastics and the genetic modification of plants and animals are examples of this remaking. These ideas are now reflected in the dominant Western world view outlined in Table 3.

These world views should not be viewed as reflecting all people's views or even the majority of people's views. It is merely an illustration of a particular outlook considered to dominate a society at a particular time; there may or may not be social consensus of this outlook. Significant diversity exists in world views. Many current environmental social movements, for example, actively challenge the idea of humans remaking nature. La Vía Campesina is a vocal global movement of farmers who reject this industrialized world view (Desmarais 2007) and will be discussed further below. Organic farmers also actively reject the industrialized worldview; important institutions such as the Canadian Wheat Board have stated that their customers reject genetically modified crops; therefore they do not accept the remaking of nature (Canadian Wheat Board 2004).

A description of an environmentalist world view is illustrated in *New Ecological Paradigm* (Catton and Dunlap 1978). Catton and Dunlap posit that through much of history, those studying society ignored the biophysical environment and embraced the human exemptionalism paradigm. One reason for this was to avoid the unethical and unsatisfactory conclusion that the environment and climate determined health, energy and mental processes such as intelligence, genius and power (Huntington 1915), which, combined

Table 3 Major Assumptions of Key Environmental World Views

	Dominant Western World View	Human Exemptionalism Paradigm	New Ecological Paradigm
Assumptions about the nature of human beings:	People are fundamentally different from all other creatures on Earth, over which they have dominion.	Humans have a cultural heritage in addition to (and distinct from) their genetic inheritance and thus are quite unlike all other animal species.	While humans have exceptional characteristics (such as culture and technology), they remain one among many species that are interdependently involved in the global ecosystem.
Assumptions about social causation	People are masters of their destiny; they can choose their goals and learn to do whatever is necessary to achieve them.	Social and cultural factors (including technology) are the major determinants of human affairs.	Human affairs are influenced not only by social and cultural factors, but also by intricate linkages of cause, effect and feedback in the web of nature; thus purposive human actions have many unintended consequences.
Assumptions about the context of human society:	The world is vast, and thus provides unlimited opportunities for humans.	Social and cultural environments are the crucial context for human affairs, and the biophysical environment is largely irrelevant	Humans live and are dependent on a finite biophysical environment that imposes potent physical and biological restraints on human affairs.
Assumptions about constraints on human society	The history of humanity is one of progress; for every problem there is a solution and thus progress need never cease.	Culture is cumulative; thus technological and social progress can continue indefinitely, making all social problems ultimately soluble.	Although the inventiveness of humans and the powers derived there from may seem for a while to extend carrying capacity limits, ecological laws cannot be repealed.

Source: Dunlap 2002: 333.

with theories of Darwinism, resulted in forms of "scientific racism" and ethnocentricism (Hannigan 1995: 2).

The human exemptionalism paradigm appears to have many parallels to the world view of the industrial age described above. Humans are exempt or independent from their environment as technology allowed them to manipulate and control that environment to suit their needs. As such we could understand modern industrial society without consideration of its biophysical base, and therefore environmental phenomena were irrelevant to the study of human society. In contrast, the new ecological paradigm outlook regards humans as one among many interrelated species and concerns itself with the consequences of human activity for the environment. Less faith is placed on technology and human progress solving environmental problems.

Catton and Dunlap argued that the emergence of environmentalism challenged the inherently anthropocentric (human-centred) world view of the human exemptionalism paradigm, and an alternative, the new ecological paradigm, emerged, emphasizing the ecological foundation of human societies. The new ecological paradigm recognizes that humans live within a finite biophysical environment and seeks to reduce human impact on the environment by consuming less.

These paradigms outline a proposed history of dominant world views — from an industrial world view and/or human exemptionalist orientation to one embracing a more ecological perspective. Adopting an ecological perspective such as that of the new ecological paradigm changes the conception of justice to one of ecological justice wherein plants and animals are included in our consideration. Consider the case of La Vía Campesina (described in the box below). Although this social movement does not go so far as to acknowledge the rights of plants and animals *per se*, it is an example of a new ecological paradigm acknowledging the interconnection of people with their biophysical environment and also the rights of these people to self-determination.

Envisioning the new ecological paradigm or change in the current institutional structure of Canadian society is challenging. Social movements, such as La Vía Campesina, and often non-profit organizations seek to effect this

La Vía Campesina

La Vía Campesina was formed in 1993 as the Uruguay Round of the General Agreement on Trade and Tariffs (GATT) negotiations were drawing to a close. Initially bringing together forty-five farm organizations, the movement now embraces 149 organizations of peasants, rural women, small and medium-scale farmers, indigenous agrarian communities and rural workers from sixty-nine countries in Asia, the Americas, Europe and Africa.

La Vía Campesina claims that the globalization of an industrial model of agriculture, together with increased liberalization of the food trade, is leading to the destruction of biodiversity and subsequent loss of cultural diversity, further degradation of the environment, increased disparity and greater impoverishment in the countryside everywhere. It argues that neo-liberal policies are sustained by human rights abuses and increased violence in the countryside — geared specifically to intimidate peasants — while economic liberalization facilitates the corporatization of agriculture, endangers national food security and threatens the livelihood and very survival of peasant families. As a result, peasant and farm families everywhere in the North and the South are "disappeared" and rural communities are decimated. There is ample evidence to support these claims.

La Vía Campesina formed in the North and South around common objectives: an explicit rejection of this neo-liberal model of rural development, an outright refusal to be excluded from agricultural policy development and a firm determination to work together to build viable alternatives based on social justice and human rights.

The concept of food sovereignty is at the heart of La Vía Campesina's alternative model of development, and the movement sees it as the only viable solution to current global food, energy and environmental crises (Desmarais 2007). Food sovereignty — first introduced by La Vía Campesina at events surrounding the World Food Summit held in Rome in 1996 — is a prerequisite to realizing the human right to food; it entails people's right to define their agricultural and food policy. Most importantly, food sovereignty includes farmers' and peasants' "right to produce our own food in our own territory" and "the right of consumers to be able to decide what they consume and how and by whom it is produced" (La Vía Campesina 2000: 125, 132).

La Vía Campesina's international efforts are leading to important shifts in the debate around food and agriculture. The concept of food sovereignty has spread widely and is now embraced by local, national and international movements around the world. The concept is also being explored by global institutions such as the Food and Agricultural Organization of the United Nations (FAO).[1] Recent reports to the United Nations Commission on Human Rights advocate food sovereignty to ensure people's human right to food and food security (Ziegler 2003 and 2004). The concept of peasant rights re-entered the international arena when, in the spring of 2004, under the leadership of the Federation of Indonesian Peasant Unions (FSPI), La Vía Campesina petitioned the United Nations Commission on Human Rights for the development of a charter or convention on peasants' rights. As well, some national governments are adopting the concept: Nepal is proposing to integrate food sovereignty into its national constitution while Bolivia, Venezuela and Mali are exploring how it can form the basis of national policies. (Annette Aurélie Desmarais, University of Regina)

Note

1. In 2003, following the World Food Summit: Five Years Later (2002), the FAO formally recognized the International Planning Committee for Food Sovereignty, a global network of non-governmental organizations and social movements, as its main civil society interlocutor for follow-up to the World Food Summit.

change by altering public opinion. Another example is Greenpeace, which was founded by a small team of Canadian activists in 1971 who set sail to "bear witness" to the U.S. underground nuclear testing in Amchitka, a tiny island off the west coast of Alaska in an earthquake-prone region. Their boat was intercepted prior to arrival but this sparked a flurry of public interest and nuclear testing ended in this area the same year. Now, 2.8 million people support Greenpeace and its vision to use non-violent, creative confrontation to expose global environmental problems and force solutions essential to a green and peaceful future (Greenpeace 2010).

After examining in more detail the environmental state of affairs in Canada, we will assess the degree to which our environment has been and is protected and, thus, the degree to which Canadian society has embraced the new ecological paradigm.

The State of the Canadian Environment

In Canada the environment has a place of importance, partly due to its countless rivers and lakes, forests and coasts and the vast areas of sparsely populated wilderness. With their diverse multicultural makeup, one of the notable convergences of Canadian people is our passion for the environment. Together with multiculturalism, the environment is cited as one of two unifying Canadian values (Angus 1997), and environmental protection has been found in one study to be an emerging part of Canada's fundamental moral beliefs (Nevitte 1996). However, the poor state of the Canadian environment doesn't reflect this revered status.

Various research studies have found that Canada has a poor record for wasting its water resources, polluting its air, allowing the use of harmful pesticides and failing to manage Canada's biodiversity (evidenced by Canada's loss of fish stocks). A University of Victoria study, which analyzed the Organization for Economic Cooperation and Development's (OECD) ranking of countries in relation to the environment, concluded that Canada was second last, better than only the United States in respect of environmental stewardship (Boyd 2001). The OECD gathers information on Canada in addition to twenty-eight other industrialized nations and tracks Canada's environmental performance based on several environmental indicators. Canada is among the three worst countries in the OECD on nine indicators: emissions of greenhouse gases, sulphur dioxide, carbon monoxide and volatile organic compounds; consumption of water and energy; energy efficiency; volume of timber logged; and generation of nuclear waste. Canada's economy is among the dirtiest and least efficient in the industrialized world in that it generates more pollution and uses much more energy to produce a given amount of economic output than other OECD countries (Boyd 2003: 6). In the 2008 OECD ranking, Canada remains in its dismal position on many of these indictors (OECD 2008).

Canadians have a toxic effect on their environment. A study completed in 2004 concluded that in the year 2002 Canadians released into their environment 4,244,614,425 kg of air contaminant pollutants which included 274 toxic chemicals with known neurotoxins including lead and mercury. Canadians also sent 54,202,6464 kg of pollutants off site to sewage treatment plants and energy recovery and treatment facilities while 1,226,553,508 kg of pollutants were sent to another facility for recycling (Pollution Watch 2004: 5). In 2002, 39,515,265 kg of chemicals were released into water. These chemicals are considered by the Canadian Environmental Protection Agency as toxic; this is 51 percent of all chemicals released in 2002 (Pollution Watch 2004: 15). In 2002 Canadian facilities released 3,723,470,288 kg of chemicals suspected to harm the respiratory system (enough pollutants to fill railroad cars from Ottawa to Fredericton). Over 96 percent of all releases were suspected respiratory toxins. The Ontario Medical Association estimates that 1900 premature deaths occur every year in Ontario, while 9800 hospital admissions, 13,000 emergency room visits and 47 million minor illness days occur every year because of air pollutants (OMA 2000: iii). Canada's performance isn't improving as these statistics showed a 49 percent increase from 1995 to 2002 (Pollution Watch 2004: 5).

When thinking about this Canadian environmental crisis it is important to situate oneself within the crisis and not just blame government for inadequate regulations or poor enforcement and business for damaging production processes. As an example, electricity, necessary for all forms of modern industrialization as well as survival during the Canadian winter, is often produced through a coal-fired generation plant. The coal burned in the power plant would have to be mined from the Earth, creating disruption to the surface including the mining of any other metals or substances in the coal strata which would then be discarded. Coal would be burned to produce the electricity and in this process harmful particulates, such as CO_2 and other contaminants, would be released into the atmosphere. The sulphuric and nitric acids released would form acid rain and damage the forests and freshwater sources in an area at a great range away from the power plant. Damage to the water affects fish, killing less hardy fish and leaving the handful of species still living in acidified water accumulating mercury in their body tissue. Birds and mammals (including humans) living off of these fish then develop mercury poisoning. In the United States, fish in roughly 50,000 lakes, streams and ponds contain levels of mercury that are harmful to humans (Glick 2000). In Saskatchewan, the culprit is SaskPower, listed by Pollution Probe in the pollution statistics cited (Pollution Watch 2004: 16). However, it is the residents and the industries within Saskatchewan consuming the electricity produced by SaskPower.

Self Test

Is the real environment the same as our cognized environment?
In the industrial world view do people control nature, or remake it?
Why is the Canadian environment in such a sorry state, given the value that Canadians place on it?

The tragic state of the Canadian environment calls out for redress, especially in light of the importance Canadians place on their environment. The analysis of world views allows consideration of different perspectives that exist in relation to the environment, which is an important first step in exploring environmental justice, but it seems to reduce the discussion to a debate between differing values of nature, progress and industrial development. Another dimension is essential: the dimension of environmental inequality. People experience the environment and, more particularly, environmental degradation unequally and in disproportionate ways. For example, mercury released into water from industrial processing is experienced disproportionately. Aboriginal people living downstream from industrial processing plants in Ontario have been, for the past forty years, and still are being poisoned by high levels of mercury in their water, resulting in Minamata Disease, the symptoms of which are a loss of motor control, speech, memory, vision and hearing and the development of cerebral palsy (Harada 2005). Only 38 percent of the cases were accepted by the Mercury Disability Board in Ontario (Harada 2005). Studies have confirmed the failure of the Canadian government to protect against mercury poisoning in specifically rural, sparsely populated locations (Gilbertson 2009), which are home to many Aboriginal people.

Adding this layer of information and concern about the environment allows us to move into a realm of substantive environmental justice, or ensuring that all people experience fair, healthy relationships with their environment. The following section will start with a narrow legal and procedural definition of environmental justice, akin to formal justice, the first perspective of justice of this book. Later sections of the chapter will expand to a definition allowing for substantive or distributive environmental justice, followed by an ethical environmental practice.

What is Environmental Justice?

Main Points

As you read, highlight the answers to these questions:
What is environmental justice?
Is any definition of environmental justice wrong? Inadequate?
If we are to solve the problem of our degrading environment, how must we define environmental justice?

Environmental justice can be defined narrowly or broadly, depending on context and political persuasion. Defined narrowly, environmental justice is reflected in our laws and regulations which have been adapted over the years to provide legal redress for environmental injustice. In this regard, remedial action is provided in law to correct an injustice imposed on a specific person or group of people (often a minority group).

For people who suffer environmental harm, environmental law and procedural environmental justice envisions three rights: the right to information, the right to a hearing and the right to compensation (Cutter 2006: 249). This definition is really about simple procedural or process equity, or addressing the direct causal mechanisms of inequity. This conception of environmental justice reflects a formal legalistic approach to environmental justice (termed "legal environmental justice") wherein the government is responsible for passing necessary legislation to protect the environment and people affected by pollution or environmental contamination can access remedies in court. Environmental justice in this definition is akin to formal or procedural justice as it entails remedies available to all who access the legal justice system.

Some of the earliest environmental justice movements in North America were led by groups of people combating a specific, hazardous, environmental practice in their locale, relying on the media and a legalistic approach. These groups and their actions encapsulate this definition of environmental justice. Often these groups were made up of people with low socio-economic status and represented a racial minority. In the U.S., the environmental justice movement's genesis is thought to have been in 1982 in Warren County, North Carolina. Here, the state selected a site to host a hazardous waste landfill containing 30,000 cubic yards of PCB contaminated soil. Residents, rural, poor and primarily Black, were joined in their protests by national civil rights groups, environmental groups, clergy and the Black Congressional Caucus. This group of Black Americans of lower socio-economic status was not protected from a hazardous environmental practice (the storage of PCBs) and its resultant adverse health effects. Studies surrounding this event confirmed environmental racism: the perspective, voices and wishes of these poor, marginalized Black people were not heard and the landfill was approved by the Environmental Protection Agency (Cutter 2006: 252).

This narrow definition of environmental justice focuses on negatively affected groups and grants them remedies in the event they are adversely affected. Although the principles of protection from environmental degradation and prevention of pollution are espoused, the actor in charge of attaining these principles is arguably the state through the passage and enforcement of laws and regulations. A high onus rests on individuals to bring court actions to enforce their rights.

This conception of environmental justice is still very important today.

Remedies available to people through the common law for damage to their health have been supplemented with statutory remedies in environmental protection legislation to make the commencement of these lawsuits easier. These measures have had only limited success. Bringing a court action for environmental damage always happens after the damage has been done. The process is slow, time consuming and very expensive. Scientific proof is required that the defendant (or person being sued) caused the environmental damage and that the damage harmed the person(s) bringing the lawsuit. Proof is required on a balance of probabilities. These factors impede access to justice and create significant barriers for the courts to play an effective role in protecting the environment.

This legalistic approach to environmental justice is also reflected in the emergence in government departments or ministries of environment in the 1970s and the plethora of environmental protection legislation passed by various governments since then. Legislation includes environmental protection acts, clean air acts, endangered species acts, hazardous substances acts and pest control acts, to name a few. Regardless of the number of pieces of legislation passed, the environment continues to be degraded at an increasing rate. Contributing to this is the fact that although voluminous, environmental legislation is an inconsistent patchwork of rules. This legislation allows excessive discretion of environmental protection officers to do nothing and is generally inadequately implemented and enforced (Boyd 2003: 228–38).

During the massive government cutbacks of the 1980s and 1990s, and the emerging neo-conservative political strategy of neo-liberalism, environment departments were the subject of some of the deepest cuts and, as a result, enforcement actions have reduced. For instance, the number of inspections carried out annually under the Canadian *Environmental Protection Act, 1999* fell during the 1990s from two thousand to seven hundred (Benidickson 1997: 123). Of known violations only a handful are prosecuted. Government reports acknowledge that hundreds of companies and municipalities regularly break environmental laws without being prosecuted (Christie 2000). Legal environmental justice is elusive. Courts are not generally accessible due to cost and time delay and governments are inactive due to budget constraints. Formal legal environmental justice should be expanded such that the following principles of environmental justice are guaranteed:

- protection from environmental degradation;
- prevention of adverse health impacts as a result of deteriorating environmental conditions before the harm occurs, not afterwards;
- appropriate assignment of culpability for environmental harm and shifting the burden of proof of contamination. Polluters should have to

prove they are not polluting (or causing harm) instead of people having to prove that polluters are; and

- compensation for the impacts of environmental degradation with targeted remedial action and resources.

Distributive or Substantive Environmental Justice

The distribution of societal benefits (such as wealth, income or good health) and societal ills (such as pollution, unsavoury work or risks of accidents) is another key aspect of environmental justice. Justice theorist John Rawls espoused that a fair distribution of societal goods could be arrived at by pretending one is behind a veil of ignorance and one's own life chances and circumstances are not yet determined — the principle of "maximin." Without the personal bias of being either wealthy (and wanting to maintain that wealth) or being poor (and wanting a better status), one would then philosophize about how a just society would allocate its goods.

In respect of the environment, focus is on the distribution of both the costs and benefits from development processes, or the utilization of Earth's natural resources for producing goods. The benefits or goods produced from the Earth's natural resources include everything from wood for building houses and furniture, cotton and silk for clothing, food to feed us and oil, coal and natural gas for manufacturing other goods, running our cars, making plastics. The costs of the production of these goods include such things as pollution, global warming, environmental degradation, the loss of natural habitat for plants and animals and the contamination of water.

A distributive environmental justice perspective would argue that environmental ills such as pollution have been inequitably distributed as predominantly marginalized people experience disadvantage through the contamination of their environments (Dobson 1998) but do not have the benefits of development through access to an equitable share of resource revenues. The disproportionate effects of environmental degradation on people and places are illustrated aptly in a global context. Southwest Nigeria is the home of the Ogoni people and the place Shell has been pumping oil since 1958. Although Shell has made considerable profit in the past decades, the Ogoni people live without adequate roads, electricity and water in a wasteland of environmental degradation from Shell's pumping activities (Watts 2001: 195). While the Ogoni people have lived in deplorable conditions, Shell has profited and North Americans have driven their vehicles with very reasonable gas prices.

Environmental inequity, such as that illustrated by the Nigerian example, originates from two major sources of dissimilarity: social and generational. Social equity refers to the role of social and economic factors (class, race, gender, ethnicity and political power) in environmental degradation and resource consumption. Classism, racism and sexism all contribute as well to social inequalities. Generational equity is the framework of norms to bring justice to future generations from current and past practices. For the Ogoni people, they currently live in poverty, their oil is depleting and future generations will not have oil as a resource with the potential to eliminate their poverty. Generational equity would ensure that this generation does not deplete resources and degrade the environment such that the next generation cannot attain the current standard of living. Adding these considerations to the conception of environmental justice broadens environmental justice to include aspects of distributive justice. This broad definition of environmental justice and its inclusion of social equity entails an expansion of distributive justice so that the next generation is encompassed.

While this approach to environmental justice illustrates the inequity of current global distribution and draws attention to the need for fairer distribution, it does not assist in the development of a mechanism for doing so. If, as John Rawls suggested, there was no personal bias, issues of the distribution of costs and benefits could be fairly decided. However, no such societal institution yet incorporates Rawls' principle of maximin. The next form of environmental justice responds to the questions surrounding the process and mechanisms of decision-making.

Lastly, this distributive approach to justice fails to question the current determinants, relationships and methods of producing goods. How many goods produced, the varieties of goods produced and the farming and industrial processes of producing goods in our society that damage the environment are all factors which are assumed as constant and predetermined. Adding social and generational equity and sustainability helps to address this shortfall. Social and generational equity concerns begin the process of inquiry into why our generation requires all of our goods and material wealth and whether this materialism is at the expense of future generations. This consideration of equity is addressed in the section on ethical practice.

Participatory Environmental Justice

A common theme emerging among struggles for social justice and ecological reform and among social movements for environmental justice is the call for the democratization of political institutions and the processes for decision-making (Schlosberg 2004; Adkin 2009; Fraser 2005). Many terms reflect this idea, including "deliberative democracy," "participatory justice," "green democracy" and "ecological citizenship." All envision local people and communities playing a greater role in making decisions affecting the environment, which include decisions about what economic developments occur close to them and how the environmental effects of these developments are mitigated (Anand 2004). Participatory environmental justice ensures everyone the ability to contribute to environmental decisions affecting community (both local and global), risks and benefits (Shrader-Frechette 2002: 24).

Many in this current struggle for participatory environmental justice recognize that environmental degradation and cost is experienced by those who are economically and racially marginalized or experience the "politics of difference" (Schlosberg 2004). This conception of justice recognizes and encourages the diversity of participants and experiences in affected communities. Facilitating a respectful dialogue that incorporates these diverse perspectives to achieve consensual decisions is a practice of participatory environmental justice. As such, a plurality of interests and knowledge are recognized, which allows different sorts of knowledges to be opened up and engenders different environmental decision-making processes. It is then possible to value the traditional ecological knowledge that Indigenous communities hold within a framework that appreciates plurality (McLean 2007).

Supporting participatory environmental justice is Vandana Shiva, a social activist from India who writes about the experience of injustice in India and the lack of participatory environmental justice. The people of India, she argues, have been marginalized historically through three waves: colonialism by Britain; the "development" discourse post-World War II; and, finally, in the last few decades, free trade. These global transformations have resulted in homogenization or a loss of diversity. This diversity ranges from genetic diversity (with the expansion of genetically engineered crops or monocultures) to diverse social systems and specifically methods of local self-organizing, self-governing and self-provisioning. Rejecting genetically engineered plant species and maintaining the diversity of local farmers and local seeds is important to sustaining life. Vandana Shiva argues that intolerance to diversity is the biggest threat to peace and what is needed are communities with the freedom to self-organize and self-govern, recognizing and respecting difference and diversity (Shiva 1997).

Recognizing diverse local knowledge, as espoused by Vandana Shiva, implicitly involves an aspect of participation in order that local knowledges can be expressed and understood. Schlosberg argues that meaningful participation through consultations, feedback mechanisms, public review processes and activist modes are important for environmental justice (Schlosberg 2004: 518). Allowing this participation, which examines fair processes for the distribution of goods and benefits and the "fairness" of distribution, remedies the key inadequacies of distributive environmental justice. Including different local knowledges in this approach to environmental justice goes further than formal notions of justice. Schlosberg argues for a "trivalent" conception of justice that involves a focus on the three interlocking and overlapping themes of justice: recognition (of different local knowledges), distribution and participation (Schlosberg 2004: 521).

Aspects of this theory of justice (particularly participation and recognition of diverse interests or groups) are recognized in current environmental laws. Every province and the federal government have environmental assessment legislation. Although somewhat diverse, this legislation requires that a development (such as the building of a power line or a hydro electric dam) cannot proceed without the environmental impacts considered and plans to reduce impact on the environment developed. Depending on the severity of the impact on the environment, a development may be screened by an environment department or it may require public consultation and advertisement. Although this appears to be important legislation involving the public's participation in development decisions affecting the environment, in practice, many developments are never assessed. This is partly due to the discretionary nature of the legislation. In one study of the developments that were assessed, over 99.9 percent of the screenings did not involve the public (CEAA 2000). For instance, in 1996 Ottawa refused to conduct an environmental assessment of the sale of nuclear reactors to China, even though Ottawa was providing a $1.5 billion loan guarantee (Howlett 2001). It is also extremely rare that any project does not proceed (Boyd 2003: 151). For example, in 1997–98, 5,042 out of 5,047 projects were approved (CEAA 1997; 1998; 1999). Development is favoured over a principle such as sustainability (or delaying the development of a resource to preserve that resource for future generations).

Another problem of current participatory processes is that although the principle of inclusion of all participants in the process is paramount, current processes often do not recognize that certain voices are effectively marginalized and these processes continue to perpetuate the power imbalances which exist in our society. A study of participatory governance and decision-making regarding forest governance in Alberta noted that the process served to isolate the community decision-making forum from larger public spheres, making it easier for corporate and government interests to dominate and preventing local conflicts from connecting to broader social movements (Adkin 2009: 302). However, in another Alberta example, participatory environmental processes did result in a curtailment of development because of negative impacts on water (Alberta Environment 2005: 6).

Aspects of all the environmental justice dimensions discussed so far (legal, procedural, distributive and participatory) are reflected in Canadian laws and practices However, the combination currently employed in Canada does not adequately address the current state of our environment as the environment continues to deteriorate. Legal and procedural environmental justice occurs in a haphazard manner; distributive justice only ignites discussion on fair distribution and doesn't solve the issue; and participatory initiatives emerging presume an ability to participate (which is not always the case) and may not address power imbalances. As a result, something more than participatory environmental justice is needed in defining and advancing environmental justice.

Self-Test

What is legal or procedural environmental justice and what are its shortcomings?
How can distributive environmental justice be achieved?
Does participatory justice envision aspects of distributive justice?

Including an Environmental Ethical Practice

In order to overcome participatory processes simply repeating the hegemonic power structures already present in society, the ethical principle of "leximin" must be added as a practice. According to this principle, the concerns of the "neediest" must be taken into account (Paavola, Adger and Huz 2006: 274). This is similar to Rawls' principle of "maximin" (or the idea that the prospects of the least well-off will be maximized if people make decisions behind a "veil of ignorance" wherein they set aside their own personal life situation). Within the context of environmental decision-making, the "neediest" or least favoured are those experiencing a disproportionate share of environmental burdens, pollution and climate change risks. These are generally marginalized and oppressed people and also perhaps future generations who will exist in an environment impacted by decisions made by the current generation.

Summary Points

Legal environmental justice is ensuring our laws protect our environment and allowing timely and effective redress for people harmed as a result of damage to the environment.
A sustainable future requires that all forms of environmental justice are reflected in substantial ways in our society. Achieving environmental justice requires consistent actions by us as individuals, by social movements and on all political fronts locally, nationally and internationally to achieve environmental equity.
Social environmental justice requires all forms of justice and the incorporation of the principle of "leximin."

The consideration of the environmental issue of climate change illustrates the need to adopt the ethical practice of "leximin." Human-induced climate change has become a very real and significant threat to the environment and sustainability. The cause of climate change is disproportionately attributable to the developed world, which includes Canada, the United States and Europe, but many of the most severe effects will be experienced by the developing world. Small island states are some of the countries which will be most significantly affected, with sea level rise reducing their land mass, storm surges, coastal erosion and the compromise of water resources and fisheries on which they depend for food (Mimura et al. 2007). Because these small islands are already poor they will not have access to the necessary resources to adapt to these changes. One study concludes that, if unchecked,

Climate Change

It is now indisputable that the Earth's climate is changing due to the activities of humans. Because of our reliance on energy for our production of food, materials and transportation, we have emitted greenhouse gases, including CO_2, into our environment in amounts vastly greater than would have been emitted through natural processes. This excess of CO_2 is contributing to global warming. Not only will there be increased average temperatures, but there will also be increased precipitation in some areas, increased intensity and frequency of droughts, floods and severe storms and as yet unforeseen abrupt changes and extreme climatic events (Sauchyn et al. 2007; IPCC 2007). Not only will changes in climate be different in different areas of the world, but the impacts on people in those areas will be different. Rising sea levels may cause people in small island states and coastal regions to lose their land. They will have to migrate to other areas, sometimes other countries, causing potential conflict. The number of people who will live in water-stressed countries is expected to get much larger. Already, food-insecure regions are expected to see radical declines in agricultural yields (IPCC 2007).

Negative impacts of climate change will not be experienced equally. Already, vulnerable people have limited capacity to adapt to climate change and, consequently, will suffer the most. These people in countries like Africa, Bangladesh and the Maldives are not the people who have contributed to the emissions of CO_2 but will suffer the worst consequences in our current global system. Stated another way, while Canada, the United States and the European Union have, historically and currently, the largest industrial development and made significant contributions to CO_2 emissions, they will nevertheless have access to resources (such as money or technology) to adapt to the changing climate.

Climate change will have impacts in Canada from reduced stream flow in rivers, increased temperature variability with warming trends and changing ecosystems (Lemmen et al. 2008). Communities vulnerable to this changing climate are those most likely to be exposed, to be more sensitive to changing climate and who possess limited capacity for adaptation (Adger and Kelly 1999). Within Canada, impacts will be felt inordinately by poor and marginalized people who are unable, because of a lack of resources, to adapt to the changing climate. As an example, farmers in the prairie provinces who are dependent on weather for successful crops will be impacted. Particularly impacted are farmers who lack resources such as access to money to make necessary adjustments in farming practices or purchase expensive irrigation equipment to maintain viability.

Contributors to climate change are individuals who in their everyday decisions are heating or air conditioning their homes, driving their cars and participating in other activities that burn fossil fuels which contribute to global warming. The people living in small, vulnerable island states and other countries that will be impacted the most severely by climate change are not the ones significantly contributing to the burning of fossil fuels. An ethical practice of environmental justice in relation to climate change entails individual people making individual changes to lessen carbon-emitting activities and, in this way, protect the most vulnerable people from predicted climate change harm. An ethical practice of environmental justice at the institutional level might entail the adoption of a regulatory climate regime which would effectively limit emissions and reduce anticipated climate change in the future.

climate change will become a major obstacle to continued poverty reduction for these vulnerable countries such as the Maldives or Kiribati (Stern 2007).

Social Environmental Justice

Environmental justice illustrates and encompasses many of the themes, disciplines and theoretical approaches to studying justice elaborated on in other chapters of this book. The very important area of legal environmental justice or procedural justice is akin to formal justice. Laws, regulations and civil court actions are important for people seeking redress (or compensation) and protection from environmental degradation. However, this is not the only practice of environmental justice. Just as studying justice is not just about studying law, studying environmental justice is more than studying environmental laws.

Understanding what is meant by the "environment" and what is included in our analysis of environmental justice is important. The environment includes more than pristine undeveloped environments; it includes our everyday, rural, urban, park, agriculture and work environments, to name a few. Thinking about the reciprocal relationship humans have with the environment is also important; humans both affect and are affected by their environments. Our health, well being and livelihoods are often determined by our environment.

Distributive or substantive environmental justice (the second theme of justice of this book) focuses on the distribution of benefits and costs or ills of the environment and its resources. On its own, this study has many shortcomings as it fails to challenge how distribution is determined and the fundamental materialism of the current structures of distribution. Participatory environmental justice offers the solution by allowing people to participate in and decide on the distribution of costs and benefits. However, the danger of this is that marginalized people continue to be marginalized; the hegemonic power structures of society continue to operate in the small, participatory environmental decision-making bodies. Adopting a philosophy of the principle of "leximin," which is envisioned in the third theme of this book, ethical practice, alleviates this. Including the interests of future generations expands the environmental justice problematic. Much more study, writing and thought on implementing this approach is required. If the pursuit of environmental justice is approached with an ethical practice, utilizing participatory processes and envisioning distributive justice, ultimately environmental laws will encompass a structure in which environmental justice can be achieved.

If the current climate change emission reduction debate were reconsidered incorporating principles of environmental justice (other than just legal environmental justice), a very different result would occur than has to date. Concerns expressed that climate change CO_2 emission reductions may result in reduced economic growth and military security would be replaced with a discussion of the global community, social inequality (regarding class, race and gender) and perhaps concern for future generations and the true sustainability of our future.

Summary Points

Environmental justice is built through participatory processes (at all levels of government) which include and respect a diverse membership and make special allowance not to simply repeat hegemonic power structures.

This is done by these participatory processes adopting an ethical practice of "leximin" or taking into account the position of the least favoured or neediest in such a manner that fair distribution of benefits and costs of developing the environment can be realized.

Ultimately this realization will be achieved through reformation and expression in laws at the state/provincial, nation state and, ultimately, international level.

Glossary

cognized environment – an environment defined and interpreted by humans.

distributive environmental justice – a fair distribution of societal goods or benefits (wealth, income or good health) and societal ills or burdens (pollution, unsavoury work or risks of accidents), incorporating notions of John Rawls.

ecological justice – a conception of justice that expands the relevant players beyond humans to include animals and plants and other aspects of the environment into the justice equation.

environmental equity – a fair adjustment of the distribution of resource development such that its benefits and costs are fairly dispersed globally.

environmental racism – the inequitable allocation of environmental burdens, including pollution, and the impacts of climate change on disadvantaged communities constituted by populations of racial and/or ethnic minorities.

hegemonic – a process or practice which continues or perpetuates hegemony.

hegemony – a process by which dominant groups maintain their power and domination over less powerful groups, usually with the less powerful group's consent and support.

legal environmental justice – predominantly procedural justice and includes laws, regulations and civil court actions which are important for people seeking either redress (including compensation) or protection from future environmental degradation. Legal environmental justice is that justice which can be attained through jurisprudential law by accessing legal tools (court actions and agreements) and institutions (international and domestic tribunals and courts).

leximin – the principle that a person holding the least favoured position, or the neediest person in society, should have their interests taken into account in decision-making.

maximin – a justice criterion proposed by Rawls (1971) that social systems should be designed in order to maximize the position of those who will be worst off in order to achieve justice.

participatory environmental justice – the resolution of environment issues through the meaningful participation of a representative group of people expressing a plurality of perspectives and knowledges in respect of the distribution of environmental costs and benefits.

sustainability – ensuring that decisions surrounding our environment preserve it and its resources for future generations.

world view – the totality of a group of people's cultural beliefs and belief systems about the world and reality.

Part III

Legal Justice

Margot A. Hurlbert

Although law should not be seen as synonymous with justice, it is a significant structure impacting justice overall. Law, in Canada and elsewhere, constitutes a significant part of formal or procedural justice. Legal rules provide the basis of individual rights, of our relationships with others in society and of the freedoms from state interference, including freedom of thought, expression and religion. Legal process provides the basis for procedural justice through the right to a fair trial, full notice of a case made against an individual and the guarantee of enough time to respond to legal actions and processes (such as being dismissed from employment). The aim of pursuing legal justice in this section is not to review or outline all of the elements of the law or formal legal justice. That is the aim of learning how to practise law, the predominant focus of law schools or the jurisprudence approach to law and justice. In this section the focus lies on law as a social institution that is created, maintained and experienced by people — and that often recreates the power imbalances in society.

Some basic elements of the structure and function of law are covered in this part: human rights (Chapter Eight), equality rights (Chapter Nine), and the sources and structure of law and the court system (Chapter Ten). However, the concern of those chapters is substantive justice and its achievements. Chapter Eight, for example, explores the notion that in order for human rights, such as the right to an education or an adequate standard of living, to be met, substantive justice or distributive justice must be achieved. Examining the international human rights architecture and its shortcomings helps explain the lack of progress in achieving these rights and substantive justice. Chapter Eight also introduces social movements and their important contribution to advancing human rights, a theme that will be picked up on and illustrated in Chapter Nine with respect to women's equality rights organizations.

It is in regards to equality rights that Canadian courts have grappled most with the concepts of formal and substantive justice. These terms, and their treatment in Canadian court cases asserting equality rights, are a fertile area for investigating the differences and interrelationship between formal and substantive justice. In some instances the achievement of equality requires the rejection of formal equality and advancement of substantive equality. While the focus of Chapter Eight is on women, equality issues regarding Aboriginal people, people with disabilities and sexual orientation are included.

Chapters Nine and Ten also discuss the dialectic between lived law and the jurisprudence approach to law and legal principles. Often people's lived experience is very different from the jurisprudential aims and aspirations of equality. Building on the proposition that law is not always the same as justice, the living law approach recognizes that law operates as a social system and is constituted, lived and applied by people. Viewing law as a social system expands discussions of law into an analysis of its place in society and its role in social justice.

Chapter Eleven introduces the structure, concepts and principles of the criminal justice system (CJS) in Canada. Starting with a discussion about what crime is and how it is defined, the main focus of this chapter is the formal, procedural and corrective aspirations of criminal justice, the first theme of justice. A systems perspective is used to address criminal justice, a somewhat different perspective from other authors in this section. From this perspective, a key issue is procedure and procedural justice; more specifically, the authors examine the extent to which the CJS implements its promise of procedural fairness from first contact with police through trials to incarceration. It is noted that the use of the CJS in Canada, and particularly in the U.S., has been rising rapidly. Despite falling crime rates, more and more people are being arrested, tried and incarcerated.

One issue, particularly relevant to Canadian justice, that gives rise to such an examination, is the relationship between Aboriginal people and Canada's CJS. The experiences of many Aboriginal people in contact with the law have not been positive. In fact, over at least the last two decades, many commissions and inquiries have been created to examine the CJS at the federal and provincial levels as a result of specific events involving Aboriginal people. These reports have relatively consistent conclusions and recommendations: the "failure of the justice system" is a result of the fundamentally different world views of Aboriginal and non-Aboriginal people with respect to the substantive content of justice and the process of achieving justice (Royal Commission on Aboriginal People 1995; Hamilton 1991; Cawsey 1991; Linn 1992, Ontario Commission on Systemic Racism and the Criminal Justice System 1995). There are, the authors of Chapter Eleven note, problems with the procedures in the CJS but, they conclude, it does fulfill its role of crime control.

Conclusions reached throughout Part Three illustrate the inability of our current legal system to achieve substantive justice. The human right to an adequate standard of living isn't met in Canada or internationally;

barriers exist in law to achieve substantive equality; and the CJS increasingly incarcerates Aboriginal people. A new paradigm of justice is required. This paradigm isn't a new organization, a new government department or a new law. In pursuing justice a new paradigm entails a new way of thinking about justice and the achievement of justice. This paradigm gives weight to all three of the themes of justice: formal justice, substantive justice and ethical practice.

8

Human Rights

Margot A. Hurlbert

At the end of this chapter, you will be able to:

- Describe the historical context and generations of human rights
- Outline challenges of international law-making
- Understand the fundamentals of the right to development and the right to peace and the process for achieving these rights
- Understand the sources of Canadian human rights law and its relationship to international human rights law

Often we associate human rights with criminal justice rights such as the right to a lawyer, the right to remain silent and the freedom from unreasonable search and seizure. These are important rights but only a small representation of the variety and depth of human rights that exist. Human rights have importance both in criminal law with respect to the right of an accused person to counsel, trial without unreasonable delay and to be free from unreasonable search and seizure, but also in the area of social justice with rights to security of the person and international rights to clean water, food and housing, as well as rights of development and peace.

It is important to understand human rights both nationally and internationally for the effective advocacy of people within the justice system. For instance, Maher Arar, a Canadian citizen, was apprehended in the United States (with the assistance of Canadian security officials) when passing through the airport in New York while travelling home from a holiday in Tunis with his family. He was detained two weeks in solitary confinement without accessing a lawyer or being charged on suspicions of being a member of Al Qaeda. The United States then deported him to Syria where he was tortured. He has been found by authorities in Syria, and Canada to be innocent. For advocates lobbying on his behalf, knowing the Canadian justice system, Mr. Arar's human rights as a Canadian and his international right not to be tortured, were instrumental in securing his eventual release. Knowledge of rights is essential for individuals to demand recognition of their rights and promote respect for rights. The importance of human rights post-9/11 can't be over-emphasized. The increase in the depth and breadth of security and anti-terrorism laws since 2001 requires constant vigilance to prevent human rights violations.

Often social groups and social movements advance a particular human right and are able to make strides for the advancement of justice in society through this process. Examples of this can be seen locally and historically with the suffragists' struggle at the beginning of the twentieth century for women's right to vote, and the Québécois' struggle for sovereign status. Examining human rights both internationally and nationally is enlightening in understanding the strengths and limitations of Canadian human rights law and practice. While Canada has agreed to many fundamental principles of human rights, law-making bodies (courts and legislatures) have been reticent in recognizing these rights in Canadian law.

Rights in Historical Context

Main Points

As you read, highlight the answers to these questions:
Why is the period after World War II significant in respect of the study of rights?
Why is the Magna Carta significant to Canadian rights?
Do the same rights exist simultaneously in different legal instruments?

The expression "human rights" has only been a part of everyday language since World War II and the founding of the United Nations in 1945. This is not to say that the concept of rights was not in existence prior to 1945. On the contrary, in Western societies the topic of rights had been the focus for such philosophers as Socrates, Plato, the Stoics and Aristotle in centuries past. Prior to 1945, discussion had centred on natural rights and the rights of people. It was after 1945 that these rights came to be called "human rights."

The idea of human rights can be traced back to documents such as the *Magna Carta*, of 1215, which bound the king of England to the law. In this way the king could not make any order or directive he wished but only those within the confines of the law. One of the most important features of the *Magna Carta* was the limiting of the king's ability to imprison at a whim. A right of "habeas corpus" (which is Latin, meaning "you shall have the body") was introduced in this document, which allowed a remedy for people who were unlawfully imprisoned by the king to be freed upon application to the court. This writ (a legal document akin to a petition or claim) was first used in 1305 in England (Blackstone 1768) and most famously in 1771 in order to free a Black slave, Somersett (Hill 2004). This right is reflected in the *Canadian Charter of Rights and Freedoms*, which states that "Everyone has the right on arrest or detention (c) to have the validity of the detention determined by way of *habeas corpus* and to be released if the detention is not lawful" (section 8c). Other important precursors to current human rights are the English *Bill of Rights* (1689) and the French *Declaration on the Rights of Man and Citizen* (1789).

Early European philosophers also espoused the importance of liberty rights and influenced some of the first recognized rights. John Locke (1632–1704), for example, focused on the development of the idea of the "self" and planted the seeds of liberalism (or individualism) and its importance. The liberty rights generated by this philosophy were of a civil and political nature and included the right of individuals to choice, freedom from interference by the state, freedom from unreasonable detention, freedom of expression and freedom from torture. The influence of this generation of rights is illustrated in the American *Declaration of Independence* (1776), which states:

> We hold these truths to be self-evident, that all men (*sic*) are created equal, that they are endowed by their Creator with certain unalienable Rights, that among these are Life, Liberty and the pursuit of Happiness. (Kinsella 1982: 16)

These rights exist in Canada as well and are independent of particular people, places and times and are duplicated in different spheres. They simultaneously exist and are protected in the common law, in the Canadian Constitution and in international law. These liberty rights pre-existed the *Canadian Charter of Rights and Freedoms* in the common law Canadians inherited from the British legal system. Because the right of *habeas corpus* existed in British common law, it also existed in Canada because of our country's colonial status and later adoption of all British common law upon achievement of nationhood. These rights were also included in the *Universal Declaration of Human Rights* (UDHR) of the United Nations in 1948 as well as the precursor document, the United Nations Charter of 1945. The UDHR and the United Nations Charter are only resolutions of the General Assembly of the United Nations; they are not formally ratified, legally binding treaties. These documents can't necessarily be relied on as binding authority by courts of law but can only provide guidance. Finally, some of these rights were also enshrined in the *Canadian Charter of Rights and Freedoms* in 1982.

The UDHR was the result of world leaders collaborating after World War II. The world community was reeling from the atrocities committed during that war and consequently successfully developed and agreed upon a framework highlighting human rights and individual dignity. This framework was subsequently ratified and endorsed by countries individually, including Canada. Article 1 of the UDHR states:

> All human beings are born free and equal in dignity and rights. They are endowed with reason and conscience and should act towards one another in a spirit of brotherhood (*sic*).

Summary Points

The rights of people have been an evolving subject of law and study for centuries.
After World War II the term "human rights" emerged and the world community agreed to the UDHR.
Canada inherited Britain's legal system and tradition, including common law rights.
Numerous instruments contain rights, including the *Magna Carta* (1215), the UDHR (1948) and the *Canadian Charter of Rights and Freedoms* (1982).

A Brief Overview of the United Nations

Main Points

As you read, highlight the answers to these questions:
How does a nation state influence a person's rights?
Which human rights regime currently exists?
What are the generations of rights?
Are the distinctions drawn from the generation of rights accurate?

The United Nations replaced a defunct League of Nations, which had been established in 1919 by the allied victors of World War I: the United Kingdom, the United States, France, Italy and Japan. Fifty-one nation states (countries) came together initially to form the U.N. and established a charter outlining its purpose. Once the U.N. Charter was adopted in 1948, the U.N. Commission began drafting treaties that would implement, in substantive and enforceable terms, the more general commitments of the UDHR.

It was decided that two separate covenants should be drawn up, each devoted to a different aspect of human rights. The International Covenant on Civil and Political Rights enumerates the liberty-oriented rights that a state must not interfere with, such as freedom of expression, conscience and association. The International Covenant on Economic, Social and Cultural Rights addresses aspects of the UDHR that pertain to people's basic rights such as food, shelter and health care. There are also many more acts and conventions such as the *Convention on the Prevention and Punishment of the Crime of Genocide* 1948, the *Convention on the Political Rights of Women* 1953 and the *Convention on the Rights of the Child* 1989.

There are five main organs of the U.N., each of which, with one exception, is based at the U.N. headquarters in New York City:

The General Assembly – (192 members) this body makes resolutions on the basis of two-third majority votes. Resolutions are not enforceable by international law.

The Security Council – responsible for peacekeeping, interventions and sanctions against warring or rogue states. For instance, peacekeeping missions were lead in the Congo from 1960–1973, Rwanda from 1993–1996, and Bosnia in 1995. There are five veto power permanent members. (This is probably intended to ensure that the interests of the Western industrialized nations are not jeopardized by the General Assembly).

The Economic and Social Council – made up of fifty-four members elected for three-year periods to oversee specialist agencies dealing with economic, social and humanitarian issues. One such agency is the Commission on Human Rights.

The International Court of Justice – this court is based in The Hague and seeks to resolve conflicts between states by the law instead of by force.

The Secretariat – this is the administrative centre of the U.N. headed by the secretary-general with a staff of around 8,900 from 160 countries (O'Byrne 2003: 82).

The Generations of Rights

The first generation of rights is often described as "liberty" rights (or civil and political rights): freedom from interference by the state as well as the right to equality. Although the American Declaration of Independence, quoted above, states that people have the right of equality, this had been interpreted in a very different fashion prior to 1948. For many years it did not include a right to equality for women (until in the early twentieth century when they obtained the right to vote) and in 1948 laws segregating Black people still existed in many countries. The 1948 UDHR made it clear that equality rights applied to women and racial and ethnic minorities as well as others. In 1948 the UDHR also contained the second generation of rights and a precursor of the third generation of rights.

The first generation of rights, or civil and political rights, is viewed as directly endowed upon individuals and involve the state refraining from interfering with these rights. Sometimes these are described as cost-free or "negative" rights because of this general inaction. Conversely, the second generation of rights is described as positive rights as they require positive action on the part of the state in the form of national policies and programs and the expenditure of resources. These rights are progressive in nature in that each state agrees to undertake steps, based on their available resources, in order to move to realizing the full rights to education, an adequate standard of living and so on.

However, these distinctions, while illustrative, are not entirely accurate. For instance, in order to realize the right of free speech, a first generation right, a state may have to provide and promote the "public space" and channels of communication where the right can be recognized free from interference from others. In respect of the second generation right of education, a state may have to refrain from interfering in the parents' right to inculcate values in their child. The two sets of rights are interrelated, interdependent and indivisible. Without basic social and economic standards, the rights to free speech and assembly, or civil and political first generation rights, are meaningless.

The recognition of this interconnection has resulted in two conclusions. First, rights are not hierarchical, but are indivisible and interdependent, and the protection and promotion of one set of rights and fundamental freedoms cannot exempt the state from doing the same for other rights (resolution 32/130 of the General Assembly, December 16, 1977). Secondly, instead of focusing on individual rights in conflict with one another, what is often required is a focus on principles and norms setting the foundation for human rights. For instance, in 1987 the General Assembly in its Resolution on the indivisibility and interdependence of economic, social, cultural, civil and political rights stated:

> Recalling that in the Preambles to the International Covenants on Human Rights, it is recognized that the ideal of free human beings enjoying freedom from fear and want can only be achieved if conditions are created whereby persons may enjoy their economic, social and cultural rights, as well as their civil and political rights. (Stener and Alston 2000: 268)

Over time, the traditional formulation of the first and second generation of rights was criticized as incapable of addressing key global issues of poverty, famine and health. This led to the identification of a third generation of rights and the realization that rights rely on the action of all actors, public and private alike, not just the state. Examples of this generation are the rights to a clean environment, the rights of communities, the right of self-determination and the right to development.

The third generation of rights are described as those of "solidarity." These are best understood in relation to the changing place of the nation state in the last half of the twentieth century. They were foreshadowed by Article 28 of the 1948 UDHR, which proclaimed that everyone is entitled to a social and international order in which the rights set out in the UDHR are fully realized. Three relate to the emergence of Third World nationalism and demand for a global redistribution of wealth, including the right to participate in and benefit from the common heritage of humankind, the right to political, economic, social and cultural self-determination and the right to economic and social development. The other three third generation rights include the rights to peace, a healthy and balanced environment and to humanitarian disaster relief. These rights suggest the ineffectiveness of the nation state in providing these services.

In order to attain the objectives of the second and third generation of rights the U.N. has a system of setting objectives and monitoring compliance.

The limitation of "progressive realization" is applied to the *International Covenant on Economic, Social and Cultural Rights*. This means that it is recognized that some governments can't immediately meet and satiate their peoples' rights to such things as food, shelter and health care. Consequently, it is recognized that compliance will be recognized if the nation is progressively realizing these rights. Nevertheless, governments are required to immediately:

- take steps that are deliberate, concrete and targeted as clearly as possible towards the obligations described in the Covenant; and
- guarantee that rights will be exercised without discrimination.

The fourth generation of rights are those on the cutting edge of science, such as the right to the beginning and end of life (bioethics) or the right to die. They may include the granting of rights to non-humans — animals, flora and fauna. The emergence of rights to non-humans can be seen in legislation surrounding endangered species. These rights are still under development and not all scholars recognize this fourth generation (Wenz 1988).

The Decline of the Nation State

The UDHR also introduced an important new principle in the notion that the relations between nation states and their own citizens should be a matter of international concern and not the exclusive purview of the sovereign states. This was a small step in the direction of weakening the sovereignty of the nation state. While nation states are instrumental in determining the quality of rights experienced by their citizens, the UDHR meant they would not be the sole determinant. This subtle shift in power is meant to protect people from the potential for the state to abuse its power.

Human rights regimes (or structures for governing human rights na-

Table 4 The Generations of Rights

First Generation	**Second Generation**	**Third Generation**	**Fourth Generation**
Liberty rights: civil and political rights	Social, economic and cultural rights	Solidarity rights	New frontier
Negative rights	Positive rights	Negative and positive rights	Increasing the entities with rights (plants, animals, the unborn)
Examples: The freedom of conscience (religion), association and expression	Examples: The right to education, health care and a standard of living	Examples: The right to economic and social development and peace	Examples: The rights of animals not to be inhumanely experimented on and the rights of endangered species

tionally and internationally) can be seen as a continuum of three types of international society:

> *Statist* – "The traditional statist model sees human rights as principally a matter of sovereign national jurisdiction… statists… insist that human rights remain principally a matter of sovereign national jurisdiction and a largely peripheral concern of international (inter-state) relations."
> *Cosmopolitan* – "A cosmopolitan model starts with individuals, who are seen more as members of a single global political community (cosmopolis) than as citizens of states… Cosmopolitans often see international organizations and certain transnational NGOs as representatives of an inchoate global community of mankind [sic]."
> *Internationalist* – "Internationalists accept the centrality of states and sovereignty in international relations, but stress international social practices (such as international law and the rules and procedures of diplomacy) that regulate inter-state relations. This body of formal and informal restrictions on the original sovereignty of states creates an international social order, an anarchical society of states." (Bull quoted in Donnelly 1994: 202–03)

It is not possible to conclude that the current world order of international human rights is reflected in any one of these three models. The statist and the cosmopolitan models represent two extremes on a continuum while the internationalist model reflects aspects of both. Donnelly asserts that there currently exists a relatively weak internationalist model. The last half century of human rights violations illustrate that only modest and international societal constraints on state sovereignty exist (203). This is illustrated by the genocides that have occurred in Rwanda (1994, 800,000 deaths), Cambodia (1975–1979, 2 million deaths) and Bosnia-Herzegovina (1992–1995, 200,000 deaths). Despite these discouraging incidents, many people and organizations such as Amnesty International and Oxfam continue to advance the agenda of human rights internationally, aiming for a stronger internationalist, or perhaps cosmopolitan, model of human rights. International societal constraints are created through political pressure (a country or its leader voluntarily meeting international standards) or through international law.

Treaties and International Customary Law

Main Points

As you read, highlight the answers to these questions:

What are the elements necessary for a practice to form the basis of a customary international law?

What is the difference between a treaty and a customary international law?

Treaties and custom are the two principal sources of international law (Currie 2001: 83). Treaties or international agreements have the advantage of offering clarity and speed with which international law may be created or advanced. However, their disadvantage is that they only bind parties who sign the treaty and consent to be bound. The U.N., with its enormous institutional apparatus, including the International Court of Justice, is the product of the widely ratified multilateral treaty, *Charter of the United Nations*. Other examples of treaties include the *Convention on the Rights of the Child*, the *Convention against Torture* and the *General Agreement on Tariffs and Trade*.

Customary international law is rooted in what states actually believe is legally required (rather than what they have expressly agreed to). It is inductive or based on actual practice, so it is not very precise or finely tuned. This means it is necessary to examine how states have operated in different circumstances in the past in order to draw conclusions about what the established customary practice is; it is derived from patterns of state conduct. By nature it is conservative (as it trails behind actual state behaviour and is not at the forefront of handling new claims such as environmental climate change).

In order for a rule of customary international law to exist, two elements must be present. The first element is the actual behaviour of states, or the "objective" or "material" element of customary international law. The actual behaviour must be both general and uniform.

In order to be "general," it must be shown that a sufficient number of states adhere to the given practice which is being asserted as "customary." This is a clear derogation from the previous source of international law requiring "consent" of a participating nation and a fruitful practice area for international lawyers as it creates much debate about whether something is sufficiently "general." Examples of such practice include crimes against humanity, war crime, piracy, genocide and slavery. Many of these general practices were codified in the *Hague Conventions* of 1889 and 1907.

In order to be "uniform" the actual practice among practising states must have a degree of consistency or homogeneity. There is no established threshold of what qualifies as "general" or "uniform." Thus, it is time-consuming to prepare and present arguments to persuade international judges when such a threshold has been met. However, evidence of practice is amassed through national legislation, opinions of national legal advisors, diplomatic correspondence and the practice of international organizations (United Nations 1957). If, for example, the Canadian government continued to refuse to endorse international Indigenous rights, a good argument could have been formulated that Canada's recognition of Aboriginal rights in its Constitution was evidence of a Canadian custom of recognizing Indigenous rights.

The second element is the actual belief by the state that the practice is legally obligatory in character. This is the "subjective" or "psychological" element of customary international law (Currie 2001: 163). Establishing this legal test can be an arduous process. Examples of issues where customary international law has been argued include trying to resolve maritime boundaries in respect of continental shelves (*North Sea Continental Shelf Cases*) and laws of war (before they were codified into treaty).

Summary Points

Treaties offer clarity and speed in making international law.
Customary international law has two elements: objective behaviour and subjective belief that the behaviour is legally obligatory.

Making International Law Binding

What is required for international agreements or treaties to become binding on states? The reason a true cosmopolitan model of human rights does not yet exist is partly because of the onerous requirements that must be fulfilled for international agreements to become binding on nation states. It is not possible for a body such as the United Nations to agree to a right in principle and for it to be automatically binding on all nation states. A delicate balance exists in international human rights law and justice between principles of state sovereignty and respect for human rights. This delicate balance has evolved from 1945 and the UDHR. Currently, governments' human rights abuses in some parts of the world are areas of attention where issues of state sovereignty and international human rights interact. Non-governmental organizations such as Human Rights Watch and activists such as Ian Smilie are documenting the abuses of the Zimbabwe government, which is responsible for killing small-scale diamond miners who are mining illegally (with the added fear their activities fuel the civil war) while at the same time running mining operations for funding that rely on forced child labour (Smilie 2009). How to solve this situation is by no means clear.

The UDHR is only a declaration and thus was not intended to bind states at the time it was proclaimed. In order to bind states legally, the states must enter into a treaty in accordance with their national law, sign the treaty and pass state laws adopting and implementing the subject matter of the treaty. An example of the complexity of this process can be seen by Canada's historical commitment by Prime Minster Chrétien to enter into the Kyoto Protocol on global warming and climate change in 2002. This commitment was voted on in the House of Commons and a motion was passed that Canada would implement its commitment. However, no laws doing so were ever passed and an election changed the Canadian government in 2006. Although Canada committed to the Kyoto Protocol, a decade later Canada is still struggling with its international climate change commitments.

An example of where international law was applied in direct contradiction to state law occurred with the trial of war criminals after World War II. During

World War II Germany had many laws validating its poor treatment of Jewish people. At the time the UDHR did not yet exist. However, Nazi war criminals were tried in international criminal courts. This is partly because natural law principles against genocide were relied on by the court, overriding Hitler's national laws. Laws against genocide were, in principle, seen as customary international law. Again, this is an illustration of the complexity of this area of law and justice that eludes description in tight legalistic rules and procedures.

Some aspects of the UDHR are now part of customary international law and binding even though they are only reflected in a declaration (Hannum 1995–1996). For instance the right to food, clothing and housing contained in Article 25 has not been recognized in Canada as illustrated in the Gosselin case discussed below. As such, the UDHR has evolved into something more binding than originally intended: a highly visible and widely recognized expression of moral and political standards and a measure against which compliance with and respect for international human rights principles can be judged (Henkin 1990: 19).

Some international human rights instruments become so entrenched in international norms that they become customary international law without meeting all treaty requirements.

Summary Points

To make a treaty binding, a state must do the following:

- sign the treaty;
- pass state laws adopting the treaty;
- pass state laws implementing the treaty; and
- enter into the treaty in accordance with their national law.

The Right to Development

Often development, especially in the Western world, is thought of in terms of economic development, the creation of jobs, industry and wealth. However, development can be defined quite differently, especially in the non-Western world. For example, the right to development includes the rights to both economic and social development. In the last two decades of the twentieth century, development thinking shifted from a growth-oriented model based on economics and the generation of profit to a human development model defined as a process of enhancing human capabilities that acknowledge intrinsic and mutually reinforcing links between development and human rights (Andreassen and Marks 2006: vi).

The right to development has evolved and emerged into the concept of the rights-based approach to development, which in the words of the Office of the High Commissioner for Human Rights is:

> the operational expression of the inextricable link between development and human rights. A rights-based approach is a conceptual framework

> for the process of human development that is normatively based on international human rights standards and operationally directed to promoting and protecting human rights. The rights-based approach integrates the norms, standards and principles of the international human rights system into the plans, policies and processes of development. (Robinson 2001: para. 19)

The rights-based approach to development is based on a respect for human rights and contains aspects of social justice, equity, empowerment, accountability and participation. Often the international legal regime for human rights is criticized as being largely "Western" in terms of values and emphasis and not recognizing non-Western values or conceptions of human rights as they exist in Africa or Islam (Etzioni 1996: 235). The right to development is much more than the Western conception of the spread of a capitalist model of business. Sustainable human development as defined by the United Nations Development Programme is:

> Expanding the choices for all people in society. This means that men and women — particularly the poor and vulnerable — are at the centre of the development process. It also means "protection of the life opportunities of future generations... and... the natural systems on which all life depends." (UNDP 1997: n.p.)

In order to circumvent this aspect of the U.N. notion of the right to development, nations supporting the spread of capitalism have created and dominated other international governance organizations including the International Monetary Fund, World Trade Organization and World Bank. These organizations perpetuate and advance capitalist notions of development.

The central purpose of development (utilizing the United Nations Development Programme's definition of development) is the creation of an enabling environment in which all can enjoy long, healthy and creative lives. Like other human rights, in order to be effective, the right to development requires a degree of justiciability (or enforcement through court litigation) and feasibility to be achieved. Feasibility envisions such thing as having resources, people and effective governments, all of which may differ from nation to nation. Thus, effectiveness depends on an appropriate mix of rights and obligations in legislation and actions to promote the realization of the right to development.

Adopting the right into a country's law is not enough. Positive political action for achievement is required. Considerable work in explaining this positive political action has occurred in defining aspects of sustainable human development and best practice of good governance. The U.N. has gone on to outline five aspects of sustainable human development as (UNDP 1996):

> *Empowerment* – the expansion of men's and women's capabilities and choices increases their ability to exercise those choices free of hunger, want and deprivation. It also increases their opportunity to participate in, or endorse, decision-making affecting their lives.
> *Cooperation* – with a sense of belonging important for personal fulfillment, well being and a sense of purpose and meaning, human development is concerned with the ways in which people work together and interact.
> *Equity* – the expansion of capabilities and opportunities means more than income — it also means equity, such as an educational system to which everybody should have access.
> *Sustainability* – the needs of this generation must be met without compromising the right of future generations to be free of poverty and deprivation and to exercise their basic capabilities.
> *Security* – particularly the security of livelihood. People need to be freed from threats, such as disease or repression, and from sudden harmful disruption in their lives.

The United Nations Development Programme goes even further to list characteristics of "good governance" to achieve sustainable human development as participation (of all on a broad basis), the rule of law (which is fair and enforced impartially), transparency (built on the free flow of information), responsiveness (of institutions to stakeholders), consensus orientation (where possible) and equity (to provide opportunities for all to improve or maintain their well being) (UNDP 1996). It is evident that these characteristics of good governance, necessary in achieving the right of social and economic development in a nation state, cannot exist in a nation engaged in civil war. Considerable linkages exist in the principles for attaining sustainable development and those principles for attaining peace.

Many academic writers have gone further to define the essential obligation to the right to development as one of not causing damage or harm. In this regard, governments should not "initiate or support policies or institutional arrangements, whether domestic or international, which systematically damage any country's economic development, or encourage a markedly unequal form of that development" (Beetham 2006: 95). In contradiction to this, many Western nations, such as Canada and the United States, support the International Monetary Fund and World Trade Organization, whose structural adjustment policies have exactly these negative effects of encouraging unequal development through requiring government program reductions (Klein 2008).

Another expression of the essential obligation to the right to development is that the international community should act in ways that alter unjust institutional structures (Salomon 2006: 117). These positive obligations are aimed at not furthering or perpetuating the growing inequality or income gap between the rich and the poor. As outlined previously, the third generation of rights involves acknowledging that the achievement of these rights involves more than just actions by the state. Non-state actors, individuals, non-profit organizations and corporations must all be involved. This is a marked evolution from what many Western people believed several decades ago, that development of the Third World equated with expansion of the First World's economic business in a growth-orientated model of development.

Summary Points

Development is not simply the Western view of economic development.
The United Nations Development Programme defines development as expanding the choices for all people in society.
To achieve sustainable human development four aspects are required: empowerment, cooperation, sustainability and security.

The Right to Peace

The international commitment to peace can be illustrated in the Kellogg-Briand Pact of 1928 where the participating nations agreed that "the settlement of solution of all disputes or conflicts of whatever nature or of whatever origin they may be, which may arise among them, shall never be sought except by pacific means." (Donnelly 2003: 7–13) This commitment was again confirmed in Chapter VI of the U.N. Charter in 1948, wherein the member states committed to the peaceful settlement of disputes and the Security Council was given a clear role in promoting this approach to international conflict resolution.

These international obligations show a commitment to peace, or the absence of war. This is often termed a "negative" peace or the absence of violence. However, peace can also be characterized in positive terms as "the capacity to handle conflict creatively and non-violently" (Galtung 1998). This capacity refers to the existence of equitable, participatory and stable social institutions that are able to resolve conflict in a constructive, non-violent manner. Linkages between this capacity for peace and the practices of restorative justice found in the concluding chapter are significant and will be revisited there. Lasting peace is more complex than simply the absence of violence (or negative peace). It involves fostering the ability of people in local and global communities to build peace, often termed, "peace-building." This is the establishment of equitable, participatory and stable political institutions as well as economic, social and cultural conditions that guarantee diversity and a minimal standard of well being for the protection of the vulnerable. This last principle reflects the ethical practice of justice, or protecting the interests of the vulnerable.

The conditions required in a nation state for positive peace have similarities to those required for development. Empowerment, cooperation, equity and security were requirements for development; equity and cooperation are key components of a society engaged in peace-building. The overlapping of these conditions for both peace and development illustrate that the third generation of rights is more than just an itemized list of rights held by global citizens for which realization would depend on the Western model of remedies available in a court of justice. These third generation rights, or rights of solidarity, illustrate the importance of viewing international rights as positive obligations or responsibilities which have a direct bearing on ensuring that negative rights (such as the right to peace, the right to freedom of expression, conscience and association) can be exercised by the individual.

Attaining the third generation of rights entails rethinking the current form of internationalist order and improving it or moving to a cosmopolitan order. Engaging in a process of global dialogue to advance this exercise would be required. Attaining truly universal peace reflecting the third generation of human rights consists of bridging the chaotic state system to a world order that incorporates effective global governance reflecting human rights. It also consists of adopting principles of cooperation, not confrontation (or dividing material stakes of conflicts based on the power of one's military).

Summary Points

The right to peace is more than the right to be free from violence.

Peace-building requires equitable, participatory, stable political institutions as well as conditions guaranteeing diversity and a minimal standard of well being for protection of the vulnerable.

The U.N. employs a system of progressive realization for monitoring a nation's progress at achieving positive rights.

Social Movements

Main Points

As you read, highlight the answers to these questions:

What is the importance of social movements in relation to global human rights? Does Canada have the same rights in its domestic law as contained in the UDHR?

What are the implications of Canada not having recognized certain rights such as the right to water or food?

An important step in migrating away from a statist model of international human rights has been not only the development of the U.N. and its structure but also the emergence and increasing number of social movements or issue-based organizations. Examples of these include the World Wildlife Fund, Greenpeace and Amnesty International. This transformation over the

Table 5 Conditions Needed to Attain the Right to Peace, Sustainable Human Development and Factors of Good Governance for Achieving Sustainable Human Development

Goal	Peace	Sustainable human development	Good governance to achieve sustainable human development
Condition	Empowerment	Empowerment	Participation
	Cooperation	Cooperation	Consensus orientation and responsiveness
	Equity	Equity	Equity
	Security	Security	Rule of law
		Sustainability	Transparency

last fifty years marks a shift from nation state politics (and established political parties) to global politics (and issue-based campaigning organizations) (O'Byrne 2003: 93). Many of these movements are concerned with human rights and take their claims directly to the U.N. and individual nation states.

Social movements have been critical for advancing human rights and pursuing substantive justice. This will be further evidenced by the discussion of women and the advancement of equality rights in Chapter Nine.

Human Rights Law

Because of Canada's colonial development, British law applied to Canada as a colony and, with this, all of the British recognition of human rights already mentioned in such documents as the *Magna Carta*. However, as any social institution, the law has continued to evolve and develop since Canada attained status as a sovereign state. Saskatchewan was the first province to pass a human rights act, the *Saskatchewan Bill of Rights Act*, 1947, which predated the UDHR. The current Act (*Saskatchewan Human Rights Code*) states that the central aims are:

> To promote recognition of the inherent dignity and the equal inalienable rights of all members of the human family; and to further public policy in Saskatchewan that every person is free and equal in dignity and rights and to discourage and eliminate discrimination.

This Act was only binding in the province of Saskatchewan (although other provinces eventually passed their own human rights acts) and was not binding on the federal government or, consequently, any of the pieces of federal legislation. The federal government eventually passed its own human

Human Rights and Social Movements

You would be hard pressed to find much evidence of progress made on human rights if you looked only at governments. Most often, advancements in human rights are rooted in the actions of social movements. Take, for example, the abolition of the slave trade and slavery as institutionalized practices. These were abolished as a result of two kinds of social movements: on the one hand, religiously or morally based groups of people worked together in abolition societies to put pressure on their governments to end slavery; and, on the other hand, slaves organized themselves and mounted significant slave rebellions, which eventually helped lead to the end of slavery.

There are countless cases of social movements that have led to fundamental change as they claimed new political, economic and social rights. Some of these include:

- Amnesty International's campaign in the 1970s helped spur the development of the international convention against torture;
- non-governmental organizations (NGOS) were instrumental in getting an international, non-binding declaration on children's rights turned into the legally binding *Convention of the Rights of the Child*;
- social movements launched the International Campaign to Ban Landmines and pushed for the adoption of the *Convention on the Prohibition, Stockpiling, Production and Transfer of Anti-Personnel Mines and on Their Destruction* (otherwise known as the Ottawa Convention, signed in Ottawa in 1997);
- civil society organizations spearheaded the creation of the International Criminal Court;
- activism and mobilization among Indigenous communities concerned with access to and control over traditional territories and cultures in many parts of the world led to the recent adoption of the U.N. *Declaration of Indigenous Rights;* and
- the U.N. declaration condemning violence against women (including domestic violence) is a direct result of women's movements that worked for decades to make the issue of violence against women a political and human rights issue.

While the formal definitions of social movements differ slightly, most analysts agree that social movements are a main source of political conflict and social change. Social movements emerge as groups of ordinary people who form a collective identity, articulate collective interests based on shared values and engage in non-violent, collective action in efforts to effect social change. In doing so, social movements are involved in political struggles as they seek to alter the norms, policies and structures that affect peoples' everyday lives.

In essence, social movements attempt to reshape society based on certain values and morals. It is important to note that not all social movements are engaged in political struggles for social justice and human rights. Some, like the Ku Klux Klan, work to protect and enhance the privilege and power of an already privileged minority sector of society. Human rights movements, however, challenge the status quo as they engage in a struggle for equitable distribution of resources and power.

How do social movements effect social change? Social movements are often involved in non-institutional collective action. That is, instead of relying only on lobbying government officials, social movements also engage in demonstrations, protests, civil disobedience, sit-downs and so on. In doing so, social movements aim to change the general public's opinion about what governments and policymakers should do and how the world should be. The most effective social movements use credible information and moral authority to "frame" their political demands. Framing involves presenting an issue in a specific way so that it creates a greater understanding of the justice claims involved and builds support for mobilization, action and change. Numerous progressive social movements for social justice around the world now frame their demands in the context of human rights. As such, social movements are key agents of social change as they force the general public, governments and institutions to pay more attention to human rights.[1] (Annette Desmarais, University of Regina)

Note

1. Informative social movement sources include Snow, Burke, Worden and Benford 2008 and Benford and Snow 2000.

rights legislation to govern federal acts. However, problems of enforceability existed at both the provincial and federal levels as governments could still pass legislation in contravention of the principles contained in these human rights statutes. It was not until 1982 when the *Canadian Charter of Rights and Freedoms* was adopted as a Constitutional document that theses rights attained the higher status able to overrule other pieces of legislation.

The UDHR has been very influential in the global community (Flowers 2008) and also on the Canadian federal government. It provided the foundation for many human rights conventions that have been entered into by countries as binding agreements. It also influenced such documents as the *Canadian Charter of Rights and Freedoms*, which became part of Canada's Constitution in 1982. The Canadian Charter contains many rights similar to the UDHR. However, not all rights contained in the UDHR appear in the Canadian Charter.

It should be remembered that the UDHR and the U.N. Charter are only resolutions of the General Assembly of the United Nations; they are not formally ratified, legally binding treaties. These documents can't necessarily be relied on as binding authority by courts of law but can only provide guidance. At times, courts will find the provisions contained in them to be customary international law and incorporate them into the law of the state; but not all of the time. The case of *Gosselin* v. *Québec* illustrates this lack of legal force of U.N. declarations of human rights.

Article 25 of the UDHR states that a person has the right to "a standard of living adequate for the health and well being of himself (*sic*) and of his family, including food, clothing, housing and medical care and necessary social service." In the Supreme Court of Canada, Louise Gosselin argued that the government of Québec violated her right to life, liberty and security of the person and to equality, as stated in sections 7 and 15 of the Charter, when it reduced welfare benefits to young people and mandated program involvement as an eligibility requirement. The Charter does not contain specific rights to such things as food, clothing and housing; the closest provision was the right to "life, liberty and security of the person" contained in section 7. The UDHR was not raised (again, because it is not a legally binding treaty). Louise Gosselin argued that the $170 per month as social assistance allotted to her by the Government of Québec was impossible to live on. Try to imagine living and paying for food, rent, clothing and any other expenses on this monthly sum. The Supreme Court of Canada determined that section 7 of the Charter (the right to life, liberty and security of the person) did not create a positive obligation on governments to guarantee adequate living standards. This case illustrates some of the hurdles to effective litigation of human rights through the courts. It also illustrates the importance of the global community and social movements, as indicated in the case study, in encouraging and mobilizing for the achievement of human rights through positive action by not only nation states, but individuals, non-profit organizations, corporations and other entities. Just as importantly, this case illustrates that human rights are developed not by courts and litigation, but by political struggle by social movements. Given the Supreme Court of Canada ruling, it seems obvious that the important step is to have the government define life, liberty and security as including the right to an standard of adequate living.

Although Canada prides itself in the equality provisions of its Charter and the fact that the rights envisioned in the Charter apply to all equally, there isn't a right to the economic security of a bare subsistence level of living that would be consistent with social justice. Many are of the opinion that combating poverty and providing basic living standards would allow the poor and marginalized to escape the social structures limiting their success and contributing to their involvement with the criminal justice system.

For many, justice is about respecting people and allowing them to flourish in a community supportive of all their rights. These rights include the right to have their basic human needs met through adequate food, water and housing. Without these basic human rights how can any meaning be given to the right to vote or the freedom of expression?

Summary Points

After World War II, provinces and Parliament enacted human rights statutes.
In 1982 the *Canadian Charter of Rights and Freedoms* enshrined human rights in Canada's Constitution.
Canada's Charter has been found in case law not to create a positive obligation on governments to guarantee an adequate standard of living.

International Indigenous Rights

In 2007 the U.N. adopted the *Declaration on the Rights of Indigenous Peoples*. At this time, Canada refused to endorse this Declaration. Chuck Strahl, the minister responsible, cited as reasons that the Declaration was "not balanced" and "inconsistent with the Charter." However, in response, Paul Joffe, who was part of the legal team promoting the Declaration, stated, "The government's argument that the declaration goes against the Charter simply doesn't stand up" (CBC 2007). The *Declaration on the Rights of Indigenous Peoples* protects self-determination and autonomy or self-government for Indigenous people on matters relating to internal and local affairs in Article 3 as well as means or finances allowing for autonomous functions. Article 8 specifically provides that Indigenous people will not be assimilated and Article 10 provides they will not forcibly be removed from their land. None of these provisions would create new legal rights for Canada's Aboriginal people.

In an about-face, the governor general in the 2010 throne speech promised that Canada would give recognition to the Declaration. Specifically, it was stated:

> A growing number of states have given qualified recognition to the United Nations Declaration on the Rights of Indigenous Peoples. Our Government will take steps to endorse this aspirational document in a manner fully consistent with Canada's Constitution and laws. (Canada 2010: 19)

However, in yet another abrupt about face, the Harper government argued before a Canadian Human Rights Tribunal case later in 2010 that the Declaration was "meaningless in Canada and shouldn't be used to determine the human rights challenge" (Robson 2010). Canada's record on both respecting Aboriginal rights and supporting international human rights would appear to be less than exemplary and a very good illustration of the lack of legal standing of anything less than legally binding treaties containing very specific enforcement mechanisms. As well, Canada is very far from being a true cosmopolitan state and continues to replicate a much more traditional statist model.

Human Rights and Social Justice

Liberty rights have been recognized in Canada for many years. However, second and third generation rights including the right to an adequate standard of living (as discussed in Chapter Four) and a sustainable environment (as discussed in Chapter Seven) are not recognized. These second and third generation rights encompass aspects of social justice and ethical practice. The advancement of these rights will require continued action by social movements and activists to engage public opinion and sway government policy.

Human rights laws emanate from the three sources of law: the Constitution, Parliament and the courts. There are Constitutional rights in the Charter, there are statutory rights in the human rights legislation of provincial legislatures and the federal Parliament, and there are many court decisions that have expanded on the meaning and application of the rights in the Constitutional documents and legislation. Human rights issues can be argued in courts of law and quasi-judicial tribunals. International human rights are not always enforceable human rights in a nation. In order to be enforceable they must be found in a court as a customary international law or have been agreed to in a treaty together with all of the necessary requirements to make the rights enforceable in Canada.

Locally, principles of international human rights often are not reflected in Canadian law. Conversely, principles of Canadian law are not committed to in international law, such as in the case of Indigenous rights. Both of these examples illustrate state reluctance to advance human rights, limits of legislation and human rights being taken for granted. People, non-profit organizations (such as Amnesty International or Oxfam) and social movements (such as the women's movement or Via Campesina) are essential for the protection and advancement of human rights. The next chapter will illustrate this in respect of equality rights.

Glossary

cosmopolitan – a model of international society where international organizations determine the human rights of people all over the world.

customary international law – law that is evidenced by a sufficient number of states adhering to its practice, with a degree of consistency or homogeneity, such that there is a subjective belief that the practice is law.

declaration – statements of intent not usually binding.

development – a process enhancing human capabilities to maximize human flourishing in a socially just manner.

generations of rights – a method of describing and categorizing human rights loosely by time period and characteristics such as being positive, negative or community rights.

human rights – a term used since the end of World War II to describe the rights of all people, including civil, political, economic and social rights.

internationalist – a model of international society where international social practices and nation states operate in balance.

peace – the absence of war and the capacity to handle conflict creatively.

statist – a model of international society where the state has ultimate authority to determine the human rights of its citizens.

UDHR – *Universal Declaration of Human Rights*; adopted and proclaimed by the U.N. in 1948, this document sets out agreed principles and norms surrounding human rights to be respected and advanced by member nations.

United Nations – an international organization founded in 1945 by international treaty and committed to maintaining international peace and security and comprising of several institutions including the General Assembly, Security Council and International Court of Justice.

9

Equality Rights and Justice

Marilou McPhedran

At the end of this chapter, you will be able to:

- Understand differing approaches to defining equality in Canada and internationally
- Discuss how equality theory and jurisprudence have influenced the justice system
- Appreciate the difference between equality rights in theory and "lived rights"

> "Rights"... is still deliciously empowering to say. It is the magic wand of visibility and invisibility, of inclusion and exclusion, of power, and no power. The concept of rights, both positive and negative, is also the marker of our citizenship, our relation to others. (Williams 1991: 153)

This chapter explores the concept of equality as an essential component of justice at the provincial, national and international levels. Examples are provided and topics for thought and discussion are introduced to help integrate the notion of equality with that of justice and human rights and to assess the usefulness of the concept of equality in the pursuit of justice. Until the 1980s, the term "Constitutional equality rights" was unknown in this country. The human rights we now associate with the *Canadian Charter of Rights and Freedoms*, Part 1 of the *Constitution Act, 1982*, and provincial/territorial human rights codes were introduced conceptually in the human rights parlance of the founding of the United Nations (U.N.), following the atrocities of World War II. But the concept of "rights" goes much further back. In 1817, the philosopher Hegel observed:

> Whether what is called ancient *right and constitution* is actually right or not cannot depend on its antiquity. For the abolition of human sacrifice, of slavery, of feudal despotism and innumerable other infamies was also the abolition of what had been an ancient right. (cited in Habermas 1973: 122)

Chapter Eight discussed the advent of human rights as articulated in the first and overarching policy of the U.N. — the *Universal Declaration of Human Right* (UDHR). Although the Declaration is not legally enforceable, because it is a high-level policy statement, or "declaration," it has had tremendous influence in the thinking behind legal definitions of rights, considered essential to building civilized societies sustained by the rule of law. Dating back to the *Magna Carta* (1215), the rule of law is part of the British common law tradition, adopted in Canada and other countries — particularly members of the British Commonwealth — holding that law should be written down and applied consistently rather than at the whim of monarchs or governments. For 115 years (from 1867 to 1982) Canada operated with a common law constitution and without a constitutionally entrenched bill of rights that defined equality.

What Is Equality?

Main Points

As you read, highlight the answers to these questions:
What is the origin of "equality"?
When was the concept of the human right of "equality" created?
How and why did Canada entrench equality rights in the Charter?
How are the various types of justice (for example, criminal justice, civil justice and restorative justice) informed by definitions of equality or equality values? Is equality an essential component of justice?
Has the status of equality seekers in Canada improved since s.15 of the *Charter* was activated in 1985?

In Chapter One we were encouraged to set aside our normative thinking and reach for a deeper understanding of justice. Similar "rules of engagement" apply in the study of equality. Since we generally think within the confines of our own values, norms and experiences, we must honestly acknowledge our own centrism, especially within our social context (for example, ethnocentrism). For instance, a legal challenge must approach the issue of a provincially appointed marriage commissioner who refuses to officiate at same-sex marriage ceremonies from more than one perspective, since both freedom of religion and freedom from discrimination on the basis of sexual orientation are covered by s.15 of the *Charter* and provincial human rights statutes. Perspectives to consider include local and international human rights norms and questions such as whether it is necessary to fire the marriage commissioner in order to enforce the rights of the same-sex couple.

Since majority viewpoints do not always resemble justice, equality analysis must reach beyond personal experience to consider the perspectives and lived experiences of members of marginalized populations — both *within* the particular population and *between* that population and society-at-large: for example, as a woman member of the Muslim community in Regina, Saskatchewan, Canada; and as a Muslim in Regina compared to other populations in Regina, in Saskatchewan and in Canada.

A thorough study of equality cannot be limited to the law. Equality has meaning and is a concept "beyond the law," and our understanding of equality is informed by other disciplines, including philosophy, history, economics, sociology, religious studies and criminology.

Formal versus Substantive Equality

In *Ethica Nichomacea*, Aristotle concluded that equality was achieved by treating likes alike and unlikes unalike. Aristotle's reasoning is at the root of what we today consider to be the principle of "formal equality." The Aristotelian-derived formula of "same = equal" has proven problematic — particularly for equality seekers. Clearly, women are different from men, persons living with a disability are different from those who do not, and Aboriginal Canadians are a different people than non-Aboriginal Canadians. So, according to Aristotle, do their differences define them as "unlike" and therefore they are to be treated unequally? Does inequality mean different treatment for likes, same treatment for unlikes? Perhaps the best known application of the Aristotelian approach is found in the American Constitutional Fourteenth Amendment terms, which require equality claimants to be "similarly situated" before they will be considered eligible to pursue their equality claim. MacKinnon (2006: 107) challenges this approach:

> But what if social life is unequal? Legal equality then becomes a formula for reinforcing, magnifying, and rigidifying the social inequalities it purports to be equalizing and might have rectified.

While "formal" equality requires that claimants must be "similarly situated," the approach in international human rights law is different and can be seen as a strong influence in the first Canadian *Charter* cases, decided under Chief Justice Brian Dickson in the 1980s, which led to the distinction between "formal" and "substantive" equality (Young 1990: 199–200). "Substantive" equality requires recognizing the inherent value of each individual human being, and assessing the impact of alleged discrimination demands more thought and inquiry than the formulaic approach where judges apply the same formal equality analysis to all cases.

Constitutional Equality in Canada

Constitutions are considered to be the supreme law of the land for defining the limits of governmental powers. The Canadian Constitution is the source for legally defining the division of powers among federal, provincial, territorial and municipal governments — such as which level of government can tax what, which has responsibility for health care and which is responsible for the military. When defining a liberty or freedom, the Constitutional question is whether there are any explicit limits on the power of governments to constrain certain liberties that are particularly important to people, such as the freedom to practise their religion or freedom of expression.

Prior to passing the *Constitution Act, 1982*, with its entrenched *Charter*, there were few national legally enshrined rights guarantees in Canada. The British common law position on people's liberty is that individuals are free to do whatever the law does not prohibit — which may suit most people as long as their government does not pass oppressive laws. However, the common law does not explicitly guarantee that governments must respect certain individual rights and freedoms. Compared to an explicit Constitutional guarantee of a freedom (for example, freedom of expression/speech), the common law scope of an individual's freedom is that we have as much liberty as remains *after* we obey any laws that governments may have enacted to restrict that freedom. In the common law tradition, governments would not be acting outside their power if they took away certain freedoms or rights because there are no clear rules or principles that forbid such governmental actions. Constitutional rights may be described as legally protected "spaces" in the justice system that allow people to claim freedoms that are considered essential to a democracy — in other words, to have choices and to be able to live their rights.

Rights are used to defend our liberties. Historically, rights were not guaranteed widely; civil rights and liberties were available to those privileged enough to own property. The right of African Americans in the southern United States to vote was a major organizing focus of the social movement against racial segregation, which gained momentum in the 1960s, commonly known as the "civil rights movement." This focus on civil rights raised awareness worldwide about the connections between citizenship and the basic human rights set out in 1948 in the *Universal Declaration of Human Rights*. Therein, rights are defined as *equal* and *inalienable*, meaning that they are the inherent rights of *every* human, *because* they are human and *regardless*

Balancing Individual and Collective Rights

When Alberta made photographs on drivers' licences mandatory, members of the Hutterian Brethren of Wilson Colony, who sincerely believed that the second of the Ten Commandments of the Christian/Judaic faiths prohibits them from having their photographs willingly taken, began proceedings against the Alberta government, alleging breach of their religious freedom. The Supreme Court of Canada (SCC) in *Hutterian Brethren of Wilson Colony* v. *Alberta* (2009) overruled the decisions made in the Alberta courts that had decided in favour of the Hutterian members. Balancing competing interests, the SCC concluded that Alberta's universal photo requirement did not limit freedom of religion more than was required to meet the important goal of minimizing identity theft. Using the language of section 1, the SCC held that this infringement was a "reasonable limit prescribed by law" and was "reasonably justified" in Canada as "a free and democratic society."

of their immutable personal characteristics, such as race. The first lines of the preamble to the UDHR state:

> Whereas recognition of the inherent dignity and of the equal and inalienable rights of all members of the human family is the foundation of freedom, justice and peace in the world…

Legal rights are rights recognized by law and therefore enforceable in courts. In Canada today, legal rights include equality rights. But what is the connection between constitutions, rights and liberties or freedoms? In everyday terms, liberty or freedom means the ability to do something if we want to do it, as long as it does not hurt others and is not illegal; this includes the freedom *not* to do something, not to be subjected to certain governmental requirements. Judges are tasked with trying to balance rights in the best interest of our society, and they often reach different conclusions as to which governmental actions are unconstitutional.

Does Equality Include Economic and Social Rights?
The UDHR introduced the idea of economic, social and cultural rights, such as the freedom to work; the right to an adequate standard of living, which includes food, clothing, shelter, medical care and social services; the right to education; and the right to cultural life in the community (Articles 22–27). While the *Charter* does guarantee equality rights, specific social and economic rights are not listed in s.15. Canadian judicial decisions where aspects of poverty

Human Rights and Poverty in Canada

Three of the more compelling examples of Canadian judicial reasoning on poverty that demonstrate a judicial "disconnect" to the reality of those who live "below the poverty line" are Gosselin v. Québec (Attorney General) [2002] 4 S.C.R. 429, Federated Anti-Poverty Groups of B.C. v. Vancouver (City) [2002] B.C.J. No. 493 and Masse v. Ontario (Ministry of Community and Social Services) (1996), 134 D.L.R. (4th) 20, 35 C.R.R. (2d) 44 (Ont. Div. Ct.); leave to appeal to C.A. denied [1996] O.J. No. 1526; leave to appeal to S.C.C. denied [1996] S.C.C.A. No. 373. In the Gosselin and Masse cases, one from Québec and the other from Ontario, poor citizens argued that their Charter rights were violated because their governments kept social assistance benefits below subsistence levels. The judges favoured the governments — in Masse, government cutbacks were found to be acceptable; and in Gosselin, the claimant lost because she was under thirty and did not participate in a provincial workfare program for youth. In Federated Anti-Poverty Groups of B.C. v. Vancouver (City) [2002] B.C.J. No. 493, the British Columbia Supreme Court upheld a Vancouver bylaw restricting areas where panhandling was allowed, finding that it did not violate the rights of poor people who begged to their freedom of expression under section 2 of the Charter or to their access to fundamental justice under section 7.

Equality under International Law

Social and economic rights are not very "popular" with most governments. Of the three parts of the U.N. *International Bill of Rights (IBR)*, the rights defined in the *International Covenant on Economic, Social and Cultural Rights* (ICESCR) are the least implemented. This gap in implementation is primarily due to the financial implications on government budgets and policies of the broad sweep of ICESCR guarantees, including:

- equal rights for men and women (article 3),
- right to work, and just and favourable work conditions thereof (articles 6, 7),
- right to social security and social insurance (article 9),
- right to an adequate standard of living (article 11),
- right to the highest attainable standard of physical and mental health (article 12)
- right to education (article 13).

Also a part of the IBR, the *International Covenant on Civil and Political Rights* (ICCPR) offers a range of equality protections, such as "the equal right of men and women to the enjoyment of all civil and political rights set forth in the present Covenant," including:

- right to determine political status and pursue economic, social and cultural development Article 1(1)),
- right to life (Article 6),
- freedom from torture, cruel, inhuman and degrading treatment (Article 7),
- right to liberty and security (Article 9),
- right to dignified, human and respectful treatment (Article 10),
- freedom of movement (Article 12),
- equality before courts and tribunals (Article 14(1)),
- freedom of thought, conscience and religion (Article 18),
- freedom of association (Article 22),
- right to participate in public affairs, vote and be elected, and become a member of the public service (Article 25), and
- equality before the law and entitlement to equal protections under the law (Article 26).

have been central to the issues to be decided have not been encouraging to the notion that Canadians have social and economic rights or that protection from discrimination on the basis of "poverty" should be included as a s.15 equality right in the *Charter*. The "five faces" of oppression, often mirrored in poverty, include exploitation, marginalization, powerlessness, cultural imperialism and violence (where violence against a particular group is accepted more than when directed to more advantaged groups) (Young 1990: 199–200).

Brodsky and Day (2002: 200) argue that it is incumbent on the Canadian government to observe and implement the rights set out in both the

International Covenant on Social and Cultural Rights (ICESCR) and the *International Covenant on Civil and Political Rights* (ICCPR) because one set of rights cannot be implemented without the other. Essentially, civil and political rights for disadvantaged Canadians are not achievable unless they have the capacity to be full citizens, which comes with economic and social rights. Conservative Senator Noel Kinsella (2008: 16) writes that there is already a *de facto* "charter of social rights" in Canada, achieved through combining the 1999 federal/provincial/territorial Social Union Framework Agreement (SUFA) goal to "ensure access for all Canadians…to essential social programs and services of reasonably comparable quality" with s.36 of the Constitution. SUFA commits to:

- promoting equal opportunities for the well being of Canadians;
- furthering the economic development to reduce disparity in opportunities; and
- providing essential public services of reasonable quality to all Canadians.

Amartya Sen (1988: 57–68), a Nobel Laureate in economics, observed that poverty is often not the failure of economic production but rather of "entitlement systems," whereby the rights claimed by the most vulnerable in society to such basics as food and housing are devalued relative to the property-oriented rights claimed by more privileged people, with more capacity to actualize their own rights.

As discussed in Chapter One, John Rawls in his 1971 book, *A Theory of Justice*, proposed a new version of social contract theory, stating that we must rethink what a just society is from the ground up, putting aside our individual interests. In the Canadian context, Pierre Elliott Trudeau, who identified the federal-provincial Constitutional reform process as a priority when he became justice minister in 1968, was influenced by the ideas of his law professor Frank Scott. While neither used the term "equality rights," Scott taught and wrote (prior to Rawls and Sen) about his vision of Canada and the need for rights to be applied equally — describing the "just society" that can be found in Trudeau's later reform arguments.

In the 1980s and 1990s, arguments were increasingly made that traditional theories of social justice failed to address the necessity of confronting sexism (for example, Baines and Eberts 1981; MacKinnon 1991); building tolerant, multicultural societies (for example, Taylor 1994; Kymlicka 1995) and racism (Razack 1998)).

Made in Canada Equality Rights

An understanding of how equality rights came to be in the *Charter* begins with a discussion of the longstanding leadership of Canadian women on the issue. After decades of battles in courts and parliaments, much of what women gained in the articulation of sex equality extended the notion of "equality rights" to include and benefit other equality seeking groups in Canadian society. The examination of women's struggle for equality in the Canadian political sphere must recognize that the federation model of government was not imported to Canada. Aboriginal self-government was well developed when Europeans immigrated. For example, the Iroquois Confederacy, in which women held significant positions of authority, straddled what we now see as the American border and served as a model for some aspects of Canadian federalism.

With the 1982 patriation of Canada's Constitution and the advent of the *Charter*, equality seekers — including advocates for women, people with disabilities, Aboriginal peoples and other racialized minorities, such as Japanese-Canadians interned in World War II — successfully pressured parliamentarians to ensure that the *Charter* committed to more than mere formal equality and individualistic rights. Dobrowolsky (2009: 205) notes:

> Women's rights groups, in particular, were celebrated for both tightening up the wording and broadening the intent of section 15, as well as adding an entirely new equality provision, section 28, to Canada's *Charter of Rights and Freedoms*.

But the quest of Canadian women's rights advocates for equality began long before the Constitutional negotiations of the 1970s and 1980s. In what has come to be known as the Persons Case (*Edwards v. Canada (Attorney General),* [1929]), the first court battle focused on the exclusionary definition of "persons" that the SCC applied to wording in the *British North America Act* (BNA) of 1867:

> Unlike the Iroquoian model of federal governance, women had been excluded when the "Fathers of Confederation" met in Charlottetown to craft the *BNA*. Litigating to secure a fairer place in the affairs of the nation, more than eighty years ago five women launched the Persons Case and what has been termed a "tradition of Canadian women using the judicial system to advance equality rights." (Falardeau-Ramsay 1998: 8)

Early Fighters for Equality: The Famous Five in the Persons Case

In 1916, Emily Murphy (not a lawyer) presided over the new Women's Police Court as the first woman police magistrate in the British Empire until a male lawyer challenged her jurisdiction to hear his case because, as a woman, she could not have been lawfully appointed. On August 27, 1927, Murphy called on four other Alberta-based women — Nellie McClung, Henrietta Muir Edwards, Louise Crummy McKinney and Irene Parlby — to sign a petition under the *Supreme Court of Canada Act*, asking for the Supreme Court's answer to a crucial question, which eventually became worded as: "Does the word 'person' in section 24 of the *British North America Act*, include female 'persons'?"

On April 24th, 1928, Chief Justice Anglin, for a unanimous SCC, answered in the negative, holding that the BNA was limited by the period in which it had been passed, noting the exclusive use of male pronouns and that there was no English precedent of women appointed to the British House of Lords. He concluded:

> Women are not eligible for appointment by the Governor General to the Senate of Canada under section 24 of the *British North America Act*, 1867, because they are not "qualified persons" within the meaning of that section (*Reference as to the Meaning of the Word "Persons" in Section 24 of the British North America Act, 1867*, [1928]. S.C.R.276)

The only recourse open to the five women petitioners was to convince the government to legislate in their favour or, since at that time the SCC was subject to the judicial review of the Judicial Committee of the Privy Council of England, to appeal. On October 18, 1929, Lord Chancellor Sankey of the British Privy Council provided a significantly different unanimous answer, overruling the SCC:

> And to those who would ask why the word [persons] should include female, the obvious answer is, why should it not?" (*Reference as to the Meaning of the Word "Persons in Section 24 of the British North America Act, 1867*, [1928] S.C.R.276, reversed in *Edwards v. Canada (A.G.)*, [1930] A.C.124 (P.C)).

Canadian Bill of Rights, 1960

The *Canadian Bill of Rights* (CBR 1960, c.44) was a "recognition and declaration of the rights and freedoms" championed by one of the few prime ministers from western Canada, the Rt. Hon. John G. Diefenbaker of Saskatchewan. Following World War II, numerous women subsumed personal frustrations, having experienced considerable autonomy in the war years. Soon their economic and social grievances surfaced, creating an environment where Canadian women in the mid-1960s were asking questions about their lives

> **Persons Case Commemoration**
>
> October 18 is now officially celebrated in Canada as Persons Day, commemorated by the annual awarding of a governor general's medal to five long-time activist women (as well as an award for youth leaders) and Legal Education and Action Fund (LEAF) Breakfasts across Canada.

and about their "status" as women. In response to pressure from women's organizations and questioning commentary in the media, Prime Minister Lester B. Pearson appointed the Royal Commission on the Status of Women in the early months of Canada's centennial year, 1967, asking the commissioners to

> inquire into the status of women in Canada and to recommend what steps might by taken by the Federal Government to ensure for women equal opportunities with men in all aspects of Canadian identity. (CBC Radio and Television Archives n.d.: 14)

Expectations that "justice" included women's equality were rising, as was optimism that the CBR (which is still a law in Canada) would deliver. Section 1 of Part I of the CBR states:

> There have existed and shall continue to exist without discrimination by reason of race, national origin, colour, religion or sex, the following human rights and fundamental freedoms, namely… the right of the individual to equality before the law and the protection of the law.

However, judicial interpretation was largely cautious and unhelpful to equality seekers who tried to claim their rights under the CBR. The following decisions under the CBR delineate differences between interpretations of "justice" and the "law."

Aboriginal Women and the Indian Act

Aboriginal women married to non-Aboriginal men felt the unfair sting of the CBR in *Canada (Attorney General) v. Lavell*, when federal *Indian Act* provisions denying status were upheld in a 1974 SCC decision. Counsel for Jeanette Lavell and Yvonne Bédard argued that s.12(1)(b) discriminated on the basis of sex against women of Indian status, who lost that status upon marriage to a non-Indian, but permitted a status man to extend status to his non-Indian wife and in turn to their children.

This decision prompted a dramatic activist response involving a group of Aboriginal women who left the Tobique Reserve in New Brunswick with their small children, fathered by non-status men, to walk in protest to Ottawa. One of their leaders, Sandra Lovelace (now Senator Lovelace-Nichols), a

Maliseet woman of the reserve, gained international attention when she petitioned the United Nations Human Rights Committee, alleging violations by Canada under the *Optional Protocol to the International Covenant on Civil and Political Rights,* to which Canada had just acceded (G.A. Res. 2200 (XXI), 1966). Canada defended the legislation. Embarrassed internationally by the U.N. finding that the federal law contravened the rights of Aboriginal women (*Lovelace v. Canada,* 1981), Canada moved slowly, even with sustained lobbying from a wide range of women's groups. Nearly ten years after the march from Tobique, in 1981 the government enacted partial redress, leaving Aboriginal women's rights at the discretion of bands, which could ask the government to exempt them from s.12(1)(b) (Bayefsky 1982).

Women's "Routine" Work

In *Murdoch v. Murdoch* [1975], dismissing more than twenty-five years of ranching with her husband in Alberta, the SCC awarded Irene Murdoch just two hundred dollars a month, agreeing with the trial judge that the "routine" work of "any ranch wife" was not enough to create a legal claim to the matrimonial property. Women across Canada identified with Murdoch and mobilized to demand their property rights. By 1980 every province and territory had passed family law amendments as a result of women discovering and flexing their collective political "muscle."

Gender Neutral Pregnancy?

Stella Bliss lived in British Columbia when she was fired because she was pregnant. After her baby was born, she actively sought, but did not find, appropriate employment, and so, having determined that she met the regular criteria, applied for unemployment insurance benefits. The Unemplyment Insurance Commission refused her application because she had been pregnant when she lost her job and she did not meet the more stringent criteria applied to pregnancy benefits in the legislation. In *Bliss v. A.G. Canada,* (1979), Bliss's *pro bono* lawyers argued before the Federal Court of Appeal and the SCC that the higher legislative bar for pregnant women discriminated on the basis of sex. To the dismay of women's groups, both courts rejected this argument in favour of the Aristotelian formal equality notion that all pregnant women were equally denied regular benefits due to a legitimate gender neutral distinction based on nature — not between men and women, but between pregnant and non-pregnant persons.

Reacting to Losses under the CBR

When Prime Minister Trudeau announced his determination to "bring home" the Canadian Constitution and to entrench within it a charter of rights and freedoms, the platform for women's Constitutional activism had already been framed by the judicial use of the CBR to deny the discrimination rampant in women's daily lives. When the draft charter was released in 1980, the federally appointed members of the Canadian Advisory Council on the Status of Women launched a public education campaign on the Constitution, led by its president, Doris Anderson. British Columbia, Alberta, Saskatchewan, Québec, New Brunswick, Nova Scotia, Newfoundland and the Yukon had all enacted new laws or amendments to their family property regimes in 1979–80, preceded by the Northwest Territories, Ontario and Manitoba. So, when a women's Constitutional battle broke out in January 1981, prompting Doris Anderson to resign in a very public manner, many grassroots women had a sense that making politicians respond was an achievable prospect, and the women's movement had both human and organizational infrastructure in place and on the alert. In her article on the impact of the "ad hoc" women's Constitutional conference and lobby that sprang up in early 1981, Collins (1981: 22) reported:

> The issue — whether women would have a share in the future of the nation.... As Linda Ryan-Nye says, there seemed to be a peculiar readiness to speak with one voice: "A lot of us sensed it and not just in the organized women's movement. It had been building.... this shoddy treatment of a strong and honest woman at the same time as denying us our rights as citizens... Boom."

Canadian Constitutional Trialogue on Equality

So how did Canadians end up with equality rights guaranteed in a bill of human rights entrenched in the supreme law of the land — the Constitution? It is important to remember that governments make laws and governments are made up of people. Constitutions are built by people — but only certain people. It's helpful to understand the background and context to the introduction of the *Charter* and how it took years from when the first draft charter, with "non-discrimination" provisions, was introduced in 1968 at a federal/provincial first ministers' conference until more than a decade later, when "equality rights" became a topic of broad public concern and televised debates and were introduced into the proposed *Charter* in 1981. Journalist Graham Fraser (2002) offers this retrospective on events leading up to the *Charter:*

> In April 1968, a year after becoming justice minister, Trudeau was prime minister and the agenda he had had as justice minister acquired a new importance. Within three years, a *Charter* ["Victoria Charter"] had been written and quietly negotiated with Québec's new Liberal premier, Robert Bourassa. Fundamental liberties would be guaranteed and language rights would be protected in every province. But the Victoria *Charter* ultimately failed when Bourassa withdrew his support.

The Struggle for Equality Rights in the Charter

Prime Minister Pierre Trudeau envisioned a statement of rights and freedoms as part of the new Constitution that would provide "guarantees" for people in Canada (mostly Canadian citizens, with some exceptions) in a stronger manner than in the 1960 *Canadian Bill of Rights*, which was limited to federal laws, was not applicable to provincial statutes and could be amended at any time, because it was not an entrenched part of the Constitution. However, "equality rights" was not a term used in any of the drafts of the *Charter* developed by government officials or political leaders from the 1960s through to 1981, although one of the arguments for accepting the Trudeau government's "people's package" for Constitutional reform was that an entrenched charter would apply to governments across Canada and thus rights would be equally available. Equality rights in the charter came out of the grassroots mobilization of people and groups in Canada — mostly women's rights organizations and representatives of people living with disabilities.

Accounts of this struggle vary; perspectives differed depending on the position of the participant in the Constitution-building processes. Initially, the Trudeau government was not prepared to "open up" the process, but public pressure convinced the government to name a special joint committee of the Senate and of the House of Commons on the Constitution in 1980, with members drawn from all the parties of both houses of Parliament — co-chaired by M.P. Serge Joyal from Québec and Senator Harry Hays from Alberta. For the first time in Canada, a parliamentary committee was televised, and millions of Canadians paid attention to what was happening at the hearings. Senator Hays made news when he addressed the National Action Committee on the Status of Women (NAC) executives (with this author present) in the following manner:

> I want to thank you girls (*sic*) for your presentation. We're honoured to have you here. But I wonder why you don't have anything in here for babies or children. All you girls are going to be working and who's going to look after them? (in Watson and Barber 1988: 141)

After months of presentations by concerned citizens and their organizations to the Special Joint Committee, Attorney General Jean Chrétien announced major changes to section 15 in January 1981. Dawson (2006: 31) and Lepofsky (1998: 156) wrote firsthand accounts of what went into these changes, including altering the title to "equality rights," creating an opening for non-enumerated or analogous grounds of discrimination, reversing the order of "age" and "sex" and adding another enumerated ground — "mental or physical disability." The attorney general attributed the title change to "Equality Rights" to a (now defunct) federal body called the Canadian Advisory Council on the Status of Women (CACSW), then chaired by Doris

Anderson, with Mary Eberts acting as her legal counsel (Senate and House of Commons 1981).

The "spark" that galvanized Canadian women's Constitutional activism was when Doris Anderson abruptly resigned in January 1981, in public protest against what she considered to be government interference in the women's Constitutional conference being organized by the CACSW. Again, perspectives on what happened vary, but the aptly named Ad Hoc Committee of Canadian Women on the Constitution ("Ad Hoc Committee" or "Ad Hockers") took responsibility for organizing an alternative conference — to be surprised when more than 1,300 women found their way to Ottawa on Valentine's Day in 1981. Run by consensus, the conference produced resolutions that guided ensuing months of lobbying for amendments to the draft Constitution to strengthen equality rights (Kome 1983).

It was this unprecedented public engagement in the 1980s Canadian Constitution building process that gave rise to the term "trialogue" to describe and validate citizens and their organizations as key contributors. Constitutional scholars Hogg and Bushell (1997, 2007) used the term "Charter dialogue" to describe the bilateral dynamic between legislators in drafting and adopting the *Charter*, complemented by judges using their authority under the *Charter* to interpret what the written words actually meant when applied to real-life problems and challenges to the *Charter* brought before the courts. In arguing for a more inclusive understanding of how the Canadian Constitution was built and is sustained, McPhedran (2005: 14) introduced the "trialogue" metaphor to acknowledge the ongoing engagement and influence of social movements in the drafting of Constitutional text and in securing equality rights in sections 15 and 28 of the *Charter*:

> Too often, judges and politicians fail to appreciate that Canadians invested in an equality-based constitutional democracy — often engaging directly through interventions in Parliament and in the courts — have turned the dynamic into a *trialogue*; surely one of the most significant outcomes of the s.15 impact on Canadian society.

The *Canadian Charter of Rights and Freedoms* is a bill of rights consisting of 34 sections entrenched within the *Constitution Act, 1982,* which, in effect, reintroduced all of Canada's statutory Constitutional law, including the *British North America Act, 1867.* Prime Minister Pierre Elliot Trudeau stated at the proclamation ceremony for the *Constitution Act, 1982* on April 17, 1982:

> We now have a *Charter* which defines the kind of country in which we wish to live, and guarantees the basic rights and freedoms which each of us shall enjoy as a citizen of Canada. It upholds the equality of women, and the rights of disabled persons. (Library and Archives Canada n.d.)

Women's determination to strengthen *Charter* equality rights was honed by the harsh fact that the cases brought by women in the 1970s seeking equality protections under the *Canadian Bill of Rights* were all lost. In the early 1980s, when the new *Constitution Act* and the *Charter* were being drafted to effect patriation to Canada, Canadians watched as American women were losing their battle to include the "Equal Rights Amendment (ERA)" in their Constitution. Canadian women saw how Canadian judges followed American judges (using the Fourteenth Amendment equal protections for race- and sex-based discrimination) in foisting notions of formal equality on women. The ultimate wording of the equality sections of the *Charter* was substantially different from the drafts that had caused such concern.

Efforts to ensure that the new Constitutional equality rights actually made a difference in the daily lives of equality seekers took many forms after the *Constitution Act, 1982* was activated. Since s.32 of the *Charter* imposed a three-year moratorium on people being able to use s.15, during the moratorium, from 1982 through 1985, a number of preparations were made, including publication of the first textbook on equality rights (Bayefsky and Eberts 1985) and the formation of a new organization, LEAF (the Women's Legal Education and Action Fund) — launching what Manfredi (2004: 49) describes as the women's "microconstitutional campaign for substantive equality." LEAF — founded in 1985 by some of the "Ad Hockers" — has been involved in more equality cases than any other non-governmental organization in Canada, attempting to ensure that equality is interpreted by the courts through a "gender impact lens" even when the case has not focused on women. For example, in 1989, the first major Supreme Court decision interpreting s.15, *Andrews v. Law Society of British Columbia* [1989], was brought by a White male lawyer, but LEAF was granted intervener status to make arguments that became reflected in the Court's decision that section 15(1) and (2) of the *Charter* should benefit those who have been historically disadvantaged, thus preventing arguments, based on American cases of "reverse discrimination," from those who traditionally benefited from legislation developed by privileged classes. Five principles that continue to frame Canadian discussions of Constitutional equality were established in the *Andrews* decision.

First, the Court emphasized that equality cannot be reduced to sameness of treatment.... laws that treat everyone the same — laws that are "facially neutral" — may be discriminatory in their impact. This is referred to as "adverse effects discrimination." Second, the American "similarly situated" test based on the Aristotelian notion of formal equality, was rejected as a reliable guide to the interpretation of s.15. Third, the actual effects of a challenged law or practice should be the focus of the analysis. It is not necessary to establish intentional or purposeful discrimination. Fourth, to make out

Table 6 Equality Protections and Limitations in the *Charter*

Equality Protection	Limitations of Equality Protection
Equality of Women and Men **Preamble** Whereas respect for the dignity of human beings, equality of women and men, and recognition of their rights and freedoms constitute the foundation of justice, liberty and peace;	*Reasonable Limits* **s.1** The *Canadian Charter of Rights and Freedoms* guarantees the rights and freedoms set out in it subject only to such reasonable limits prescribed by law as can be demonstrably justified in a free and democratic society.
Equality before and under Law and Equal Protection and Benefit of Law s.**15** (1) Every individual is equal before and under the law and has the right to the equal protection and equal benefit of the law without discrimination and, in particular, without discrimination based on race, national or ethnic origin, colour, religion, sex, age or mental or physical disability. *Affirmative Action Programs* **s.15**(2) Subsection (1) does not preclude any law, program or activity that has as its object the amelioration of conditions of disadvantaged individuals or groups including those that are disadvantaged because of race, national or ethnic origin, colour, religion, sex, age or mental or physical disability. *Rights Guaranteed Equally to Both Sexes* s.**28** Notwithstanding anything in this Charter, the rights and freedoms referred to in it are guaranteed equally to male and female persons.	*Exception* s.**32**(2) Notwithstanding subsection (1), section 15 shall not have effect until three years after this section comes into force. *Exception where Express Declaration* s.**33**(1) Parliament or the legislature of a province may expressly declare in an Act of Parliament or of the legislature, as the case may be, that the Act or a provision thereof shall operate notwithstanding a provision included in section 2 or sections 7 to 15 of this Charter. *Operation of Exception* **s.33**(2) An Act or a provision of an Act in respect of which a declaration made under this section is in effect shall have such operation as it would have but for the provision of this *Charter* referred to in the declaration.

Equality Protection	Limitations of Equality Protection
	Five Year Limitation **s.33**(3) A declaration made under subsection (1) shall cease to have effect five years after it comes into force or on such earlier date as may be specified in the declaration. *Re-enactment* **s.33**(4) Parliament or the legislature of a province may re-enact a declaration made under subsection (1). *Five Year Limitation* **s.33**(5) Subsection (3) applies in respect of a re-enactment made under subsection (4).

a violation of s.15, the claimant must establish differential treatment that amounts to discrimination on the basis of a personal characteristic that is either listed as a prohibited ground of discrimination in s.15 ("enumerated") or that is analogous to the listed grounds (as eventually happened in the equality cases brought on the basis of sexual orientation). Fifth, a personal characteristic will be accepted as an analogous ground if it shares the essential features of the personal characteristics listed in s.15.

Ten years after *Andrews*, in its 1999 decision in *Nancy Law v. Canada (Minister of Employment and Immigration)*, the Supreme Court of Canada unanimously reformulated the *Andrews* test, stating that burdensome differences in treatment on the basis of prohibited grounds are discriminatory *only if they can reasonably be said to violate "human dignity."* Although the term "dignity" is nowhere to be found in the *Charter*, it figures prominently in the international human rights treaties and has become significant in many Canadian judicial interpretations of equality.

Unfortunately, many of those decisions have gone against the equality seekers who brought their claims to the courts (Petter 1987). Nancy Law was married to a man quite a bit older, and when he died, she relied on the protection in s.15(1) against discrimination on the basis of age, because the benefits allowed to her as a spouse under the age of thirty-five were less than for those over that age. Nancy Law lost her case. This one decision has generated hundreds of pages of commentary and speculation. Through its *Nancy Law* decision, the Court established a tougher test for claimants — requiring the additional step of proving to the Court that their human dignity has been impaired — as an addition to the *Andrews* principles summarized above. The Court still applied a comparative test, but it came down to being what the Court decided a "reasonable person" in the position of the claimant would/should feel about their dignity being impaired, not necessarily what the claimant actually did feel about the impact of the alleged discrimination.

Petter (1987: 857, 860), a "*Charter* critic," expressed the following years before the *Nancy Law* decision:

> The argument is that, while sold to the public as part of a "people's package," the Canadian *Charter of Rights and Freedoms* is a regressive instrument more likely to undermine than to advance the interests of socially and economically disadvantaged Canadians.... The negative nature of *Charter* rights combined with this selective view of state action remove from *Charter* scrutiny the major source of inequality in our society — the unequal distribution of property entitlements among private parties.

In *R. v. Kapp* (2008 SCC, 41), the Supreme Court changed its approach again — described by Ryder (2008) as "Taking Section 15 Back to the Future"— and returned to the test in the *Andrews* case of almost two decades earlier, prompting cautious optimism among equality rights advocates.

When Is a Charter Guarantee Not a Guarantee?

When section 1 of the draft Canadian Constitution was introduced, deep concern was expressed before the Special Joint Committee and in the media that it did not protect rights, allowing governments to place too many limitations on rights. Many names were given to section 1 to illustrate that it was a problem, including the "Mack Truck clause" and the "bathtub clause" because it would make it too easy for politicians to "run over" or "pull the plug" on human rights. Justice Minister Chrétien introduced a number of changes to the section until it reached its current wording:

> The Canadian *Charter of Rights and Freedoms* guarantees the rights and freedoms set out in it subject only to such reasonable limits as are generally accepted in a free and democratic society with a parliamentary system of government.

Opting Out of Charter Rights — Section 33 Override

Ironically, section 33 of the *Charter*, introduced much later in the Constitutional negotiations, gave to governments a much clearer authority to opt out of rights than the much-scrutinized section 1. The Latin term for a clause like s.33 of the *Charter* is *non obstante*, or "notwithstanding," because this clause functions like an optional legislative "override" on the rights specified in s.33(1) of the *Charter* — all of the fundamental freedoms in s.2, all of the legal rights in sections 7 through 14 and the equality rights in s.15 (but not the sex equality guarantee in s.28). Section 33 makes it clear that there is no tight "guarantee" in the face of this governmental power.

How did the so many rights in the *Charter* become potentially "unentrenched"? One of the earliest suggestions for such a clause came from Harvard-based Canadian law professor Paul Weiler (1980: 231), who urged:

> We should entrench our fundamental rights in the Canadian Constitution in order to give them the legal and symbolic authority which would be conducive to their flourishing. But we should include in the Constitutional Bill of Rights the kind of *non obstante* provision now contained in our statutory bill.... In typical Canadian fashion, I propose a compromise, between the British version of full-fledged parliamentary sovereignty and the American version of full-fledged judicial authority over Constitutional matters.

The fundamental difference between section 1 and section 33 is that section 1 requires balancing of the rights and freedoms identified in the *Charter* with the needs and values of a free and democratic society, but section 33 empowers governments to decline to respect specific rights and freedoms listed in the *Charter*.

However, Hogg and Bushell (1997: 75) assessed the likelihood of s.33 being used often by governments as slim, even though there is nothing in law to stop them, "because of the development of a political climate of resistance to its use." Another possible contest between *non obstante* powers in the *Charter* has yet to unfold — there is another override still operative: the sex equality guarantee in s.28, which is not subject to s.33 in the way that equality rights in s.15 are, but a case is yet to arise (Kome 1982).

Statutory

Federal, Provincial and Territorial Human Rights

In 1947, Saskatchewan became the first North American government to enact a general human rights statute — soon after the United Nations was founded in 1945, at the close of World War II. Now human rights mechanisms, created by statute, such as human rights commissions and tribunals, operate nationally and in every province and territory in Canada, each with its own enabling legislation. For example, the national legislation, the *Canadian Human Rights Act*, prohibits discrimination on eleven grounds: disability, race, national or ethnic origin, colour, religion, age, sex, sexual orientation, marital status, family status and conviction for which a pardon has been granted.

Complaints on the specified grounds in the federal/provincial/territorial legislation are initially addressed through related bodies and their quasi-judicial tribunals, while complaints related to the *Charter* are addressed through the courts. Thus, jurisprudence (reports on the facts and outcomes of judicial and quasi-judicial decisions on cases brought to these tribunals and courts) for statutory human rights mechanisms is different from decisions by courts in Constitutional *Charter* cases. However, when a human rights tribunal decision is challenged, then the appeal moves into the same court system as the *Charter* complaints — underscoring the importance of Canadian judges at every level being well educated in human rights, including equality rights, regardless of the jurisdiction (federal, provincial or territorial).

Lived Equality

The complexity of the pursuit of equality rights in Canada is the topic of extensive commentary. The Chief Justice of the Supreme Court of Canada, the Right Honourable Beverley McLachlin (2001: 17), concluded:

> The Canadian *Charter of Rights and Freedoms* guarantees a panoply of rights.... And like most modern bills of rights, it guarantees equality. Of all the rights, this is the most difficult.

How do citizens of the world turn promises on paper — in constitutions, local and international laws — into "lived rights" that make a positive difference in their daily lives? This chapter discusses how grassroots engagement altered the *Canadian Charter of Rights and Freedoms* and Canadian Constitutional jurisprudence. Real life examples of "equality lived" through active s.15 claims, based on the protected grounds specified in s.15 equality rights, as well as the analogous ground of sexual orientation, which was "read in" by the Supreme Court, demonstrate the complexity and imperfections in the pursuit of justice based on equality rights. However, these setbacks should not be taken as a message to "give up" on justice or equality. Consider the alternatives. In the examples that follow, look for information that gives a practical perspective on how important it is for information and evidence — from the perspective of the equality seekers — to be presented to judges in the course of a hearing, before they make their decision. Because judges are supposed to make their decisions only on the evidence presented to them, this is a challenging but crucial aspect of the strategic litigation undertaken by sophisticated equality-focused organizations like Egale, the Council of Canadians with Disabilities, the Native Women's Association of Canada and most frequently, LEAF, often in collaboration with other equality-seeking groups.

The importance of judges having the best available evidence on which to base their decisions is unlikely to draw debate. But the value of equality-based organizations being allowed by judges to bring information and evidence in their role as "interveners" in key cases (because they are not one of the parties to the case) is less settled. A notion that frontline expertise provided to the Court through interventions should be invalidated as that of "special interest" groups — such as Constitutional rights advocates — seems to be gaining ground. Such a notion is derived from an elitist perspective. Rights are just words on paper unless they can be beneficially experienced — unless they can be lived. Interventions before the Court are a form of inclusion that is consistent with Canadian *Charter* values, and this produces knowledge that is essential in equality cases — if only because judges are among our most privileged and protected of citizens.

The interconnection of rights guarantees in the *Charter* and in statutory human rights law has emerged in case after case. In the examples of "lived rights" that follow, the relationship between equality rights and other rights and freedoms in the *Charter* exposes how inequality is compounded by other prohibited grounds of discrimination, such as Aboriginal status, disability or sexual orientation.

Aboriginal People

The following excerpt from a speech by Senator Lillian Quan Dyck (2007 n.p.), one of two Aboriginal women senators in Canada at the time, captures the tension inherent in *Charter* promises and the different reality often experienced:

> I am proud to be a Canadian. Canadians have much to be proud of; our nation believes it and passes legislation that provides for basic fundamental freedoms and equality of its citizens. On the one hand I know this to be true, yet at the same time I know for some of us it is not necessarily true. As I look at the history of federal legislation and how it affected my family and others like me, the ideals of our country and the reality of our lives do not necessarily match up. There is a political and cognitive dissonance.

Senator Dyck went on to speak of how her mother, an Aboriginal woman, qualified as a "status Indian" under the *Indian Act*, but Canadian law dictated that she lost her status when she married a non-Indian. This is an illustration of how the intersection of rights and personal characteristics — in this case, gender, race and culture — necessitates a balancing with Aboriginal sovereignty.

When she was national speaker of the Native Women's Association of Canada (NWAC), Gail Stacey-Moore (1991) noted how Aboriginal women's equality advocates often experienced significant resistance from influential leaders within a number of important bodies, such as governments, academia and the media, and how Aboriginal women have been legally, politically and socially subordinated by the federal government and by Aboriginal governments. Canadian legal scholar Douglas Sanders (1985: 569), soon after the *Canadian Charter of Rights and Freedoms* was activated in the early 1980s, reasoned:

> If Canadians are serious about cultural autonomy for aboriginal collectivities, then sexual discrimination should be acceptable so long as it authentically reflects the continuing traditions of the communities.

By contrast, some twenty years later, then National Chief Phil Fontaine (2001) of the Assembly of First Nations stated:

> The strength, knowledge, and capacity of our women leaders must be heard and honoured by all First Nations, and all Canadians.

Disability

The most significant recent success for equality seekers came in *Council of Canadians with Disabilities v.* VIA *Rail Canada Inc.* [2007], "which affirms the universal application of human rights principles and the right to equality for people with disabilities" (Manitoba Human Rights Commission 2007). However, counsel for the Council of Canadians with Disabilities (CCD), David Baker and Sarah Godwin (2008: 61) caution that the success of the case almost bankrupted the CCD and that governmental resistance does not seem to have been reduced by the decision.

In an earlier turning point for disability rights, *Eldridge v. British Columbia (Attorney General)* [1997], the CCD intervened, as did LEAF, in coalition with the Disabled Women's Network of Canada, to convince the Supreme Court that the government was obligated to fund sign language as part of its promise to provide medical services to all residents of the province.

Sexual Orientation

Until 1969, the *Criminal Code of Canada* contained an offence that effectively criminalized homosexuality. Now, the human rights architecture in Canada (federal, provincial, territorial and, in some places, municipal) holds that sexual orientation is not an acceptable ground of discrimination and complaint mechanisms are provided — but nowhere in the *Charter* will you find an explicit protection against discrimination on the basis of sexual orientation. The answer to this Constitutional puzzle lies in the open wording of s.15 and the s.24 "remedies" power given to Canadian judges in the *Charter* to decide on appropriate remedies, including what has come to known as "reading in rights" that are not specifically listed in s.15.

Douglas Elliott (2006: 98), counsel in a number of sexual orientation cases, including *Hislop v. Canada (Attorney General)* (2007), which extended same-sex pension benefits, observed how the shift in society toward equality rights for lesbian, gay, bisexual and transgendered (LGBT) Canadians was influenced by the *Charter:*

> So long as growing public support did not move the politicians, the only way to move them would be through the courts.... All of these cases accepted that sexual orientation was an analogous ground, but most of the early cases ended in failure.... The public began to conceive of the issues in terms of the human rights model, and countervailing arguments based on the "sin" or "medical" models began to be viewed as antiquated at best and bigoted at worst.... The question of sexual orientation as an analogous ground finally reached the Supreme Court of Canada in the famous Egan case. A majority of the Court found that discrimination against same-sex couples was an infringement of section 15(1).... However, a different majority upheld the impugned law under section 1. It would be the last time that section 1 would be relied upon to reach that result, but it was a bitter blow at the time.

In 1996, the Alberta Court of Appeal ruled against Delwin Vriend, a teacher who was fired when it was discovered that he was gay. The Alberta *Individual Rights Protection Act* did not include "sexual orientation," so Vriend sued the Alberta government, arguing that the appropriate remedy was for "sexual orientation" to be read into the Alberta statute. The Supreme Court agreed, overruling the Alberta Court of Appeal:

> As a remedy, the words "sexual orientation" should be read into the prohibited grounds of discrimination in these provisions. (para. 497)

Although his government fought Vriend at every stage of the case, Alberta premier Ralph Klein surprised many when he announced in 1998 that he would not use his legislative majority to override the Court by activating s.33 of the *Charter*, and he acceded to the requirement that his province's human rights legislation should prohibit discrimination on the basis of sexual orientation. Elliott (2006: 112–3) describes the importance of the wide-ranging political and legal battle over the legalization of same-sex marriage in the federal government's Bill C-38:

> Parliament relented and passed Bill C-38, but only after a long and difficult political battle... in the process, we had moved the political goalposts.... Canadians had firmly embraced the human rights model embodied in the Charter.

Sex Equality

The world over, in courts and beyond, control over women's bodies is the crux of equality struggles. Much of the equality jurisprudence has been related to sexual assault. In *R. v. Seaboyer* [1991], legislation that women fought for — known as the "rape shield" — was struck down, but this loss in court galvanized public concern and paved the way for subsequent pro-victim legal amendments by Parliament — another example of the crucial contribution citizens make to law reform. In *O'Connor* [1995] (a Catholic priest who sexually assaulted Aboriginal women under his authority in residential school and as their employer), the compelling dissent from Justice L'Heureux-Dubé led to major amendments expanding the understanding of Constitutional rights beyond those who are accused of sexual crimes. *R v. Ewanchuk* [1999] generated the "no means no" legislation on sexual assault when an Alberta appeal court judge (ironically, the grandson of Nellie McClung, one of the Famous Five in the Persons Case) was overruled by a stinging opinion penned by Justice L'Heureux-Dubé. Public mobilization was triggered by personal and professional criticism of her by prominent defence counsel and Judge McClung in the media. In *R. v. Darrach* [2000] — another challenge to rape shield provisions in the *Criminal Code* — women's Constitutional equality rights figured prominently, but the protective legislation was upheld. The various "sides" have different perceptions of fundamental rights in the *Charter*, but all sides have passionately engaged the criminal legal system in these cases. It has been an exhilarating and exhausting series of steps forward and back. More often than not, public engagement has had real impact in broadening the courts' and Parliament's perspectives on just whose rights and freedoms are at stake in sexual assault cases and what constitutes a truly "fair trial."

Assessments on the extent to which s.15 equality rights in the courts have been the source of progress for women are mixed. Dobrowolsky (2009) and Bashevkin (2009) determine the political sphere to be equally as important as the courts for women's equality gains.

Equality Rights and Justice

As in the pursuit of justice, the path to equality is not only through the courts and the *Charter*. Following the *Nancy Law* case, most equality-seeking claims were lost before the Supreme Court. Soon after that decision, Beverly Baines (2000: 71–73) predicted that the Court's unusually unanimous decision in *Law* would create additional barriers through which equality-seeking litigants would have difficulty passing. Broad judicial latitude for subjective assessment of others' reality is exposed in the split decision in *Gosselin v. Québec (Attorney General)* 2002 S.C.C. 84, where the Chief Justice (para. 68), for the majority, applied the *Law* test in dismissing a class action on behalf of the majority of young, entrenched unemployed in Québec: "This is not a case where the complainant group suffered from pre-existing disadvantage and stigmatization."

In the *Canadian Foundation for Children, Youth and the Law v. Canada (Attorney General)* [2004] — the "spanking" case on assaults by parents protected under the *Criminal Code of Canada*, the Court held that such assaults on children — which would be illegal if committed on other adults — were not a violation

Ethical Considerations

"Two central issues for ethical analysis of equality are: Why equality? Equality of what? The two questions are distinct but thoroughly interdependent. We cannot begin to defend or criticize equality without knowing what on earth we are talking about, i.e., equality of what features (incomes, opportunities, wealths, achievements, freedoms, rights" (Amartya Sen 1980: 256).

Unequal Distribution of Wealth — In *World Poverty and Human Rights: Cosmopolitan Responsibilities and Reforms* (2002), philosopher Thomas Pogge argues that individuals from affluent countries were directly or indirectly responsible for the millions of annual preventable deaths of individuals in developing countries arising from an inability to access the requisite resources. The unequal distribution of wealth within societies raises a heatedly debated ethical question. Do affluent individuals and countries have an ethical obligation to instill elements of substantive equality into society?

Affirmative Action for Substantive Equality — Affirmative action (sometimes called reverse discrimination in the United States), defined in s.15(2) of the *Charter,* is allowed to rebalance the effects of inequality that arise from discrimination of historically disadvantaged groups to provide members of these groups with substantively equal opportunities for success in education, business, politics and other realms of life.

Resolving Competition between Rights — Although rights and freedoms are guaranteed under the *Charter*, guaranteeing one right or freedom for a certain individual can infringe on the enjoyment of rights and freedoms for others. For instance, a juror who exercises his or her freedom of expression by discussing the trial in progress could infringe the right to a fair trial for the accused. Reconciling competing outcomes of the enjoyment of rights and freedoms is a delicate balance that judges must decide within the ethical and legal framework of the Constitution.

of children's s.15 rights. On the other hand, in *Dickie v. Dickie* [2007], the Supreme Court held that parents who refuse to comply with family court orders for support of their families (about 97 percent being men) can be held in contempt of court. It is clear that the *Charter* has changed Canada — s.15 equality rights and s.15 equality values intersect with Canadian perceptions and concerns. A Trudeau Foundation poll (Environics 2006) found that 49 percent of the population felt immigrants should be free to maintain their religious and cultural practices in Canada, but the vast majority (81percent) also felt that gender equality "trumps" multiculturalism — an opinion shared almost equally across demographic, income, education, age and gender lines. The *Charter* is a contract between Canadians and their governments. Another Trudeau Foundation poll (Environics 2010) revealed an intergenerational difference in viewing responsibility for justice — 70 percent of young adults believed that current Canadian governments are responsible for addressing human rights violations committed by previous governments, compared with only 47 percent of Canadians sixty and over.

Nevertheless, there is concern that a negative shift in the impact of how the courts are dealing with equality rights is emerging — from constructive to damaging — from s.15 acting as a beacon to illuminate and value the struggles against inequality in ordinary lives, to s.15 becoming the laser that burns away access to justice.

Glossary

British common law – developed from British court decisions (beginning in 1066 with the Norman Conquest) that set precedents, which are referred to in future cases of a similar nature. Parliament can pass new laws that overrule existing precedents. All federal and provincial law in Canada is based on the common law system, except for Québec (which is based on civil law).

Canadian Bill of Rights — a statute in 1960 to guarantee certain rights to individuals in Canada,

Charter of Rights and Freedoms – guarantees rights and freedoms to individuals in Canada and protects against infringement, subject to the limitations set out therein.

Constitution – outline of the division of powers and authorities of the provincial and federal governments in Canada.

Constitutional equality – equality protections entrenched within the Constitution

cultural imperialism – the norms of the dominant group are assumed to be those of everyone.

discrimination – different treatment of an individual on the basis of a prohibited ground of discrimination, such as national or ethnic origin, colour, religion, age, sex, sexual orientation, marital status, family status, physical or mental disability and pardoned criminal conviction.

entitlement systems – the rights claimed by the most vulnerable in society to such basics as food and housing are devalued relative to the property-oriented rights claimed by more privileged people.

entrench – to give legal effect by inserting within a piece of legislation.

formal equality – equal treatment for all (i.e., likes treated alike; "unalikes" treated alike).

infringement – a violation of an individual's rights and freedoms as protected under the Constitution or other laws.

jus cogens – non-derogable international customary law.

rights, lived– the beneficial experience of rights that results in positive changes in daily life.

rights, collective – rights belonging to a group of individuals.

rights, individual – rights belonging to individuals.

rights, negative – right to refrain from taking a particular action.
rights, positive – right to take a particular action; may impose a duty on governments.
substantive equality – allowing different treatment if necessary to achieve equalizing effect, resulting in fairer outcomes or lived rights.
unconstitutional – contravenes the principles set out within the Constitution.

Acknowledgements

I dedicate this chapter to my "*Charter* babies" Jonathan Jacob and David Kitson, with thanks to my teachers on equality: Bev Baines, Mary Eberts, Peter Hogg, Claire L'Heureux-Dubé, Michele Landsberg, Catharine MacKinnon, Nancy Ruth and LEAF, Bruce Ryder; to my former colleagues at U. of Saskatchewan College of Law: Norm Zlotkin and Mark Carter, to Margot Hurlbert for inviting and editing this chapter, and to my indefatigable research tag team over two years: Sarah E. Sharp, Adele Domenco, Aaron Swanson and Christina Szurlej.

10

Law and Justice

Margot A. Hurlbert

At the end of this chapter, you will be able to:

- Understand the jurisprudence approach to studying the law and also think of the law as a social system
- Describe Canadian court structures, the sources of law and the difference between civil and criminal law
- Understand several perspectives on studying law as a social system
- Understand how the law interrelates to formal and substantive justice
- Build an ethical practice through the critical analysis of the law

It is important to understand that law is a social system, like any other (for example, our system of reproduction, part of which is the family, or our system of education, part of which are schools). One way societies institutionalize particular views of justice is through their legal system. The critical analysis of the institution of law allows its weaknesses, inconsistencies and inequities to be revealed, which is an important first step in not taking the justice of the legal system for granted and in advocating for social justice change.

Legal justice, or the justice that emerges from the legal system and the workings of its component parts (such as courts and written laws), is regarded by some as the ultimate expression of justice. An issue such as whether an Aboriginal person can hunt is thought dependent on various licensing acts and land ownership issues; an issue such as whether a credit company can charge 30 percent interest for cashing a paycheque is dependent on whether the law allows such a high interest rate. If it does, then according to this approach to justice, receiving $69 for a $100 paycheque is unjust while receiving $70 is just.

Wading through licensing regulations, ownership issues and credit legislation are all tasks of accessing the law. Law schools in North America study the law in this manner, as internal to itself, a rational, orderly system much like an exact science, where specific legal questions always have specific legal answers generated within the legal system. This is a "jurisprudence" approach to the study of law. Most people think of the law in this jurisprudential way, as an institution which dispenses justice in an unbiased manner, without favour or ill will. The definition of the law and legal rules begins with the state and proceeds on the assumptions that legal decision-making is rational and that legal processes are legitimate and essential to social order (Milovanovic 1988). The law is presented as a formal and coherent body of rules, doctrines and principles concerned with interpretation of acts, case readings and legal doctrines. The law constitutes itself through textual manifestations of legal decisions, judgments and opinions (Banakar 2005: 22). This is often described as the "official version of the law" (Naffine 1990: 12), and this approach informs formal justice, the first theme of justice of this book. Formal justice is partly composed of the coherent body of rules embodied in jurisprudence law.

Legal "justice" is much a broader concept than this starting point for formal justice and treating equals equally. Justice is much more than solving a problematic situation or conflict between people by applying the set of rules encompassed in the law. Justice is also constituted by considerations of substantive justice (treating unequals unequally) and ethical practice (the second and third themes of this book). In order to expand the study of law and justice, first we must recognize that the normativity, moral and philosophical perspectives reflected in the law are debatable and debated; next we must undertake a critical analysis of the law's influence on relations between people, especially in light of unequal power and social structures in society. In the example of the Aboriginal hunter, a narrow review of provincial licensing acts disregards promises of hunting rights made in the late nineteenth century through treaties, the fact that an Aboriginal hunting right pre-existed colonization and a history of oppression and colonization of Aboriginal people. These justice arguments are expanding the law to recognize Aboriginal rights previously unrecognized by the courts, and they illustrate the importance of an expanded study of legal justice from the traditional jurisprudence approach taught at law schools. Through this process, substantive justice is discovered; unequal or different situations can be treated differently. However, more than this is also needed. To truly begin to treat unequals unequally or achieve substantive justice, sometimes we need to go outside of our formal structure of legal justice. A structure of legal justice constructed by different people, such as Aboriginal people, is needed. Consider the following perspective.

Because Canadian law is taught, practised and dispensed based on the jurisprudence approach, only a limited amount of societal change can occur within the confines of the Canadian legal system. Recognizing and empowering Aboriginal people and their customs often occurs outside the legal system. Aboriginal legal scholars document their experience of attending law school and their shock at learning concepts of "property" law. An example is the state owning all land because the land was legally vacant upon discovery by Europeans, or the "doctrine of discovery" (Martin 2002:

229). Obviously Aboriginal people occupied the land at this time. Through acquiring jurisprudence legal knowledge, these scholars challenge traditional legal assumptions (Mi'kmaq people had elaborate systems of government such that the land was "occupied" not vacant) and enable the governance of Aboriginal people in Aboriginal courts. Martin writes that victories for the Mi'kmaq have been rare or marginal at best in "newcomers' courts" and that the Mi'kmaq are resisting the legal and social structures forced upon them when the first newcomers came, challenging the economic and political powers that usurped their jurisdiction and its laws of "property." By asserting Aboriginal jurisdiction (now incrementally recognized in areas such as fishing rights and child welfare), the Mi'kmaq are building a nation-to-nation relationship with Canada (244). In this way, Mi'kmaq law exists and is practised in a sphere on its own, outside of Canadian jurisprudence law.

A solid foundation in understanding legal justice includes an appreciation of formal legal justice, including how the law is created and how it is applied. It is important to also understand the components of the legal justice system, including the court system and the difference between civil and criminal matters. Understanding substantive justice (elaborated in previous chapters) is facilitated by using different theoretical perspectives to analyze the law as a social system; this chapter reviews the approaches of structural functionalism, symbolic interactionism, conflict theory, post-structuralism and feminism. These non-jurisprudencial perspectives expose differing power relations that produce and reproduce within the structure of the law. Such perspectives inform an ethical practice to start reforming the law to attain justice for the neediest in society.

The Law as a Social System

Main Points

As you read, highlight the answers to these questions:
How does the law influence people's actions?
How do people's actions and inter-relations influence the law?
How does the law reflect economic structures of society?
What are the three important characteristics of legal courts?

The law is a social structure that represents the society within which it is situated. The law creates, produces, reflects and informs interactions and relations between people. This is a critical insight for those studying justice and has been a historical focus of study by scholars like Max Weber, Emile Durkheim and Karl Marx. This insight assists in explaining why laws differ between countries and different historical periods (a focus of Emile Durkheim). The fact that divorce can now be accessed after a couple lives separately for one year (without regard to fault for marriage breakdown), and that this type of divorce was not available fifty years ago, reflects something about change in Canadian society and relations between couples.

Weber, a lawyer by training, focused on how the law affected relations between people. Weber was concerned with interactions of people and the meaning people ascribed to these interactions. He outlined the characteristics of a formal rational legal system within the basis of a modern political authority as part of a more general theory of sociology. In theorizing about order and conduct in society, Weber (1922: 319) analyzed, contrasted and distinguished "custom" (a practice valid because of practical convenience), "convention" (a practice valid through external guarantee) and "law" (a practice externally guaranteed through a specialized staff expressly in charge of compliance). These concepts form a continuum of not mutually exclusive categories, the boundaries of which are fluid and often imperceptible. A custom might be the first person walking through a door holding it open for another; a convention is having only one intimate partner at a time (the breach of which is met with disapproval but no legal sanction); and a law, not speeding or committing murder. Weber distinguished between substantive rationalization, which is based on certain values and conceptions of justice, and formal rationalization, which rests on general rules and procedures. Maintaining one monogamous intimate relationship at a time would qualify as substantive rationalization. People often regard their intimate partner's infidelity as unjust. This action would only qualify as formal rationalization if one were legally married (and breach of this rule entitled one to divorce). This distinction similarly holds between substantive and procedural justice. Formal rationalization reflects the conception of formal or procedural justice and is enshrined in law; substantive rationalization relates to substantive justice or treating people and groups of people differently to achieve justice. This justice is not always reflected in law but sometimes is.

Durkheim (1893) conceived of the law as the most important observable manifestation of the collective consciousness and its transformation. As such it was a visible symbol of social solidarity, and he used it as a methodology to study society. Although parallels can be seen to Weber's work, Durkheim concentrated on laws and behaviours of groups, as opposed to a more micro approach on how individuals interpreted specific actions. There are parallels between Durkheim's work and later analysis using a structural functionalist lens. Expanding on some of Durkheim's principles, Sorokin (1957) distinguished between official law (obligatory law norms protected and enforced by authoritative power of government) and unofficial law (or law norms not politically overseen but restricted to other groups). A similar conception was made earlier by Ehrlich (1913), who referred to the "living law" as the whole of law dominating social life (even though it may not have been posited in legal propositions and juristic law). Living law could be observed in various aspects of everyday life, whether legally recognized as such or not.

Although Marx (1848: 475) did not write specifically on the topic of legal justice, his ideas on the law within his perspective of historical materialism have been influential. As outlined in Chapter Two, Marx asserted that the economic conditions of society (the base of society) determine what type of state will develop. In a capitalist society, the state operates on behalf of the capitalist class (the bourgeoisie) to secure their economic rights and privileges and to moderate class conflict. For Marx, the state was part of what he called the superstructure of society. He similarly viewed the law and legal system as an instrument of control serving bourgeois interests. Rather than endorsing the principle of the rule of law (which holds that it is just for the law to be applied equally and fairly to all), Marx maintained that capitalist law actually enhances the conditions of inequality that exist in capitalist society. The legal system in capitalism contributes to, as well as legitimates, the inequalities that exist as a result of capitalist economic conditions. Individualized rights of freedom benefit those who own while disfavouring those who are without property. In the final analysis and at a fundamental level, the law will protect the economic interests of capitalists and the well off. Formal equality (granted in law by treating various parties who are in contract with one another or with the state as equal) contributes to developing and sustaining the economic inequalities that exist among legal subjects. Although formal legal equality is not a complete sham, it is more easily accessed by those with economic means. As such, the law takes the form of a bourgeois ideology. Its ultimate triumph is that the ideology of capitalist law becomes widely accepted, even among those members of society who are economically disadvantaged and subject to inequalities (Marx 1842). Marx laid the foundation for analyzing the law and inequality based on power imbalances in society, discussed below.

The study of law as a social system is a topic too vast to cover here. However, with some basic legal justice information, including the court structure, the distinction between civil and criminal matters, and the sources of law, we can begin such an analysis.

Structure of the Court System

If people are unable to resolve their conflicts, the ultimate forum of resolution is a court of law. At first the variety and diversity of courts may appear complex. Yet, there are really just three important court characteristics: the government creating it (provincial/territorial or federal), its place in the hierarchy of courts (whether it is a court of first instance or an appeal court) and what types of matters it can deal with (for example, criminal matters, family divorce matters or human rights complaints).

Provincial/Territorial Courts

There is considerable diversity in the ten provincial and three territorial court systems. Generally, however, there are two types of courts, those dealing with criminal matters and those dealing with all other matters (termed "civil," which is explained in more detail later). (In Nunavut, the Nunavut Court of Justice deals with both civil and criminal matters.) The names given in each province differ. For example, the civil court is the Court of Queen's Bench in Saskatchewan, Alberta, Manitoba and New Brunswick and is almost identical to the Supreme Court (trial division) in Ontario, the Northwest Territories and Yukon and the Cour Supérieur in Québec. These are the courts where trials take place in most of the matters which are not criminal and also the more serious criminal matters not dealt with by the lower criminal courts, such as murder. When a party to one of these trials believes the judge hearing the matter made an error, an appeal may be made to an appeal court. This court is called the Court of Appeal in Alberta, British Columbia, Manitoba, New Brunswick, Ontario, Québec and Saskatchewan, and the Appeal (or Appellate) Division of the Supreme Court in other provinces. Most criminal trials occur in criminal courts, termed provincial and territorial courts (although in some provinces, for example, Alberta, New Brunswick and Saskatchewan, these have been amalgamated with the superior courts).

In some instances, such as in Ontario and Saskatchewan, divisions or branches known as family courts and juvenile courts have been created to handle specific kinds of cases. Saskatchewan even has specialized courts such as criminal courts which operate in the Cree or Dene language, and many provinces have therapeutic courts for drug offenders and courts which deal exclusively with domestic violence.

Federal Courts

The only federally constituted courts in Canada are the Federal Court of Canada, the Federal Court of Appeal and the Supreme Court of Canada. The Federal Court of Canada hears and decides legal disputes arising in the federal domain, including claims against the Government of Canada and citizenship, taxation, immigration, copyright and patent issues. Appeals from this court are taken to the Federal Court of Appeal. The Supreme Court of Canada hears appeals from provincial appeal courts and from the Federal Court of Appeal and is the final judicial authority on the entire body of Canadian law, including the civil law of Québec. It is presided over by nine judges, appointed by the federal government.

Quasi-Judicial Tribunals

The federal and provincial governments also create quasi-judicial tribunals to handle specialized cases such as trade union matters and complaints arising from human rights abuses, occupational health and safety and workers' compensation. Although the details of structure and function vary from province to province, these bodies are limited to the authority invested in them by statute and do not have all of the power that a court of law would have; thus they are "quasi" or "partly" judicial. Decisions and awards by quasi-judicial bodies are in all cases subject to some review by courts of law. These bodies, which often take the form of administrative tribunals, are usually characterized by:

- a concern with some form of specialization of subject matter, for example, human rights, collective bargaining or contract terminations;
- judicial procedures in establishing facts, calling witnesses and arriving at conclusions; and
- the authority to decide the dispute.

In a strictly jurisprudence approach to the study of law, the rules regarding court hierarchy are essential. The Supreme Court of Canada is the highest court in the land, and its judgements are binding on all other courts. Similarly, within a province or territory, quasi-judicial tribunals must follow decisions of courts of law, and all courts follow decisions of courts of appeal. A broader study of justice recognizes this normative ordering of hierarchical decision-making but does not take it for granted. Rather, an alternative approach identifies and studies the inconsistencies, resistance and restructuring occurring between the lived experience of the people participating in the various places where disputes are resolved and the way in which those unofficial forums of dispute resolution and courts visualize or construct those lives and relationships. Some scholars have termed this broader approach to studying the social system of law "legal pluralism" (Merry 1988, 2008), and it has been used to analyze systems of legal ordering in relation to tuna courts in Tokyo (Feldman 2006) and business instruments (letters of credit, export credit insurance, etc.) in the United States (Levit 2005). Other possible new areas of study might be the lived experience of people participating in the therapeutic drug or domestic violence courts, both relatively recent creations in the legal system.

The origin of legal pluralism is in the study of colonial societies (Merry 1988: 874). In the imperial/colonial context, many scholars reject the law-centredness of traditional studies of jurisprudence law and argue that not all law takes place in courts. Researchers document the symbols of law operating in unofficial forums of dispute resolution incorporating the law and legal traditions of the colonized. As an example, Pospisil (1979) studied the people of New Guinea and wrote a classic text on Indigenous law.

The Court System of Canada

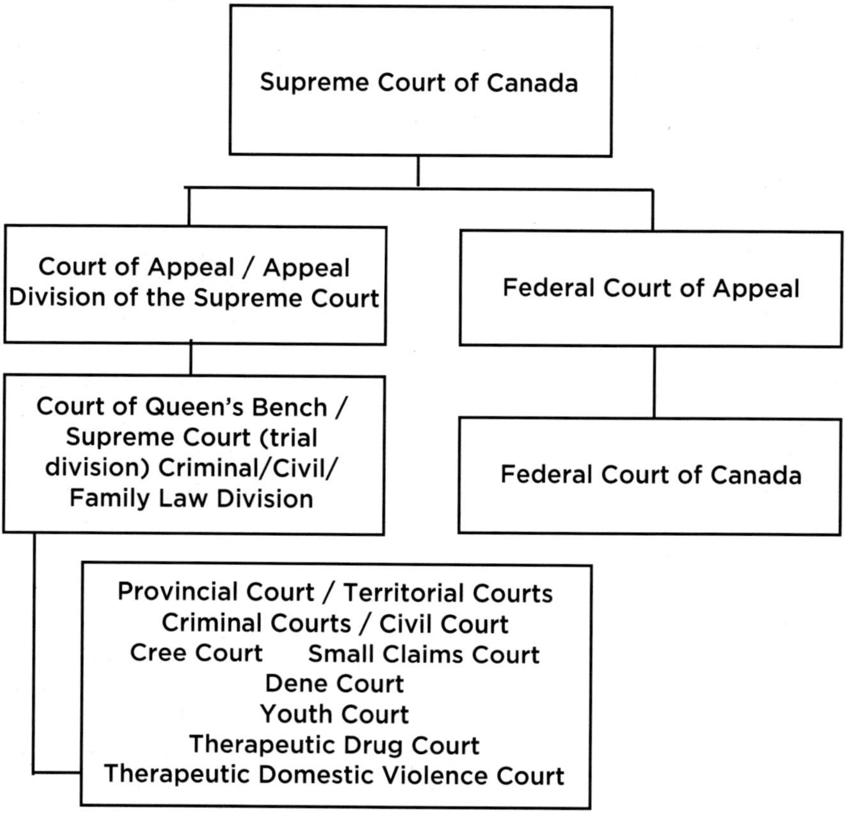

Criminal Law and Civil Law

Courts are divided between those that deal with criminal cases and those that deal with all other matters, called civil cases. The legal system makes a sharp distinction between criminal and civil matters. A jurisprudence approach to the determination of what is "criminal" is based on Constitutional law. The federal government has the official legal authority to decide what is or is not criminal, pursuant to section 91(27) of the *British North America Act, 1867* or Canada's Constitution. Most of our criminal law is embodied in the *Criminal Code.* One Canadian authority states: "Criminal law can be defined in many ways but it is essentially a prohibition coupled with a penalty" (Beckton 1982: 2). MacKay (1984: 204) states: "Criminal matters involve disputes between individuals and the state." The gist of these definitions is that society, through government, determines what is harmful or undesirable and uses the sanctions of fines and/or imprisonment to enforce its view. In terms of the legal system, criminal misbehaviour is behaviour that is deemed in law to be the most harmful to individuals and society. Thus, the state actually defines these behaviours as transgressions against the state itself.

In studying justice, however, an additional concern is analyzing what particular actions by which particular actors are designated by society as "criminal" or "not criminal." Or as civil rather than criminal. Why is loitering in a public place a crime? What is the socio-economic status of people who are charged with this offence? Why is it a crime to carry a concealed weapon in Canada but not the United States? A broader study of justice concerns itself with exploring these questions and how dominant, powerful groups and interests determine what activities and actions are illegal. Consider the following examples of what our society deems criminal and not criminal.

Like any aspect of the law, determining what is or is not a crime is an exercise in social construction. The delineation of something as "criminal" is based on social norms and power and effected by a combination of social, actors including judges and legislatures (see the Sources of Law section below). Thinking critically about what constitutes a "crime" requires careful consideration of what harms are done and what is morally reprehensible.

Corporate "Death"

Individuals comprise the overwhelming majority of cases proceeding through the criminal justice system. Occasionally an individual is charged for a crime committed in the course of their employment or business, such as fraud in a business transaction or criminal breach of trust as a result of wrongfully taking money. Examples include better known cases such as Martha Stewart and Sir Conrad Black. Corporations, although regarded as "individuals" according to the law, are rarely, if ever, charged for crimes. Realistically, given that a corporation's main and primary goal is the accumulation of profit, and not a moral existence, this warrants further exploration. Here are a few specific cases:

Asbestos: The health dangers of asbestos have been known since 1900 (exposure is linked with potentially fatal illness, scarring the lungs, stifling breath and impeding the flow of oxygen to the blood) and have been documented in medical journals as far back as 1935 as linked to cancer (Snider 2006: 187). Yet, with full knowledge of these risks, companies continue to mine asbestos, largely in Québec, exposing their workers and customers to health risks. Is the killing of people through exposure to asbestos any different from killing someone during a robbery?

Bhopal, India, and Union Carbide: In 1984 a gas leaked from storage at the plant and killed over 2,000 people and maimed over half a million more. The company, Union Carbide, cut costs, first by choosing this location where safety standards were lower than those of the United States. Then the company violated safety regulations, failed to train employees, failed to respond to warning signs and tried to deny culpability (Rajan 2001: 381).

In neither of these cases were there criminal charges. Why do we as a society not think of these actions by these corporations as "criminal"?

Most would agree that acts of violence and killing cannot be condoned and are correctly labelled (and codified) as "crime." However, consider harm in our society a bit more expansively. How many people are harmed by cigarette smoking, workplace accidents or stress, faulty products and unsafe medication? If our definition of crime is harmful behaviour or acts that cause harm to people, why are these harms not considered crimes?

Using a conflict theoretical perspective, one would argue that our law turns a blind eye to these behaviours because they relate to powerful entities in our society, large corporations. Although we like to think that everyone is treated equally before the law, the reality is that powerful groups and interests — individuals and corporations — escape the full force of the law. In this way, the law perpetuates the power structures in our society and makes it appear natural that our criminal justice system only deals with individuals killing individuals.

In a criminal case the Crown prosecutor must prove the guilt of the accused person beyond a reasonable doubt. This is not easy to define. However, reference is usually made to moral or honest certainty that a person is guilty. The usual caveat is that moral certainty does not mean absolute certainty. For instance, accused are often convicted on the basis of circumstantial or "surrounding" evidence. This means there was no evidence directly proving that they did the crime (such as a witness who saw them commit the specific offence) but rather there was evidence that they were in the vicinity or had the opportunity and motive to commit the offence. If the judge or jury is convinced based on this evidence and believe there is no reasonable doubt as to the accused's guilt, they may convict. This occurred in the case of David Milgaard. Without any direct evidence linking him to the murder of Gail Miller, he was convicted and served twenty-three years in prison. He merely had previous interaction with the police for minor offences, a bad reputation and had been in the vicinity at the time of the murder. In the summer of 1997, DNA evidence provided positive proof of his innocence (Anderson 1998: 62).

Civil law and civil cases are defined as misbehaviour that is not criminal. These cases are diverse and range from family matters, such as divorce and child custody, to disputes about trademarks, wills or wrongful dismissals from jobs. In a civil case, there is no "accused," but rather a plaintiff, or complainant, and a defendant. In these cases, the state acts to facilitate resolving a conflict between parties. The state establishes civil courts for the resolution of these disputes (courts of Queen's Bench or superior courts) and often imposes mandatory mediation at the outset in an attempt to streamline the settlement of the dispute.

In a civil case, the plaintiff need not prove beyond a reasonable doubt that the defendant is guilty (the standard of a criminal case). Instead, a lesser burden of proof is required, based on the balance of probabilities; that is, the court must answer the question of whether the allegations made by the plaintiff are probably true. An example of a civil case is a court action against a doctor for negligently performing a medical procedure. If it can be proven with greater than 50 percent probability that the doctor did not meet an acceptable standard for a medical doctor, then the doctor will be found liable. The jurisprudence approach to law assumes that both parties are more or less of equal strength. As a result there is thought to be less need to protect the litigants, and rules concerning admissibility of evidence may not be as strict as in criminal cases. The reality is, though, that many people do not have the resources to protect themselves through civil law, which can be exceedingly expensive. Injured patients, for example, almost always have less money, less stamina and access to fewer resources (such as expert medical witnesses) than doctors, who are covered by medical insurance companies and assisted by medical colleges and associations. More generally, corporations are protected more by civil law than individual citizens. Many can and do break the (civil) law, but the individuals they injure are constrained from acting by the cost of civil litigation.

Making matters worse, legitimate political activities by social activists challenging unjust actions of corporations and governments have been the subject of lawsuits by corporations and governments in an attempt to prevent opposition. These lawsuits are termed "strategic litigation against public participation," or "slapps." Slapps are civil lawsuits alleging that the activities of protesters and members of social movements have somehow caused the private corporation or government official some damage or injury. Slapps divert attention and resources away from the "real" public issue and potentially costs the defendants many dollars in legal fees (Sheldrick 2004: 49). Examples of slapps include lawsuits for civil damages for loss of reputation or court orders to prevent further communications that private corporations or government officials have alleged are "defamatory." One such lawsuit resulted when protesters handed out pamphlets titled, "What's Wrong With McDonald's? – Everything they don't want you to know" outside of McDonald's restaurants (50).

Even though criminal law and civil law are distinctly different from each other, an act by an individual may constitute at the same time both a crime and a civil wrong, or "tort," in legal terms. For example, a person committing assault against another might be charged with a crime under the *Criminal Code* and might also be sued by the victim in civil court for compensation. The concerns, proceedings and results would be very different in each case. In a criminal case, the concern relates to the accused's duty to the public to obey the law and keep peace and order in society; in a civil case the concern relates to the duty of the offender not to cause injury to another

O.J. Simpson

Consider the case of Nicole Brown and O.J. Simpson. Nicole Brown suffered violence and abuse at the hands of her ex-husband during her marriage and after her separation and divorce. O.J. Simpson was accused of murdering Nicole Brown and her friend, Ron Goldman. The criminal court found O.J. Simpson not guilty. However, the civil action by Nicole Brown's and Ron Goldman's families for wrongful death was successful. O.J. Simpson was ordered to pay damages of 33.5 million dollars (O.J. Simpson 2008).

Why would the criminal courts find O.J. Simpson not guilty of murder, while in the civil court he was found guilty of wrongful death? The reason for this has to do with the burden of proof. In the criminal trial, the prosecution had to prove that O.J. Simpson committed the murder beyond a reasonable doubt. In the civil trial, the standard of proof was only on the balance of probabilities — that is, it was easier to prove that O.J. Simpson probably killed Brown and Goldman than it was to prove that beyond a reasonable doubt.

Now consider this case in the context of social justice, not as just a jurisprudence matter. Nicole Brown was a battered spouse. As a spouse, the legal system failed to protect her from her battering husband; as a divorcee, the family law system failed to protect her and her friend from her murdering ex-husband; as a family, the law failed to provide her children and parents with justice in finding anyone guilty of her and her friend's murder. Consider whether this case illustrates the failure of our laws to regulate behaviour (for example, domestic abuse leading to murder) or whether the law and the entire legal system protect men over women. In this particular case the interests were those of a popular sports star.

individual and to pay damages when found guilty of such action. In criminal proceedings, the focus is on the behaviour of the accused, and a conviction may be decided even when no injury was caused to the victim. In a civil case, the focus of the proceedings is on both the offender and the victim and, for example, whether injury resulted to the victim, whether there was contributory cause on the part of the victim and the extent of both. These considerations are all very important in determining whether the plaintiff (victim) is allowed to succeed or whether the defendant (offender) has a right to dismissal of the lawsuit.

Summary Points

Events can have both criminal and civil consequences.

The law can be approached from a jurisprudence perspective or from a more critical perspective of critical legal scholars and feminists uncovering the power differentials of different actors in society.

The existence of corporate crime, when contrasted with the demographic of our poor people in prison, reflects the unequal power structures of our society.

Crime and Intent

In general every crime has a physical element (*actus reus*, that is, guilty or wrongful act) and a mental element (*mens rea*, that is, guilty mind). If either element is missing, then no crime is committed. The *actus reus* of a crime relates to the conduct of an accused, the consequences of that conduct and the surrounding circumstances of the conduct. In *mens rea,* the focus is on such considerations as whether the accused had the mental intent to commit the crime, that is, whether the accused foresaw the consequences of the wrongful act, was aware of the contingent circumstances and intended to cause the consequences. For example, if a person hits another without that other person's consent, they will be guilty of assault only if they intended or meant to hit the other person. If the act of hitting was an accident, no intent, *mens rea*, would exist and no criminal assault would have been committed.

In addition to intention and knowledge, a third type of *mens rea* relates to recklessness. The Supreme Court of Canada has held that a person is reckless when that person foresees the possibility of a harmful consequence and then takes the unreasonable risk that harm will not result. Stated another way, a person must be aware of the danger involved and if that person does not have awareness or foresight regarding consequences, then that person is not reckless. In addition, if the risk is reasonable to take or justifiable, the person will not be held to be reckless (*Creighton v. R.*, 1993). Hence, there is a great deal of difference between a responsible doctor who operates on a patient who, consequently, dies and an irresponsible hunter who target shoots in a public park and, consequently, kills a child at play.

The intent for recklessness and the *mens rea* previously described are called subjective *mens rea* in that it is the accused's state of mind that is important. It is for the trier of facts (judge or jury) to determine what was in the mind of the accused at the relevant time. This is contrasted with an objective intent, which is a determination of what a reasonable person in the accused's situation would have or might have believed. The jurisprudence approach to law and those practising it resolutely assert that judges and juries are capable of hearing evidence and determining what the accused did or did not believe (Roach 2009: 154). Approaching law in a critical manner and analyzing it as a social structure makes one question this (Norrie 1998: 717). How is a judge capable of determining exactly what was in an accused's mind at the time of the offence? Would a judge not always be "objectively" judging the accused or applying an "outside" standard, a standard of conduct influenced by the background and biases of the judge?

The Sources of Law

The major sources of Canadian law include the Constitution, regular statutory law (including regulations and policy) and common law. The people who actually create the law within these sources are the Canadian Parliament, the provincial legislatures and the courts. Parliament and the provincial legislatures make the law by passing statutes; courts make law through judicial decision (what we term "common law"). A jurisprudence approach simply takes these sources of law for granted — that they represent the consensus of society on what should be deemed misbehaviour and the degree of that misbehaviour. However, the discussion of how law is created in the study of justice requires deeper consideration. The law is developed within a society; thus, all aspects of society, particularly its social structure will come into play. Hence, the law must be the product of the power structure of society and develops through struggle, activism and social change. Different kinds of law may not necessarily represent actual differences in harm to individuals and society.

Constitutional Law

A country's Constitution defines the powers and limits of power that can be exercised by different levels and branches of government. It is the foundation of a country's political and legal system. It is contained in statute, so is part statutory law, but it is not "regular" statutory law because of its importance and the difficulty entailed in amending the Constitutional statutory documents.

After the occupation of the land of Aboriginal people by French and British colonists, Canada became a country, a nation state, by an act of the Parliament of Great Britain. It is noteworthy that there was no consent or participation in this by Aboriginal people. On April 17, 1982, the Constitution of Canada was patriated (or brought home from Britain). A number of important statutes, for example, the *Constitution Act, 1867* (formerly called the *British North America Act,* 1867), continue to form an important part of our Constitution. These documents (which include some thirty acts and orders) declare the Constitution of Canada to be the supreme law of Canada. They also affirm Canada's dual legal system, with provinces having jurisdiction in relation to some matters, such as property and civil rights, and the federal government over other matters, such as peace, order and good government and the criminal law. The Constitution also affirms Aboriginal rights, such as those related to the historical occupancy and use of the land by Aboriginal peoples, treaty rights and agreements between federal/provincial/territorial governments and Aboriginal groups in relation to self-government.

The *Constitution Act, 1867*, which established Canada as a federal state, continues to include in its preamble a statement that Canada is to have a Constitution similar in principle to that of the United Kingdom. This one single phrase covers a vital part of Canada's Constitution. Consequently, British Constitutional principles have been read into the *Constitution Act, 1982* as required, and Canada is full heir to British common law principles, conventions and prerogatives. For example, Canadian laws, both civil and criminal (outside of Québec), fall within the traditions of British jurisprudence; the pre-eminence of statute law over common law, or legislative supremacy, was to apply in Canada as it did in Britain; and there was no need for the *Constitution Act, 1982* to mention how our prime minister, cabinet, political parties or civil service would function. An important point to be emphasized in this context is that the *British North American Act, 1867* is not dead but still very much alive as the new (in-name-only) *Constitution Act, 1982*. Canada's Constitution, therefore, continues to be partially written and partially unwritten.

In a Western democracy such as Canada the Constitution is the final or ultimate source of law. It provides a legal framework for legislative enactments and judicial decisions at all levels of jurisdiction. Unlike regular statutory law, the written Constitution can only be amended in accordance with a formula agreed to by the federal and provincial governments.

In addition to a new *Canadian Charter of Rights and Freedoms*, the *Constitution Act, 1982* added other new provisions to our Constitution, including an affirmation of existing rights of Aboriginal peoples, the principle of equalization and the strengthening of provincial powers over resources. The addition of the *Canadian Charter of Rights and Freedoms* was important for it gave certain rights Constitutional status, protecting them from amendment and infringement by governments. The enactment of the *Canadian Charter of Rights and Freedoms* as part of Canada's written Constitution (Sections 1–34 of the *Constitution Act, 1982*) emphasizes society's increasing attention to diverse values, interpersonal tensions and fundamental rights and freedoms for all Canadians. The *Charter* protects fundamental freedoms (religion, expression, association), democratic rights (voting), mobility rights (entering, remaining or leaving the country), legal rights (life, liberty, security of a person, right to a lawyer), equality rights, language rights (English and French), minority language educational rights and Aboriginal rights. Significantly, the *Canadian Charter of Rights and Freedoms* does not include economic rights.

Statute Law

"Statute law," or written or enacted law, did not exist in British jurisprudence prior to the thirteenth century. Only with the granting of the *Magna Carta Charter* and the abolition of serfdom did statute law begin to constitute an important part of English law. In the Canadian context, statute or statutory law refers to legislative enactment, for example, the passing of an act which makes legal provision for something to be done or not to be done. Statute laws may be enacted by a government to cover circumstances not covered in existing law, to change existing law or to make existing laws more certain and ascertainable. Statutes achieve the goals of making the law accessible and written. However, the challenge is that it is very difficult to write laws which cover every circumstance and situation. As a result, judges must interpret and apply the law to various eventualities. These decisions form the basis of the common law.

Common Law

Canada, with the exception of Québec, is a "common law" state. British common law began to evolve soon after the Norman conquest of 1066, and an early Norman monarch, King Henry II, who reigned during the twelfth century, is regarded as its founder. King Henry sent judges throughout the realm to service the king's courts. The judges would travel through the country holding court in the larger villages and trading centres. The route was known as a "circuit." The appointed judges worked together, compared cases and made group decisions, thereby establishing a consistent law in the interests of the king. This coincided with the development of a penal code and prosecution of "criminal" matters on behalf of the king or state. These circuit judges began a process for the development and evolvement of one law for all of England, that is, common to all, and hence, called the common law. British common law has continued to evolve over the centuries and was brought to Canada and the United States by colonists. Hence, the common law system is shared by a number of countries, including Australia and New Zealand. Although the basic laws of these countries have similarities, many differences have evolved.

The common law is much more than an accumulation of judicial decisions over time, usually referred to as "case law." The common law is also referred to as "unwritten law," which is a misnomer because judicial decisions and precedents are systematically recorded and organized. Case law is only unwritten in the sense that it is not enacted by the legislature. However, in a technical sense, the written record — the case law — is not the law; it is only evidence of how the law applies in a specific case. In another case circumstances may be different, and a different result may occur in the application of the law. It is this feature that makes the common law dynamic and elastic, rather than rigid and unadaptable to changing times and conditions. In this manner a certain amount of substantive justice is meted out in the case law as unequal cases or those of differing circumstances are handled differently.

Where Does the Law Come From?

This trilogy of sources of law is where law is derived. A jurisprudence perspective assumes that these three sources create a logical body of rules independent of surrounding social institutions. In philosophy, there are at least three ideas about where the law comes from. These ideas have some similarities to the three sources of law just discussed. Legal positivism views the law as being created and written by governments (this is similar to the source of statute law); legal interpretation holds that the law is interpreted by judges (this is similar to the source of common law); and finally, natural law holds that the law is true for all societies or countries and has universal, unchanging and everlasting application.

In past times (such as those of Aristotle and Aquinas), some believed in the idea of "natural law." Natural law is that arising in nature or that which naturally is or ought to be. The intersection between law and morals can be described as "natural law." The Roman lawyer Cicero, drawing on Stoic philosophy, identified the following three components of natural law:

(1) true law is right reason in agreement with nature, universal application, unchanging and everlasting;
(2) it is a sin to alter or repeal or abolish natural law;
(3) God is the author and enforcing Judge of natural law. (Wacks 2006: 3)

Over time the idea of natural law has waxed and waned and been embellished. Most recently, resurgence has occurred with the United Nations' *Universal Declaration of Human Rights* and the *Canadian Charter of Rights and Freedoms*. As we learned in our introduction to international law, in order to enforce international law on a country whose government is not complying, it is necessary to regard this law as inherent and binding on everyone in this world, regardless whether the country's particular government has passed laws contradictory to this law. An example is Hitler passing the Nuremberg laws to deny Jewish people rights. This denial of rights and the apathy of people to it resulted in the eventual genocide of Jewish people by Nazi Germany in World War II. International rules and laws, which are based on "natural law" (as well as various international treaties) making genocide a criminal act, overrode the laws passed by Hitler in Germany. This example is illustrative of the tension existing between the three sources of law for philosophers, common law, statute law and natural law, which are still debated by philosophy and legal scholars today (Roach 2001).

A Canadian example of the tension of these ideas of the sources of law can be seen in the famous case of *R. v. Morgentaler* (1988) (the case which legalized abortion). The *Criminal Code* clearly made it a criminal offence to terminate a pregnancy unless the procedural requirements of the section (which required the approval of a committee at a hospital) were followed. This section was challenged on the basis of s. 7 of the *Canadian Charter of Rights and Freedoms*. It was argued that this provision of the *Criminal Code* denied women their right to life, liberty and security of the person, as the decision about whether she could have an abortion was placed with a committee and therefore inconsistent with her rights.

The Supreme Court of Canada had the task of reconciling these two laws: the *Charter* right to security and the *Criminal Code* restriction of abortion. When judges perform tasks such as the reconciliation of legal principles which results in a statute law being rendered ineffective, this is often termed as "judicial activism." The actual dispute in the Morgentaler case was over having to obtain approval of a committee for an abortion instead of a woman being empowered to make her own decisions. The latter principle and the unequal access to abortion across Canada for women resulted in the abolishment of the sections of the *Criminal Code* requiring committee approval. The Supreme Court of Canada did invite Parliament to amend the *Criminal Code* and introduce a crime of having an abortion which would meet *Charter* standards. This has not been done. As with many justice issues, this legal decision had strong support from women's organizations, yet strong opposition from groups supporting the right to life of the unborn. The court's exercise of its power of legal interpretation doesn't preclude the government's ability to pass law and thereby exercise its power of legal positivism.

Socio-legal scholars approach the issue of where laws come from, or their source, differently. American legal scholar Holmes rejected this jurisprudence approach (which he termed "legal formalism") and the proposition that judges merely find the law in legal codes, which they apply in specific cases. He recognized that judges contribute to formulating law by selecting the relevant principles and precedents of law to take into account when deciding the outcomes of cases. As a result, the judges' normative conceptions — their values, beliefs and experience — influence the law. Pound (1942, 1959) regarded the law as a form of social control and an institution which could be adapted to respond to changing societal conditions.

Another view of the sources of law can be found in the political economy and philosophy of Marx. Unlike Pound, Marx did not view the law as an institution which could be changed in order to change society. For Marx, the economic relations of society, which created and perpetuated the unequal power relations in society, required transformation. Once economic change occurred, the law or the juridical superstructure would be changed. Yet, Marx saw the state and thus the laws that it created as serving the long-term interests of the capitalist class. In the end, for Marx, theory and praxis (practice) have to come together in order to explain as well as change the world (Marx 1869). More recent conflict theorists expand this thinking to recognize that the law is a reflection of the social arrangements of power in which some groups are marginalized based on social factors and locations determined by such things as age, sex and racialization. These marginalized groups are much more likely to find themselves acting outside the law and/or being labelled as outside of the law and as "criminals." Abolishing inequalities of wealth and poverty and these social factors affecting life chances must occur if the root causes of crime are to be addressed; for these theorists, crime is that behaviour that is seen as problematic within the social power arrangements of the time (Taylor and Young 1988: 282).

In summary, the law comes from the legislatures and Parliament, which write and pass laws (the view of the legal positivist). The law is also made by judges as they perform their task of deciding cases, just as we saw with the Morgentaler case. Natural law reflects the idea that some laws arise and exist in a universal unchanging manner based on everlasting morals. No one position is correct or incorrect. In a jurisprudence approach, law comes from all three sources.

Self Test

With respect to abortion, what are the different perspectives of people on the topic and how can the courts and Parliament reconcile them?
How does the jurisprudence view of the law differ from the view that the law is a social system?
Does the concept of "natural law" have influence in society today?

Perspectives on Law and Society

Main Points

As you read, highlight the answers to these questions:
Which perspective analyzes the law in terms of power?
How can the law be analyzed as a discourse?
What examples illustrate how the law reflects society?

In the social study of the law many perspectives can be utilized. The various socio-political approaches to the structure and nature of the legal system more or less emphasize or reject a jurisprudence approach. As well, each perspective tends to lean towards either formal or substantive justice, yet all try to explain why our legal system takes the shape it does and whether or not that system is just.

Structural Functionalism

A structural functionalist perspective of the law uses a society-as-organism metaphor to illustrate the law. Key social institutions are needed for society to operate effectively, and the law (statutes, the court system, etc.) is one such institution. The law resolves the myriad of social conflicts. All societies are a combination of functions and dysfunctions. For instance, a family is a social institution, and there are dysfunctional family relationships and also functional ones. Generally over time, dysfunctions are alleviated, and institutions like the family or the law tend toward equilibrium. The law is thought to remedy dysfunction and bring any conflicts which are dysfunctional to society into alignment with societal consensus. The law does not function so much to impose one group's will on others but is seen to control, reconcile and mediate the diverse and conflicting interests of individuals and groups within society in order to maintain harmony and social integration (Vago

1994: 18). Both Pound and Durkheim, discussed earlier, are structural functionalists because of their grand macro theories of law as an institution and its place in society.

One particular legal systems theorist, Luhmann (1993), envisioned the law as a closed system (meaning a system without external influences). Luhmann endorsed the view that the practice of law and dispensation of justice through the law was completely self referential, based on statutes, legal decisions and reasoning, such that there were no outside influences. Even new scientific methods of evidence such as DNA testing didn't exist within the law until a judge determined that the methods were credible and applicable in a particular case. Luhmann's conclusions are based on the specialized actors and institutions of the law and utilize a similar logic to the jurisprudence view of law.

There are many problems with the structural functionalist perspective of the law. First, social values are rarely uniform. Interpersonal conflict is generally rooted in differing values, priorities and interests. This view also fails to explain social inequality in our society. By assuming a relatively uniform standard of values and interests, it fails to take into account the plight of those who are poor, marginalized and discriminated against. Not only can it not take into account social inequality, as it has no contribution to analyzing power dynamics in society, and it also cannot explain social change. The use of this perspective often only "reifies" (ratifies and reproduces) current laws and practices (that is, functionalists take the "official version of law" — that law is just and unbiased — for granted) or calls for harsher laws to bring dysfunctional behaviour into alignment. As well, the structural functionalist perspective assumes that all people can access the legal system to partake in its justice; the reality is that access to expensive lawyers and courts is really only available to the wealthy. However, the structural functionalist perspective does emphasize mediation and reconciliation, often used in labour-management disputes and negotiations, and other court processes, a significant component of many Western democratic societies. This perspective emphasizes a formal justice perspective and is akin to a jurisprudence approach to studying law.

Symbolic Interactionism

Expanding on Durkheim's ideas on the law as a manifestation of collective consciousness and Ehrlich's ideas, discussed earlier in the chapter, Cotterrell (1996: 29) regards the law as a social structure, both shaping and being shaped by the society in which it operates. Seen this way, the law is more than a set of codified legal rules but rather a "living law," or a set of rules actually followed by individuals in social life. Stated another way, there is what is termed an "official version of the law," but within society another structure, often called the "living law," is not only greatly influenced by the law but also informs such official endeavours as law reform. An example can be found in the highly technical area of water rights. The determination of water right priorities can be made with a technical, legalistic review of interests, dates of licences, types of use, etc. However, a study of actual behaviour in times of water conflict (or disagreement over who has priority to water during times of shortage when all people can't receive their water share) found that rules as to water priorities were largely ignored (Hurlbert 2009). This research included interviews with people affected by the water shortage and ascertained the "living law," or norms and behaviours, which resolved the conflict. Community practices of sharing and maximization of benefits were found to predominate This study shows that the official version of the law may be very different from the living law.

Although symbolic interactionism illustrates discrepancies between law in practice and its official version, it fails to analyze power differentials or provide any praxis to remedy the unequal power relations. In the water research study, an affected First Nation was omitted from the dialogue respecting water (Hurlbert 2009a: 238). In fact, from a jurisprudence, or "official version of law" viewpoint, Aboriginal water rights have not been recognized (Laidlaw 2010: 2; *Tsuu T'ina First Nation* v. *Alberta*), and as such the Crown or federal government "owns" all of the water (Hurlbert 2009b: 47) and continues to marginalize and silence Aboriginal people. Exploring the living experience of law, or the reality of social practices of water sharing, and comparing this with the official version of the law only highlights the marginalized space of Aboriginal people. Power imbalance is more aptly addressed through the conflict perspective.

Conflict

In the 1960s and 1970s, building on Marxian ideas and concepts, the analysis of social control and criminal law as important aspects of criminalization emerged. Instrumental Marxists see capitalists as having direct access to those who pass statute laws in the legislatures and Parliament because of connections among the elite. Structural Marxists see this influence as resulting because of the predominance of the economy (with the capitalists and the state actors all pursuing the advancement of the economy and maximization of profits as goals). The result of these pressures is that most often laws are passed which benefit the upper classes. Hunt (1981), for one, developed a comprehensive Marxist perspective of the law by questioning the extent to which major justice or legal ideals have not been realized in capitalist societies. Although our society espouses the idea that any person through enough hard work and determination can succeed, the reality is that the very poor people in society have limited opportunity to change their life circumstances (see Chapter Three). Hunt studied the contribution of the law as a social system, generally regarded as fair and equal, to this oppression. The starting point of Marxist analysis is not the immediate form of the law — the statutes, common law, system of courts, rules of trials and so on — which is fair on its face. Rather, the law is conceptualized in the context of a class-divided and unequal society and is viewed as reproducing the stratification of society (to use the terms of Chapter Three), involving a continuous process whereby the oppressive structures of society are shaped and reshaped. These law-inequality processes occur within specific socio-historical circumstances. The law functions as a means of domination, perpetuating the hegemony of societal structures among the social institutions and practices involved in the legal system (Hunt 1993). In simple terms, from this perspective, both what comes to be defined in law as criminal and how the criminal system operates, in the end, protect the interests of the economically dominant groups/classes. Recall the discussion above asking why behaviours of corporations that cause death are treated not as criminal but rather as violating less important regulatory laws. In a conflict analysis approach, the law/legal system in an unjust and unequal society cannot by definition be just, even if it appears to be.

Post-Structuralism

A newer perspective on the law that has emerged from the conflict tradition (more precisely from a sympathetic critique of the conflict tradition) and is based largely on the insights of Michel Foucault is post-structuralism, which sees the law is a site through which social power operates (Comack and Balfour 2004). This theoretical perspective sheds light on the perpetuation of inequality in our society. Post-structuralists view the jurisprudence approach to the law as a reproduction of dominant thinking about the social world and a perpetuation of idealized liberalism, with its preoccupation with rights of the individual. They see judges as preserving social inequality in their decision-making, rationalized by references to precedent case law (the common law) — which simply refers to an already flawed system of "justice." The prolonged preoccupation with individual rights, which is the focus of jurisprudence, fails to show how individuals are a product of both the socio-economic forces and the legal authority that put them before the law to begin with (MacDonald 2002: 31).

A post-structural perspective focuses on the way power operates through the language of the law and its practices. It compares and contrasts legal discourses (court transcripts, statutes, written court decisions, that is, internally constructed by the law) with social discourses (or institutional practices external to the law). This analysis shows that peoples' lived experience of discrimination, violence and injustice is often covered over by legal discourse. The key aspect of this analysis is that law is shown to be part of the social process through which inequality is perpetuated. Stated another way, the ways that laws are made and enforced, in the long run, protects the interests of powerful groups in society.

As an example, Razack (2002) analyzed the language or discourse in the

1995 trial of the men who murdered Pamela George, a Saulteaux (Ojibway) Nation woman. The victim is referred to as the "hooker" or prostitute, and other than for a few moments when one witness remembered her as a nice person and the mother of two children who did crafts and could cook, Pamela George never left the racially bounded space of prostitution and degeneracy when referred to during the trial. In contrast, the accused, Steven Kummerfield and Alex Ternowetsky, two White, athletic college boys, never left the place of White respectability, being referred to instead as "boys who did pretty darn stupid things" (148). The ultimate expression

The Law and Wealthy People

Elected officials often meet with constituents, interest groups and the public to discuss issues that the government is or should be considering and debating, including various laws. Instrumental and structural Marxists see this process as resulting in the powerful more often than not having their interests taken into account, often to the detriment of the rest of society. Consider the following examples:

In the modern banking system, there have always been laws preventing banks from using their depositors' money to engage in high risk financial speculation. But, in the two most recent depressions, those laws were changed. In 1910, representatives of the two most powerful banks in the United States met with the president and convinced him to go against the recommendations of his solicitor general and allow laws facilitating the speculation of banks in stock trading. These banks effectively controlled portfolios worth, in today's dollars, 850 billion dollars. These banks then became involved in increasingly risky stock market speculation which only a couple years earlier would have been illegal. As those risky stocks began to crumble in 1929, so did the banks which had been speculating with depositors' money, resulting in the Great Depression. The CEO of one of the banks continued to earn his salary of five million per annum through 1930–1932 (McQuaig and Brooks 2010).

Again in the late 1990s, banks and financial institutions flagrantly violated these same laws prohibiting their involvement in risky speculation in stocks and other sorts of financial investments and instruments, such as subprime mortgages and credit default swaps. Regulators not only failed to take any action, but in 1999, through the early part of the 2000s, after much vigorous lobbying by banks and financial corporations, governments around the world (but especially in the U.S.) repealed many of those financial regulations (this is known as deregulation — one of the outcomes of neo-conservative strategy). This eventually resulted in the subprime mortgage recession of 2008, with massive layoffs and the loss for many Americans of their homes. Many of the main lobbyists for these changes to the laws on banking were the same financial institutions that required and received the lion's share of the massive $1 trillion bailout in the U.S. Orchestrators such as John Paulson took advantage of this and emerged making 3.7 billion dollars. The deregulation that financiers like Paulson pushed so hard for legalized financial activities which only a few years earlier would have been illegal (McQuaig and Brooks 2010).

of Kummerfield's place of privilege is his reply to the Crown prosecutor when asked why he left town after his actions: "I really didn't want to be arrested or anything like that just because there are so many opportunities I had to be successful" (149). No regret was expressed for the loss of life and murder of Pamela George. Ultimately Kummerfield and Ternowetsky were sentenced to six and a half years in prison with credit for the twenty months served awaiting trial.

Similarly, Smart (1989) used the process of a rape trial to illustrate how people's experiences are translated within the legal process to become "legal relevance." Rape from the victim's standpoint is a terrifying ordeal and an experience of humiliation, degradation and violation. When testifying during the trial, the woman's experience is sifted through by the prosecutor and defence counsel to ascertain legally relevant "facts" for the determination of the guilt of the accused. Issues such as whether the woman was previously of chaste character and whether she consented by her actions (such as the manner of her dress) become the battleground of the lawyers, with the woman and her body the stuff of evidence and the purpose of the trial the ultimate disqualification of women's experiences (33). This post-structuralist approach to analyzing justice targets the law's power to define and disqualify; such an analysis uses the discourses of the law to deconstruct it. Exposing how the law operates within relationships of power and powerlessness can facilitate the emergence of a law reform strategy to assist the marginalized (164).

Smart's and Razack's work illustrates the context within which law operates in cases involving oppressed and marginalized people. Through studies such as these, sites of oppression can be identified. In this way, the dominant discourse of the official version of the law and the law's impartiality, neutrality and objectivity can be challenged and possibilities for substantive justice illuminated. Once law's mechanisms of power are revealed, then targeted actions to advance an ethical practice of leximin (the third theme of this book) can occur.

Feminism

The feminist perspective of the law has existed since the nineteenth century. Like the conflict and post-structural perspectives, it challenges the jurisprudence perspective that law is inherently just and impartial (Boyd and Sheehy 1989: 255). In analyzing the law's role in perpetuating inequality in society, Naffine (1990: 12) argues that what she calls "the official version of the law" is not coherent, logical, internally consistent and rational. In fact Naffine notes that the law reflects the "priorities of the dominant patriarchal social order" (13). Laws, to put it bluntly, have been largely written by men, for men.

Although advances have been made in recent decades, especially with the advent of the right to equality guaranteed by s.15 of the *Charter of Rights and Freedoms*, some feminists argue that many gains have been illusory. For instance, MacKinnon (1987: 1) notes a string of defeats and declines for women, including lack of effective sex-equality provisions for pay, opposition to the right to safe abortion and a movement towards sharing custody of children after separation, all which leave the ideal of women's equality before the law far from realized.

Schneider (2000: 228) explores the law and domestic violence over the last several decades, concluding that the assertion of domestic violence claims has advanced a "political conversation" and succeeded in making what used to be private, public. However, the fundamental vision of equality generated by the feminist-led movement against domestic violence has been subverted (229). Women who come forward with their experiences are seen as "unreasonable" and "difficult," and there is a tendency to view them as "sick" (pathologize them, for example, by asking why they didn't leave their abusive partners). Although intimate violence has been recognized as a public harm, the recognition is almost always couched in the discourse of individual problems, not a systemic or social one. Various kinds of quick-fix explanations and solutions in the end deny the link to gender; for example, violence against women is most often referred to as family violence, obscuring that "family" violence is mostly men abusing their female partners. As a result, "the thirty-year history of feminist lawmaking on battering reveals both the affirmative vision of equality, liberty, and freedom that has shaped legal strategy and decision-making, and the inevitable limitations of legal reform that does not take gender into account" (232).

Summary Points

The structural functionalist view of the law over exaggerates societal consensus and access to courts and legal justice.

The conflict perspective exposes the multiple actors and sites in which power is exercised and governance occurs.

The law is often a site which reproduces power structures in society, including patriarchy.

Neo-Liberalism and New Perspectives on Legal Justice

The jurisprudence approach to studying the law has parallels with neo-liberalism, an ideology and political strategy emphasizing the life choices of individuals and de-emphasizing social problems (discussed in Chapter Two). The jurisprudence approach emphasizes the application of the rational, rule-based legal system to individual cases, accentuating the life choices which have brought an individual in contact with the legal system. The social structures which contributed to the person's legal problems have very little if any relevance when analyzing their situation.

In the jurisprudence context of analyzing individual legal problems, the emphasis is on the individual and their choices in relation to their legal problems. This is consistent with the neo-conservative political strategy, which emphasize individual choice and controlling crime through harsh penalties and longer jail terms. This political strategy does not result in a reduction of government services (one of the features of neo-liberalism) but rather an increase in court and jail services. The complex relationship between neo-liberalism, emerging in the late twentieth century, and the associated political strategy of neo-conservatism has had a significant effect on the criminal justice system. Neo-conservatism calls for disciplining those who (as the middle classes see it) threaten to get out of control — the poor and people of colour (Garland 2001: 99–100)—and increasingly locking them up in jail. This strategy is espoused by Prime Minister Harper with his political agenda of getting tough on crime, imposing increasingly harsher penalties and keeping more people in jail.

The reduced ideological focus on the contribution of social problems to individuals' trouble with the law thus reduces emphasis on dealing with crime through social programs that alleviate poverty, meet the needs of troubled youths or provide early childhood special education. Government services in these areas are cut back; prison infrastructure and the criminal justice system are enlarged (Lynch and Groves 1989).

Expanding the focus of legal justice to include an analysis of the social problems associated with legal problems increases the ambit of the study of legal justice to include social justice and substantive justice. The problematic of a justice issue comes to light when the law is approached through different theoretical frameworks, including structural functionalism, symbolic interactionism and conflict theory. Individuals are viewed not just as rational actors making individual choices but as agents living and functioning in a social system, affected by the institution or social system of law, which informs and contributes to their life chances. Seeing individuals as living within a certain social context illuminates important differences in these individuals' lives and how they should be treated differently (unequals treated unequally). Viewing legal justice in this expanded way, which includes an analysis of substantive justice in addition to the procedural and formal rules enshrined in the system of law, increases the chances that reform of the law and policy will achieve justice.

Adding the dimension of power relations to the analysis of the law through a conflict, post-structural or feminist perspective and dissecting the language of the law or legal discourse furthers the problematic of a justice issue. This process of examining and analyzing legal discourse from a place of otherness or marginalization makes visible the structure of the law, which is generally described as the official version of the law and is thought to epitomize "justness" because of its perceived impartiality, neutrality and objectivity. However, through the methodology of discourse analysis, using the written text of the law and court trials, various structures of power, including ethnocentrism, patriarchy and classism, are revealed.

Such methods of analysis are important in the pursuit of justice as these structures and practices of power are usually not maliciously motivated through prejudice, false beliefs and bad attitudes, but they are institutional or societal and embedded and naturalized, so that they are often taken for granted and not questioned. These structures of power are often the least visible in day-to-day life but have a powerful effect on individuals. By revealing these dominant, or hegemonic, forms of oppression, an ethical practice at both the individual and institutional levels can be envisioned.

The result of this theoretical approach to analyzing the law is ultimately to explore how multicultural global postcolonial institutions, cultures and practices create opportunities to raise new questions, engage new dialogues and foster new discussions. In this way, through the process of raising awareness, an ethical practice of leximin emerges as does an emancipatory social project promoting positive social structural change to decentre mainstream, White, middles-class, patriarchal, dominant discourse and empower marginalized "other" discourse.

Glossary

actus reus – a Latin term denoting the objective element of a crime, or the guilty act.

appellate court – a court which sits in appeal of another court. The superior courts and Court of Queen's Bench sit as appellate courts to the provincial courts.

British North American Act, 1867 – an Act of the British Parliament which created the Dominion of Canada. It outlined Canada's system of government, modelling it after the British parliamentary system. When Canada's Constitution was patriated, or brought home to Canada in 1982, its name was changed to the *Constitution Act, 1867*.

Canadian Charter of Rights and Freedoms – a bill of rights entrenched in the Constitution of Canada. It is the first part of the *Constitution Act, 1982*, and it guarantees political and civil rights of people in Canada from policies and actions of all levels of government.

civil law – deals with matters and procedures that are other than of a criminal nature, involving compensation, damages or another form of relief.

common law – the law reflected in the decisions of judges made in court cases. The totality of these decisions is described as the common law.

constitution – system of fundamental principles by which a nation or a state is governed and the documents which comprise or embody these principles.

Constitution Act, 1867 – an Act of the British Parliament, originally called the *British North America Act, 1867* (see above).

Constitution Act, 1982 – Schedule B of the *Canada Act 1982* (U.K.) is part of the Constitution of Canada and part of Canada's process of patriating its Constitution or bringing it home from Britain.

Court of Appeal or Appeal (Appellate) Division of the Supreme Court – the appeal court for a province, which hears appeals from lower superior or Queen's Bench courts and provincial courts. Appeals from this court can be taken to the Supreme Court of Canada, if it grants leave to hear the appeal.

Court of Queen's Bench – a superior court which hears civil and criminal law cases as well as appeals from provincial courts. There are no monetary limits for claims, although usually if less than $20,000, matters would be heard in a small claims court, which is a provincial court. Appeals from this court would be taken to a court of appeal.

criminal law –deals with matters and procedures of a criminal nature.

Crown attorney (prosecutor) – a government lawyer who acts on behalf of the Crown or the state to prosecute criminals pursuant to criminal statutes such as the *Criminal Code*.

defence – an accused person in a criminal matter will present a defence to the Crown's case setting out why they are innocent.

defendant – in a civil suit this is the person against whom an action has been commenced.

Federal Court of Appeal – a court of the federal government hearing appeals from the Federal Court of Canada and other specific boards designated by the federal government.

grievances – the circumstance, act or cause of a complaint or wrong against a person.

judge – a lawyer who has been appointed by the government to be a judge of a court.

judicial decision – a decision of a judge in a court case, whether it be civil or criminal.

jurisdiction – authority given to a legal body (such as a court or tribunal) or to a political leader (prime minister) to pronounce or enforce legal matters.

jurisprudence approach – an approach to studying the law predominantly taught in law schools, with similarities to the official version of the law (see below), however, with an understanding of the vagueness and indeterminacy of the law's application. The predominant view of this approach is that law is made and determined by lawyers, judges and legislatures.

jurisprudence law – law as opined by lawyers, determined by judges and created by legislatures.

law as discourse – an approach that studies legal language, or "discourse," and how social structure and system influence what the law is, acknowledges the law as a site of both social and political power.

legal interpretation – the creation of law by judges through decisions in courts.

legal positivism – the creation of law by governments by such instruments as statutes and regulations.

living law – the law which is reflected and practised by individuals in everyday interactions between individuals (thus dominating social life). It is influenced by and influences the official version of the law.

Magna Carta Charter – an English Charter issued in 1215 limiting the king's powers. Most notably the king accepted that he could be bound by the law and could not imprison people without just cause. For the latter, a writ of *habeas corpus* was created allowing a petition to be made to a court of law for a prisoner's release for unjust imprisonment.

mens rea – a Latin term denoting one element of a crime, the guilty mind, which usually has to be proven in addition to the *actus reus*, or guilty act.

natural law – law that arises in human morals, that is, in agreement with nature, unchanging, everlasting and of universal application.

official version of the law – a version of the law presented as a formal, coherent body of rules, doctrines and principles concerned with the interpretation of statutes and previous decisions of judges (or case law) which is taught in law schools and practised by lawyers.

plaintiff – the person commencing a civil action.

principles of law – precedents, rules norms and procedures comprising the social institution and structure of the law.

provincial courts – lower courts of the provinces which hear lesser matters of criminal and civil (small claims) matters. They may be specialized courts, such as youth courts, traffic courts, therapeutic drug or domestic violence courts.

quasi-judicial – refers to a tribunal which resembles a court of law or has some attributes of a court of law, for example, a human rights tribunal.

statement of claim – a document issued by a court which commences a civil claim. After being issued, it is served on a defendant.

statute – legislation passed by the provincial legislature or the federal parliament. Usually dealing with a single subject matter, for example, *Environmental Protection Act*.

statutory law – law that is contained in a statute.

superior courts – the same as a court of Queen's Bench and Supreme Court for some provinces. Ontario uses the name "Superior Court of Justice" instead of Queen's Bench. This court hears civil and criminal law cases as well as appeals from provincial courts. There are no monetary limits for claims. Appeals from this court would be taken to a court of appeal.

Supreme Court – several provinces/territories — the Yukon, Prince Edward Island, Nova Scotia and the Northwest Territories — use the term "Supreme Court" for their superior court instead of Court of Queen's Bench.

11

The Criminal Justice System

Nicholas A. Jones and Allan L. Patenaude

At the end of this chapter, you will be able to:

- Understand various disciplinary approaches to defining crime
- Understand issues surrounding how crime is measured in Canada
- Understand two models of criminal justice processing in Canada
- Describe the critical decision-making points in the criminal justice process and the agencies involved in them (police, courts and corrections)
- Describe the sentencing philosophies employed by Canadian courts
- Critically assess the components of the criminal justice system with respect to formal justice, substantive justice and ethical practice.

The primary focus of the criminal justice system and its inherent processes is on the behaviour and sanctions of individuals. As a social institution, the system should embody the principles of fairness and equality and behave in an ethical manner. The criminal justice system has important aspects of all three frames of justice. First, formal or procedural justice is an important component of fairness and equality. Everyone has a right to a trial, a lawyer and standard procedures when interacting with the system. As well, one of the foundational concepts of the system is "corrective" justice, or fixing harm or unfortunate events in society. Modifications have been made in the criminal justice system to achieve substantive justice (the second frame of justice) by treating different situations differently; this chapter outlines many of these initiatives, such as Aboriginal policing, courts and correctional problems. Lastly, the ethical practice of the criminal justice personnel must include the assistance and protection of the most marginalized and vulnerable in society. Keeping this foremost in mind would prevent unfortunate incidents such as those documented in the Stonechild Inquiry, discussed below.

The introductory study of criminal justice often starts with an elaboration of the component parts with which a person interacting with societal institutions handling "crime" may come in contact. These institutions are illustrated as a "system," as individuals start with the institution of the police, perhaps appear before a court, enter a corrections facility and later are released. This analysis is akin to the structural functionalist perspective covered in Chapter Two. The criminal justice "system" is seen as an organism, with each component having a function. These components provide institutions of formal social control in Canada and other modern societies. In particular, this chapter focuses on: (1) the manner in which crime is defined and measured; (2) the crime control and due process models around which the criminal justice system operates; (3) how criminal offenders are processed by the criminal justice system; and (4) the components of that system through which they may or may not pass.

"What do you do with a drunken sailor?" is the opening line of the traditional Canadian naval drinking song "The North Atlantic Squadron"; it is also an interesting jumping off point for a discussion of how we handle persons who don't conform to the accepted ways of our society. Public drunkenness or intoxication is a minor legal infraction of our rules for living together in society, and the penalty might be a fine or probation. But, what if that same drunken sailor had driven a pickup truck across town? Or assaulted a passerby who made a disparaging comment about the uniform they were wearing? What should society do in cases where corporate greed leads to the death of consumers or to serious environmental damage such as that resulting from the major oil spill in the Gulf of Mexico during 2010? What should society do in more serious cases of deviance or crime?

Main Points

As you read, highlight the answers to these questions:
What is crime in Canada?
How do different disciplinary perspectives suggest we define crime?
How do we "officially" measure crime in Canada?
What factors impact people's decisions to report crime?

Defining Crime

What constitutes crime varies depending upon the disciplinary background of the person defining it, and, most importantly, there is no agreed upon definition! Legally trained Tappan (1947: 100) used a definition whereby crime was "an intentional act in violation of the criminal law (statutory and case law) committed without defense or excuse, and penalized by the state as a felony or misdemeanour." Typical of legal positivism, this definition is not without its critics. Two years later, sociologically trained Sutherland (1949: 31) modified it to include: "The essential characteristic of crime is that it is behaviour which is prohibited by the State as an injury to the State and against which the State may react, at least as a last resort, by punishment." Sutherland discussed the philosophy which underscored his definition, stating that "an unlawful act is not defined as criminal by the fact that it is punished, but by the fact that it is punishable" (35). Political definitions of crime tend to focus on the use of power by people to protect or further their own values and interests. Groups of "elites" or "moral entrepreneurs," as political sociologist Becker (1962) labelled them, use their own values and economic interests/power to define what should be punishable and to impose their views on the larger society. This idea has been explored in other chapters, notably Chapter Two, on theorizing justice, and Chapter Ten, on legal justice. Fattah (1989: 20) notes: "For the psychiatrist and the psychologist, crime is a manifestation of a personality disorder, a form of social maladjustment, a discordant reaction to the stimuli of the environment, and a disharmonious relationship between the individual and his group."

The earlier works of Sellin (1938: 21) argued against such formalized and technical definitions of crime, stating that "the unqualified acceptance of these legal definitions of the basic units or elements of criminological inquiry violates a fundamental criterion of science." Sellin was speaking about the freedom of scientists, especially social scientists, to define their terms of study and the actual study material itself. This call for the freedom to define one's field of study was taken up by Mannheim (1965), another criminologist, who claimed that any definition of crime should include anti-social behaviour. This extremely broad definition would have us include not only acts labelled as criminal but also acts which could be considered deviant.

As this discussion illustrates, definitions of crime are subject to imprecision (lack of clarity) due to a lack of agreement concerning what constitutes a crime. Definitions may vary according to the views of the persons or legislature defining and labelling a specific behaviour as criminal. Canadian criminologist Fattah (1989: 20) offers an interesting compromise between the legal and sociological perspectives. For the purposes of this discussion, we will be using Fattah's (1989: 20) definition of crime: "An act or omission regarded by a sizable segment of a given society as warranting formal intervention to control, punish and prevent such behaviour." This definition is consistent with viewing the criminal justice system as a totalizing system reflecting society and a general consensus as to what is "crime."

Measuring Crime

We don't know how much crime is actually committed, but we do know that more crime exists than is reported in official police statistics (Brantingham and Brantingham 1984; Hood and Sparks 1970; Winterdyk 2000). In addition, not every reported crime is recorded as a crime statistic. Criminologists Brantingham and Brantingham (1984: 89) offer the following six hypotheses on why many crimes go unreported:

1. A crime may be of such a subtle character that it is never known to have happened.
2. A crime might not be perceived as such.

3. A crime might not be reported because the offender is a family member, a friend, or an acquaintance.
4. A crime might not be reported because the victim believes that it was trivial or that the potential penalty is too grave for the harm done.
5. A crime might not be reported because the victim fears reprisal.
6. A crime might not be reported because the victim feels antipathy toward the police, or because the victim is also a criminal, or because the victim is embarrassed by the circumstances under which the crime occurred.

Many of these reasons appear to beg the question of how to define crime; numbers one to three aren't regarded as falling within the definition, or perhaps result from definitional imprecision, and the same applies to aspects of four and six. If non-reporting is due to many of these reasons, the issue of whether this non-reporting is important is germane and illustrative of the problematic definition of "crime." If a person doesn't regard an act as a "crime," should anything be done?

Regardless of the reasons for individuals not reporting crime to the police, our lack of knowledge concerning the actual number of crimes is compounded by the non-recording of some crime by the police. This generally involves petty offences where the officer exercised their discretion and chose to let the offender go with a warning or caution. Similarly, some police jurisdictions may decide not to record certain crimes, such as a minor theft, for political reasons or because of the cost of recording large volumes of mostly unsolvable crime (Kitsuse and Cicourel 1963; Lowman n.d.; Mawby 1990).

Using both official and unofficial sources, however, we can arrive at a "best guess" of how much crime there is in Canada. Criminologists have labelled the large amount of unrecorded crime the "dark figure of crime." The analogy of what is seen around a street lamp is useful here. Imagine that normal behaviour is most likely to occur within the clearly lit area; deviant and some criminal behaviour occurs in the shady or semi-lit area; and the majority of crime occurs in the dark area. Since we cannot clearly see what crime exists in the darkness, we cannot count it as official crime. Criminologists believe that as much as four or five times more crime occurs than is actually known by or reported to the police (Adler, Mueller and Laufer 2003; Winterdyk 2000).

The processing of criminal activity by the criminal justice system also has an impact on arriving at our guess of how much crime there is in Canada. The "crime funnel" represents an expression of this impact, as at each stage of the criminal justice process, "the crime population is transformed in character and reduced in size" (Brannigan 1984: 93). From the initial reporting of the crime through to the sentencing of an offender, even crimes which are reported to or detected by the police may disappear from the official statistics. This result is one wherein "data generated further down the funnel such as arrest numbers, charged offences, guilty verdicts or incarceration numbers are significantly different from the actual crime picture than UCR [uniform crime reports] police-recorded data" (Schmalleger, MacAllister, McKenna and Winterdyk 2000: 49).

Notwithstanding the issues with respect to reporting of crime statistics, official reports clearly demonstrate a continuous decrease in all crime categories, including violent crime, over the last decade. This decrease appears to go unnoticed by both the public and politicians, who continue to perceive crime as increasing exponentially. This perception impacts policy and legislation affecting the most marginalized of populations — the poor, youth, people living with mental illness and others. At the same time, definitions of crime in Canadian criminal legislation may reflect more the values, beliefs and economic interests/power of the elites than of the majority of citizens. The criminal justice system serves as a mechanism to enforce those interests.

Reacting to Crime

As a result of formalizing our laws and changing the notion of crime from an individual harm to a public harm, or offence against the monarch or state, Western societies began to realize that they needed formal organiza-

Figure 1 Crime Rates in Canada, 1962–2007

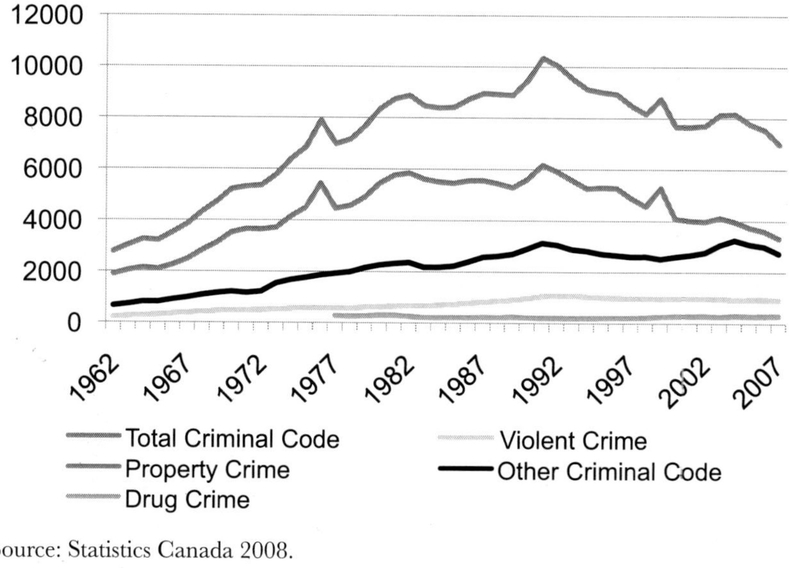

Source: Statistics Canada 2008.

tions to deal with persons (and organizations) that committed crime. To deal effectively with criminals, or so we like to believe, a modern society needs the following:

1. methods of enforcing the laws of the land;
2. methods of detecting persons who break the laws and bringing them to justice;
3. a fair and impartial way of deciding the guilt or innocence of persons accused of breaking the criminal law; and
4. methods of punishing, deterring and/or correcting the lawbreakers' behaviour.

The police generally enforce the laws and detect criminals; the courts decide their guilt or innocence and impose a sentence; and the sentence is overseen by a correctional agency. Together, these agencies are referred to as "the criminal justice system." For the purposes of this chapter, we see the criminal justice system as comprised of those agencies (police, courts and corrections) that provide formal social control of the population.

Two Models: Crime Control, Due Process or Both?

Main Points

As you read, highlight the answers to these questions:
What is the foundation upon which each model is premised?
How do the models compare with each other?

The criminal justice systems and processes found in Canada, England and the United States appear to be unsure of which goals they should pursue. They suffer from having the conflicting (or at least competing) goals of controlling crime while protecting the rights of citizens accused of committing a crime to be treated fairly and equitably. Similarly, we seek to alternatively punish and help those persons whom society has decided is a criminal. The following two models may help clarify the complex nature of the Canadian system of criminal justice.

The Crime Control Model

In his *The Limits of the Criminal Sanction*, legal scholar Packer (1968) described the U.S. system of criminal justice as having two distinct and competing goals: crime control and due process. The first goal, "crime control," seeks to ensure that the criminal justice agencies protect society by quickly detecting, arresting and convicting criminals. Fifteen years later, in *Thinking About Crime*, American political scientist Wilson (1983) attempted to provide theoretical support for the goal of crime control when he argued that criminals were not members of a poor underclass attempting to survive through criminal activity, but rather rational persons who chose crime from which to profit. More to the point, Wilson (1983: 128) argued that aggressive policing and tough sentencing practices were more practical methods in reducing crime than methods that sought to reduce poverty, improve education and tackle other social problems, which he did not believe contributed to crime.

A society pursing only the goal of crime control would operate in a utilitarian manner that seeks the greatest happiness for the greatest number of people. The words of *Star Trek's* Mr. Spock, "the needs of the many outweigh the needs of the few," express how a society operating under a crime control model might regard crime and criminals. Indeed, such a society might:

1. grant the police wide-sweeping powers to arrest and detain suspects and care very little about how the police exercise those powers (for example, coerced confessions, unauthorized surveillance and wiretaps, etc.) as long as the criminal is apprehended;
2. reduce the ability of lawyers to keep private any conversations between them and their clients or see the role of the defence counsel changed to gathering a confession and asking for a light sentence from the court;
3. impose harsher sentences for minor crime, introduce indeterminate and mandatory sentences aimed at removing more serious criminals from society for longer periods of time (or forever) and introduce the use of capital punishment; and
4. reduce the range of grounds for appealing convictions and sentences.

The Due Process Model

The second goal, "due process," seeks to ensure that the power of the state is not used in a punitive manner and that the individual citizen is protected from such abuses. Citizens in Canada, for example, receive certain processes which are due to them according to the *Charter of Rights and Freedoms,* as interpreted by the Supreme Court of Canada. What this means is that individuals are supposed to be protected from having the police, courts or correctional agencies ignore their rights to fundamental justice. A society pursuing only this goal might seek to:

1. restrict the ability of the police to arrest and detain suspects to only those instances where the police observe them committing a criminal activity or have reasonable grounds to believe they committed a crime, and limit the ability of the police to collect information about crime and criminal activities (for example, restrict the use of confessions, surveillance cameras, wiretaps, etc.);
2. require the presence and involvement of lawyers at each stage of the criminal justice process to ensure the rights of the individual are observed;

3. require the courts to release any offender whose individual rights are ignored or abused even if they are otherwise shown to be guilty of a crime; and
4. increase the range of grounds for appealing convictions and sentences.

It may be argued that no "pure" examples exist of either a crime control or due process model. Yet, while these two goals seem to be in conflict, it is possible for a criminal justice process to include elements of both crime control and due process. Indeed, this is the case in Canada, where, for example, the Supreme Court seeks to ensure that agencies involved in crime control protect individual rights. The Court does this by applying interpretations of the *Charter* to the laws and the activities of criminal justice agencies. This blended system of criminal justice occurs in most countries where the supreme law of the land is their Constitution rather than a dictator or person of "noble" birth.

In recent years, federal Conservative governments have sought to introduce laws which impose harsher penalties and mandatory sentencing for career and violent criminals in an ongoing attempt at crime control. These types of laws have sought to incapacitate serious offenders in prison for indefinite periods of time and, thus, remove their ability to commit crime. Unfortunately, these same kinds of laws (and social policy) haven't reduced crime in the United States, although they have increased the prison population in that country, which has among the highest incarceration rates in the world.

Whether a criminal justice system utilizes a crime control, due process or blended model, its operating processes function in a manner that tends primarily to reflect a formal justice approach, as discussed in previous chapters. It seeks justice by applying the tenets of procedural justice in its operation. It processes individuals through its various stages, seeking to treat each case the same way. Although at certain junctures it makes accommodations for individual circumstances, procedural fairness is the basis upon which our system of criminal justice is premised. In adopting this foundation, the system often falls short of achieving the aims of substantive justice. All individuals encountering the Canadian criminal justice system are afforded the same rights, as guaranteed by the *Charter of Rights and Freedoms;* however, these rights are not necessarily applied equally in all circumstances. Concerns regarding the application of formulaic processes that cannot or do not account for the array of individual circumstances required to achieve a broader sense of justice was a decisive factor in the emergence (or re-emergence) of restorative justice approaches to addressing crime (discussed in the next chapter).

Policing: The Law Enforcement Component

Main Points

As you read, highlight the answers to these questions:
What are the nine generally accepted roles of the police in Canada?
What decisions can/do the police make, and what is the basis upon which these decisions are permitted?
Why is police discretion argued to be necessary?

The roles of police personnel and the processes involved throughout the law enforcement component of the criminal justice system are similar across Canada, regardless of whether the police agency is municipal, regional, provincial, federal or a specialized agency such as tribal, university/campus or railway police. The roles of the police in a modern, multi-ethnic, highly urbanized society are becoming as complex as the society in which they enforce the laws.

Police in Canada are generally accepted as having a number of roles, including:

- responding to high-priority crime-related and emergency calls for service;
- responding to order-maintenance and service calls (visible police presence);
- controlling traffic (vehicle and crowd control);
- conducting preliminary investigations;
- making arrests;
- executing warrants;
- attending court;
- patrolling public gatherings (visible police presence and crowd control); and
- providing community service (creating a sense of safety and security. (Griffiths 2008: 280–1)

Throughout their performance of these roles, the police operate in a highly visible and political environment. The media, the public at large and our elected politicians review the actions of both individual officers and the law enforcement agency. The actions of individual officers, from their use of discretion in whether to arrest, or detain a suspect, the application of physical force to affect that arrest to other actions up to and including the use of deadly force may be publicized by the media in positive or negative ways. An officer who risked her life to save a child may be portrayed as a hero one day and the next day vilified as a possibly corrupt cop for accepting a free meal from a local restaurant. American policing scholar Walker (2001) noted that police agencies, due to their unique powers and authority, need review of their actions that are independent of the agency, but not independent of the local or provincial government.

Processing an Offender through the Police Services

The law enforcement component of the criminal justice system contains a number of entry- and exit-points, where decisions affect if and how an alleged offender will be processed. The police will either detect that an offence has occurred or have a suspicious incident or behaviour reported to them by a citizen. The latter is the most common method of the police becoming involved. This constitutes the first of many points where the police officer makes a decision, either alone or in conjunction with a supervisor or prosecutor, on (1) whether a crime has occurred, and if the offenders are known, whether they should be arrested, and (2) whether further investigation is required to confirm that a crime occurred and/or the identity of the offenders. Typical investigations at this point include analyzing the crime scene, interviews with victims, witnesses and/or other known criminals, and identification line-ups.

Canadian law provides the police discretion in performing their duties in many but not all circumstances. The language of the law, specifically the terminology "shall" and "may," either prohibits or permits police discretion, with the police entrusted with the responsibility of upholding the law in a fair, unbiased and equitable manner (Van Allen 2009). Permitted discretion provides an inherent flexibility in police practice that is warranted given that it is inconceivable that laws can account for the multiplicity of situations that officers may face in conducting their duties (Griffiths 2008). However, the use of discretion by police officers is subject to controversy, especially with regard to the following issues: (1) whether there is statutory authority for discretion; (2) lack of clear guidelines limiting its use; (3) its use by the least experienced police officers; and (4) its unethical or discriminatory use (Griffiths 2008; Van Allen 2009). Instances of police misuse and/or abuse of discretionary powers have become the subject of public inquiries. The consequences of police abuse of discretionary powers can be devastating for the police officer's career, destroy public confidence in the police and most importantly, detrimentally affect the individual who experienced the abuse. These issues suggest that police discretion requires mechanisms of monitoring and control.

Officer integrity and ethical conduct is a significant issue in policing. Accountability of officers for the decisions made during the course of performing their duties is both necessary and desirable. Van Allen (2009: 147) argues that "the use of integrity and ethics plays [or should play] a central role in an officer's decision-making when exercising discretion." Being ethical means doing what is right, for the right reason. It means treating people impartially, without discrimination. "Discrimination involves not only targeting someone for prosecution on the basis of race, creed, religion gender, or sexual orientation, it also involves not taking action on the basis of favouritism" (148).

In a small percentage of cases, the accused exits the process at this point since they were found to be innocent of the crime for which they were arrested or there was a lack of evidence needed to charge them with a criminal offence. The filing of criminal charges results in the case remaining in the criminal justice system, but after a brief stay that involves being charged with a criminal offence and booked into or out of police custody (with photographs and fingerprints taken), the individual exits the police component and is sent onwards to the judicial component for further processing (preliminary hearing, arraignment, bail hearing and trial).

Aboriginal Policing

Police-minority relations, in particular relations with Aboriginal people, have been a focal point of concern and contention. According to Clairmont (2006: 2), "inquiries and commissions across Canada sharply criticized how Aboriginal people were policed." Seeking to address these findings, the federal government created the First Nations Policing Policy (FNPP) in June 1991. Its stated mandate is to "provide First Nations across Canada police services that are professional, effective, culturally appropriate, and accountable to the communities that they serve."

Following the FNPP and the Royal Commission on Aboriginal Peoples (1996), numerous tripartite policing agreements have been negotiated with First Nations communities (Clairmont 2006; Griffiths 2008). This has increased the participation of Aboriginal people in policing in two primary ways: the creation of autonomous First Nations police services and recruitment of Aboriginal people into existing police services. "As of 2007, there were 142 FNPP agreements in place across the country, with 1,000 police officers (most of whom are Aboriginal) providing police services to 319 First Nations communities with a total of nearly 240,000" (Griffiths 2008: 29).

The inclusion of Aboriginal people in the police services can be argued to provide a conduit for changing from the Eurocentric worldview, which dominates the justice system in Canada (Sutherland 2002). According to Turpel-Lafond (2006: 1), "policing is a significant public sector employer, as well as an important social institution. It must fully reflect the population that it serves, lest it be fraught with challenges to its legitimacy based on a lack of confidence by some members of society." With respect to police recruitment of First Nations, Turpel-Lafond (2006: 4) notes: "The challenge for police forces is to capture this group, to attract them to service, to support them within police organizations, and to allow the culture of your policing to expand through their positive inclusion." Progress has been made in this pursuit, although it falls short of the self-declared target of representation in many regions across the country.

There have also been attempts made to address concerns regarding racism within the police services. In Regina, for example, these initiatives included: (1) support for the implementation of a citizens' review mechanism; (2) continued cooperation with the Federation of Saskatchewan Indian Nations' Special Investigations Unit; (3) continued use of appropriate diversion processes for Aboriginal youth into culturally appropriate programs; (4) development of cultural units within police services; (5) ongoing in-service cultural awareness training provided to existing members; and (6) improved screening techniques to identify possible racism in police recruits (Regina Police Service 2004).

Despite some progress, continued issues around police-Aboriginal relations have arisen since the inception of the FNPP. These issues have been well documented in inquiries and commissions, including the Aboriginal Justice Inquiry of Manitoba (1991); the Blood Tribe Policing Inquiry (Alberta 1991); the Cariboo-Chilcotin Justice Inquiry (British Columbia 1993); the Commission of Inquiry into the Shooting Death of Leo LaChance (Saskatchewan 1993); and the Inquiry into the Death of Neil Stonechild (Saskatchewan 2004).

The Commission on First Nations and Métis Peoples and Justice Reform (2004) was established in November 2002 in response to two Saskatoon police officers' treatment of an Aboriginal man, Darrel Night, in 2000. The officers "abandoned [Darrel Night] on the outskirts of the city on a bitterly cold January night in 2000. The circumstances were similar to the freezing deaths of other Aboriginal men in and around the city about the same time" (Commission 2004: 5–1). The commission made a number of recommendations specifically targeted toward the realm of policing, including: (1) implementing a strategy to eliminate racism in policing; (2) evaluation of existing cultural awareness training; (3) employment equity; (4) increasing community policing initiatives; (5) greater use of police discretion in diverting Aboriginal peoples into culturally appropriate alternatives; and (6) the provision of an Aboriginal liaison worker within the police services. These proposals recognize the state of police-Aboriginal relations and attempt to address the issues. While a great deal of work remains to be done, progress continues to be made in providing First Nations peoples and their communities with the professional, unbiased and equal police services they are entitled to receive.

Criminal Courts: The Judicial Component

Main Points

As you read, highlight the answers to these questions:

How does an accused move through Canadian courts?

Once the decision to go to trial has been made, what decisions must a trial judge make concerning the processing of the accused individual?

What are the five goals of imposing a criminal sanction in Canada? Can more than one goal be present in the same sentence and why?
What is the significance of *Regina* v. *Gladue* (1999)?

Countries with a British common law tradition, like Canada, employ an adversarial system of justice, in which lawyers (Crown prosecutors) representing the state (and supposedly the victim) argue that the accused party committed a crime and that the harm they did is worthy of punishment. On the other side, defence lawyers, representing the accused, attempt to refute those claims and/or minimize the punishment their client receives if found guilty. Determining which side best met its requirements is a federally or provincially appointed judge who can either (1) impose the most appropriate sentence upon the accused if found guilty; (2) release the accused if found not guilty; or (3) declare a mistrial if the trial procedures were violated.

Processing an Offender through the Criminal Courts

Criminal courts contain a number of decision points that affect the continued processing of accused individuals. These decision points involve the preliminary inquiry, arraignment, pre-trial detention, plea negotiation, adjudication and sentencing of criminal offenders. In Canada, the first decision point is the preliminary inquiry, at which time the Crown prosecutor must show cause (or reasons) why the accused should be tried for the criminal offence. Failure to show cause results in the dismissal of charges and release of the accused. If there is sufficient evidence to satisfy the judge that a crime may have been committed or that a conviction may be secured, the accused will be arraigned.

The judicial component becomes formally invoked at an "arraignment," which involves the reading aloud of the criminal charges against the accused and the entering of a plea of either guilty or not guilty. If the accused pleads guilty, the trial process is generally concluded and the, now guilty, party can go directly to be sentenced; this is especially the case with minor crimes. If the accused pleads not guilty, a trial date is set, and the judge decides whether the accused should be held in custody to guarantee their attendance in court or released on some form of bail or recognizance (cash or property in the former and a promise for the latter) until the trial.

Plea negotiations offer both the Crown prosecutor and defence counsel an opportunity to reduce the amount of trial processes and expenses. Such negotiations typically involve a guilty plea in return for the charges and/or sentence being reduced. Although this practice offers the accused an opportunity to avoid the stress and publicity of a trial and to take the first step towards rehabilitation by admitting their guilt, plea negotiations are not necessarily equitably or ethically applied across the board. Individuals with access to private funds, as opposed to limited legal aid funding, may employ legal counsel who are willing (for a price) to invest more effort investigating and reviewing their case before taking it to a plea negotiation. Similarly, in the case of co-accused offenders, the first accused interviewed may be presented with the opportunity to have their charges reduced or withdrawn in exchange for an agreement to testify against their partner in crime.

According to Reiman and Leighton (2010), the process of plea bargaining has an exceptionally deleterious effect on financially marginalized groups in society. These authors argue that the impact of a person's financial situation in accessing "adequate legal representation" severely hampers a defendant in the plea bargaining process. They conclude: "This means that, regardless of actual innocence or guilt, one's chances of beating the rap increase as one's income increases" (130). Despite the guarantees of legal representation outlined in Canadian law, disparities in wealth can result in significant disparities in the adequacy of the legal counsel.

Once the decision to go to trial has been made, a number of formal decisions concern the continued processing of the accused individual. The trial judge makes decisions concerning the admission of evidence, the questions that witnesses must answer, the conduct of both witnesses and opposing counsels (Crown prosecutor and defence counsel), and whether the Crown has met its burden of proving its charges on the face of the evidence beyond a reasonable doubt. The accused proceeds to the next decision point, which involves either exiting the system if found not guilty or being sentenced if found guilty. The passing of a criminal sanction, or sentence, is typically the final aspect of the judicial processing of an offender. At this point, the judge chooses to either: (1) impose a financial penalty and release the offender; (2) release the offender unconditionally or under certain conditions or restrictions back into the community; or (3) incarcerate the offender for a period of time. When dealing with major crimes that could result in significant loss of liberty, the judge will typically set a future date for sentencing. This allows time for a probation officer to prepare and submit a pre-sentence report, which will assist in determining an appropriate sentence, and/or time for the Crown prosecutor and defence counsel to speak to the court regarding the sentence.

Sentencing Philosophies

Canadian criminal courts impose punishments for committing behaviours that have been labelled criminal by Parliament. Punishments are the legal consequences of committing a crime, imposed by the state, as expressions of society's displeasure with the conduct of the offender and to prevent further crime. A number of conditions around punishment have been agreed within the Canadian criminal justice system. First, a punishment should only be imposed when we are convinced of the guilt of the person. Second, the punishment should be proportionate to the harm done by the offender. Third, punishment should only be imposed for past crimes or transgressions rather than for crime the person *might* commit in the future (Bentham 1948; Boonan 2008; Freidrichs 2001; Shichor 2006).

The reasons for imposing a punishment in Canada and in most Western societies are found within the following sentencing philosophies:

1. *Retribution*: This requires the punishment imposed on an offender to be directly proportionate to the harm done by the offender. Retribution is not the same as revenge (Morris and Rothman 1995). The concept of retribution is clear in the old adage "an eye for an eye"; it would not be acceptable to impose an indeterminate prison sentence for not paying a restaurant bill.
2. *Deterrence*: This requires that punishment imposed on an offender will be certain, swift and severe in order to influence a person not to commit a crime in the future (Griffiths and Cunningham 2000; Morris and Rothman 1995). "Specific" or "individual" deterrence is based on the notion that the unpleasantness of punishment has a preventative effect on an individual committing any future crime. "General" deterrence is the crime control goal of punishment of a single offender having a preventative effect on persons who were not punished and who will avoid committing any future crime.
3. *Rehabilitation*: This involves a range of activities based on the notion that: (1) there is something wrong with offenders that make them commit crime; (2) offenders should be treated so they can readjust to society; and (3) future crime can be prevented through treatment of the offenders (Ohlin 1974; Redekop 2008).
4. *Incapacitation*: Punishment, usually involving incarceration, seeks to prevent future crime by restraining or removing offenders from society for a specified period of time (Morris and Rothman 1995). "Selective incapacitation" targets high-risk offenders whose criminal history may be extensive, began at an early age or illustrates an escalation from minor to major crime, with numerous arrests and/or convictions; drug use and poor work and relationship histories are also considered. Typical of criminal laws embodying selective incapacitation are the so-called "three-strike laws" and habitual offender/habitual sexual offender laws. "General incapacitation" is based on the notion that long prison terms are required to protect society by removing and isolating offenders from society (Ancel 1965; Farkas and Stichman 2002).
5. *Restoration*: This is the concept that harm has been done by the offender, that individuals and the community are affected by it and that each party should be involved in correcting that harm (Braithwaite 1989; van Ness and Heetderks-Strang 1997). In restorative justice, a number of informal practices are entered into that seek to resolve conflict and

restore harmony, rather than imposing punishment alone, by involving victims, offenders and mediators rather than the formal court system.

The Canadian *Criminal Code* speaks to these sentencing philosophies as well as to the purposes for sentencing in section 718, wherein it states that "a sentence must be proportionate to the gravity of the offence and the degree of responsibility of the offender." In congruence with the sentencing philosophies, this section also declares the following purposes of sentencing: (1) denunciation, (2) deterrence, (3) public safety, (4) rehabilitation, (5) harm reparation and (6) to promote offender accountability. Section 718 also calls for the courts to take into consideration aggravating and mitigating circumstances involved in the case, the idea of consistency in sentencing (similar sentences for similar crimes) and the imposition of the least restrictive sanction.

When sentencing an offender, a judge might seek to achieve more than one sentencing goal, such as retribution and deterrence, or incapacitation and retribution. Indeed, there are a number of criminal sanctions available to a trial judge. Although some sentencing philosophies are easier than others to determine in certain sanctions, specific sentences may include more than one sanction and effect more than one crime control goal.

Addressing Aboriginal Culture in the Courts

Just as the numerous commissions and inquiries into policing and Aboriginal peoples identified systemic problems that have resulted in the over-representation of Aboriginal peoples in the criminal justice system, the Manitoba Aboriginal Justice Inquiry (1991), the Royal Commission on Aboriginal Peoples (1996) and the Saskatchewan Commission on First Nations and Métis People and Justice Reform (2004) each noted the historical conditions that contributed to increasing numbers of Aboriginal people appearing before Canadian courts. Among the problems identified by these inquiries and encountered by many Aboriginal defendants, victims and witnesses is the alien culture of the Anglo-Canadian criminal courts. As Canadian criminologist McDonnell (cited in Bennet 2000: 5) notes, there exists "a problematic relationship between rubrics emerging from one culture and practices met in another."

During the 1980s and 1990s, a few courageous judges took steps of their own to reduce the impact of the foreign culture of the courts on the trials and sentencing of Aboriginal persons. Yukon Territorial Court Judge Barry Stewart incorporated his interpretations of Aboriginal communal decision-making into his courtroom and sentencing processes. Restructuring the courtroom environment into a circular arrangement, which permitted all present to be part of the court, he permitted any community member to speak to the case once guilt had been determined. This form of "sentencing circle," as it became known, was soon incorporated into selected communities across the Northwest Territories, such as Lac La Martre by N.W.T. Territorial Court judges like Brian Bruser, and by provincial court judges such as Jean-Charles Coutu in Québec (Ross 1992; Ryan 1995).

The province with the highest number of Aboriginal people in conflict with the law, Saskatchewan, undertook a more mainstream approach in addition to the introduction of sentencing circles for Aboriginal offenders. During 2001, the province appointed a Cree-speaking jurist, Gerald Morin, and recruited Cree-speaking court staff for its northern circuit court operating out of Prince Albert. This court circuit typically

> will travel to a community on a given day, with many local residents wishing to observe. It is not unusual for 150 cases to be held per day, which can place a large strain on the personal, community, and diversionary alternatives to be implemented. These courts are structured slightly different than traditional Canadian criminal courts, with the judge in front, the prosecutor on one side, and the defendant on the other. Often the probation officer will be in attendance. Alternative options are evaluated prior to the court sessions, and recommendations are incorporated into the proceedings. (Hurlbert and McKenzie 2008: 154)

This approach was expanded during 2006 to include a Chipewyan-speaking circuit court. With all members of the court party speaking one or more Athapaskan language (Cree and/or Chipewyan), the court managed to reduce one of the major problems facing Aboriginal persons encountering the court system, namely language. Indeed, the success of that initiative was noted by the Saskatchewan Ministry of Justice and Attorney-General (2007: 15), which stated: "The ability of the Provincial Court to deal with matters in an Aboriginal language, to be sensitive to cultural and community issues and to demonstrate the ability of the justice system to address community needs is seen as positive according to initial evaluations and the response of the community or community leaders."

The Supreme Court of Canada firmly entered the Aboriginal justice fray with its decision in *Regina v. Gladue* (1999). Although section 718(2)(e) required trial judges to consider alternatives to incarceration at the time of sentencing prior to *Gladue*, the Supreme Court ruled that the unique historical and cultural circumstances of persons self-identified as Aboriginal (i.e., Indian, Inuit or Métis) as defined in section 35(2) of the *Constitution Act* (1981), must be considered at sentencing. With assistance from the attorneys-general of Canada and Ontario, four Toronto-area judges established the Toronto Gladue (Aboriginal Persons) Court in 2001 to better meet the needs of urban Aboriginal accused bail and pre-trial activities and the sentencing of convicted offenders (Knazan 2003, 2005; Whonnock 2008, 2010). Among the hallmarks of the Gladue courts are (1) a focus on rehabilitation rather solely punishment, (2) the use of expanded pre-sentence reports (known as Gladue reports), which include the accused's attachment to or detachment from Aboriginal culture as the result of colonization, residential schools and so forth and (3) the sentencing of the accused in a manner which places the offender and offence in the context of the Aboriginal community (Knazan 2003, 2005). The Gladue Courts have been reported successful and expanded to other communities in Ontario (Knazan 2005; Whonnock 2008, 2010). Note some of the conflicting evidence reported in Chapter Ten.

Although the courts in Saskatchewan and elsewhere in the West have taken positive steps to reduce the impact of the Anglo-Canadian legal culture on their Aboriginal participants, it could be argued that they merely indigenized the personnel and operating language of the court rather than changing its culture and relationship to the Aboriginal people. The Gladue courts, while still evolving, have taken the inclusion of Aboriginal values and culture into the provincial courts further than other jurisdictions in Canada.

Corrections: The Punishment/Rehabilitation Component

Main Points

As you read, highlight the answers to these questions:
What are the six roles of Canada's contemporary correctional system?
What is the primary mission of a correctional institution in Canada?
How do culturally relevant correctional programs impact Aboriginal inmates?

Both the provincial and federal correctional systems operate correctional institutions of varying security levels in which to hold offenders and provide treatment and training to the persons in their charge. In Canada, we distinguish federal inmates (sentenced to incarceration of two years or more, served in a federal penitentiary) from provincial/territorial inmates (sentenced to incarceration of less than two years, served in a provincial/territorial correctional centre or jail). The provinces and territories also hold inmates remanded into custody while awaiting trial and/or sentencing (these individuals are often referred to as "remands" or "remanded inmates").

The primary stated mission of Canada's contemporary correctional system, regardless of whether the facility is operated by a province, territory or the federal government, is to provide for the safe and secure custody of offenders for a specified period of time. The institutional correctional system's many roles include the following:

1. short-term detention of accused offenders awaiting trial and convicted offenders awaiting sentencing and/or appeal;
2. short-term detention of convicted offenders awaiting transfer to long-

term provincial/territorial and/or federal facilities;
3. provision of diagnostic and treatment services for convicted offenders serving long-term provincial/territorial and/or federal sentences;
4. provision of educational, vocational and other rehabilitative services for convicted offenders serving long-term sentences;
5. provision of pre-release planning and assistance for convicted offenders close to their statutory or discretionary release dates; and
6. provision of assistance in transitioning from incarceration to a free-world environment.

Generally, the inmate population in Canada is not comprised of middle- and upper-income individuals but rather of lower-income and Aboriginal people. This over-representation is due, in part, to the fact that an individual who commits a minor offence and has a job and a permanent residence is more likely to be subject to a fine, while an individual who commits the same offence but lacks a job or permanent residence is more likely to receive a brief period of incarceration (Reiman and Leighton 2008). This points towards the notion of crime as a social problem versus crime as an individual problem.

Institutional corrections involves a number of internal decision points that affect the treatment, education, training and health care of inmates on a daily basis. There are only two decision points, however, that affect society and other criminal justice agencies, and they are the decisions of whether to release an inmate back into the community on either (1) a temporary basis (decided by the correctional facility's managers) or (2) a long-term basis prior to completion of their sentence (decided by a federal or provincial parole board).

The other component to a modern correctional system is known as community corrections or community-based corrections and is comprised of "probation" and "parole" services. Probation offers an alternative to incarceration in which the offender is released back into the community under certain conditions and often under the supervision of a probation officer. Parole is the supervised release of incarcerated offenders back into the community to serve the remainder of their sentence under certain conditions. As of January 2010, the Correctional Service of Canada reported that 8,800 of 22,000, or 40 percent, of offenders under its correctional supervision were on parole (CSC 2010). Both services are operated on the belief that the best place for a person to learn to live properly in a community is within the community. Failure to comply with the conditions of probation or the commission of a new offence typically results in the offender being returned to the courts, which will decide what further action is required. Failure on parole typically results in the immediate return to prison to continue serving the original sentence and any new sentence that was imposed.

Aboriginal Corrections

The term "disproportionate minority confinement" (DMC) was coined during the 1960s in the U.S. to describe the over-representation of a given minority group in youth detention facilities (Conley 1994; Hsia, Bridges and McHale 2004; Pope and Feyerhern 1992). The concept of DMC has direct applicability to the Canadian correctional context, within which the confinement of Aboriginal persons is six times greater than their representation in the overall Canadian population (Perreault 2009; Statistics Canada 2009).

In response to section 80 of the *Corrections and Conditional Release Act* (1992), which states that the Correctional Service of Canada shall provide Aboriginal specific programs, CSC developed the following five major objectives with regard to Aboriginal offenders:

1. to strengthen Aboriginal offender programming;
2. to enhance the role for Aboriginal communities in corrections;
3. to increase Aboriginal human resources;
4. to enhance partnerships and relations; and
5. to ensure adequate resourcing. (Correctional Service of Canada 2006: 7)

The CSC implemented various new programs and initiatives, which included opening several new healing lodges and healing ranges in existing penitentiaries, initiating culturally appropriate treatment programs, hiring additional Aboriginal employees, including Aboriginal community development officers, developing an Aboriginal gang initiative and training existing staff to become more culturally aware and sensitive to the needs of Aboriginal offenders and communities (CSC 2006).

Programs delivered by and for Aboriginal persons, such as the In Search of Your Warrior (ISOYW) program, operated at six institutions across western Canada and one in Québec, are also needed. The ISOYW program is delivered by Aboriginal staff, elders and volunteers and combines traditional Aboriginal spirituality with Euro-Canadian cognitive-behavioural approaches to substance abuse, anger management and domestic violence (Trevethan, Moore and Allegri 2005). Among the inherent strengths of Aboriginal-designed and delivered programs are their ability to develop treatment connections with the offender in ways that mainstream, Euro-Canadian programs are unable to do and to build valuable linkages between the offender and the Aboriginal community (Braun 1998; Clairmont and Augustine 2009; Whitley 2004; Zellerer 2003). Indeed, as Whitley (2004: 17) notes, this type of program often involves "a process of re-creation, building a sense of community, embracing a set of common values and norms, together with an appreciation for collective wisdom and experience. The restorative process is a maintaining and unifying element." Trevethan et al. (2005) note several positive outcomes for program completers, many of whom reported that they were more in touch with their culture and its spiritual aspects, possessed a more positive attitude towards themselves and others and were better able to deal with the stresses of prison life. These program completers also required fewer and less-intensive correctional programming and increased their potential for early release. Recidivism rates had dropped significantly for ISOYW completers; indeed, prior to the program it was not uncommon for less than one-third of Aboriginal offenders to remain in the community, and now less than one-third were returned to the penitentiary within one year of release.

Provincial and territorial correctional systems also struggle to address the unique needs of Aboriginal offenders. The major problems facing those systems include: (1) a less stable inmate population in terms of high turnover; (2) the extremely short periods of time within which to provide quality programming; and (3) the difficulty of attracting Aboriginal elders and other resource persons due to the location of most provincial correctional facilities near urban centres. In Nunavut's Baffin Correctional Centre (BCC), some of these problems have been addressed by the high percentage of Inuit staff members, programs that seek to include both Inuit and non-Inuit cultures and extensive ties with elders and other Iqaluit residents. Unique among correctional facilities worldwide is BCC's land program, in which trained Inuit staff members take inmates "out on the land," where they use firearms and learn Inuit hunting and sealing techniques; the bounty of caribou, *muktuk* (whale) and seal is provided to local elders and hospitals, with some kept for consumption at BCC (Patenaude, DuPerron, Dillon, Friesen and Zinck 1992, 1993; Patenaude, Wood and Griffiths 1992).

The Criminal Justice System and Justice

Canada's system of criminal justice exists to ensure social control, that is, to ensure that the population complies with the criminal law and to impose a criminal sanction that will punish those individuals who are found to breach those laws in the hope that they will not commit them again. This is premised on a structural functionalist perspective of society governed by a majority, which as noted previously, is often dominated by powerful groups and interests. Learning the basics of the criminal justice system is important for foundational knowledge, but appreciating other theoretical perspectives, as are found in Chapter Two (Theorizing Justice), Chapter Six (Women) and Chapter Nine (Legal Justice), is important for critical understanding.

To perform the functions of social control, the criminal justice system is comprised of the police (to detect and apprehend suspected criminals), the courts (to determine guilt and impose sentences) and corrections (to control and treat offenders) The components of the criminal justice system seek to achieve formal justice in terms procedural fairness and the avoidance of overt discrimination. This may be seen in current criminal legislation, which doesn't distinguish between the wealth or social status of an accused person but speaks to "any person" who commits the crime, and in regulations and formal processes employed by the police that do not limit the interrogations of new Canadian and visitors accused of a crime to the use of English or French but require civilian and/or police interpreters whenever possible. British common law, which is the foundation of our criminal law and procedures, is based on the principle of treating similar cases in a similar manner. Likewise, correctional institutions do not segregate inmates on the basis of inherent characteristics, such as race or ethnicity, in terms of cell placement or access to programs. The current Canadian criminal justice system processes persons accused of a criminal offence from one component to another until it finishes with them and they are released back into society. Two academic models were presented here to assist the reader in understanding how people enter, move through and exit each component in the process as well as the process itself. The criminal justice system is governed by two competing goals, crime control and due process. A crime control model seeks to protect society by quickly removing and effectively punishing offenders, and a due process model seeks to ensure that society is protected in a manner that also protects the fundamental rights of each person accused of a crime from governmental excess and abuse.

Having accepted that substantive justice recognizes the inherent value of each individual and seeks to achieve both justice and fairness, there may be occasions when the criminal justice system must treat individuals differently to achieve that fairness. For example, police recruitment practices may need to envision that Aboriginal or other minority applicants may present different skill sets than those traditionally sought by recruiters. Such practices could result in an increase in the representation of minority populations within the Canadian policing community, which would likely result in an improvement in police-minority relations. The Supreme Court of Canada's decision in *Gladue* (1999) offers an example whereby the current criminal justice system, in order to achieve substantive justice, must take into account the histories of colonialization and discrimination when sentencing Aboriginal offenders. The inclusion of culturally relevant treatment programs delivered by Aboriginal elders and volunteers within correctional settings offer Aboriginal inmates the opportunity to reconnect to their culture and communities.

Regardless of whether the criminal law is just, police, courts and corrections attempt to provide equitable and fair dealings with those identified, accused and/or convicted of having committed a criminal offence. The criminal justice system was developed and adapted to meet the social control needs of an evolving Canadian society. While formal justice seeks to ensure that everyone is treated similarly with fairness and dignity and substantive justice seeks to ensure that we recognize the inherent value and dignity of the individual, neither type of justice can be achieved if the practitioners within the criminal justice system do not act ethically and with personal and professional integrity.

Self-Test

Compare and contrast two of the definitions of what constitutes crime.
What is the impact of defining crime on justice in Canada?
What are the six hypotheses about why a crime might go unreported?
What is the "dark figure" of crime and why is it important to understanding crime?
What differentiates the crime control model from the due process model of criminal justice?
What are the five general levels of policing in Canada?
How can police discretion impact "justice" both positively and negatively?
What is a preliminary inquiry and what role does it serve in our court system?
What determines whether a sentenced offender will serve their time in a federal penitentiary or provincial correctional centre?
What are the six roles of Canada's contemporary correctional system?
Choose one example regarding Aboriginal inclusion in the Canadian criminal justice system (i.e., police, courts, corrections) and explain how it demonstrates the concept of substantive justice.
Why is ethical decision-making and behaviour important for criminal justice practitioners?

Glossary

courts – the judicial branch of the criminal justice system. Their task is to process cases presented before them to determine the guilt or innocence of the accused and to determine a just sentence in the case of an accused found guilty.

corrections – the component of the criminal justice system that functions to provide for the safe and secure custody of offenders for a specified period of time as well as provide offenders with opportunities for rehabilitation and facilitate their eventual reintegration into society.

crime control model – one criminal justice model used to explain the Canadian criminal justice system's goals, this model seeks to ensure that the criminal justice agencies protect society by quickly detecting, arresting and convicting criminals. The goals of this model are observed at times to conflict with the goals of the due process model.

dark figure of crime – the amount of crime not known by or reported to the police.

deterrence (selective and general) – based on the notion that any punishment imposed on an offender will be certain, swift and severe in order to make a person not commit a crime in the future. It can be selective (the unpleasantness of punishment has a preventative effect on an individual committing any future crime) or general (the unpleasantness of punishment of a single offender will have a preventative effect on persons who were not punished and who will avoid committing any future crime).

due process model – one criminal justice model used to explain the Canadian criminal justice system's goals; this model seeks to ensure that the power of the state is not used in a punitive manner and protects the individual citizen from such abuses. The goals of this model are at times in conflict with the goals of the crime control model.

incapacitation (selective and general) – a sentencing philosophy based on punishment for past crime that seeks to prevent future crime by restraining or removing a high-risk person from society for a specified period of time, usually involving incarceration, reducing their capacity for committing additional crimes.

incarceration – in congruence with the philosophy of incapacitation, it is the act of restricting the liberty of a convicted criminal by placing them in a secure facility for the period of time defined by their sentence.

police – the law enforcement branch of the Canadian criminal justice system. This branch, empowered by the government with the legitimate use of force (even deadly), seeks to ensure that the laws of Canada are followed and social order is maintained.

punishment/sanction – the penalty that is assessed for an offender convicted of a crime.

rehabilitation – the process by which the justice system seeks to reform an offender from a being a criminal to adopting a pro-social lifestyle.

restoration/restorative justice – a model of justice that seeks a relational response to repair the harm that a crime has resulted in by including those affected by the crime in the determination of the best solution. It tends to emphasize restitution, reparation and reintegration rather than punishment.

retribution – a model of justice that emphasizes punishment as the correct response to crime. It is through punishment that social equality is re-established on the basis that the convicted offender gets what they deserve.

Part IV

Pursuing Justice

Margot A. Hurlbert

This book is called *Pursuing Justice*. Much of the first three parts are about analyzing the concept of justice and assessing the justice in our society. We have found that we come up short on substantive justice, even though we have many of the institutions of formal justice in place. However, we cannot simply throw out these institutions to achieve substantive justice. As was argued at the outset, true justice requires both formal and substantive justice. But how do we get to that point? Eliminating the oppressions in our society will go a long way to achieving justice, but not all the way. This section proposes that restorative justice can be one crucial way of achieving justice, of pursuing justice. This is because restorative justice is not just a social endpoint, an institution with formal rules, but a process within which justice itself is continually redefined and reinvented by the communities within which it resides.

Restorative justice is often defined by describing the values that characterize it: embracing conflict; recognizing that personal problems may be rooted in social problems; advocating the active participation of all people in solving conflict (what is called "experiencing agency"); and incorporating an ethic of valuing the vulnerable. Transformed into social practices, these values will not always provide the right answer, or the same answer when applied in similar conflicts, but, hopefully, a better answer that fits with the community within which conflict and harm take place.

Restorative justice is also often defined in limiting ways. One such definition describes it as follows:

> Restorative justice is an approach to justice that focuses on repairing the harm caused by crime while holding the offender responsible for his or her actions, by providing an opportunity for the parties directly affected by a crime — victim(s), offender and community — to identify and address their needs in the aftermath of a crime, and seek a resolution that affords healing, reparation and reintegration, and prevents future harm. (Cromier 2002: 3)

While some of the sentiments expressed by Cromier meet the values of restorative justice, this view is limited in several ways. First of all, it sees restorative justice as an end result rather than a process. Moreover, while restoring relationships and preventing future harm are worthy goals, how to achieve these goals is left wide open. Further flaws in this definition can be seen as often relations cannot and should not be "restored" to what they were prior to conflict. Finally, by focusing on "a crime," the application of restorative justice is limited to being an offshoot of the CJS. A much broader application of restorative justice is proposed here. Restorative justice can and must be expanded outside of the criminal context as applying to many other issues and conflicts. For example, it applies to water conflicts and other environmental disputes, as well as within the school system between teachers and students, teachers and parents, and amongst teachers. Restorative justice would also be appropriate in peace-building and attaining the right of development (as argued in Chapter Eight). Restorative justice, carefully defined, is not a program, a diversion for crimes not serious enough for criminal prosecution, or only applicable to the CJS.

Some authors utilize similar broad definitions of restorative justice but use different terms such as "transformative" justice (Morris 2000). While broad, the term "transformative" can often connote a journey to an envisioned better place, a destination. This may all be true of the practice of restorative justice — it intends to be transformative and it is a journey — however, the end state is often not necessarily a better place or an end point. Restorative justice is about balance and moving forward with healthy relationships. It is not about restoring to a previous state or relationship, but finding a place of balance where the process of restorative justice can continue to be practised. That is, the emphasis must be on the journey, not on an entirely definitive end result to be achieved.

Restorative justice, as defined herein, is a process or a method of practice with certain patterns to follow in the pursuit of justice. It is an individualized practice, but one embedded in structural practices. Achieving substantive justice requires making it one's mantra, keeping it flexible enough for a variety of situations and circumstances and remaining open to new ideas, new perspectives and change.

All three frames of justice are reflected in the definition of restorative justice and are required in order to facilitate its practice. Fair hearings, equal participation, recognition, respect and value for differing viewpoints are essential for the practice of embracing conflict, empowering agency and investigating the social problems surrounding individual problems. Ensuring such real procedural justice could, in fact, force the recognition of ethnocentrism and allow other viewpoints to be heard and be part of restorative decisions. In this sense, the voices and participation of the oppressed or marginalized, too often ignored and belittled in our society, are essential in restorative justice.

Second, the restorative justice practices of experiencing agency and embracing conflict require people to resolve their own problems, avoid delegation and actively participate in their resolution. These practices are also essential in achieving substantive justice, as the community of people involved in restorative procedures define what are fair outcomes for particular conflicts and for the community as a whole. In this way, defining what is a fair distribution of society's rewards and burdens (to use the terms of Chapter Three) gives way to a more fluid and evolving definition — one that is determined by a democratic community.

Finally, the ethics of restorative justice match the ethical practice of justice, or the third theme of justice. The interests, needs and perspectives of the marginalized must be recognized and taken into account. In Canada, the practices of formal justice most often reflected in legal justice can provide at least a foundation to facilitate the participation of the marginalized. But, restorative justice demands more of this participation. Our current practices of formal justice must be expanded and transformed to become truly participatory for the needs and perspectives of the marginalized and oppressed to be heard, recognized and accounted for. After achieving full, meaningful participation, the ethical practice of justice can occur.

This final chapter only introduces restorative justice. It is illustrated with a few examples. These examples are not exhaustive and do not do full credit to the breadth, depth and possible application of restorative justice and its potential contribution to achieving justice. Embracing and learning from conflict, participating actively in its resolution and maintaining a constant vigilance to ethical practice are all tenets of restorative justice. Utilizing and applying these tenets and practising restorative justice in everyday actions, decisions and relations can only help transform our community and world to a more just place.

12

Restorative Justice

Margot A. Hurlbert and Hirsch Greenberg

At the end of this chapter, you will be able to:

- Define restorative justice
- Apply basic restorative justice skills for resolving conflict constructively
- Outline the application of restorative justice in various contexts, including the environment, school system, criminal justice system and Aboriginal communities
- Explore the limitations and strengths of restorative justice

Conflict is a natural occurrence of people living together because everyone has different viewpoints, needs, stresses and challenges. It can end in disagreements or problematic situations (Goldman and Royot 2003: 10; Hulsman 1986: 66). Solving conflicts has always been practised in some form by societies, including such interventions as blood revenge, retribution, ritual satisfaction and restoration (Wietenkamp and Kerner 2002). In the thirteenth century, in Western societies, penal law emerged and the state took over the resolution of conflicts. It was during this time that a professional class of "conflict resolvers" — lawyers, police and judges — came into being (Wietenkamp and Kerner 2002; Christie 1977).

As people have come to rely on these professionals, they have developed a corresponding helplessness at solving their own conflicts. Worse yet, professional conflict resolvers have developed areas of exclusivity, which prevents people from solving their own conflicts and protects the livelihood of the conflict resolvers. For example, an agreement between two spouses is ineffective unless signed off by lawyers, and only lawyers certified by a professional lawyers association can practise law. This excludes others from the occupation of resolving family conflict, including their own. Thus, "conflict," as Christie (1977) puts it, comes to be like property or another asset from which money can be earned. Individuals should own their own conflicts, but, unfortunately, people seem to have given up their conflict rights to lawyers, courts, correctional institutions and the police.

Restorative justice is about reclaiming conflict — not delegating its resolution to professional resolvers. Indeed, numerous conflicts are resolved every day without the use of professionals, so in reality people are restorative justice practitioners already. Promoting and practising restorative justice means we increase the number and scope of these personally resolved conflicts.

This chapter is the culmination of the pursuit of justice. Restorative justice brings all aspects of justice together. In fact, if practised and implemented correctly, restorative justice answers the central question: what is justice? It is the restoration of relationships during and after conflict, keeping in mind that after conflict, relationships are never brought back to an "original" position; rather, relationships are re-established. Restorative justice embraces all three thematic frames of justice. It has aspects of procedural, process or formal justice in its mechanisms of application (such as victim-offender mediations); it has aspects of distributive or substantive justice because each participant has an opportunity to express themselves and their needs (victims are not left out of the process as happens in a criminal trial); and lastly, if practised properly, it is informed and constituted by an ethical practice.

What Is Restorative Justice?

Main Points

As you read highlight, the answers to these questions:
What is the definition of restorative justice?
What practices of restorative justice can you apply every day in your own life?
What skills and tools do restorative justice practitioners use?

The term "restorative justice" emerged in the 1980s in Canada to describe the type of justice being achieved by a new criminal justice practice of mediations involving victims and offenders. In 1974 the Mennonite Central Committee of Kitchener-Waterloo introduced victim-offender mediation in the early stages of the court process (Weitenkamp and Kerner 2002), and it was embraced Canada-wide in 1988 (Daubney 1988). Because of this initial criminal justice application, restorative justice is often defined within a narrow criminal context as

> a process whereby all the parties with a stake in a particular offence come together to resolve collectively how to deal with the aftermath of the offence and its implications for the future. (Marshall 1999: 5)

The weakness of this definition is in the word "offence," which limits the scope and practice of restorative justice to behaviour which has been determined as criminal within society. Whether interpersonal conflicts or even specific behaviours (like smoking marijuana or loitering in a park) are deemed "criminal" is partly decided by those with the power to make those determinations. By not introducing a critical examination of the determination of criminality, this definition leaves the practice of restorative justice as an appendage of the criminal justice system. In other words, it fails to address structural issues or recognize social problems and problems of maldistribution.

When restorative justice is applied more broadly than just the criminal justice system, it is often referred to by such terms as community justice, transformative justice, peacemaking and collaborative problem solving. We propose such a broader definition of restorative justice which encompasses aspects of social justice, or achieving justice in society. Our broader definition has the following four pillars:

1. *embracement of conflict resolution* – embraces resolving conflict or problematic situations without delegating the task to professionals;
2. *recognition of social problems* – recognizes the social problems inherent in individual conflicts. Conflict is viewed as not only an interpersonal dynamic but also as situated within the broader community and society. This means that conflict resolution may require social transformation as well as individual accountability;
3. *experience of agency* – requires individuals experiencing and affected by conflict and problematic situations to actively participate in its resolution; and
4. *ethical practice of leximin* – incorporates an ethic of doing no harm and protecting the most vulnerable in the community in order to create strong and supporting relationships.

This definition of restorative justice is a procedure for how to achieve justice, informed by an ethical practice and grounded in a critical social analysis. The application and practice of restorative justice in real life raises several issues. In this regard, Pavlich (2005: 105) argues that restorative justice, if it is practised within a homogenous community, can become a form of governance, with nothing really changing. By this he means that restorative justice merely substitutes a localized community for a distant government or judge; for example, instead of a judge ordering a convicted person to perform community service, a group of local people do. Restorative justice operates then simply as corrective justice within the criminal context or local politics. In these cases, restorative justice is being practised without employing pillars two (recognizing social problems) and four (applying the principle of leximin).

In Canada, Pavlich's criticism often doesn't apply. Practised in a local context, restorative justice can allow for Canada's diversity of cultural communities. For example, Aboriginal restorative justice institutions allow Aboriginal communities independence and freedom from being subsumed within the larger Canadian mainstream political context. In this way restorative justice promotes and protects diversity and self-determination for Aboriginal communities (this example is discussed in more detail later in the chapter).

The core principle of restorative justice is about developing and supporting relationships that are open and honest, communicative and supportive. Although the causes of problems in relationships are many and varied, most inevitably involve conflict. Therefore, the basics of restorative justice practice centre on constructive conflict resolution.

Generally, people do not like conflict, and as with anything that people do not like, they attempt to avoid it. However, at some stage all relationships experience conflict. Because of this it is important to recognize that conflict can often have positive impacts. For instance, handled properly by incorporating some of the practices of restorative justice outlined later in the chapter, conflict can promote communication as people express their feelings and wishes as a result of a disagreement or an action which has hurt them. Conflict often exposes problems and issues, and proper restorative justice practices can lead to these issues and problems being solved. At an individual level, this process can forge strong relationships and prevent the escalation of conflict into a situation causing irreparable damage to relationships or violence.

At a larger social level, conflict in society often results in positive social change. Think of the conflict surrounding the civil rights of the African-American community in the 1950s and 1960s and the reaction of those who opposed the vision of equality espoused by Martin Luther King, Jr. This conflict resulted in the changing of societal norms and laws which had directly discriminated against people on the basis of race, denying them the right to eat in certain establishments, sit in certain areas of the bus and swim in certain public swimming pools. Since the 1960s, many of these harmful exclusions have been rectified in U.S. society, as the people sought to resolve those civil rights conflicts.

On a societal level, and sometimes in our personal relationships, conflict prevents stagnation and promotes necessary changes. If we consider conflict as a learning experience, we will react to conflict as a "challenge," and our curiosity and imagination will be piqued as we ponder how to resolve it constructively, both personally and at a societal level. If restorative justice is practised as a social justice project, utilizing all four pillars of the broad definition of restorative justice, social problems can be addressed and positive social change effected.

Collaborative versus Adversarial Problem Solving

Dealing with conflict positively means responding to it in a collaborative, non-confrontational manner, which is pretty much the opposite of our "adversarial" legal/court system. In adversarial problem solving, there must be a winner and a loser, and only one view is the "truth." Often the dispute is personalized, with one side or the other being labelled as a "bad" person or group of people. In an adversarial structure, it is almost inevitable that winning will be seen as the most important thing, regardless of future impact. Those who embrace conflict as a means of solving problems believe that society's mechanisms, such as courts, tribunals and police, will stop people from utilizing such winner-take-all techniques when too many people have been hurt. Adversarial problem solvers hope no one else models their means of overcoming disputes, as it is a benefit to them to have fewer people use this approach to solving problems (Johnson and Johnson 1989, 2003; akin to "Competitors" in Barsky 2000: 42).

Collaborative problem solvers, on the other hand, believe they are responsible for their own conduct and they hope others will model their approach. Collaborative problem solving or conflict resolution espouses the view that a dispute can never actually be won if the other party believes they have lost. People and their relationships are critical, and even if a person doesn't agree with the other party, understanding their interests and views is required. Power and coercion are not substitutes for thought and understanding; careful attention must be paid to the dynamics of power. With a comprehensive understanding of each side, often a dispute can be resolved constructively through achieving a solution that meets the different needs and interests of the parties (Johnson and Johnson 1989, 2003; Barsky 2000: 42).

People have differing needs and interests depending on their values, material conditions and personal experiences of oppression. These needs and interests can be thought of as substantive (money, time and resources, for example), procedural (timeline of meetings and discussions) and psychological. The most powerful psychological needs include security, economic well being, a sense of belonging and recognition and control over one's life (Raiffa 1982: 126–32). Adversarial problem solvers most often focus on substantive needs such as money; collaborative problem solvers are cognizant of all three types of needs. Many problem solving processes fail as they do not deal with the procedural issues (that is, proper discussion of the issues and proper timing of the discussions to correspond with a person's healing process) or the psychological interests of parties (for example, receiving a genuine apology and being respected). The needs can be thought of as conjoining circles.

Given that relationships and conflict within the workplace are a reality, collaborative problem solving has personal implications and a potentially broad application in one's career. Many professions are directly involved in resolving conflict and apply these principles in their work every day: examples include teachers resolving disagreements amongst students, managers settling disputes with or between employees and restaurant workers dealing with dissatisfied customers. Many occupations would benefit from the knowledge developed within the restorative justice movement. On the other side of the coin, many academic disciplines have much to offer to the practice of restorative justice. Exploring and explaining how people think, behave, feel and physically respond to others and the world around them are some of the subjects addressed by psychological, sociological, anthropological and medical sciences, to name a few.

Practising restorative justice involves recognizing and acknowledging particular values in resolving conflict. The values we bring to the (restorative) justice table include influences that our families, friends, schools and cultural and religious affiliations all have in developing our beliefs, our moral sense of right and wrong. These values have important implications for the ways restorative justice practitioners assist others in resolving conflict constructively; they inform the practitioner's ethical practice of restorative justice. Sometimes these values have to be set aside, perhaps through open acknowledgement, and the practitioner must strive to be impartial when assisting the different parties in conflict. If the practitioner is a parent and is assisting a family in resolving a problematic parent-child situation, the practitioner's own values — for example, respect for elders or consequences for certain behaviours of youth — won't necessarily be useful in resolving the parent-child conflict. Helping people resolve conflicts must be done with a mind open to solutions that the parties (in this case the parent and child) arrive at. The different cultures, backgrounds and viewpoints of the parties are important to conflict resolution, and these are not necessarily within the knowledge of the practitioner (Oetzel et al. 2006: 571; Kruk 1997: 13). Consider the relationship principles in Table 7 and the corresponding implications for practice.

It is essential to understand the dynamics of relationships, recognize values in order to adopt an ethical restorative justice practice and possess a few basic tools to use in the practice of restorative justice. In some circumstances, such as domestic violence, the practitioner cannot be impartial. Consider the following example.

Family group conferencing integrates issues of domestic and child abuse into a restorative justice practice. A conference or meeting is held with family members, child welfare professionals, service providers and community members (perhaps from the police, schools, shelters, health services or cultural organizations) to discuss the needs of a family experiencing violence. Without such a restorative justice practice, the approach may be fragmented, with child welfare workers apprehending children being exposed to domestic violence and/or suffering violence themselves and women accessing shelters or interacting with police, courts and lawyers. Bringing all the individuals together in a restorative justice practice has been found to result to fewer family separations, fewer children being taken into care and fewer families having members fleeing the home out of fear (Pennel and Burford 2000: 143). In addition, restorative justice practices help address the social problem of discrimination against women by establishing organizations to hold family

Table 7 Relationship Building

Relationship Principle	Implications for Practice
Our realties are separate	By presenting their perspectives, participants begin the process of understanding each other's point of view.
Everybody has different pictures	While participants may engage with each other in a common process, the expected outcomes/pictures may be different for each.
We try to understand the other person's view of the world	Participation is not predicated on the assumption that participants must see events in the same way but rather that there will be respect for each other's point of view and acceptance that some level of harm resulted in the crime behaviour.
All behaviour is purposeful	For example, while crime behaviour is a negative social norm, for the perpetrator it had purpose (for example, fun, money).
I can't control others	Victims, in part, want to hear the offender's point of view, why they committed the crime, and to explain the harm which resulted. That is, why did the offender make the choices they did?
I can only control myself	Relationships should not be based on the assumption: "If you do what I want, I will forgive you." The victim-offender relationship should result in respect, dignity and acceptance of each other as members of the human community. This may or may not entail jail sentences, community work, etc.
Collaboration and consensus create new options	Successful relationships can evolve if the participants agree that overcoming problems together can be reached through consensus rather than coercion, punishment or threats.
Unlimited resources	Outcomes are based on the creativity and resourcefulness of those involved rather than looking outside of the participants for a "saviour."
Maximum degrees of freedom	Flexibility to create new forms of relationship renewal is essential. Cookie-cutter approaches to restorative justice cannot fit every possible circumstance.
Win/win mental model	Relationship building at the end of the day is about finding win/win solutions. All participants should be satisfied with the outcome.

Source: Adapted from Glasser 1998.

group conferences, carrying out plans arrived at in family group conferences for keeping women safe and strengthening women's autonomy and leadership through involvement in the creation and maintenance of these organizations. Most importantly, women's leadership roles within the family are strengthened, and the norms and practices of gender discrimination in private, hierarchical families (resulting in violence against women) are reduced or ended (Pennel and Burford 2002: 114). The restorative justice practice allows women control over their situation, something given up if only the state is utilized to criminally prosecute the offender.

Elements of Restorative Justice Practice

Certain ethical practices are paramount in restorative conflict resolution. For instance, if two parties to a conflict are going to feel an outcome is just, the mediator will need to be impartial and not support one person's side over the other's. A mediator's values and biases must be set aside in order to truly listen to each perspective (Smith, Young and Anderson 1996: 30). Similarly, a mediator mustn't have a conflict of interest in relation to the parties' dispute (Smith, Young, Ish and Anderson 1996: 30). A teacher resolving a dispute between students would have a conflict of interest if one of the students was their child. Confidentiality and allowing people to resolve their own differences without a mediator imposing their views or solutions are also paramount ethical practices (Smith et al. 1996: 31)

Gustafson (2007: 1), an eminent restorative justice practitioner and author, quotes a trauma survivor who addressed the June 2003 International Restorative Justice Conference in Vancouver, B.C., to answer the question, "what is practitioner competence in restorative justice?":

> Restorative Justice needs to be rooted in values like: creating no further harms, safety, listening, validating, and empowering people to seek healing and restoration in their own way and timing. It needs to flow out of developing relationships between the clients and the practitioners. People respond to being honoured and loved and you can't fake this.... RJ done well requires a huge time commitment and consistent care. When doing RJ in cases of serious crime it can be life risking and consequently life changing. So full of risks and rewards. The hardest pain imaginable faced and the biggest relief!!! ("Margaret," an adult survivor of violent sexual assaults in her mid-teens)

Competence is an integral part of the practice in restorative justice. Competence goes beyond being good at relating to friends, family and acquaintances. It is the capacity to empathize in ways that facilitate connecting individuals with themselves (self-reflection) and with others (changing behaviours). It is the capacity to go beyond technical or recipe interventions or personal opinion by evolving adaptive practices to fit the unique circumstances of the individuals involved in restorative justice.

When people tell their story — for example, a victim relating how they were affected by a robbery or natural disaster — they may experience an important aspect of repairing the harm. Herman (1997: 3) calls this fundamental aspect of recovery "reconstructing the trauma story." Additional aspects of helping a person recover include establishing a safe environment, facilitating restoration of connections to family, friends and community, and providing practical and material help, as well as moral and spiritual guidance (Herman 1997: 3; Van Ness and Strong 2006: 96). Victims often recount their story among families and friends, in our homes or at the office. Not only can a knowledgeable, sensitive and trained practitioner truly hearing someone's story, they can often provide perspectives and information families and friends are unable to offer. For example, a family member of an offender may excuse an individual's act, rather than assisting to resolve the factors which led to a conflict or a crime. Thus, the relationship between a victim or an offender and a practitioner is one among many.

In many contexts, including the criminal justice system, storytelling is an effective intervention that permits offenders, victims and their families and/or communities to express their perspectives in non-threatening ways. Storytelling can be used to present information, clarify a point, support someone's perspective and crystallize and shape ideas. Storytelling promotes understanding, appreciation and respect for the feelings (for example, anger) and physiological symptoms (for example, insomnia) of victims and offenders in response to the conflict.

Herman (1997: 134) highlights the importance, in the practice of restorative justice, of the practitioner's competence in assessing an individual's ability to both function autonomously on a day-to-day level and to make healthy life decisions. Strak and Flitcraft, in working with women who experience domestic violence, define autonomy as "a sense of separateness, flexibility, and self-possession sufficient to define one's interest" (cited Herman 1997: 134). They define empowerment as "the convergence of individual support and autonomy" (134). Empowerment occurs then, when an individual's harm is acknowledged by others, including the offender, and independent change is inspired.

Another perspective on empowerment in restorative justice is explained by elder Phil Gatensby (2007) of the Raven Clan, Inland Tlinget Nation, in his training circles:

> Gathering Power is a transformational experience designed to create the opportunity for participants to come to a greater understanding of themselves and the world around them. Gathering Power uncovers the treasure chest of resources that lies within each of us. It will bring an

> awareness of the dynamics of power and how to harness our power in order to address the ongoing struggles and the imbalances human beings are challenged with each day.

Dynamic power refers to the relationship each of us has to nature, including to each other. This power or life force is ever-changing, sometimes allowing us to gain direction over our life and sometimes the opposite, causing us to lose control over life events for a period of time, such as when a trauma — for example, a physical assault — occurs.

The above discussion looks at restorative justice practice and skills as they relate to individual circumstances. What if individuals are a member of a minority group and they experience the trauma of racism? McCaslin (2005: 89) discusses how Indigenous people respond to trauma at a community level, describing a single criminal act as a sign of "imbalance within the community as a whole — imbalances that effect everyone." She explains that the criminal actions of an individual are more a warning sign that "the essential fabric of the community is starting to unwind" (89). She goes on to propose that to heal — repair the harm done by generations of colonizers — "we must confront multigenerational internalized trauma, oppression, colonized attitudes and habits, racism, pressures to assimilate and the ongoing degeneration of people and culture" (89). She uses the Hollow Water First Nation, a reserve on Lake Winnipeg, as an example of harm being healed beyond individual circumstances:

> Whatever aspects of harm we face, our communities are central to how we respond to them. For us, healing is about bringing the community back into the picture. It is about communities finding their own solutions. Communities can view problems as opportunities for seeing more clearly how we have drifted out of balance. The challenges give us a chance to work toward a balance that grows from our traditions and is not imposed from without. When others use our challenges as an excuse to impose their ways, we are weakened. (89–90)

The work of the Hollow Water First Nation is discussed further below.

Restorative justice practices are applicable to resolving conflict at individual and societal levels. These applications share the following in common: recognizing the harm caused, recognizing the dignity, strength and spirit of the individual or community and re-establishing autonomy (or in the case of Indigenous peoples, self-determination). In this way, restorative justice encompasses the third frame of justice, ethical practice, which involves taking into account the needs of the marginalized and oppressed, whether they be individuals or groups.

Self Test

Is there any value in the adversarial problem solving method?
Can narrowly defined restorative justice tackle social problems?
Can a restorative justice practitioner ever set aside their values and prejudices and be impartial?

Restorative Justice Applications

The following examples illustrate some of the diverse applications of restorative justice.

Restorative Water Justice

Conflict occurs in relation to our environment and our sources of water on a daily basis. On the news we see such examples as an environmental group protesting the destruction of forests, or a First Nation demonstrating against the building of a pipeline. The common dynamic sees the forces of development pitted against concern for the preservation and sustainability of our environment. For example, the tar sands in Northern Alberta pollute nearby waters and impact communities downstream (Smandych and Kueneman 2010: 104). In times of water drought in Alberta, not all licensed water users have enough water. Conflict over water scarcity and its resulting degradation of quality is becoming increasingly common, with such conflicts often resulting in criminal consequences (Rojas et al. 2009: 237; Environment Canada 2002).

Two people were criminally charged and sentenced in Walkerton, Ontario, when several people died and 2,500 people fell ill in the year 2000 due to an outbreak of a highly dangerous strain of E. coli bacteria in the town water supply. In 2001, in North Battleford, more than 7,000 people fell ill, with fifty hospitalized, when the town's water supply became tainted with the cryptosporidium bacterium. These outbreaks were traced to the failure of the water treatment plants to treat solids in the water resulting from livestock grazing upstream. These incidents reflect a reliance on government to provide an element necessary for human survival, drinking water, and a host of regulatory mechanisms to ensure people's health, backed by threat of criminal consequences. Simply charging the water treatment operators and managers with criminal offences reflects our neo-liberal individualized society, which fails to recognize the social problem in the situation: the impact of development (in this circumstance, agriculture) on the environment.

Both the North Battleford and Walkerton inquiries concluded that changes in the way water was managed were needed; specifically, we must concentrate on protecting the sources of our water supplies (O'Connor 2002; Laing 2003; GWP 2000; Conference Board of Canada 2005; Pollution Probe 2007). This change in water management is a transformation from the historical reliance on government for water and its management, with regulations and criminal charges for mistakes made by employees and municipalities; it shares the same family of practices as that of restorative justice, as described below.

Concerned community members, environmentalists, conservationists, farmers and members of urban and rural municipalities have been involved in water issues for many years. Community engagement has been consistent, although terminology for these groups varies between and within provinces: in Manitoba conservation districts consider impacts on water; in Alberta river basin councils or watershed alliances perform these tasks; and in Saskatchewan the term is watershed groups (hereafter all called "watershed advisory groups"). Across Canada provinces have been increasingly involving these groups and creating new ones in water source protection planning, partially as a result of the Walkerton and North Battleford crises (Hurlbert 2009). In Alberta watershed advisory groups formulated plans which resulted in a moratorium on the issuance of further water licences in the South Saskatchewan River Basin, effectively halting development in order to protect the aquatic environment (Alberta Environment 2005: 6). In Manitoba the same theme appears with the acknowledgement in watershed planning that there are pressures due to a growing economy and that the plan must ensure the sustainable management of watershed resources; in addition, the plan must help define what is important to the community (Turtle Mountain 2006: 4). Further evidence of the important application of local knowledge is that the Turtle Mountain Conservation District is reviewing applications for drainage licensing requirements for the Manitoba Watershed Stewardship (Government of Manitoba 2009: 1). In the future it is anticipated that the district will have a greater ability to comment on licensing conditions once a surface water management plan is completed. In these ways, the Alberta local groups are responding to the conflict of water shortage and the Manitoba local group is responding to the conflict of water excess or potential flooding.

The creation and utilization of local watershed advisory groups to manage local water resources (also termed integrated water resource management) instead of delegating or relying on government or private business is a significant international theme (UNWWDR 2006; GWP 2000). This form of water governance seeks to develop a consensus-based vision and decision-making process, defined as "a process, which promotes the coordinated development and management of water, land and related resources in order to maximize the resultant economic and social welfare in an equitable manner without compromising the sustainability of vital ecosystems" (GWP 2000). The benefits in this form of water governance are:

- a commitment by the local people to the implementation of adopted decisions;
- the incorporation of local community practices, values and knowledge into decisions respecting the use of water resources;
- the recognition of the true value of impacts resulting from water decisions; and
- adaptive, quick and flexible response to issues (Brooks 2002; Hickey and Mohan 2004).

This form of governance restores justice in respect of water and the impacts of people on water. It allows people to solve their own problems in relation to water instead of leaving this matter to the government and professionals or private companies. Local watershed advisory groups can actively participate in the resolution of conflicts surrounding water and the environment and protect the environment while balancing the need for development. However, the following obstacles to this process of involving local watershed advisory groups have been identified:

- tokenism, or the province not giving the group a significant role;
- the myth of "community," or the belief that a community is a coherent and cohesive body;
- fundamental lack of resources (both economic and social) to allow the group to undertake significant activity;
- critical lack of knowledge about the actual process of this form of water governance (or the practices of restorative justice) and how to successfully facilitate it (Smith 2008; Solanes and Jouravlev 2006: 55);
- inadequate institutional and legal frameworks; and
- lack of political willingness to embrace the new paradigms (Figueres et al. 2003; Gleick 2006; Hillman 2008).

Further research is needed into the watershed advisory groups to see if they are achieving their goals (arguably akin to those of restorative justice — empowered community decision-making). It could be that more work is needed on ensuring a broad representative membership of the community. Perhaps these groups need to incorporate the ethic of doing no harm or protecting the most powerless and vulnerable in society. Also, as noted, a lack of knowledge about the actual process of this form of governance and how to facilitate it may obstruct achieving restorative justice.

Restorative Justice in Schools

It is increasingly recognized that restorative justice has an important application within schools. This is partly due to the growing awareness that punishments, such as detention and suspensions, only aggravate issues such as bullying, violence, poor academic performance and parental apathy (Porter 2007: 1). As a result, educators are exploring restorative justice practices as ways to create safe, supportive learning environments. Teachers and administrators are adopting restorative justice practices not only to replace punishment but also in respect of facilitating relations among and between students, teachers, the school administration and parents. The examples below illustrate how these practices have changed the very nature or "soul" of the school.

Educators have been incorporating restorative justice practice into the school setting since the 1990s. While the term "restorative justice" was not common early in this time period, the use of alternatives to punishment (especially corporal punishment) and suspension is well documented (Redekop 2008). Educators realized that traditional punishment detracts from the fundamental goal of developing a centred, balanced young person with self-discipline to do things such as to show up on time and adopt patterns of behaviour to work in large groups outside the family. Punishment creates anger and reduces self-esteem and is counter-productive to the development of the child (Ginott 1972: 147–48). Focus on consequences and other esteem-building measures has been deemed superior to punishment for decades.

Some advocates, such as Glasser (1969, 1998), have moved beyond consequence-oriented approaches to a complete rejection of all methods used to control student behaviour (cited in Redekkop 2008: 200). Glasser, for example, rejects facilitated mediation because, once invoked, it imposes constraints on young people, as two students and a mediator must arrive at a consensual resolution of an issue. This forces a student to do or not do something to end the mediation. Instead, Glasser argues for facilitated personal reflection or internal control of choices. This would entail a student learning about the impact of their behaviour on their fellow student and having the choice of their actions in the future (obviously behaviour with criminal or disruptive aspects will have consequences). Students' own internalized change will self-regulate future behaviours, thus, potentially mitigating future negative results (such as harm to themselves or others). Other scholars are still debating whether mediation is a form of external control.

Elizabeth McCollum, an eighth grade teacher, said "that the approach (circles with students) has provided an open line of communication, allowing students to feel safe" (quoted in Mirsky 2004: 1). Several anti-bullying initiatives now include constructive dispute resolution circles for students. These measures can change the entire school culture. At Holy Innocents School in Philadelphia, a student proclaimed: "There's someone in the eighth grade who's being mistreated, who will not speak up for him or herself, and I won't tolerate it" (1), clearly illustrating that the process can facilitate the ethical practice of assisting the less powerful.

One study found that using "punishment" had the following impacts on the whole school, not least the teachers:

> Staff were determined to carry out the punishment and physical confrontation ensued.... The sense of community was eroding. Staff-pupil relationships changed to an "us and them" situation, vandalism and antisocial behaviour increased dramatically. Staff suffered rising levels of stress, and absenteeism and turnover increased. (Boulton and Mirsky, 2006: 1)

The SaferSanerSchools program at Holy Innocents also uses circles for faculty meetings.

Restorative justice principles have not only helped change teaching practices in relation to dealing with student misbehaviour and teacher-to-teacher relations but have also been applied in inter-student contexts and encouraging positive parental participation. Jenni Lyenna, a counsellor at Princess Margaret Secondary School in Surrey, B.C., explained how at one time the "bullying was common and news of fights planned or happening were a given" (Huge and Lyenna 2004: 2) and that the school adopted a restorative justice intervention process: "We preferred to work with students and their families rather than suspend them or kick them out" (3).

Improvements in schools after implementing restorative justice practices are well documented. A report from the International Institute for Restorative Practices, Graduate School, *Schools Implementing Restorative Practices,* covering six U.S., two Canadian and two British schools, reports the number of students suspended, incidents/infractions [for example, bullying] and school initiated sanctions. The findings, covering a two- to four-year period in which restorative justice practices were implemented, uncovered dramatic declines in these numbers. For example, in West Philadelphia High School, violent incidents were down 52 percent in 2007–2008 compared to the previous year (Mirsky 2009: 7).

Canadian, British, Australian and U.S. schools, as described by Boulton and Mirsky (2006), Hugh and Lynnea (2004), Adams (2008) and others, could support the central tenet that "restorative practice can become a way of sensing the soul of a school" (Welden 2008). Restorative justice allows a school's academic and social culture to emerge (McCold, in Porter 2007: 1). Restorative justice practice in schools is not a panacea for disruptive behaviour, poor academic performance or families' non-participation in school activities. Rather, it is a model which offers a coherent multidimensional approach to problem-solving the complex nature of negative school environments and traditional reward-and-punishment responses.

Restorative Justice in the Criminal Justice System

A traditional criminal justice perspective is that crime is an "offence" committed by someone in violation of a law of the state and that punishment is required to redress the situation. Restorative justice, on the other hand, views crime as a violation of trust and a disruption of relationships. The restorative justice context is concerned with how the action that constituted the "crime" harmed the people involved, including such things as how it breached their trust and feelings of well being and security. Such violation creates obligations to make things right. Restorative justice involves the victim, the offender and the community in a search for solutions that promote repair, reconciliation and reassurance. Marshall (1999: 5) defines restorative justice as follows:

> Restorative justice is a process whereby all the parties with a stake in a particular offence come together to resolve collectively how to deal with the aftermath of the offence and its implications for the future.... Restorative justice is every action that is primarily oriented toward doing justice by repairing the harm that has been caused by a crime.

Instead of approaching crime as a matter of breaking the law or offending against the state, restorative justice regards it as an injury to a person. As a result, it entails the repair of the damage the crime has caused. The victim and offender are encouraged to play active parts in this process, not simply watch the players of the criminal justice system — the police, lawyers, and court personnel — handle their situation.

The application of restorative justice within the criminal justice system has been formally implemented through legislative amendments. The *Criminal Code* of Canada (CCC) refers to such alternative practices as "measures other than judicial proceedings under this *Act* used to deal with a person who is eighteen years of age or over and alleged to have committed an offence." With regard to young offenders, the *Youth Criminal Justice Act* (YCJA) provides for the use of extrajudicial measures for youth between the ages of twelve and seventeen. Both these "alternative measures" and "extrajudicial measures" are meant to be forms of restorative justice interventions, which include non-punitive strategies such as peacekeeping, community and family justice forums, transformative justice and mediation.

In studying restorative justice, it is often helpful to contrast it with the traditional retributive approach to criminal justice (see Table 8). The retributive approach is largely justified by assumptions that claim a deterrence value in punishment. The Canadian public assesses the criminal justice system by whether it convicts and punishes adequately those whom they believe to be guilty (Paciocco 1999: 11). The criminal justice system feeds this perception that the sentencing and incarceration of offenders reduces crime through deterring or removing criminals from society (14). In respect to deterrence, the 1987 Canadian Sentencing Commission gave up on both "specific deterrence," punishment that prevents offenders from reoffending (based on research on rates of recidivism or repeat offending), and also "general deterrence," or the intimidation of other people from offending. These findings are confirmed by other research (Redekop 2008: 81; Roberts and Grossman 2004; Andrews et al. 1990: 393). As most crime is not based on a rational decision-making process, with an informed weighing of the pros and cons, it seems evident that deterrence is a small, if existent at all, effect of sentencing to prison.

Incarceration does incapacitate or remove offenders from harming others in society for a limited period of time — however, at great financial cost. For example, for federal penitentiary inmates, the cost is $343,810 per annum for women, $223,687 for men in maximum security and $140,527 for men in minimum security (Office of the Parliamentary Budge Officer 2010: 94). These findings demonstrate that the criminal justice system has made a false promise to Canadians that the sanction of incarceration protects the public and reduces the amount of crime. It is not surprising that, in terms of crime rates and their pattern in Canada, mainstream criminal justice responses have had limited success.

Table 8 Retributive versus Restorative Justice Approaches

Retributive	Restorative
Crime is act against the state	Crime is act against a person
Criminal justice system controls crime	Crime control lies primarily in the community
Offender accountability defined as taking punishment	Accountability defined as assuming responsibility and taking action to repair harm
Crime is an individual act with individual responsibility	Crime has individual and social dimensions of responsibility
Punishment is effective as threat of it deters crime and changes behaviour	Punishment alone is not effective in changing behaviour and is disruptive to community harmony and good relationships
Offender is defined by deficits	Victims are central to the process of resolving a crime
Focus on blame/guilt	Offender is defined by capacity to make reparation
Adversarial	Focus on problem solving, on future
Imposition of pain to punish and deter/prevent	Emphasis on dialogue and negotiation
Community on sideline, represented abstractly by state	Restitution as a means of restoring both parties
Response focused on offender's past behaviour	Community is facilitator
Dependence upon proxy professionals	Response focused on harmful consequences of offender's behaviour and emphasis on future
	Direct involvement by participants

Source: Winterdyk and King 1999: 298.

It has been apparent since the 1970s that rehabilitation efforts have been largely unsuccessful in prisons, but it is also the case that programs have been underfunded, understaffed and inadequate (Paciocco 1999: 23). In 1977, a report of the Solicitor General of Canada (1977) acknowledged that as educational centres, Canadian prisons were most effective in educating less experienced, less hardened offenders to be more difficult and professional criminals. The reasons for this dynamic are not difficult to imagine and were articulated by the Le Dain Commission (1973: 59), which noted that criminalization "results from confining offenders together in a closed society in which a criminal subculture develops." It has also been noted that prisons are a recruitment centre for organized gangs, which research confirms continues to be the case (Boe 2003; Correctional Service Canada 2004).

Not only does the criminal justice system have limited impact in redirecting people who are in trouble with the law, it also provides limited assistance to those who have suffered because of "criminal" actions

Victims of crime, in particular, have lost their right to participate in the criminal justice system, as Crown prosecutors, police and lawyers now handle criminal complaints for them. Restorative justice seeks to restore the right of the participants (victims, offenders, families, communities) to participate (Christie 1977). This involves a paradigm shift about how crime is defined — from the "breaking of laws" toward causing harm to people. Thus, restorative justice tools are used to build damaged relationships caused by harmful behaviours. "The principle of repair — justice requires that we work to heal victims, offenders, and communities that have been injured by crime" (Van Ness and Strong 1997, cited in Brazmore and Schiff 2005: 152). The purpose or goal of a restorative justice intervention is to resolve the harm and to create new, positive relationships among the participants.

Summary Points

Making a decision to be a collaborative problem solver is to adopt a restorative justice practice.

A restorative justice practitioner's competence requires an ethical practice. This includes not solving people's problems for them, respecting confidentiality and not taking sides in a dispute. It also involves embracing the principle of leximin, or protecting the powerless and vulnerable.

Restorative justice can be practised in one's personal life and in many careers, including policing, corrections, teaching, business and social work.

Research confirms that prison neither deters people from committing crime nor reduces crime. Once this misconception is acknowledged, people often are more understanding of a restorative justice approach.

Aboriginal Restorative Justice Institutions

Aboriginal people have shown significant initiative and innovation in developing their own restorative justice models and institutions. The parallels between

Victims in the Criminal Justice System

Think about what victims in the criminal justice system must experience. First they have to contact the police and have a person charged with a criminal offence. Then they have a lengthy wait for a prosecutor to proceed with the charge. Their first notice that this has been done is often when they themselves are served with a subpoena to appear on a date and time at the criminal court. The Crown prosecutor may have dozens of matters to deal with on that particular day so will probably spend only a few minutes with them. They will be placed on the witness stand, questioned by the prosecutor and then cross-examined by the defence counsel. If there is a conviction, sentencing will usually be done at a later date. Although the victim might have f led a victim impact statement, which may be read by the judge, sentencing is solely within the discretion of the Judge.

Jane's partner was charged with assaulting her. She was not sure whether she wanted assistance from Victim Services. Jane said she didn't have any safety concerns and that indeed she wanted to have "no contact" removed from the court ordered conditions. The Victim Services worker met with Jane the next day. The day afterward, Jane was assaulted again by her partner (court conditions were unchanged at this time). The Victim Services worker re-contacted Jane and she was now prepared to accept services. As the worker and the victim built up a positive working relationship, Jane revealed more information about the two assaults and her partner's drinking.

Jane's partner entered a guilty plea on one of the charges and the Crown prosecutor stayed the second assault charge because Jane's partner was willing to enter a domestic violence program. During the program he appeared to be doing quite well. The Victim Services worker periodically checked in with Jane. She did not want any conditions removed at this time. She said: "things were going well and I am not with him." The domestic violence program was for a twenty-four-week period.

A few weeks before the end of program, Jane's partner assaulted her again. It turned out that they had been having regular contact. Jane now stated that she had genuine safety concerns and wanted the court conditions to remain in place. The Victim Services worker informed the Crown prosecutor of the new concerns, which resulted in Jane's partner being held in remand (jail). He was later released.

Twelve days after the report of the last assault, Jane told the Victim Service's worker she was pregnant with her partner's baby and that she no longer wanted the court conditions to remain. In addition, she said she was planning on recanting her statement to the police because "the baby needs a father that is not in jail."

Despite the best of intentions, often processes facilitated through the criminal justice system don't meet the needs of real people.

Aboriginal culture and restorative justice are striking, so much so that some have said that Aboriginal cultures were the true founders of restorative justice (Redekop 2008: 114). At the same time as restorative justice initiatives were emerging in the 1970s in the mainstream criminal justice system, the following developments supported the reformation of Aboriginal justice institutions:

- recognition that the criminal justice system was failing Aboriginal people, as evidenced by high incarceration rates and systemic discrimination against Aboriginal people (Hurlbert and MacKenzie 2008);
- assertion of the inherent right to self-government by Aboriginal people, which for some Aboriginal people means separate justice systems founded on traditional justice practised in Aboriginal communities (Ross 2006); and
- recognition of Aboriginal rights, first with statements made by Supreme Court of Canada judges in the *Calder v. A.-G. of British Columbia* case and later section 35 of the *Constitution Act, 1982*.

The practice of traditional Aboriginal justice prior to colonization is consistent with restorative justice; it was social control through consensus decision-making based upon local tribal customs (Boldt and Long 1984: 543). Traditions centring on the Creator and the teachings of the elders, oral traditions and storytelling informed many of the diverse Aboriginal justice practices in North America (Guemple 1980; Vanderburgh 1988). Despite the differences between First Nations, the underlying principles were the same: regarding the individual as an integral part of the community, a dispersal of decision-making influence among many people, a reliance on consensus decision-making and a belief that people can neither be assisted nor understood as long as they are seen as isolated individuals (Hurlbert 2009). These principles are congruent with restorative justice, yet specific to the Aboriginal community practising them. Much from traditional Aboriginal justice informs restorative justice.

Self-government, Aboriginal policing, Aboriginal courts and sentencing circles have each developed and contributed changes in justice for Aboriginal people. It is difficult to go beyond general statements about Indigenous justice because of the risk of overgeneralization and stereotyping. Aboriginal restorative justice is a local institution, based on the community within which it is practised; there is no universal blueprint for all Aboriginal peoples (Zellerer and Cunneen 2001: 249).

Many Aboriginal communities have commenced community justice programs at the level of policing, the gateway to the criminal justice system. Police can be important actors in restorative justice as they can and do exercise a good deal of discretion in determining how conflicts are resolved. Often they can resolve a matter without involving criminal charges and courts. First Nations policing occurs through Aboriginal communities establishing either their own self-administered police service or partnership agreements with the federal and provincial/territorial governments (Government of Saskatchewan n.d.: 17). The establishment of Aboriginal policing has the potential to address deficiencies of the Canadian criminal justice system for Aboriginal people. Griffiths and Cunningham (2003: 75) note the following benefits of Aboriginal policing programs:

- decreased number of arrests;
- decreased tension when an Aboriginal police officer is involved; and
- better police response because of the combination of an officer's knowledge of and commitment to the community with his/her police training.

Restorative justice practices and initiatives which are sensitive to Aboriginal peoples' cultures are increasingly available. This is partly due to the creation of Aboriginal community organizations capable of performing restorative justice initiatives, available through most criminal courts, as well as mediation and sentencing diversion. Most institutions are patterned after justice circles; however, some other highly innovative institutions have also developed.

Justice circles initially emerged with First Nations in Canada and are now widely practised throughout the criminal justice system (Zehr 2002: 50). Four possibilities exist for the utilization of the justice circles modelled on Aboriginal tradition to resolve a community issue. The first is for the parties or community to access a justice circle for the resolution of an issue prior to the involvement of the police or courts. In the second possible use, after the criminal justice system is involved, a criminal charge may be diverted and withdrawn through the use of mediation diversion. This is also termed "alternative measures" or "victim-offender mediation." The third use happens once a guilty plea is entered, and the circle is used for sentencing purposes. This may take the form of a sentence advisory committee, an elders or community sentencing panel or a sentencing circle. The fourth main use of a justice circle is to assist in the reintegration of an individual into the community once their period of incarceration is at an end (Hurlbert and MacKenzie 2008).

The following criteria for a sentencing circle have been largely accepted in court cases (such as *R.* v. *Joseyounen*, 1995; *R.* v. *Alaku*, 1993; and *R.* v. *Moses*, 1992):

- voluntary agreement by accused to have recommendations as part of the judge's consideration;

- willingness of victim to participate;
- resolution of disputed facts;
- acceptance of responsibility by offender for their actions;
- guilty plea;
- community support for the offender and willingness to be involved in the process on behalf of the accused;
- victim has had meaningful input; and
- demonstrated sincere intention of accused to be rehabilitated and to participate meaningfully in rehabilitation.

In Saskatchewan, for example, the sentencing circle is generally opened by a prayer, and the defence and Crown agree on the facts. The Crown prosecutor, defence counsel, judge, accused, victim and their families (sometimes the police as well) speak one at a time going around the circle until finally a proposal is agreed upon. The end of the sentencing circle discussion is typically declared by the circle participants, not the judge (Peterson 2000). Practice over the years has found pre-charge diversion useful, but post-charge sentencing circles very time consuming and less embraced by the community (Hurlbert and McKenzie 2008). Many First Nation community-based justice programs exist in order to facilitate the usage of these circles of justice.

The Tsuu T'ina First Nation outside of Calgary has successfully created a peacemaking court, which sits on reserve lands and has operated since 2000. The Tsuu T'ina elders initiated the establishment of the court and advised that the traditional approach to dealing with conflict was to heal offenders to behave properly and restore offender-victim relationships (Mandaman 2003). The court is the result of investigation by the First Nation into alternative criminal justice solutions, followed by lobbying and negotiations with both provincial and federal governments. The court is staffed by Aboriginal people.

The peacemaking court has the full jurisdiction of an Alberta provincial court. The protocols of court, however, reflect Tsuu T'ina tradition. Court is held in a chamber representing the circle of a teepee and is commenced with a smudging ceremony, which is a sacred pledge of truth to the Creator. In some diversions, healing ceremonies are held instead of payment of fines. In one, peacemaking was ended with a pipe ceremony, a vow by the participant to the Creator. All peacemaking ends with an elders panel for the Tsuu T'ina people, who hold the elders in high regard and their directions mandatory. Many checks and balances exist within the peacemaking process. The accused must choose peacemaking, and a court worker tasked with making peace must be agreeable, along with the Crown prosecutor, who refers the matter, and the judge, who adjourns the case to allow for peacemaking. Although the Tsuu T'ina Nation members can elect not to utilize the peacemaking court, the community members are using it.

When the peacemaking court was originally established, the elders determined that it would not handle sexual assault, homicide, prostitution and domestic violence. However, the court has expanded and now includes a holistic approach to domestic violence, which includes professional counsellors, peacemaking and healing. As with all other matters in which peacemaking is used, the accused must take responsibility for the incident and the victim must agree to participate.

The Tsuu T'ina court is important as it establishes the success of Aboriginal community justice. Some argue that systemic racism and inequality will only be eliminated through initiatives like these and a fully recognized inherent Aboriginal right to self-determination, including an independent Aboriginal justice system (Ross 2006).

In the mid-1980s, in Hollow Water, Manitoba, a healing system for sexual abuse was developed by four First Nation communities; it is known as the Hollow Water First Nation Community Holistic Circle Healing (often referred to only as Hollow Water). Given Hollow Water's colonial and residential school legacy, the community had an issue of child and sexual abuse, which it was determined to tackle head-on instead of utilizing the mainstream criminal justice process of sentencing and incarceration. First Nation members are still charged with an offence and have to plead guilty in order to access the Hollow Water program. Thus, Hollow Water is a combination of a sentencing circle and reintegration of the offender back into the community, the third and fourth types of justice circles outlined previously. However, sentencing is delayed if the accused agrees to participate in the program. Failure to remain in the program results in a return to the regular court system and most likely incarceration. When the accused has proceeded through the healing program, they appear in court for sentencing, and the team from the community presents a report to the judge about the accused's sincerity and effort and how much work, if any, still needs to be done (Goff 2004: 75).

The healing process is a thirteen-step program based on the seven Midewin teachings of the Anishnabe people, which also integrates elements of a number of federally and provincially funded services. The process holistically involves victims, victimizers and their families and creates spiritual, physical, emotional and intellectual benefits throughout the community. The process involves disclosure by the victimizer and ensures safety and support for the victim, followed by circles with the victim and victimizer and preparatory meetings with their families, leading to a special gathering/sentencing circle, and ending with a cleansing ceremony.

Between 1986 and 1995, only five offenders selected to be tried by Western courts; forty-eight others chose to enter the healing program (Goff 2004: 75). From the program's inception in 2001, 107 victimizers and between 400 and 500 victims participated in the program. Charges dealt with were primarily sexual offences, but included other charges, such as break and enter and second-degree murder. In 1997, the reserve had a population of 708, which is anticipated to be 1038 by 2016 (Couture, Parker, Couture and Laboucane 2001).

A holistic cost/benefit evaluation of Hollow Water was conducted using a participatory action research study. The study concluded that governments contributed a total of $2.4 million, and, in comparison, the cost of government-run services would have been from $6 million to $16 million. In addition, government-run services would have neither the community capacity building nor the healing effect of the Hollow Water process.

The recidivism rate for the Hollow Water project was found to be 2 percent compared to the national average of 13 percent for sex offenders. Value-added benefits included improved child health, more educational attainment by community members, improved parenting skills, empowerment of individuals, broadening of community resources, increased community responsibility, return to traditional ceremony, decrease in overall violence and overall healing of the intergenerational pain resulting from colonization (Hansen 2001).

Does Restorative Justice Work?

Restorative justice is not a panacea for all of the shortcomings of the criminal justice system. In fact, Woolford (2009: Chapter Seven) argues that restorative justice may be just another form of punishment because the practice of restorative justice within the criminal justice system is one of co-optation. This criticism may be well founded if applied only to a narrow definition of restorative justice, that is, used for minor, first offences within the criminal justice system. Two main groups also criticize restorative justice: those who support more severe penalties for people who commit crime and certain victims groups. With respect to the former, often the media sensationalize a case and polarize public opinion such that a harsh penalty, regardless of the sentencing circle recommendation, is imposed (Coolican 2009). With respect to the latter, some women's groups have concluded that restorative justice should not be used in cases of domestic violence (Cameron 2006). In particular, Aboriginal women's groups have been very vocal against restorative justice. Teressa Nahanee (1995: 362), a member of the Squamish Indian Nation and adviser to the Native Women Association of Canada, states: "The use of elders' circles has not been effective in deterring violent crimes against women." The Manitoba Justice Inquiry (cited in Smith 1993: 34–35) confirms this:

> The unwillingness of chiefs and council to address the plight of women and children suffering abuse at the hands of husbands and fathers is

quite alarming. The failure of Aboriginal government leaders to deal at all with the problem of domestic abuse is unconscionable. Their silence and failure to act actually contribute to the problem

Some studies report a significant minority of victims who felt worse after a restorative justice conference, upset over something said or feeling disrespected. However, these victims were greatly outnumbered by ones who felt healing (Braithwaite 2002: 49). There is a high victim approval of restorative justice experiences, although the approval is lower than that assessed by other participants in the process, such as offenders and community members (47). Restorative justice programs have a wide variation on the level of victim participation. Victims in restorative justice programs were more satisfied than victims whose cases went to court, and they also experienced reduced fear and increased emotional restoration (51).

To answer the question of whether restorative justice works, we must first answer the question, "Works at what"? The goals of restorative justice are the reduction of crime and the restoration of the victim, offender and community. The focus on whether restorative justice is working would naturally be twofold. First, it would assess whether this restoration of the parties had occurred. The second aspect of assessment would be to determine the effectiveness of restorative justice in respect of crime reduction.

Offenders were also more likely to be satisfied with how their cases were handled compared with those proceeding through the criminal justice system. Studies show that offenders had a much higher completion rate for following through with restitution obligations to victims (restoring victims to the condition they were in prior to the crime) or making reparations and fulfilling compensation agreements than those who were ordered through the mainstream criminal justice system to make victim restitution (Braithwaite 2002: 54).

Statistical evaluation shows that restorative justice initiatives reduce reoffending, or recidivism (Latimer, Dowden and Muise 2001). Several meta-analyses have been conducted on the research of recidivism rates after restorative justice. These analyses combine results from between fourteen and forty-six individual studies of programs of restorative justice. The studies confirm that restorative justice reduces reoffending by amounts averaging 3, 7 and 8 percent of traditional criminal justice system responses (Latimer, Dowden and Muise 2001; Bonta, Wallace-Capretta and Rooney 2002; Bonta, Wallace-Capretta and Rooney 1998; and Roberts 1995). This means that individuals who completed a restorative justice program had between 3 and 8 percent less likelihood to reoffend than individuals who experienced sentences resulting from mainstream criminal justice.

Results improve when restorative justice is combined with rehabilitation programs for offenders, and even more promise is shown with culturally appropriate institutions for Aboriginal people. Although more research is needed, it is proposed that further support should be given to holistic and culturally specific restorative justice programs. Based on available research, those restorative justice programs which combine culturally appropriate institutions and components to combat socio-economic factors will have the best results. From this review, restorative justice initiatives have an important place in the Canadian criminal justice system for both Aboriginals and non-Aboriginals.

Self Test

Darren Huenemann was an upper middle class student at a Victoria, B.C., high school. He was considered to be a nice kid and a "good boy." He was doted on by his mother and grandmother, who instilled in him middle-class, materialistic values. Darren talked with friends about killing his grandmother and mother to get a very large inheritance. They thought he was joking. He was not. Eventually he convinced two friends, who were dazzled by his lifestyle, to kill the two women in return for money and status as his "special friends." He told the boys when and where the women would be together at his grandmother's home and how to get into the house. On October 5, 1990, the boys entered the grandmother's Vancouver home, beat and stabbed the women to death and took the money from the house. They disposed of the weapons on the ferry ride back to Victoria. The trail leading to Darren's conviction is complex but resulted mainly from his early boasting about the plan to a friend. Darren was found guilty of first-degree murder. (Source: Silverman and Kennedy 1993: 165–6)

Josh is twelve-year-old student. One day he came to school with the leg of chair that had been wrapped with tape at one end. The principal and the police resource officer became involved. Upon interviewing Josh, the police resource officer learned that the "weapon" was for "protection." Josh told him that he was afraid of George, another student in school, who was looking to beat him up. When asked why George was planning to beat him up, he explained that his brother, Brian had beat up George for stealing his (Brian's) bike. George couldn't beat up Brian, and wanting revenge, George decided to get even by beating up Josh, Brian's younger brother.

From a restorative justice perspective, were there any winners and losers in the above situations?

If you were to develop a restorative justice intervention in these two cases, who would you involve and why?

What steps might you envision taking?

Restorative Justice and Social Justice

This chapter introduces the principles and practices of restorative justice. Restorative justice is used in a wide context, in personal life decisions every day and in different professions and contexts, such as schools and workplaces. One of the predominant areas of restorative justice practice is in the criminal justice system, where it is contrasted with the principles of retributive justice (the norm in the traditional criminal justice system). Within this context, a narrow definition of restorative justice is usually employed; this limits the potential for a full restorative justice practice. This chapter argues for a restorative justice definition and practice employing themes and concepts of social justice. This expanded view of restorative justice has the following four pillars:

1. Embracement of conflict — Restorative justice entails embracing conflict or problematic situations and solving conflict without delegating the task to professionals (lawyers, government and the police).
2. Recognition of social problems — Conflict is viewed as not only an interpersonal dynamic or problem between individuals but is also situated within the broader community, such that social problems which contributed to and were encompassed within the interpersonal conflict are recognized.
3. Experience of agency — Individuals experiencing and affected by conflict and problematic situations actively participate in its resolution.
4. Ethical practice of leximin — An ethic of doing no harm and protecting the most powerless and vulnerable in our community is practised in order to create strong and supporting relationships.

This definition of restorative justice is illustrated with the practices of local water advisory groups in the environmental context, within the school context and within circles of justice in the criminal context. However, these processes must also be informed by an ethical practice, to ensure justice, and grounded in a critical social analysis, in which social problems are recognized, to prevent a fragmented, limiting, individualized approach. Also required are active participation by members of the community and an embracement of conflict as a learning opportunity. If all four pillars are fully employed, the shortcomings of restorative justice can be reduced and the benefits of restorative justice made accessible to all.

Glossary

collaborative – a style of human interaction focusing on respectful dialogue and achieving mutual understanding, cooperation and solutions which meet as many human needs as possible.

community – generally a collection of people in a geographical area. Within this chapter community is usually referring to a group of people interacting in a given geographical area, such as a First Nation reserve, a village, town or city, or perhaps a rural area. Within Chapter Seven, environmental justice, the global community, or all people living in the biosphere of earth, was discussed.

competence – having suitable or sufficient skill, knowledge, experience etc. for some purpose — here specifically, the practice of restorative justice.

confidentiality — speaking, writing, acting on, etc. in strict privacy or secrecy.

conflict of interest — the professional's primary commitment is to the individual participants, the process and the purpose or goal of the intervention (Smith et al. 1996: 30). If the professional is in conflict with (or favours) any participants, the process or purpose they should withdraw.

deterrence – discouragement from acting or proceeding.

extrajudicial measures – ways that young persons can be diverted from or kept out of the youth criminal justice system. If the police decide to use one of these measures, they will not lay a charge against the youth and the youth will not have to go to court. Alternatively, a prosecutor or judge can determine to use extrajudicial measures. Unlike going to court, where the judge makes all the decisions, some extrajudicial measures allow the youth and people who have been affected by the youth's actions to participate in the decision-making.

impartiality – While we all live with our own biases — values and knowledge of the world around us — the impartial professional recognizes their own biases and is able to avoid prejudicial interventions favouring individual participants (Smith, Young, Ish and Anderson 1996: 30)

justice circles – used in Aboriginal traditions to resolve a community issue. There are four possibilities for the utilization of the circles of justice: 1) for the parties or community to resolve a dispute prior to the involvement of the police or courts; 2) after the criminal justice system is accessed, a criminal charge may be diverted and the charge withdrawn through the use of mediation diversion; 3) once a guilty plea is entered, the circle may be used for sentencing purposes; 4) to assist the reintegration of an individual in the community once their period of incarceration is at an end.

knowledge-based practice – the understanding many disciplines might offer to explain crime behaviours based on scientific, evidence-based practices and theories.

mediation – the act of bringing about an agreement, accord, truce, peace, etc. as an intermediary between parties by compromise, reconciliation, removal of misunderstanding, etc.

peacemaking court – created by the Tsuu T'ina First Nation outside of Calgary, Alberta. The Tsuu T'ina elders initiated the court and advised that the traditional approach to dealing with conflict was to heal offenders to behave properly and restore offender-victim relationships (Mandaman 2003). The court is staffed by Aboriginal people, and Aboriginal traditions are incorporated into the traditional provincial court practices.

procedural interests – needs relating to the process by which the dispute is resolved.

psychological interests – needs regarding how one feels about the problem and solution.

recidivism – reoffending.

rehabilitation – restore to a good condition, operation or management or re-establish the good reputation of a person.

retributive approach – views crime as an individual act against the state. The criminal justice system controls crime, and offender accountability is defined as taking punishment. The punishment is effective as a threat if it deters crime and punishment changes behaviour. The focus of retributive justice is on blame and guilt.

restorative approach – views crime as an act against a person and has individual and social dimensions of responsibility. Crime control lies primarily in the community, and accountability is defined as assuming responsibility and taking action to repair harm. Restorative justice views punishment alone as not effective in changing behaviour and as disruptive to community harmony and good relationships. Victims are central to the process of resolving a crime.

self-administered police services – under the First Nations Policing Policy (FNPP), the federal and provincial governments work with First Nations to negotiate agreements for police services that meet the specific needs of each community. These agreements aim to strengthen public security and personal safety; increase responsibility and accountability; and build new partnerships with First Nations based on trust, mutual respect and participation in decision-making. Police services must be responsive, accessible, effective, regulated and accountable through bodies that are representative of the communities they serve.

storytelling – an effective intervention that permits offenders, victims and their families and/or communities to express their perspectives in non-threatening ways. Storytelling may be defined as presenting information, clarifying a point, supporting someone's perspective and/or crystallizing and shaping ideas. Storytelling promotes an understanding, appreciation and a respect for the thoughts and behaviours of victims and offenders.

self-determinism – describes participation as voluntary (Smith, Young, Ish and Anderson 1996: 31). Practitioners ensure all agreements in resolving the conflict are voluntary.

substantive interests – needs such as money, time and resources.

value-based practice – the influence of our families, friends, schools, cultural and religious affiliations in developing our beliefs, our moral sense of right and wrong.

References

Aboriginal Justice Inquiry of Manitoba. (1991). *Report of the Aboriginal Justice Inquiry of Manitoba*. (vols. 1–3). A.C. Hamilton & C.M. Sinclair (eds.). Aboriginal Justice Inquiry of Manitoba. Winnipeg, MB.

Adams, C. (2008). "The talk-it-out solution: How we promote safety? Try getting rid of the metal detectors." *Scholastic Administrator* Nov/Dec.

Adger, N., and P.M. Kelly. (1999). "Social vulnerability to climate change and the architecture of entitlements." *Mitigation and Adaptation Strategies for Global Climate Change* 4, 253–66.

Adkin, L.E. (2009). "Democracy from the trenches: environmental conflicts and ecological citizenship." In L.E. Adkin (ed.), *Environmental conflict and democracy in Canada* (pp. 315-336). Vancouver, BC: UBC Press.

___. (2009). *Environmental conflict and democracy in Canada*. Vancouver, BC: UBC Press.

Adler, F., G.O.W. Mueller, and W.S. Laufer. (2003). *Criminal justice: An introduction* (third ed.). New York: McGraw-Hill.

Alberta. (1991). *Report of the commission of inquiry on policing in relation to the blood tribe*. (Vols. 1–2). C.H. Rolf, Chairperson. Edmonton, AB: The Commission.

Alberta Environment. (2005). "Approved water management plan for the South Saskatchewan River Basin in Alberta." October 18 draft. Retrieved October 2005 from <http://www3.gov.ab.ca/env/water/regions/ssrb/pdf/Draft_SSRB_Plan.pdf>.

Anand, R. (2004). *International environmental justice: A north-nouth dimension*. Hampshire, England: Ashgate.

Ancel, M. (1965). *Social defence: A modern approach to criminal problems*. London, U.K.: Routledge & Kegan Paul.

Anderson, B., and D. Anderson. (1998). *Manufacturing guilt: Wrongful convictions in Canada*. Halifax, NS: Fernwood.

Anderson, J.T.M. (1918). *The education of the new-Canadian: A treatise on Canada's greatest educational problem*. Toronto, ON: J.M. Dent.

Andreassen, B.A. and S.P. Marks (eds.). (2006). *Development as a human right: Legal, political and economic dimensions*. Cambridge, MA: Harvard University Press.

Andrews, D.A., I. Zinger, R. Hoge, J. Bonta, P. Gendreau and F. Cullen. (1990). "Does correctional treatment work?: A clinically relevant and psychologically informed meta-analysis.' *Criminology* 28, 393–404.

Angus, I. (1997). *A border within: National identity, cultural plurality and wilderness*. Montreal, QC: McGill-Queen's University Press.

Aristotle. (1985). *Nicomachean ethics: The various types of justice*. (H. Hachett, trans.) Indianapolis, IN: Terence Irwin.

Assembly of First Nations. (2009). "*First Nations control of First Nations education: It's our vision, it's our time.*" <http://64.26.129.156/calltoaction/Documents/FNCFNE.pdf>.

Auditor General of Canada. (2003). *Report of the Auditor General to the House of Commons; Chapter 4 Correctional Services of Canada; Reintegration of women offenders*. Ottawa, ON:

Minister of Public Works & Government Services.

Babooram, A. (2008). "The changing profile of adults in custody, 2006/2007." *Juristat*, catalogue no. 85-002X. Ottawa, ON: Statistics Canada, Canadian Centre for Justice Studies. Retrieved September 6, 2009 from <http://www.statcan.gc.ca/pub/85-002-x/2008010/article/10732-eng.htm#a6>.

Baier, A. (1986). "Trust and anti-trust." *Ethics* 96, 231–60.

Baines, B. (2006). "Equality, comparison, discrimination, status." In F. Faraday, M. Denike and M.K. Stephenson (eds.), *Making equality rights real: Securing substantive equality under the Charter.* Toronto, ON: Irwin Books.

Baines, B., and M. Eberts. (1981). "Women, human rights and the Constitution." In A.D. Doerr and M. Carrier (eds.), *Women and the Constitution in Canada* (p.31). Ottawa, ON: Canadian Advisory Council on the Status of Women.

Baker, D., and S. Godwin. (2008). "All aboard! The Supreme Court of Canada confirms that Canadians with disabilities have substantive equality rights." *Saskatchewan Law Review,* 71(1): 39-77.

Balfour, G. (2006). "Regulating women and girls." In G. Balfour and E. Comack (eds.), *Criminalizing women: Gender and (in)justice in neo-liberal times* (pp.153-173). Halifax, NS: Fernwood Press.

___. (2008). "Falling between the cracks of retributive and restorative justice: The victimization and punishment of aboriginal women." *Feminist Criminology* 3(2): 101–20.

Balfour, G., and E. Comack (eds.). (2006). *Criminalizing women: Gender and (in)justice in neoliberal times.* Halifax, NS: Fernwood Press.

Balfour, G., and J. DuMont. (2009). "Confronting restorative justice in neo-liberal times: Legal and rape narratives in conditional sentencing." Presented at "sexual assault law, practice and activism in a post-Jane Doe Era." University of Ottawa Press.

___. (2011). "Confronting restorative justice: Legal and rape narratives in conditional sentencing." In Elizabeth Sheehy (ed.), *Sexual assault, practice, activism in a post Jane Doe era.* University of Ottawa Press.

Banakar, R., and M. Travers. (2005). *Theory and method in socio-legal research.* Oxford: Hart.

Bannerji, H. (2000). *The dark side of the nation: Essays on multiculturalism, nationalism and gender.* Toronto, ON: Canadian Scholars' Press.

Barrera, J. (2009). "Big companies wield too much power, says poll." *Leader Post,* January 2: A 8.

Barsky, A.E. (2000). *Conflict resolution for the helping professions.* Scarborough, ON: Thomson Learning.

Bashevkin, S. (2009). *Women, power, and politics: The hidden story of Canada's unfinished democracy.* Toronto, ON: Oxford University Press.

Battle, K., M. Mendelson and S. Torjman. (2006). *Towards a new architecture for Canada's adult benefits.* Ottawa, ON: Caledon Institute of Social Policy.

Bayefsky, A. (1982). "The Human Rights Committee and the case of Sandra Lovelace." *Canadian Yearbook of International Law* 120, 244–46.

Bayefsky, A., and M. Eberts. (1985). *Equality rights and the Canadian Charter of Rights and Freedoms.* Toronto, ON: Carswell.

Beasley, C. (1999). *What is feminism? An introduction to feminist theory.* London: Sage.

Beauchesne, E. (2008). "Gap between rich and poor growing: Stats Can." *National Post* May 1. Retrieved September 4, 2009 from <http://www.nationalpost.com/nationalpost/story.html?id=485124>.

___. (2008). "Canada's wealthy benefit most from tax cuts, OECD finds." *Financial Post*

March 24. CanWest News Service.

Beaujot, R. (2004). *Delayed life transitions: Trends and implications*. Ottawa: Vanier Institute of the Family.

Becker, H.S. (1963). *Outsiders: Studies in the sociology of deviance*. New York, NY: Free Press.

Beckton, C.F. (1982). *The labour and the media.* Toronto, ON: Carswell.

Beetham, D. (2006). "The right to development and its corresponding obligations." In B.A. Andreassen and S. P. Marks (eds.), *Development as a human right: Legal, political and economic dimensions* (p.79). Cambridge, MA: Harvard University Press.

Benford, R., and D. Snow. (2000). "Framing processes and social movements: An overview and assessment." *Annual Review of Sociology* 26: 611–39.

Benidickson, J. (1997). *Environmental law*. Toronto, ON: Irwin Law.

Bennet, N. (2000). "Improving partnerships with Aboriginal communities." *Forum on Corrections Research* 12(1): 5–6.

Bentham, J. (1948 [1823]). *A fragment on government and an introduction to the principles of morals and legislation*. Oxford: Basil Blackford.

Bisharat, G.E. (2003). "Democracy — or colonialism in Iraq?" Retrieved June 21, 2010 from <http://www.commondreams.org/views03/0306-03.htm>.

Blackstone, W. (1768). *Commentaries on the laws of England* 3: 129–37.

Blatchford, C. (2009). "What are little girls made of these days?" *Globe and Mail* August 12.

Boe, R., M. Naketh, B. Vuong, R. Sinclair and C. Cousineau. (2003). "The changing profiles of the federal inmate population: 1997 to 2002." Research report R-132, Ottawa, ON: Ontario Correctional Service in Canada.

Boldt, M., and J.A. Long. (1984). "Tribal traditions and European-Western political ideologies: The dilemma of Canada's Native Indians." *Canadian Journal of Political Science* 17(3): 537–53.

Bonta, J., S. Wallace-Capretta and J. Rooney. (1998). *Restorative justice: An evaluation of the restorative resolutions project*. Ottawa, ON: Solicitor General Canada.

Bonta, J., S. Wallace-Capretta, J. Rooney and K. McAnoy. (2002). "An outcome evaluation of a restorative justice alternative to incarceration." *Contemporary Justice Review* 5, 4: 319–38 Retrieved June 25, 2008 from <www.psepc0sppcc.gc.ca/res/cor/sum/cprs200301_1-en.asp>.

Boonan, D. (2008). *The problem of punishment*. Cambridge: Cambridge University Press.

Boulton, J., and L. Mirsky. (2006). *Restorative practices as a tool for organizational change: The Bessels Leigh School. February 23.* International Institute for Restorative Practices. Retrieved February 23, 2006 from <http://www.iirp.edu/article_detail.php?article_id=NTMx>.

Boyd, D.R. (2001). *Canada vs. the OECD: An environmental comparison*. Victoria, BC: Eco-Research Chair of Environmental Law and Policy, University of Victoria. Retrieved May1, 2009 from <http://www.environmentalindicators.com/htdocs/PDF/CanadavsOECD.pdf>.

___. (2003). *Unnatural law*. Vancouver, BC: UBC Press.

Boyd, S.C. (2006). "Representations of women in the drug trade." In G. Balfour and E. Comack (eds), *Criminalizing women: Gender and (in)justice in neo-liberal times* (pp.131–51). Halifax, NS: Fernwood Press.

Boyd, S., and E. Sheehy. (1989). "Overview: Feminism and the law in Canada." In T. Caputo, M. Kennedy, C. Reasons and A. Brannigan (eds.), *Law and society: A critical perspective* (pp. 255–70). Toronto, ON: Harcourt Brace Jovanovich.

Boyko, J. (1998). *Last steps to freedom: The evolution of Canadian racism* (rev. ed.). Winnipeg, MB: J. Gordon Shillingford.

Braithwaite, J. (1989). *Crime, shame and reintegration*. Cambridge, U.K.: Cambridge University Press.

___. (2001). *Restorative justice and responsive regulation*. Oxford: Oxford University Press.

___. (2002). *Restorative justice and responsive regulation*. New York, NY: Oxford University Press.

Brannigan, A. (1984). *Crimes, courts and corrections: An introduction to crime and social control in Canada*. Toronto, ON: Holt, Rinehart & Winston of Canada.

Brantingham, P.J., and P.L. Brantingham. (1984). *Patterns in crime*. New York: Macmillan.

Braun, C. (1998). "Colonization, destruction, and renewal: Stories from Aboriginal men at the Pe'Sakastew Centre." Unpublished master's thesis, University of Saskatchewan. Saskatoon, SK.

Brodsky, G., and S. Day. (2002). "Beyond the social and economics rights debate: Substantive equality speaks to poverty." *Canadian Journal of Women and the Law* 14(1): 185–220.

Bronowski, J. (1973). *The ascent of man*. Boston MA: Little Brown.

Brooks, D.B. (2002). *Water, local-level management*. Ottawa, ON: International Development Research Centre.

Brownlee, J. (2005). *Ruling Canada: Corporate cohesion and democracy*. Halifax, NS: Fernwood.

Busby, K. (1999). "Not a victim until a conviction is entered: Sexual violence prosecutions and legal truth." In E. Comack (ed.), *Locating law: Race/class/gender connections* (pp. 260–88). Halifax, NS: Fernwood.

California Newsreel. (2003a). "The difference between us." In *Race: The power of an illusion*. Volume 1.

___. (2003b). "Where race lives: A tale of two families." In *Race: The Power of an Illusion*. Retrieved May 14, 2004 from <http://www.pbs.org/race/006_WhereRaceLives/006_02-taleoftwo.htm>.

Cameron, A. (2006). "Stopping the violence: Canadian feminist debates on restorative justice and intimate violence." *Theoretical Criminology* 10(1): 49–66.

Campaign 2000. (2005). "Decision time in Canada: Let's make poverty history: 2005 Report card on child poverty in Canada." Retrieved February 12, 2008 from <http://www.campaign2000.ca/rc/rc05/05NationalReportCard.pdf>.

Campbell, B., and G. Marchildon (eds.). (2007). *Medicare: facts, myths, problems, promise*. Toronto, ON: James Lorimer.

Canada Centre for Policy Alternative. (2010). "Growing gap updates." Retrieved August 25, 2010 from <http://www.policyalternatives.ca/projects/growing-gap/>.

Canada, Governor General. (2010). "A stronger Canada: A stronger economy, now and for the future." Speech from the Throne, March 3, 40th Parliament, 3rd session, library and archives Canada cataloguing in publication. Retrieved from <http://www.speech.gc.ca/grfx/docs/sft-ddt-2010_e.pdf>.

Canadian Association of Elizabeth Fry Societies (CAEFS). (2009). "Fact sheet 2009." Retrieved August 15, 2009 from <http://www.elizabethfry.ca/eweek09/factsht.htm>.

Canadian Council of Provincial Child and Youth Advocates. (2010). "Aboriginal children and youth in Canada: Canada must do better." Retrieved June 24, 2010 from <http://www.cdpdj.qc.ca/en/publications/docs/aboriginal_children_youth_advocates_position_paper_2010.pdf>.

Canadian Heritage, Government of Canada. (2004). *Canadian diversity: Respecting our differences*. Retrieved March 14, 2008 from <http://www.pch.gc.ca/progs/multi/respect_e.cfm>.

Canadian Human Rights Commission. (2003). *Protecting their rights: A systematic review of human rights in correctional services for federally sentenced women*. Ottawa, ON: Canadian Human Rights Commission.

Canadian Sentencing Commission. (1987). *Sentencing reform: A Canadian approach*. Ottawa, ON: Ministry of Supply and Services.

Canadian Wheat Board. (2004). "Customer opposition to GM wheat growing." Retrieved June 3, 2009 from <http://www.cwb.ca/public/en/newsroom/releases/2004/031804.jsp>.

Carroll, W.K. (2005). *Corporate power in a globalizing world*. Don Mills, ON: Oxford University Press.

Catton, W.R., and R.E. Dunlap. (1978). *Environmental sociology: A new paradigm. American Sociologist* 13: 41.

Cawsey, R.A. Mr. Justice. (1991). *Report of the Task Force on the Criminal Justice System and its impact on the Indian and Metis people of Alberta*, March 1991, vol. 1. Edmonton: Alberta Government Publications. Retrieved August 24, 2010 from <http://www.justice.gov.ab.ca/publications/default.aspx?id=2679>.

CBA (Canadian Bar Association). (2006). "CBA decries cuts to court challenges program and Law Commission of Canada." Retrieved June 28, 2010, from <http://www.cba.org/CBA/News/2006_Releases/2006-09-26_cuts.aspx>.

CBC (Canadian Broadcasting Corporation). (2007). "Canada votes 'no' as UN native rights declaration passes." Retrieved September, 13, 2007 from <http://www.cbc.ca/canada/story/2007/09/13/canada-indigenous.html>.

___. (2007). "Immigration: Quickfacts." Retrieved January 15, 2008 from <http://www.cbc.ca/news/background/immigration/quickfacts.html>.

___. (2007). "In depth immigration: Immigration in Canada: from 1947 to 2017." Retrieved January 15, 2008 from <http://www.cbc.ca/news/background/immigration/index.html>.

CBC Radio and Television Archives. "Equality first: The Royal Commission on the Status of Women." Retrieved 26 August 2010, from <http://archives.cbc.ca/politics/rights_freedoms/topics/86>.

CEAA (Canadian Environmental Assessment Agency. (1997). *Annual report*. Ottawa, ON: Minister of Public Works & Government Services.

___. (1998). *Annual report*. Ottawa, ON: Minister of Public Works & Government Services.

___. (1999). *Annual report*. Ottawa, ON: Minister of Public Works & Government Services.

___. (2000). "Review of the Canadian Environmental Assessment Act: A discussion paper for public consultation." Ottawa, ON: Minister of Public Works & Government Services.

Centre for Social Justice. (2007–2010). "Key issue: Aboriginal issues." Retrieved August 25, 2010 from <http://www.socialjustice.org/index.php?page=aboriginal-issues>.

Centre for Studies in Food Security (n.d.). "Food security further defined." Ryerson University Press. Retrieved August 25, 2010 from <http://www.ryerson.ca/foodsecurity/definition/fsdefinedmore/>.

Cheon, A., and C. Regehr. (2006). "Restorative justice models in cases of intimate partner violence: Reviewing the evidence." *Victims and Offenders* 1(4): 369–94.

Christie, E. (2000). *Pulping the law: How pulp mills are ruining Canadian waters with impunity.* Toronto, ON: Sierra Legal Defence Fund.

Christie, N. (1977). "Conflicts as property." *British Journal of Criminology* 17 (1): 1.

"Circles." Directed by Shanti Thakun, produced by Mark Zannis, executive producer Don Haig. National Film Board of Canada Montreal Quebec 2006.

Clairmont, D. (2006). "Aboriginal policing in Canada: An overview of developments in First Nations." Halifax, NS: *Atlantic Institute of Criminology*, Dalhousie University.

Clairmont, D., and T. Augustine. (2009). "Advancing the strategic justice plan in Elsipogtog: The relevance of First Nation and other initiatives for increased effectiveness and community ownership." Final report. Halifax, NS: *Atlantic Institute of Criminology*, Dalhousie University.

Cohen, G.A. (1988). *History, labour, and freedom: Themes from Marx.* New York: Oxford University Press.

Coker, D. (2006). "Restorative justice: Navajo peacemaking and domestic violence." *Theoretical Criminology* 10(1): 67–85.

Collins, A. (1981)." Which way to Ottawa? A special report on the women's conference on the Constitution." *Homemaker's Magazine* 22.

Comack, E. (1996). *Women in trouble.* Halifax, NS: Fernwood.

____. (2000). "Women and crime." In R. Linden (ed.), *Criminology: A Canadian perspective.* Toronto, ON: Harcourt Brace.

____. (2006). *Locating law, race class gender sexuality connections* (second ed.). Halifax, NS: Fernwood Publishing.

Comack, E., and G. Balfour. (2004). *The power to criminalize: Volence, inequality and the law.* Halifax, NS: Fernwood Publishing.

Commission of Inquiry into the Shooting Death of Leo Lachance. (1993). *Report of the Commission of inquiry into the shooting death of Leo Lachance.* Justice E.N. Hughes, Chairperson. Regina, SK: The Commission.

Communitarianism. (2009). *Stanford wncyclopedia of philosophy.* Retrieved August 25, 2009 from <http://plato.stanford.edu/entries/communitarianism/>.

Conference Board of Canada. (2005). "Water pressure is building in Canada." *InsideEdge* Winter: 16.

Conley, D.J. (1994). "Adding color to a black and white picture: Using qualitative data to explain racial disproportionality in the juvenile justice system." *Journal of Research in Crime and Delinquency* (31)2: 135–48.

Cooley, C.H. (1902). *Human nature and the social order.* New York: Scribner's.

Coolican, L. (2009). "Pauchay gets 3 years: Drunk father left house in -50 wind chill with two toddlers dressed only in shirts and diapers. Both froze to death in the cold." *Leader Post.* March 7. Retrieved March 7, 2009 from <http://www.leaderpost.com/news/Pauchay+gets+years/1363937/story.html>.

Correctional Service of Canada. (2004). *A profile and examination of gang affiliation within the federally sentenced offender population.* Ottawa, ON: Correctional Service Canada.

____. (2010). *Statistics: Key facts and figures.* Ottawa, ON: Research Branch, Correctional Service of Canada.

Cotterrell, R. (1996). *Law's community: Legal theory in sociological perspective.* Oxford: Clarendon Press.

County Galway. (2005). "Local poverty profile 2005 (Appendix III: Deprivation and its spatial articulation in the Republic of Ireland)." Galway County Council. Galway, Ireland: Retrieved September 12, 2009, from <http://www.galway.ie/

en/Services/CommunityEnterpriseEconomicDevelopment/SocialInclusion/Reports/PovertyProfile/>.

Couture, J., T. Parker, R. Couture and P. Laboucane. (2001). "A cost-benefit analysis of hollow water's community holistic circle healing process." Ottawa, ON: Aboriginal Corrections Policy Unity, Solicitor of Canada. Retrieved June 24, 2008 from <www.sgc.gc.ca/EPub/AboCor/eAPC2001>.

Crank, J.P. (2003). *Imagining justice.* Cincinnati, OH: Anderson.

Cromier, R.B. (2002). "Restorative justice: Directions and principles – Developments in Canada." A paper sponsored by the International Centre for Criminal Law Reform and Criminal Justice Policy, and presented at the Technical Assistance Workshop of the Programme Network of Institutes at the 11th Session of the Commission on Crime Prevention and Criminal Justice, held in Vienna from April 16 to 25, 2002.

Cunliffe, E., and A. Cameron. (2007). "Writing the circle: Judicially convened sentencing circles and the textual organization of criminal justice." *Canadian Journal of Women and the Law* 19(1): 1–35.

Currie, J. (2001). *Public international law.* Ottawa, ON: Irwin Law.

Cutter, S.L. (2006). "Race, class and environmental justice." In S.L. Cutter, *Hazards, vulnerability and environmental justice* (pp. 249–61). London: Earthscan.

Daly, K. (1994). "Criminal law and justice system practices as racist, white, and racialized." *Washington & Lee Law Review* 51: 431.

Daly, K., and J. Stubbs. (2006). "Feminist engagement with restorative justice." *Theoretical Criminology* 10(1): 9–28.

Daubney, D., and M.P. Chairman. (1988). "Taking responsibility." Report of the standing committee on justice and solicitor general on its review of sentencing, conditional release and related aspects of correction, Ottawa, ON.

Davis, K., and W. Moore. (1945). "Some principles of stratification." *American Sociological Review* 10(April): 242–49.

Dawson, M. (2006). "The making of section 15 of the Charter." *Journal of Law & Equality* 5(25): 31.

Desmarais, A.A. (2007). *Globalization and the power of peasants: La Vía Campesina.* Halifax, NS: Fernwood & Pluto Books.

Dickinson, H.D. (2002). "Mental health policy in Canada: What's the problem?" In B. Singh Bolaria and Harley D. Dickinson (eds.), *Health, illness, and health care in Canada* (third ed.) Scarborough, ON: Nelson.

Dignity for All: The Campaign for a Poverty Free Canada. (n.d). "About dignity for all." Retrieved August 25, 2010 from <http://www.dignityforall.ca/en/about-dignity-all>.

Dobrowolsky, A. (2009). *Women and public policy in Canada: Neoliberalism and after?* Toronto, ON: Oxford University Press.

Dobson, A. (1998). *Justice and the environment: Conceptions of environmental sustainability and theories of distributive justice.* Oxford: Oxford University Press.

Donnelly, J. (1994). "Human rights and international organizations: States sovereignty, and the international community." In F. Kratochwil and E.D. Mansfield (eds.), *International organization: A reader.* New York: Harper- Collins.

___. (2003). *Universal human rights in theory and practice (*second ed.). Ithaca, NY: Cornell University Press.

Drislane, R., and G. Parkinson. (2005). *Nelson criminology dictionary.* Toronto, ON: Nelson

Thomson Learning.
Du Mont J., T. Forte., and R. Badgely. (2008). "Does the punishment fit the crime? Judicial sentencing in adolescent and adult sexual assault cases." *Medicine and Law* 27(2): 477–98.
Dunlap, R.E. (2002). "Paradigms, theories, and environmental sociology." In R.E. Dunlap, F.H. Buttel, P. Dickens and A. Gijswijt (eds.), *Sociological theory and the environment, classical foundations, contemporary insights* (pp. 329–50). Oxford: Rowman & Littlefield.
Durkheim, E. (1951 [1897]). *Suicide*. New York: Free Press.
___. (1964 [1893]). *The division of labour in society.* New York: Free Press.
___. (1965 [1895]). "The rules of the sociological method." (S.A. Soloway and J.H. Mueller, trans.). New York: Free Press.
Dworkin, R. (1973). "The original position." *University of Chicago Law Review* 40, 500–33.
Dyck, L.Q. (2007). *Debates of the Senate* (Hansard), February 13, 1st Session, 39th Parliament, Volume 143, Issue 69, Debate on second reading of Bill S-4, to amend the Constitution Act, 1867 (Senate tenure).
Ehrlich, E. (1962 [1913]). *Fundamental principles of the sociology of law.* New York: Russell & Russell.
Elders' Panel: Aboriginal Justice. (2002). "Indian communication arts, First Nations University of Canada (FNUC)." Available in DVD through the FNUC library.
Elliott, D. (2006). "Secrets of the lavender mafia: Personal reflections on social activism and the Charter." *Journal of Law and Equality* 5: 98.
Engels, F. (2000 [1878]). "Against arm-chair justice from *anti-duhring*." In R.C. Solomon and M.C. Murphy (eds.), *What is justice? Classic and contemporary readings* (pp. 174–75). New York: Oxford University Press.
English Indices of Deprivation. (2007). "Communities and local government publications (summary)." West Yorkshire, UK. Retrieved September 12, 2007 from <http://www.communities.gov.uk/documents/communities/pdf/576659.pdf>.
Environics Poll. (2006). "Complete poll results." Conducted from Sept. 18–Oct. 12, 2006 for the Trudeau Foundation. Retrieved August 20, 2010 from <www.trudeaufoundation.ca>.
Environment Canada. (2002). "Urban water indicators: Municipal water use and wastewater treatment." <http:// www.ec.gc.ca/soer-ree/English/Indicators?issues?Urb_H2O>.
Erikson, K.T. (1966). *Wayward puritans.* New York: Willey.
Etzioni, A. (1995). "Old chestnuts and new spurs." In A. Etzioni (ed.), *New communitarian thinking: Persons, virtues, institutions, and communities*. Charlottesville, VA: University Press of Virginia.
___. (1996). *The new golden rules: Community and morality in a democratic society*. New York: Basic Books.
Falardeau-Ramsay, M. (1998). "Gender equality and the law." *Canadian Woman Studies* 19(1–2): 52–53.
Farkas, M.A., and A. Stichman. (2002). "Sex offender laws: Can treatment, punishment, incapacitation, and public safety be reconciled?" Criminal Justice Review 27(2): 256–83.
Fattah, E. (1989). *Introduction to criminology.* Burnaby, BC: School of Criminology, Simon Fraser University.
Feagin, J.R. (2006). *Systemic racism: A theory of oppression.* New York: Routledge.
Federation of Saskatchewan Indian Nations. (2009). "Justice." Retrieved August 25,

2009 from <http://www.fsin.com/justice/vision.html>.

Feldman, E.A. (2006). "The tuna court: Law and norms in the world's premier fish market." *California Law Review* 94: 313.

Fellows, M.L., and S.H. Razorback. (1998). "The race to innocence: Confronting hierarchical relations among women." *Journal of Gender, Race and Justice* 1(2): 335–52.

Figueres, C., C. Tortajada and J. Rockstrom. (2003). *Rethinking water management: Innovative approaches to contemporary issues*. London: Earthscan.

Firestone, S. (1970). *The dialectic of sex: The case for feminist revolution*. New York: Morrow.

Flelury, D., and M. Fortin. (2006). "When working is not enough to escape poverty: An analysis of Canada's working poor (August 2006)." Human Resources and Social Development Canada working paper series. Retrieved August 28, 2010 from <http://www.hrsdc.gc.ca/eng/cs/sp/sdc/pkrf/publications/research/SP-630-06-06/page20.shtml>.

Fleras, A., and J.L. Elliott. (1992). *Multiculturalism in Canada: The challenge of diversity.* Toronto, ON: Nelson.

Flowers, N. (2008). "Human rights here and now: Celebrating the universal declaration of human rights." Retrieved June 30, 2009 from <http://www1.umn.edu/humanrts/edumat/hreduseries/hereandnow/Default.htm>.

Fontaine, P. (2001). "Statement for International Women's Day, March 8, 2004." Assembly of First Nations National Indian Brotherhood.

Foucault, M. (1978). *The history of sexuality, volume I* (R. Hurley, trans.). New York: Pantheon Books.

___. (1979). "Governmentality." *Ideology & consciousness* 6: 5–21.

___. (1997). "Ethics: subjectivity and truth." In P. Rabinow (ed.), New York: New Press.

Fraser, G. (2002). "The fight for Canada's rights." *Toronto Star*. April 14. Retrieved June 27, 2010 from <http://archives.vigile.net/ds-federation/docs/02-4-14-fraser-3-1982.html>.

Fraser, N. (2005). "Reframing justice in a globalizing world." *New Left Review* 36, 69–88.

Freiler, C., L. Rothman and P. Barata. (2004). *Pathways to progress: Structural solutions to address child poverty*. Toronto, ON: Campaign 2000.

Galabuzi, G.E. (2006). *Canada's economic apartheid: The social exclusion of racialized groups in the new century*. Toronto, ON: Canadian Scholar's Press.

Galtung, J. (1998). "Conflict transformation by peaceful means (the transcend method): A manual prepared for the United Nations disaster management training program, transcend: A peace and development network." Retrieved June 28, 2009 from <www.transcend.org/trmanpar.htm>.

Garland, D. (2001). *The culture of control: Crime and social order in contemporary society*. Oxford: Oxford University Press.

Ghorayshi, P. (2007). "Unholy alliances: The discourse of globalization and our global future." In L. Samuelson and W.A. Antony (eds.), *Power and resistance* (fourth ed.) (pp. 215–41). Halifax, NS: Fernwood,

Gilbertson, M. (2009). "Index of congenital minamata disease in Canadian areas of concern in the Great Lakes: An eco-social epidemiological approach." *Journal of Environmental Science and Health* part C, 27(4): 246–75.

Gingrich, P. (2009). "Boom and bust: The growing income gap in Saskatchewan." *Canadian Centre for Policy Alternatives*. Regina, SK: Retrieved September 9, 2009 from <http://www.policyalternatives.ca/~ASSETS/DOCUMENT/Saskatchewan_Pubs/2009/Boom_and_Bust_Sept_01_09.pdf>.

Ginott, H. (1972). *Between teacher and child*. New York: MacMillan. Quoted in P. Redekop (2008), *Changing paradigms, punishment and restorative discipline*, Scottdale, PA: Herald Press.

Glasser, W. (1969). *Schools without failure*. New York: Harper & Row.

___. (1998). *Choice theory: A new psychology for personal freedom*. New York: Harper Perennial.

Gleick, P. (2006). *The world's water, 2006–2007: Biannual report on the world's freshwater resources*. Washington, DC: Island Press.

Glick, P. (2000). "The toll from coal." *National Wildlife Federation*, p.1. Retrieved June 1, 2009 from <www.nwf.org/washingtondc/resources.html>.

Goff, C. (2004). *Criminal Justice in Canada* (third ed.). Winnipeg, MB: Thomson Nelson.

Goffman, E. (1963). *Stigma: Notes on the management of spoiled identity*. Englewood Cliffs, NJ: Prentice Hall.

Goldberg, D.T. (1993). *Racist culture: Philosophy and the politics of meaning*. Oxford: Blackwell Publishers.

Goldman, A., and J. Royot. (2003). *Negotiation theory and practice*. The Hague, Netherlands: Kluwer Law International.

Government of Canada. (2010). "Strategic plan for Aboriginal corrections." Corrections Canada. Retrieved January, 2010 from <http://www.csc-scc.gc.ca/text/prgrm/abinit/plan06-eng.shtml>.

Government of Manitoba. (2009). *Conservation districts of Manitoba 2008–2009 annual report*. Manitoba. Retrieved from <http://www.gov.mb.ca/waterstewardship/agencies/cd/cd_annual_report2008-2009.pdf>

Government of Saskatchewan. (n.d.). "Creating healthy, just, prosperous and safe Saskatchewan: A response to the commission on First Nation and Metis peoples and justice reference." Retrieved June 25, 2008 from <www.publictions.gov.sk.ca/detailscfm?p=9870>.

Gowans, C. (2008). "Moral relativism." *Stanford encyclopedia of philosophy*. Retrieved June 5, 2010 from <http://plato.stanford.edu/entries/moral-relativism/>.

Grabb, E. (2002). *Theories of social inequality* (fourth ed.). Toronto, ON: Thomson Nelson.

Greenpeace International. (2010). "Questions about green peace in general." Amsterdam, Netherlands: Retrieved from <http://www.greenpeace.org/international/en/about/faq_old/questions-about-greenpeace-in/>.

Griffiths, C.T. (2008). *Canadian police work* (second ed.). Toronto, ON: Nelson.

Griffiths C.T., and A.H. Cunningham. (2003). *Canadian criminal justice* (second ed.). Toronto, ON: Harcourt Brace.

Guard, J., and W. Antony (eds.). (2009). *Bankruptcies & bailouts*. Halifax, NS: Fernwood.

Guemple, L. (1980). "Growing old in Inuit society." In V.W. Marshall (ed.), *Aging in Canada, social perspectives* (pp. 95–102). Don Mills, ON: Fitzhenry & Whiteside.

Gustafson, D. (2007). "Facing the question." A workshop on a palaver on praxis: The marriage of restorative justice theory and practice following the June 2003 International Restorative Justice Conference in Vancouver, BC: Retrieved April 2008 from <http://www.csc-scc.gc.ca/text/rj/rj2007/pdf/7_e.pdf>.

GWP (Global Water Partnership). (2000). *GWP annual report*. Retrieved from <www.gwpforum.org/servlet/PSP?:NodeID=263&iFronNode/D=102>.

Habermas, J. (1973). *Theory and practice*. Boston: Beacon Press.

Hachett, R.D., P.K. Bycio and P.A. Hausadorf. (1994). "Further assessment of Meyer and Allen's 1991 three components model of organizational commitment." *Journal of Applied Psychology* 79: 240–50.

Hagan, J., J. Simpson and A.R. Gillis. (1987). "Class in the household: A power-control theory of gender and delinquency." *American Journal of Sociology* 92: 788–816.

Handel, M., W. Asikinack and J. Mulvale (co-producers). (2002). *Elders' panel: Aboriginal justice* (in video and DVD format). Regina SK: Dept. of Indigenous Studies, First National University of Canada and Dept. of Justice Studies, University of Regina.

Hannigan, J. (1995). *Environmental sociology* (second ed.). New York: Routledge.

Hannum, H. (1995–1996). "The status of the Universal Declaration of Human Rights in national and international law." *Georgia Journal of International and Comparative Law* 25: 317–52.

Hanson, R.K. (2001). *Age and sexual recidivism: A comparison of rapists and child molesters.* Ottawa, ON: Solicitor General.

Harada, M. (2005). "The global lessons of minimata disease: An introduction to minamata studies." *Advances in Bioethics* 8: 299–335.

Harper, C.L. (2004). *Environment and society: Human perspectives on environmental issues* (third ed.), New Jersey, NJ: Pearson Prentice Hall.

Hay, D.I. (2009). "Poverty reduction policies and programs in Canada." *Canadian Council on Social Development.* Ottawa, ON: Retrieved August 30, 2009 from <http://www.ccsd.ca/SDR2009/Reports/Canada_Report_FINAL.pdf>.

Health Canada. (1999). *Statistical report on the health of Canadians.* Retrieved April 25, 2009 from <http://www.hc-sc.gc.ca/hppb/phdd/report/state/eng/over.html>.

___. (2005). *A statistical profile on the health of First Nations in Canada for the year 2000.* Ottawa, ON: Health Canada.

Heffernan, W., and J. Kleinig. (2000). *From social justice to criminal justice: Poverty and the administration of criminal law.* New York: Oxford University Press

Henkin, L. (1990). *The age of rights.* Columbia, NY: Columbia University Press.

Henry, F., and C. Tator. (2006). *The colour of democracy: Racism in Canadian society* (third ed.). Toronto, ON: Nelson Thomson Learning.

Henry, F., C. Tator, W. Mattis and T. Rees. (2000). *The colour of democracy: Racism in Canadian society* (second ed.) (pp. 15–33). Toronto, ON: Harcourt.

Henton, D. (2010). "Oilsands 'doomed' if duck charges stick, Syncrude tells court." *Leader Post,* April 28.

Herman, J. (1997). *Trauma and recovery: The aftermath of violence: From domestic violence to political terror.* New York: Basic Books.

Hewitt, P. (2009). "MR likened to 'Fatal Attraction' character." *CNews* July 15. Retrieved September 29, 2009 from <http://cnews.canoe.ca/CNEWS/Crime/2009/07/14/10125576-cp.html>.

Hickey, S., and G. Mohan. (2004). "Towards participation as transformation: Critical themes and challenges." In Hickey and Mohan, *Participation: From tyranny to transformation? Exploring new approaches to participation in development.* London: Zed Books.

Hill, G.B. (2004). *Life of Johnson* (Volume 3). Kessinger.

Hillman, M., and R. Howitt. (2008). "Institutional change in natural resource management in New South Wales, Australia, sustaining capacity and justice." *Local Environment* 13(1): 55–66.

Hobbes, T. (2000). "The state of nature and the laws of nature, from *Leviathan* (1651)." In R.C. Solomon and M.C. Murphy (eds.), *What is justice? Classic and contemporary readings* (pp. 63–73). New York: Oxford University Press.

Hogg, P.W., and A.A. Bushell. (1997). "The *Charter* dialogue between courts and legislatures (or perhaps the *Charter* of rights isn't such a bad thing after all)." *Osgoode*

Hall Law Journal 35: 75–124.
Hogg, P.W., A.A.Bushell and W.K. Wright. (2007). "*Charter* dialogue revisited — or 'much ado about metaphors'." *Osgoode Hall Law Journal* 45: 1–65.
Hood, R.G., and R.F. Sparks. (1970). *Key issues in criminology*. London: Weidenfield & Nicolson.
hooks, B. (1992). "Eating the other." *In black looks: Race and representation* (pp. 21–39). Toronto, ON: Between the Lines.
Howlett, M. (ed.). (2001). *Canadian forest policy: Adapting to change*. Toronto, ON: University of Toronto Press.
Hsia, H., G.S. Bridges and R. McHale. (2004). *Disproportionate minority confinement — 2002 update*. Washington, DC: U.S. Department of Justice.
Hudson, B. (2002). "Restorative justice and gendered violence: Diversion or effective justice." *British Journal of Criminology* 42: 616–34.
Hugh, R., and J. Lynnea. (2004). *Restorative justice in schools in Surrey, British Columbia.* Fifth International Conference on *Conferencing and Circles.*
Hulsman, L.H.C. (1986). "Critical criminology and the concept of crime." *Contemporary Crisis* 10: 63–80.
Hunt, A.J. (1981). "Marxism and the analysis of law." In A. Podgorecki and C.J. Whelan (eds.), *Sociological approaches to law* (pp. 91–109). New York: St Martin's Press.
____. (1993). *Explorations in law and society: Toward a constitutive theory of law*. New York: Routledge.
Huntington, E. (1915). *Civilization and climate: World power and evolution and the character of races.* New Haven, CT: Yale University Press.
Hurlbert, M.A. (2009). "An analysis of trends related to the adaptation of water law to the challenge of climate change: Experience from Canada." *International Journal of Climate Change Strategies and Management* 1(3): 230–40.
____. (2009a). "The adaptation of water law to climate change." *International Journal of Climate Change Strategies and Management* 1(3): 230–40.
____. (2009b). "Comparative water governance in the four Western Provinces." *Prairie Forum* (special edition on climate change) 34(1): 45–77.
Hurlbert, M.A., and J. MacKenzie. (2008). "Making structural changes in criminal justice." In J. Whyte (ed.), *Moving toward justice: Legal traditions and Aboriginal justice.* Saskatoon, SK: Purich.
____. (2008). "The criminal justice system and Aboriginal people." In J. Whyte (ed.), *Moving toward justice: Legal traditions and Aboriginal justice* (pp. 142–59). Saskatoon, SK: Purich.
Hurtig, M. (2002). *The vanishing country: Is it too late to save Canada?* Toronto, ON: McClelland & Stewart.
IPCC (Intergovernmental Panel on Climate Change). (2007). "Climate change 2007: Synthesis report." AR4 synthesis report, summary for policymakers, an assessment of the *Intergovernmental Panel on Climate Change*. Valencia, Spain: Retrieved June 15, 2009 from <www.ipcc.ch/pdf/assessment-report>.
Johnson, D.W., and R.T. Johnson. (1989). *Cooperation and competition: Theory and research.* Edna, MN: Interaction.
____. (2003). "Social interdependence: The interrelationships among theory, research and practice." March. University of Minnesota: Center for Cooperative Learning
Johnson, R. (2008). "Kant's moral philosophy." *Stanford encyclopedia of philosophy.* Retrieved June 5, 2010 from <http://plato.stanford.edu/entries/kant-moral/>.

Kendall, D., R. Linden and J. Lothian Murray. (2008). *Sociology in our times: The essentials* (fourth ed., Canadian). Toronto, ON: Nelson Thomson Learning.

Kerbo, H.R. (2006). *Social stratification and inequality: Class conflict in historical, comparative, and global perspective.* New York: McGraw Hill Higher Education.

Kinewesquao [C. Richardson]. "Métis experiences of social work practices." In S. Strega and S.A. Esquao [J. Carrière] (eds.), *Walking this path together: Anti-racist and anti-oppressive child welfare practices* (pp.110–26). Halifax, NS: Fernwood.

Kinsella, N. (1982). "Tomorrow's rights in the mirror of history." In G. Gall, *Civil liberties in Canada: Entering the 1980s* (pp. 3–50). Toronto, ON: Butterworths.

___. (2008). "Can Canada afford a *Charter* of social and economic rights? Toward a Canadian social Charter." *Saskatchewan Law Review* 71(1): 7–22.

Kitsuse, J.I., and A.V. Cicourel. (1963). "A note on the use of official statistics." *Social Problems* 11(1): 131–39.

Klein, N. (2007). *The shock doctrine: The rise of disaster capitalism.* Toronto, ON: Alfred A. Knopf.

___. (2008). *The shock doctrine: The rise of disaster capitalism.* New York: Henry Holt.

Kline, M. (1994). "The colour of law: ideological representations of First Nations in legal discourse." *Social and Legal Studies* 3: 451–76.

Knazan, B. (2003). "Sentencing Aboriginal offenders in a large city: The Gladue (Aboriginal Persons) courts." A paper presented at the national judicial institute, Aboriginal law seminar, January 23–25, 2000, at Calgary, AB.

___. (2005). "The Gladue (Aboriginal Persons) courts: An update." A paper presented at the national judicial institute, Aboriginal law seminar, April, 2005, at St. John's, NF.

Knuttila, M. (2002). *Introducing sociology: A critical perspective.* Don Mills, ON: Oxford University Press.

Kome, P. (1983). *The taking of twenty eight: Women challenge the Constitution.* Toronto, ON: Women's Press.

Kong, R., and K. AuCoin. (2008). "Female offenders in Canada." *Juristat.* Ottawa, ON: Statistics Canada.

Kruk, E. (1997). "Introduction." In E. Kruk (ed.), *Mediation and conflict resolution in social work and the human services.* Chicago: Nelson-Hall.

Kymlicka, W. (1995). *Multicultural citizenship: A liberal theory of minority rights.* New York: Oxford University Press.

___. (1995). *The rights of minority cultures.* Oxford: Oxford University Press.

La Vía Campesina. (2000). "Food sovereignty and international trade." Position paper approved at the third international conference of La Vía Campesina, Bangalore, India. (October 3–6).

Lacey, N. (1998). "Unspeakable subjects: Impossible rights: Sexuality, integrity, and criminal law." *Canadian Journal of Law and Jurisprudence* 11(1): 47–68.

Laidlaw, D.K. (2010). "Water rights and water stewardship: What about Aboriginal people?" *Canadian Institute of Resources Law* 107.

Laing, R. (2003). "Report of the Commission of inquiry into matters related to the safety of the public drinking water in the city of North Battleford, Saskatchewan." Regina: Queen's Printer.

Laishes, J. (2002). *The 2002 mental health strategy for women offenders: Women offender program, correctional service Canada.* Retrieved October 17, 2008 from <www.csc-scc.gc.ca/text/prgrm/fsw/mhealth/4-eng.shtml>.

Latimer, J., C. Dowden and D. Muise. (2001). *The effectiveness of restorative justice practices:*

A meta-analysis. Ottawa, ON: Department of Justice.

____. (2005). "The effectiveness of restorative justice practices: A meta-analysis." *Prison Journal* 85(2): 127–44.

Le Dain Commission. (1973). *Final report of the Commission of inquiry into the non-medical use of drugs*. Ottawa, ON: Information Canada.

Lemke, T. (2001). "The birth of bio-politics: Michael Foucault's lectures at the College de France on neo-liberal governmentality." *Economy and Society* 30(2): 190–207.

Lemmen, D.S., F.J. Warren, J. Lacroix and E. Bush (eds). (2008). *From impacts to adaptation: Canada in a changing climate 2007*. Ottawa, ON: Government of Canada. Retrieved June 3, 2009 from <http://adaptation.nrcan.gc.ca/assess/2007/toc_e.php>.

Lentin, A. (2009). "Competing anti-racisms and the interpretation of racism in the post-multicultural era." In S.P. Hier, D. Lett and B. Singh Bolaria (eds.), *Racism and justice: Critical dialogue on the politics of identity, inequality, and change* (pp. 189–206). Halifax, NS: Fernwood.

Lepofsky, M.D. (1998). "The Charter's guarantee of equality to people with disabilities: How well is it working?" *Windsor Yearbook of Access to Justice* 16(55): 156.

Levit, J. K. (2005). "A bottom-up approach to international lawmaking: The tale of three trade finance instruments." *Yale Journal of International Law* 30: 125.

Lexchin, J. (2002). "Profits first: The pharmaceutical industry in Canada." In B.S. Bolaria and H.D. Dickinson (eds.), *Health, illness and health care in Canada* (third ed.). Scarborough, ON: Nelson.

Library and Archives Canada. (n.d.). "Prime Minister Pierre Elliott Trudeau proclamation ceremony speech April 17, 1982." Retrieved February 28, 2011 from <www.lac-bac.gc/ca>.

Lightman, E., A. Mitchell and B. Wilson. (2008). *Poverty is making us sick: A comprehensive survey of income and health in Canada*. Toronto, ON: Wellesley institute and community social planning council of Toronto. Retrieved September 9, 2009 from <http://www.socialwork.utoronto.ca/Assets/SANE/Poverty+making+us+sick.pdf>.

Locke, J. (2000 [1690]). "The state of nature and the social contract: From second treatise on government." In R.C. Solomon and M.C. Murphy (eds.), *What is justice? Classic and contemporary readings* (pp. 74–80). New York: Oxford University Press.

Lowman, J. (n.d.). *Police practices and crime rates*. Burnaby, BC: School of Criminology, Simon Fraser University.

Luhmann, N. (1993). 2004. *Law as a social system*. Oxford: Oxford University Press.

Lynch, M.J., and B.W. Groves. (1989). *A primer in radical criminology*. Albany, NY: Harrow and Heston.

MacDonald, G.M. (2002). *Social context & social location in the sociology of law*. Peterborough, ON: Broadview Press.

MacIntyre, A. (1981). *After virtue.* Notre Dame, IN: University of Notre Dame Press.

MacKay, A.W. (1984). *Education law in Canada.* Toronto, ON: Emond-Montgomery.

Mackey, E. (1999). *The house of difference: Cultural politics and national identity in Canada.* New York: Routledge.

MacKinnon, C. (1987). *Feminism unmodified: Discourses on life and law*. Cambridge: Harvard University Press.

____. (1991). *Toward a feminist theory of state*. Cambridge: Harvard University Press.

____. (2006). *Are women human? And other international dialogues*. Boston: Harvard University Press.

Mandamin, T.L.S. (2003). "Peacemaking and the Tsuu T'ina court." *Justice as Healing*

Newsletter 8(1): 1.

Manfredi, C.P. (2004). *Feminist activism in the Supreme Court: Legal mobilization and the women's legal education and action fund*. Vancouver, BC: University of British Columbia Press.

Manitoba. (1991). *Public inquiry into the administration of justice and Aboriginal people, (Aboriginal justice inquiry)* (Vols. 1–2). Winnipeg, MB: Queen's Printer.

Manitoba Human Rights Commission. (2007). *Council of Canadians with Disabilities v. Via Rail Canada: Decision ensures equality and freedom from discrimination*. March 23. Retrieved July 4, 2010 from <http://www.gov.mb.ca/hrc/publications/news_releases/pdf/03_23_07.pdf>.

Mannheim, H. (1965). *Comparative criminology*. Boston, MA: Houghton-Mifflin.

Marshall, K. (2006). "Converging gender roles." *Perspectives* 5–17. Statistics Canada Catalogue no. 75-001-XIE.

Marshall, T.F. (1999). *Restorative justice: An overview*. London, UK: Home Office, Research Development and Statistics Directorate. <http://www.homeoffice.gov.uk/rds/pdfs/occ-resjus.pdf>.

Martin, M. (2002). "The Crown owns all the land?" In G.M. MacDonald, *Social context & social location in the sociology of law* (pp. 229–46). Peterborough, ON: Broadview Press.

Martinez, E., and A. Garcia. (2007). *What is neo-liberalism?* Global Economy 101, global exchange. Retrieved June 29, 2009 from <http://www.globalexchange.org/campaigns/econ101/neoliberalDefined.html>.

Marx, K. (1842). "Debates on the law on thefts of wood." Supplement to the *Rheinische Zeitung*, October–November. <www.marxists.org/archive/marx/works/1842/10/25.htm>.

___. (1869). "Report of the general council on the right of inheritance." Written on behalf of the International Workingmen's Association. <www.marxists.org/histor/international/iwma/documents/1869/inheritance-report.htm>.

Marx, K., and E. Fredrick. (1846). "The German ideology." In *Marx Engels collected works* (Vol. 5) (1976). New York: International Publishers.

___. (1848). *The communist manifesto*. New York: Washington Square Press.

Matthew, chapter 5 verses 6 and 10. In Haydock's *Catholic Bible commentary*. (1859 edition). Retrieved August 28, 2010 from <http://haydock1859.tripod.com/id19.html>.

Mawby, R.I. (1989). "Policing and the criminal area." In D.J. Evans and D.T. Herbert (eds.), *The geography of crime* (pp.260–81). London: Routledge.

___. (1990). *Comparative policing issues: The British and American system in international perspective*. London: Unwin Hyman.

McCaslin, W. (2005). "Introduction: Reweaving the fabrics of life." In W. McCalsin (ed.), *Justice as healing: Indigenous ways*. St. Paul, MN. Living Justice Press.

McCulloch, B. (2008). "Harper pledges to get tough on crime." Newstalk 650 CKOM, September 23 <http://www.newstalk650.com/story/20080923/6126>.

McGillivray, A., and B. Comaskey. (1999). *Black eyes all the time: Intimate violence, Aboriginal women and the justice system*. Toronto, ON: University of Toronto Press.

McIntosh, P. (1988). "White privilege: Unpacking the invisible knapsack." Retrieved November 12, 2007 from <http://www.case.edu/president/aaction/UnpackingTheKnapsack.pdf>.

McLachlin, B. (2001). "Equality: The most difficult right." *Supreme Court Law Review* 14(2d): 17.

McLean, J. (2007). "Water injustices and potential remedies in indigenous rural contexts: A water justice analysis." *Environmentalist* 27: 25–38.

McPhedran, M. (2005). "Reflections on the 20th anniversary of section 15: The impact of s. 15 on Canadian society equality rights: Beacon or laser?" *National Journal of Constitutional Law* 19: 7–29.

Mead, G.H. (1934). *Mind, self and society*. C.W. Morris (ed.). Chicago, IL: University of Chicago Press.

Merry, S.E. (1988). "Legal pluralism." *Law & Society Review* 22: 869–95.

___. (2008). "International law and sociologic scholarship: Toward a spatial global legal pluralism." Special issue: Law and society reconsidered. *Studies in Law, Politics, and Society* 41: 149–68.

Merton, R.K. (1938). "Social structure and anomie." *American Sociological Review* 3: 672–82.

___. (1968). *Social theory and social structure*. New York: Free Press.

Mills, C.W. (1959). *The sociological imagination*. New York: Oxford University Press.

Milovanovic, D. (1988). *A primer in the sociology of law*. New York: Harrow & Heston.

Mimura, N., L. Nurse, R.F. McLean, L.J. Agard, P.L. Briguglio, R. Payet and G. Sem. (2007). "Small islands." Contribution of working group II to the fourth assessment report of the Intergovernmental Panel on Climate Change. In M.L. Parry, O.F Canziani, J.P. Palutikof, P.J. Van Der Linden and C.E. Hanson (eds.), *Climate change 2007: Impacts, adaptation and vulnerability* (pp. 687–716). Cambridge: Cambridge University Press.

Mirsky, L. (2004). "Transforming school culture: An update. International Institute for Restorative Practices." December 7. Bethlehem, PA. Retrieved August 28, 2010 from <http://www.safersanerschools.org/articles.html?articleId=395>.

___. (2009). "Restorative practices and the transformation at West Philadelphia High School. International Institute for Restorative Practices." June 22. Bethlehem, PA. Retrieved August 28, 2010 from <http://www.safersanerschools.org/articles.html?articleId=609>.

Mitura, V., and R.D. Bollman. (2003). "The health of rural Canadians: A rural-urban comparison of health indicators." *Rural and Small Town Canada Analysis Bulletin* 4(6).

Moller O.S. (1989). *Justice, gender and the family*. New York: Basic Books.

Mooney, L.A., D. Knox, C. Schacht and M.M. Holmes. (2008). *Understanding social problems* (third ed. Canadian). Toronto, ON: Nelson Thomson Learning.

Morris, A. (2002). "Critiquing the critics: A brief response to critics of restorative justice." *British Journal of Criminology* 42: 596–615.

Morris, N., and D.J. Rothman. (1995). *The Oxford history of the prison: The practice of punishment in western society*. Oxford: Oxford University Press.

Mullaly, B. (2002). *Challenging oppression: A critical social work approach*. Toronto, ON: Oxford University Press.

Mulvale, J.P. (2007). "Enough to live on: The case for guaranteed income and the end of the growth economy." *Briarpatch* 36, 7(November): 29–33. Retrieved September 12, 2007 from <http://briarpatchmagazine.com/enough-to-live-on/>.

___. (2008a) "Basic income and the Canadian welfare state: Exploring the realms of possibility." *Basic Income Studies* 3, 1 (Article 6). Retrieved September, 2009 from <http://www.bepress.com/bis/vol3/iss1/art6/>.

___. (2008b). "Desperately seeking a new model of economic security for Canada: The basic income approach." *Canadian Social Work/Travail Social Canadian* 10(1): 8–28.

Naffine, N. (1990). *Law and the sexes: Explorations in feminist jurisprudence*. Sydney, Australia:

Allen & Unwin.

Nahanee, T. (1994). "Sexual assault of Inuit females: A comment on 'cultural bias'." In J. Roberts and R.M. Mohr (eds.), *Confronting sexual assault: A decade of legal and social change*. Toronto, ON: University of Toronto Press.

___. (1995). "Dancing with a gorilla: Aboriginal women, justice and the *Charter*." In *Aboriginal peoples and the justice system: Royal Commission on Aboriginal Peoples.* Ottawa, ON: Canada Communications Group.

NCW (National Council of Welfare). (2007a). "Poverty statistics 2004." <http://www.ncwcnbes.net/documents/researchpublications/ResearchProjects/PovertyProfile/2004/PovertyRates-TrendsENG.pdf>.

___. (2007b). *Solving poverty: Four cornerstones of a workable national strategy for Canada* (Vol. 126). Ottawa, ON: NCW. Retrieved September 12, 2009 from <http://www.ncwcnbes.net/en/research/antipoverty-antipauvrete.html>.

___. (2008) *Draft outline of a presentation concerning the study on poverty presented to the Standing Committee on Human Resources, Social Development, and Persons with Disabilities* [cited January 13, 2011]. Available at <http://www.ncw.gc.ca/l.3bd.2t.1ils@-eng.jsp?lid=24>.

Nelson, A. (2006). *Gender in Canada* (third ed.). Toronto: Pearson Prentice Hall.

Nevitte, N. (1996). *The decline of deference: Canadian value change in cross-national perspective*. Peterborough, ON: Broadview Press.

New York Times. (2008). "O.J. Simpson." October 4, updated December 3.

NFU (National Farmers Union). (2005). *The farm crisis: Its causes and solutions.* National Farmers Union's submission to the Ministers of Agriculture, Kananaskis Alberta. Saskatoon, SK: Retrieved September, 2009 from <http://www.nfu.ca/briefs/2005/Ministers_of_Ag_brief_FOUR.pdf>.

Nightingale, M. (1991). "Judicial attitudes and differential treatment: Native women in sexual assault cases." *Ottawa Law Review* 23(1): 71–86.

Nikiforuk, A. (2008). *Tar sands: Dirty oil and the future of the continent*. Vancouver, BC: Greystone Books.

Nisbet, R.A. (1969). "The twilight of authority." *The Public Interest* 15 (spring): 3–9.

Norrie, A. (1998). "The limits of justice: Finding fault in the criminal law." In M.S. Archer (ed.), *Critical Realism, Essential Readings* (pp 702–22). New York: Routledge.

Nozick, R. (1974). *The entitlement theory: Anarchy, state, and utopia*. New York: Basic Books.

Nussbaum, M. (1999). *Sex and social justice*. New York: Oxford University Press.

O'Byrne, D.J. (2003). *Human rights, an introduction*. Essex, UK: Pearson Education.

O'Connor, D. (2002). "Report of the Walkerton Commission of Inquiry." Retrieved September 24, 2007 from <http://www.attorneygeneral.jus.gov.on.ca/english/about/pubs/walkerton/part1/>.

OECD (Organization for Economic Cooperation and Development). (2008). *OECD key environmental indicators*. Paris, France: OECD Environment Directorate.

Office of the Parliamentary Budge Officer. (2010). *The funding requirement and impact of the "Truth in Sentencing Act" on the correctional system in Canada*. Ottawa, ON: Office of the Parliamentary Budget Officer.

Ohlin, L. (1974). "Correctional strategies in conflict." *Proceedings of the American Philosophical Society* 118(3): 248–53.

OMA (Ontario Medical Association). (2000). "Phase II: Estimating health and economic damages, illness costs of air pollution." Toronto, ON: Retrieved from <https://www.oma.org/Resources/Documents/2000IllnessCostsOfAirPollution.pdf>.

Ontario Human Rights Commission. (2003). *Paying the price: The human cost of racial profiling.* October 21. Toronto, ON: Human Rights Commission.

Oztel, J.G., B. Arcos, P. Mabizila, A.M. Weinman and Q. Zhang. (2006). "Historical, political and spiritual factors of conflict: Understanding conflict perspectives and communication in the Muslim world, China, Columbia and South Africa." In J.G. Oetzel and S. Ting-Toomey (eds.), *The Sage handbook of conflict communication: Integrating theory, research and practice.* Thousand Oaks, CA: Sage.

Paavola, J., W.N. Adger and S. Huz. (2006). "Multi-faceted justice in adaptation to climate change." In W.N. Adger, J. Paavola, S. Huq and M.J. Mace (eds.), *Fairness in adaptation to climate change* (pp. 263–77). Cambridge, MA: MIT Press.

Paciocco, D.M. (1999). *Getting away with murder: The Canadian criminal justice system.* Toronto, ON: Irwin Law.

Packer, H. (1968). *The limits of the criminal sanction.* California, ON: Stanford University Press.

Paperny, A.M., and S. Minogue. (2009). *Globe and Mail*, August 14: A1.

Parsons, T. (1937). *The structure of social action* (Vol. 1). New York: Free Press.

___. (1951). *The social system.* New York: Free Press.

Pateman, C. (1998). "Democracy, freedom and special rights." In D. Boucher and P. Kelly (eds.), *Social justice: From hume to walzer.* New York: Routledge.

Patenaude, A.L., W.A. DuPerron, J.M. Dillon, D.N. Friesen and D.B. Zinck. (1992). "Corrections in Canada's Northwest Territories: Balancing individual, institutional and community needs, Part I." *American Jails* 6(5): 73–78.

___. (1993). "Corrections in Canada's Northwest Territories: Balancing individual, institutional and community needs, Part II." *American Jails* 6(6): 71–75.

Patenaude, A.L., D.S. Wood and C.T. Griffiths. (1992). "Indigenous peoples in Canadian corrections: Critical issues and the prospects for 'localized' corrections." *Journal of Contemporary Criminal Justice* 8(2): 114–36.

Pavlich, G. (2005). *Governing paradoxes of restorative justice.* London: GlassHouse Press.

Peirce, J., and K. Bentham. (2007). *Canadian industrial relations* (third ed.). Toronto, ON: Pearson Prentice Hall.

Pennell, J., and G. Burford. (2000). "Family group decision making: Protecting children and women." *Child Welfare* Mar Apr 79(2): 131–59.

___. (2002). "Feminist praxis: Making family group conferencing work." In H. Strang and J. Braithwaite (eds.), *Restorative justice and family violence.* Cambridge: Cambridge University Press.

Perreault, S. (2009). "The incarceration of Aboriginal people in adult correctional services." *Juristat* 29(3). Ottawa, ON: Statistics Canada.

Peterson, M.R. (2000). "Developing a restorative justice programme." *Justice as Healing* 5(4), Part II. Native Law Centre of Canada.

Petter, A. (1987). "Immaculate deception: The Charter's hidden agenda." *The Advocate* 45: 857–67.

Phillips, N., and C. Hardy. (2002). *Discourse analysis: Investigating processes of social construction.* Thousand Oaks, CA: Sage.

Picot, G., F. Hou and S. Coulombe. (2007). "Chronic low income and low-income dynamics among recent immigrants." *Statistics Canada.* Analytical studies research paper series, 11F0019NIE, no. 294.

Plato, (1982). *The republic.* (G.M.A. Grube, trans.). Indianapolis, IN: Hachett.

Pogge, T.W. (2002). *World poverty and human rights: Cosmopolitan responsibilities and reforms.*

Cambridge: Polity Press.
___. (2008). "Moral universalism and global economic justice." In T. Brooks (ed.), *The global justice reader.* Malden, MA: Blackwell.
Pojman, L.P. (2006). *Justice*. Upper Saddle River, NJ: Pearson Prentice Hill.
Pollock, O. (1978). *The criminality of women*. Westport, CT: Greenwood Press.
Pollack, S., V. Green and A. Allspach. (2005). *Women charged with domestic violence in Toronto: The unintended consequences of mandatory charge policies.* Toronto, ON: Woman Abuse Council of Toronto.
Pollock, S. (n.d.). "You can't have it both ways: punishment and treatment of imprisoned women." *Journal of Progressive Human Services* 20(2): 112–29.
Pollution Probe. (2007). "Towards a vision and strategy for water management in Canada." Final report of the water policy in Canada national workshop series. Victoria, BC: Polis Project on Ecological Governance.
Pollution Watch. (2004). "Shattering the myth of pollution progress in Canada: A national report." < http://www.pollutionwatch.org/pub/pollutionwatch%20 national%20report_english_ebook.pdf>.
Pope, C., and W. Feyerhern. (1992). *Minorities and the juvenile justice system*. Washington, DC: Office of Juvenile Justice and Delinquency Prevention, U.S. Department of Justice.
Porter, A.J. (2007). "Restorative practices in schools: Research reveals power of restorative approach, part I." April 27. *Restorative Practices eForum*. Retrieved August 4, 2007 from <http://www.safersanerschools.org/library/schoolresearch1.html>.
Porter, J. (1970). *The vertical mosaic: An analysis of social class and power in Canada*. Toronto: University of Toronto Press.
Poser, W.J. (n.d.). *The names of the First Nations languages of British Columbia.* Retrieved June 20, 2010 from <http://www.billpower.org/Papers/bclgnames.pdf>.
Pospisil, L. (1979). "Legally induced culture change in New Guinea." In R. Pound (1942), *Social control through law* (pp. 127–44). New Haven, CT: Yale University Press.
Pound, R. (1959). *Jurisprudence* (Vols. 1–5). St. Paul, MN: West.
Pruegger, V., D. Cook and S. Richter-Salomons. (2009). *Inequality in Calgary: The racialization of poverty.* City of Calgary, community and neighbourhood services. Retrieved on June 10, 2010 from <http://www.calgary.ca/docgallery/bu/cns/inequality_in_calgary.pdf>.
Raiffa, H. (1982). *The art and science of negotiation.* Cambridge, MA: Belknap Press of Harvard University Press.
Rajan, S.R. (2001). "Towards a metaphysics of environmental violence: The case of the Bhopal gas disaster." In N.L. Peluso and M. Watts (eds.), *Violent environments* (pp. 380–98). Ithaca, NY: Cornell University Press.
Raphael, D.D. (2001). *Concepts of justice*. Oxford: Clarendon Press.
___. (2007). *Poverty and policy in Canada: Implications for health and quality of life.* Toronto, ON: Canadian Scholars' Press.
___. (2010). *About Canada: Health and illness*. Winnipeg: Fernwood Publishing.
Rawls, J. (1971). *A theory of justice.* Cambridge: Harvard University Press.
Razack, S. (1998). *Looking white people in the eye: Gender, race and culture in courtrooms and classrooms.* Toronto, ON: University of Toronto Press.
___. (2000). "Gendered racial violence and spatialized justice: The murder of Pamela George." *Canadian Journal of Law and Society* 15(2): 91–130.
___. (2002), "Gendered racial violence and spatialized justice: The murder of Pamela

George." In S. Razack (ed.), *Race space and the law: Unmapping a white settler society.* Toronto, ON: Between the Lines.

Redekop, P. (2008). *Changing paradigms: Punishment and restorative discipline.* Waterloo, ON: Herald Press.

Regina Leader-Post. (2007). "KKK revived, with strong Regina ties." August 27. Retrieved August 27, 2007 from <http://www.canada.com/reginaleaderpost/news/story.html?id=01bbc304-6a89-481a-8184-2cb2c4bef98d>

Regina Police Service. (2004). *The Regina police service response to the recommendations of the Commission on First Nation and Métis people and justice reform.* (December 16) Regina, SK: Regina Police Service.

Reiman, J., and P. Leighton. (2010). *The rich get richer and the poor get prison: Ideology, class and criminal justice* (ninth ed.). Toronto, ON: Allyn & Bacon.

Roach, K. (2001). *The supreme court on trial: Judicial activism or democratic dialogue.* Toronto, ON: Irwin Law.

___. (2009). *Criminal law.* Toronto, ON: Irwin Law.

Roberts, J.V., and M.G. Grossman (eds.). (2004). *Criminal justice in Canada* (pp. 289–303). Scarborough, ON: Thomson Nelson.

Roberts, J.V., and K. Roach. (2005). "Conditional sentences and the perspectives of crime victims: A socio-legal analysis." *Queens Law Journal* 30: 560.

Roberts, T. (1995). *Evaluation of the victim-offender mediation project: Langley, B.C.* Ottawa, ON: Solicitor General Canada.

Robinson, M. (2001). "Bridging the gap between human rights and development: From normative principles to operational relevance." *United Nations High Commissioner for Human Rights.* Washington, DC: World Bank.

Robson, M. (2010). "Stand on funding reversed." *Leader Post.* Retrieved June 4, 2010 from <www.leaderpost.com/news/Standfunding reversed/3111067/story.html>.

Rogin, M. (1996). *Blackface, white noise: Jewish immigrants in the Hollywood melting pot.* Los Angeles, CA: University of California Press.

Rojas, A., L. Magzul, G.P. Marchildon and B. Reyes. (2009). "The Oldman River dam conflict: Adaptation and institutional learning." *Prairie Forum* (34)1: 235–60.

Rosaldo, R. (1989). *Culture and truth: The remaking of social analysis.* Boston, MA: Beacon Press.

Ross, D.P., K.J. Scott and P.J. Smith. (2000). *The Canadian fact book on poverty.* Ottawa, ON: Canadian Council on Social Development.

Ross, R. (2006). *Returning to the teachings: Exploring Aboriginal justice.* Toronto, ON: Penguin Books.

___. (1992). *Dancing with a ghost: Exploring Indian reality.* Markham, ON: Octopus.

Ross, R.J.S., and K.C. Trachte. (1990). *Global capitalism: The new leviathan.* Albany, NY: SUNY Press.

Rousseau, J.J. (2000). "Excerpts from *on the social contract* (1762)." In R.C. Solomon and M.C. Murphy (eds.), *What is justice? Classic and contemporary readings* (pp. 89–94). New York: Oxford University Press.

Rousseau, Jean-Jacques. (1959–95). *Oeuvres complètes* Vol III, pg. 361. (ed. B. Gagnebin and M. Raymond). Paris: Editions Gallimard.

___. "From the state of nature to citizenship." From *A discourse on the origins of inequality* (1754) and *On the social contract* (1762) (D. Cress, trans. 1983). Indianapolis, IN: Hackett.

Royal Commission on Aboriginal Peoples. (1995). *Bridging the cultural divide: A report on*

Aboriginal people and criminal justice in Canada. René Dussault & Georges Erasmus, Co-Chairs. Ottawa, ON: Royal Commission on Aboriginal Peoples.

Ryan, J. (1995). *Doing things the right way: Dene traditional justice in Lac La Martre, N.W.T.* Calgary, AB: University of Calgary Press & the Arctic Institute of North America.

Ryder, B. (2008). "*Taking Section 15 back to the future.*" *The Court.* Toronto: Osgoode Hall Law School. Accessed February 28, 2011 from <http://www.thecourt.ca/2008/07/02/r-v-kapp-taking-section-15-back-to-the-future/>.

Said, E. (1978). *Orientalism.* New York: Random House.

Salomon, M.E. (2006). "International human rights obligations in context: Structural obstacles and the demands of global justice." In B.A. Andreassen, P. Stephen and S.P. Marks (eds.), *Development as a human right: Legal, political and economic dimensions.* Cambridge: Harvard University Press.

Sanders, D. (1985). "The renewal of Indian special status." In A. Bayefsky and M. Eberts (eds.), *Equality rights and the Canadian Charter of Rights and Freedoms* (p. 529). Toronto, ON: Carswell.

Sarlo, C. (2008). *What is poverty? Providing clarity for Canada.* Vancouver, BC: Fraser Institute. May. Retrieved August 29, 2009 from <http://www.statcan.gc.ca/pub/75f0002m/75f0002m2006004-eng.pdf>.

Saskatchewan. (2004). *Report of the Commission of unquiry into matters relating to the death of Neil Stonechild.* Justice D.H. Wright, Commissioner. Regina, SK: Saskatchewan Department of Justice.

___. (2004). *Report of the Commission on First Nations and Métis peoples and justice reform.* (Vols. 1–2) W. Littlechild, Chairperson. Regina, SK: Saskatchewan Department of Justice.

___. (2007). *Northern access to justice committee: Final report.* Regina, SK: Ministry of Justice and Attorney-General.

Sauchyn, D., and S. Kulshreshtha. (2007). "The prairies." In D.S. Lemmen, F.J. Warren, J. Lacroix and E. Bush (eds.), *From impacts to adaptation: Canada in a changing climate 2007.* Ottawa, ON: Government of Canada.

Saunders, R. (2005). *Lifting the boats: Policies to make work pay.* Ottawa, ON: Canadian Centre for Policy Alternatives. Retrieved September 9, 2009 from <http://www.cprn.org/documents/37297_en.pdf>.

Schlosberg, D. (2004). "Reconceiving environmental justice: Global movements and political theories." *Environmental Politics* 13(3): 517–40.

Schmalleger, F., D. MacAllister, P.F. McKenna and J. Winterdyk. (2000). *Canadian criminal justice today: An introductory text for the twenty-first century.* Toronto, ON: Prentice-Hall.

Schneider, E.M. (2000). *Battered women and feminist lawmaking.* London: Yale University Press.

Schwartz, H., R.D. Jerone and S.K. Olnick. (1962). "Two studies of legal stigma." *Social Problems* 10: 133–38.

Scott, K. (2009). "Poverty reduction policies and programs: Social development report series." Canadian Council on Social Development. Retrieved August 24, 2010 from <http://www.ccsd.ca/SDR2009/SDR-2009.html>.

___. (n.d.) *The world we have: Towards a new social architecture.* Ottawa, ON: Canadian Council on Social Development.

Sears, A. (2005). *A good book in theory: A guide to theoretical thinking.* Peterborough, ON: Broadview Press.

Segall, A., and N. Chappell. (2000). *Health and health care in Canada.* Toronto, ON:

Prentice-Hall.
Sellin, T. (1938). *Culture, conflict & crime.* New York: Social Science Research Council.
Sen, A. (1980). "Equality of what?" In S. McMurrin (ed.), *Tanner lectures on human values.* Cambridge: Cambridge University Press. Retrieved August 10, 2010 from <http://philosophy.ucsd.edu/faculty/rarneson/Courses/SENeqofcapacity.pdf>.
___. (1988). "Property and hunger." *Economics and Philosophy* 4: 57–68. Reprinted in W. Cragg and C. Koggel, (2005), *Contemporary Moral Issues* (fifth ed.), (p. 402), Toronto, ON: McGraw-Hill Ryerson; and in S. Boyd, G. Brodsky, S. Day and M. Young, (2007), *Poverty, rights, social citizenship and legal activism* (p. 77), Vancouver, BC: University of British Columbia Press.
Senate & House of Commons. (1981). *Minutes of proceedings and evidence of the special joint committee of the Senate and of the House of Commons on the Constitution of Canada.* January 12. 32nd Parliament, 1st Sess., issue no. I.
Sheldrick, B. (2004). *Perils and possibilities: Social activism and the law.* Winnipeg: Fernwood.
Shichor, D. (2006). *The meaning and nature of punishment.* Long Grove, IL: Waveland Press.
Shiva, V. (1997). *Biopiracy: The plunder of nature and knowledge.* Cambridge, MA: South End Press.
Shrader-Frechette, K. (2002). *Environmental justice: Creating equality, reclaiming democracy.* New York: Oxford University Press.
Silverman, R., and L. Kennedy. (1993). *Deadly murder in Canada.* Toronto, ON: Nelson.
Sinclair, M. (2009). Chairperson, Truth and Reconciliation Commission of Canada (TRC), speaking to Assembly of First Nations annual general meeting in Calgary, July 22. Retrieved August 25, 2010 from <http://www.trc.ca/websites/trcinstitution/index.php?p=3>.
Sluiter, L. (2009). *Clean clothes: A global movement to end sweatshops.* London, UK: Pluto Press.
Smandych, R., and R. Kueneman. (2010). "The Canadian Alberta tar sands: A case study of state-corporate environmental crime." In R. White (ed.), *Global environmental harm: Criminological perspectives* (pp. 87–109). Portland, OR: Willan.
Smart, C. (1989). *Feminism and the power of law.* London: Routledge.
___. (1992). "The woman of legal discourse." *Social and Legal Studies* 1: 29–44.
Smillie, I. (2009). "Zimbabwe, diamonds and the wrong side of history." *Human Rights Watch.* Partnership Africa Canada.
Smith, A. (1976 [1776]). *An inquiry into the nature and causes of the wealth of nations* (R.H. Campbell and A.S. Skinner, eds.). Oxford: Oxford University Press. <http://oll.libertyfund.org/?option=com_staticxt&staticfile=show.php%3Ftitle=220>
Smith, A., J. Young, B. Ish and J. Anderson. (1996). "Common ground mediation trainers." (Unpublished). Saskatoon, SK.
Smith, D. (1993). *The seventh fire.* Toronto, ON: Key Porter Books.
Smith, J.L. (2008). "A critical appreciation of the 'bottom-up' approach to sustainable water management: embracing complexity rather than desirability." *Local Environment* 13(4): 353–66.
Smith, L.T. (1999). *Decolonizing methodologies: Research and indigenous peoples.* New York: Zed Books.
Snider, L. (1994). "Feminism, punishment, and the potential for empowerment." *Canadian Journal of Law and Society* 9(1): 75–104.
___. (1998). "Understanding the second great confinement." *Queen's Quarterly* 105(1): 29–46.
___. (2006). "Relocating law: Making corporate crime disappear." In E. Comack

Ungerleider, C. (2009). "Racism, justice, and social cohesion in Canada." In S.P. Hier, D. Lett and B.S. Bolaria (eds.), *Racism and justice: Critical dialogue on the politics of identity, inequality, and change* (pp. 173–88). Halifax, NS: Fernwood.

UN OHCHR (United Nations Office of the High Commissioner for Human Rights). 2004. *Human rights and poverty reduction: A conceptual framework.* New York: United Nations. Retrieved August 13, 2009 from <http://www.unhcr.org/refworld/category,LEGAL,OHCHR,,,46ce95c32,0.html.>

UNDP (United Nation Development Program). (1996). "Governance for sustainable human development." Retrieved August 25, 2010 from <http://mirror.undp.org/magnet/policy/chapter1.htm>.

___. (1997). "Governance for sustainable development: A UNDP policy document." Retrieved June 30, 2009 from <http://magnet.undp.org/policy/>.

United Nations. (1948). *Universal declaration of human rights.* GA Res. 217A (III), 3d Sess. Supp. No.13, U.N. Doc. A/810. December 10. Retrieved June 28, 2010, from <http://www.udhr.org/UDHR/default.htm>.

___. (2007). *Declaration of the rights of Indigenous peoples,* G.A. Res. 61/295, U.N. Doc. A/RES/61/295 7. September 13. Retrieved June 28, 2010 from <http://www2.ohchr.org/english/issues/indigenous/declaration.htm>.

UNWWDR (United Nations World Water Development Report). (2006). *Water, a shared responsibility* (report 2). United Nations Educational Scientific and Cultural Organization. New York: Berghahn Books.

Vago, S. (1994). *Law and society* (fourth ed.). Upper Saddle River, NJ: Prentice Hall.

Valverde, M. (1991). *The age of light, soap, and water: Moral reform in English Canada, 1885–1925.* Toronto, ON: McClelland & Stewart.

Van Allen, B. (2009). *Police powers: Law, order and accountability.* Toronto, ON: Pearson Education.

Van Ness, D., and K.H. Strong. (1997). "Looking back and moving forward: Conclusions, implications, and agenda for future research." Cincinnati, OH: Anderson. In G. Brazemore and M. Schiff (eds.), (2005), *Juvenile justice reform and restorative justice: Building theory and policy from practices.* Portland, OR: Willan.

___. (1997). *Restoring justice.* Cincinnati, OH: Anderson.

___. (2006). *Restoring justice: An introduction to restorative justice.* Cincinnati, OH: LexisNexis/Anderson.

Van Parijs, P. (2004). "A basic income for all: A brief defense. To secure real freedom, grant everyone a subsistence income." In L. Groot, *Basic income, unemployment and compensatory justice* (pp. 11–24). Boston, MA: Kluwer Academic.

Van Teijlingen, E.R., G.W. Louis, P.G. McCaffery and M. Porter. (2000). *Midwifery and the medicalization of childbirth: Comparative perspectives.* Hauppauge, NY: Nova Science.

Vanderburgh, R.M. (1988). "The impact of government support for Indian culture on Canada's aged Indians." In E. Rathbone-McCuan and B. Havens (eds.), *North American Elders: United States and Canadian perspectives* (pp. 221–34). New York: Greenwood Press.

Veenstra, G. (2009). "Social inequality and health." In E.G. Grabb (2002), *Theories of social inequality* (fourth ed). Scarborough, ON: Nelson Thomson Learning.

Visual Economics. (2010). "Unemployment rates around the world." <http://www.visualeconomics.com/unemployment-rates-around-the-world/>.

Wacks, R. (2006). *Philosophy of law: A very short introduction.* Oxford: Oxford University Press.

Walker, S. (2001). *Police accountability: The role of citizen oversight*. Belmont, CA: Wadsworth.

Wallace, M. (2009). "Police-reported crime statistics in Canada, 2008." *Juristat* 29 (3), catalogue no. 85-002-X.

Walzer, M. (1983). *Spheres of justice*. New York: Basic Books.

Watts, M. (2001). "Petro-violence: Community, extraction, and political ecology of a mythic commodity." In N.L. Peluso and M. Watts (eds.), *Violent environments* (pp. 189–212). Ithaca, NY: Cornell University Press.

Weber, M. (1978 [1922]). *Economy and society: An outline of interpretive sociology* (G. Roth and C. Wittich, eds.). Berkeley, CA: University of California Press.

Weiler, P.C. (1980). "Of judges and rights, or should Canada have a constitutional bill of rights?" *Dalhousie Review* (205), Summer.

Weitekamp, E., and H.J. Kerner (eds.). (2002). *Restorative justice: Theoretical foundations*. Cullompton, U.K: Willan.

Welden, L.M. (2008). *Restorative practices in Australia's schools: Stronger relationships and multi-school summits help schools "be and learn" together.* International Institute for Restorative Practices. Retrieved January 14, 2008 from <www.iirp.org>.

Wellesley Institute (n.d.). "Overview." Retrieved August 25, 2010 from <http://wellesleyinstitute.com/issues/housing-and-homelessness/overview>.

Wenz, P.S. (1988). *Environmental justice*. Albany: State University of New York Press.

Wetherell, M., and J. Potter. (1992). *Mapping the language of racism: Discourse and the legitimation of exploitation.* New York: Columbia University Press.

Whitley, C. (2004). "Programs for Aboriginal offenders: Lessons from the educational experience." Paper presented at the international society for the reform of criminal law (August), Montreal, QC.

Whonnock, K. (2008). *Aboriginal courts in Canada*. Calgary, AB: The Scow Institute.

___. (2010). "The status of Aboriginal courts in Canada." A paper presented at the western criminology articulation meetings (May 27–28), Terrance, BC.

Wilkins, L.T. (1965). *Social deviance: Social policy, action, and research*. Englewood Cliffs, NJ: Prentice Hall.

Williams, P.J. (1991). *The Alchemy of race and rights.* Boston, MA: Harvard University Press.

Williams, R.M. (1960). *American society: A sociological interpretation.* New York: Knopf.

Wilson, J. (1983). *Thinking about crime.* New York: Vintage Press.

Wilson, S.J. (2001). "Paid work, jobs and the illusion of economic security." In Nancy Mandell (ed.), *Feminist issues: Race, class, and sexuality* (third ed.). Toronto: Pearson.

Winterdyk, J.A. (2000). *Canadian criminology*. Scarborough, ON: Prentice-Hall Canada.

Woodsworth, J.S. (1909). "Strangers within our gates: Or coming Canadians." Retrieved June 11, 2009 from <http://www.archive.org/stream/strangerswithino00wooduoft#page/10/mode/2up>.

Woolford, A. (2009). *The politics of restorative justice*. Halifax, NS: Fernwood.

Wright, D.H. (2004). "Report of the Commission of inquiry in to matters relating to the death of Neil Stonechild." <www.cbc.ca/news/background/stonechild/stonechild_report.pdf>.

Yablonsky, L., and M.R. Haskell. (1988). *Juvenile delinquency* (fourth ed.). New York: Harper & Row.

Young, I.M. (1990). *Justice and the politics of difference*. Princeton: Princeton University Press.

Young, M., and J.P. Mulvale. (2009). *Economic security in Canada: The possibilities and prospects of guaranteed income proposals*. Vancouver, BC: Canadian Centre for Policy

Alternatives (BC Office).
Zehr, H. (2002). *The little book of restorative justice*. Intercourse, PA: Good Books.
___. (2004). "Commentary: Restorative justice: Beyond victim-offender mediation." *Conflict Resolution Quarterly* 22(1–2): 305–15.
Zellerer, E. (2003). "Culturally competent programs: The first family violence program for Aboriginal men in prison." *Prison Journal* 83(2): 171–90.
Zellerer, E., and C. Cunneen. (2001). *Restorative justice, Indigenous justice, and human rights restorative community justice*. Cincinnati, OH: Anderson.
Ziegler, J. (2003). "Report by the special rapporteur on the right to food: Mission to Brazil." United Nations Commission on Human Rights, fifty-ninth session, 3 January, E/CN.4/2003/54/Add.1.
___. (2004). "Report submitted by the special Rapporteur on the right to food, in accordance with commission on human rights resolution 2003/25." United Nations Commission on Human Rights, Sixtieth session, February 9, C/CN.4/2004/10.

Statutes

British North America Act, 1867, 30-31 Vict., c. 3 (U.K.).
Canadian Charter of Rights and Freedoms, Part 1 of the *Constitution Act, 1982*, being Schedule B to the *Canada Act 1982*, (U.K.), 1982, c. 11.
Charter of the United Nations, 26 June 1945, Can. T.S. 1945 No. 7 (entered into force 24 October 1945) and annexed Statute of the International Court of Justice, 26 June 1945, Can. T. S. 1945 No. 7 (entered into force 24 October 1945).
Constitution Act, 1867 , (U.K.), 30 & 31 Victoria, c. 3.
Constitution Act, 1982, being Schedule B to the *Canada Act 1982* (U.K.), 1982, c. 11
Corrections and Conditional Release Act, R.S.C. 1992, c.20.
Criminal Code, R.S.C. 1985, c. C-46.
Indian Act (1876).
Saskatchewan Human Rights Code S.S. 1979, c. S-24.1.
Universal Declaration of Human Rights, G.A. Res 217A (III), U.N. Doc. A/810 (Dec. 10, 1948 [UDHR]
Youth Criminal Justice Act, S.C. 2002, c. 1.

Cases

A.G. Canada v. *Lavell* [1974] S.C.R. 1349.
Andrews v. Law Society of British Columbia, [1989] 1 SCR 143
Bliss v. Canada (Attorney General) [1979] 1 S.C.R. 183
Canadian Foundation for Children, Youth and the Law v. *Canada (Attorney General)*, 2004 SCC 4, [2004] 1 S.C.R. 76.
Council of Canadians with Disabilities v. *VIA Rail Canada Inc.*, 2007 SCC 15, [2007] 1 S.C.R. 650.
Creighton v. *R.* [1993] 3 S.C.R. 3
Dickie v. *Dickie*, 2007 SCC 8, [2007] 1 S.C.R. 346.
Edwards v. *Canada (Attorney General)*, [1928] S.C.R. 276, 1928 Carswell Nat 35 (S.C.C.), reversed (1929), [1930] A.C. 124, 1929 Carswell Nat 2 (Canada P.C).
Eldridge v. *British Columbia (Attorney General)*, [1997] 3 S.C.R. 624, 151 D.L.R (5th) 577.
Federated Anti-Poverty Groups of B.C. v. *Vancouver (City)* [2002] B.C.J. No. 493.

Gosselin v. *Quebec (Attorney General)* [2002] 4 S.C.R. 429.
Hislop v. Canada (Attorney General), [2007] 1 S.C.R. 429
Lovelace v. Canada (1981), Report of the Human Rights Committee, GAOR 36th Sess., Supp. No.40 (AQ/36/40), Annex XVIII, 166.
Masse v. Ontario (Ministry of Community and Social Services) (1996), 134 D.L.R. (4th) 20, 35 C.R.R. (2d) 44 (Ont. Div. Ct.); leave to appeal to C.A. denied [1996] O.J. No. 1526; leave to appeal to S.C.C. denied [1996] S.C.C.A. No. 373. In the *Murdoch v. Murdoch* [1985].
Nancy Law v. Canada (Minister of Employment and Immigration) [1999] 1 S.C.R. 497.
O`Connor [1995]
North Sea Continental Shelf Cases (Federal Republic of Germany v. Denmark; *Federal Republic of Germany v. The Netherlands*, [1969] I.C.J. Rep. 3)
R. v. Alaku (1993), 112 Dominion Law Reports (4th) 732 (Court of Quebec).
R. v. Darrach, [2000] 2 S.C.R. 443
R. v. Ewanchuk, [1999] 1 S.C.R. 330
R. v. Gladue, [1999] 1 S.R.C. 688.
R. v. Hamilton and Mason 2003 Canadian Legal Information Institute 2862 (Ontario Superior Court), [191-198].
R. v. Joseyounen, [1995] 6 Western Weekly Reports 38, (Saskatchewan Provincial Court).
R. v. Kummerfield [1998] 9 W.W.R. 619 (Sask. C.A.); (1998) 163 Sask. R. 257 (Q.B.).
R. v. Morgentaler [1988] 1 S.C.R. 30.
R. v. Moses [1992] 3 Canadian National Law Reports 116 (Yukon Territorial Court).
R. v. O'Connor, [1995] 4 S.C.R. 411
R. v. Seaboyer; R. v. Gayme, 1991 [1991] 2 Superior Court Report. 577.
Vriend v. Alberta, [1998] 1 S.C.R. 493, [1998] S.C.J. No. 29, 156 D.L.R. (4th) 385.